"The Chagossians were brutally expelled from their Indian Ocean home by UK officials who referred to them as 'Tarzans and Men Fridays'. In 2008 Lord Hoffmann denied their right of return, casting them as incapable of living 'Crusoe-like'. The declaration of a 'no take' Marine Protected Area in 2010 further limited their conditions of return. As this language reveals, the expulsion and exile of the Chagossians repeats the gestures and practices of unbridled colonial power; and shows the complicity of law and science. But as the essays and artistic works in this book show, the collusion of successive US and UK governments are resisted effectively at every turn. How are empires and nations created and remade? Can a fully decolonised nation avoid marginalising an ethnic or indigenous minority? How are environmental and 'green' agendas deployed for neo-colonial ends? This timely and multi-disciplinary book addresses these urgent questions that apply well beyond the fate of the Chagossians."

Stewart Motha, *Professor of Law,*
Birkbeck, University of London, UK

"This extraordinary, polyvocal anthology amply documents the historic case of the Chagos islanders and their grotesque treatment at the hands of successive British Governments. It is an indispensable resource that illuminates the juridical, geopolitical, cultural and human dimensions of this long-running scandal. Anybody interested in the persistent politics of empire and colony has much to learn much from it."

Paul Gilroy, *Professor of the Humanities,*
University College London, UK

"Urgent and uncompromising, this multilayered volume is a powerful reminder of Chagossians' on-going resistance to British and US colonisation in the 21st century."

Olivette Otele, *Distinguished Research*
Professor of the Legacies and Memory of Slavery,
SOAS, London, UK

Challenges and Prospects for the Chagos Archipelago

Challenges and Prospects for the Chagos Archipelago considers the origins, challenges, and future of Chagos, bringing together leading experts and academics specialising in differing aspects of the Chagos dispute.

In 1965, as part of negotiations leading to Mauritian independence in 1968, the UK government excised the Chagos Archipelago from the colony of Mauritius to form part of a new overseas territory, the British Indian Ocean Territory (BIOT). The UK then set about removing the population of the Chagos Islands in order to allow the United States to construct a military base. As a consequence of the UK's acquisition of the Chagos Islands and the expulsion of the Chagossian population, there has been wide-ranging litigation brought by Mauritius and the Chagossians. This has reached the International Court of Justice, the United Nations General Assembly, the European Court of Human Rights, and the UK Supreme Court. This book offers a wide-ranging debate between experts and practitioners, including those of Chagossian and Mauritian heritage, touching upon key developments and offering an inclusive approach that transcends traditional disciplinary silos. Issues such as international and constitutional law, human rights, colonialism, and decolonisation, using creative writing to express the experience of banishment, international relations, environmentalism, and globalisation, will be explored as part of a dialogue that sheds new light on the Chagos dispute. Edited by experts on Chagos, the contributors are drawn from across the globe, and all have a distinctive take on what has happened, what it means for the world and the region, and how Chagos will both shape and be shaped by the future.

This book will be of great interest to students, academics and researchers from across the humanities and social sciences, including political science, international relations, law, sociology, socio-legal studies, human rights, social anthropology, indigenous rights, history, colonialism, postcolonialism, and cultural studies, as well as practitioners, policymakers, and general readers who are interested in Chagos.

Laura Jeffery is Professor of Anthropology of Migration in the School of Social and Political Sciences at the University of Edinburgh, UK. She has worked with the Chagossian community since 2002, and is author of *Chagos islanders in Mauritius and the UK: Forced Displacement and Onward Migration.*

Chris Monaghan is Head of Law and Principal Lecturer in Law at the University of Worcester, UK. He has interests in the Chagos Islands legal dispute, Constitutional Law, the role of Parliament, executive accountability, and the global use of impeachment.

Mairi O'Gorman is a social anthropologist who holds a PhD from the University of Edinburgh, UK. Her doctoral thesis, *Tree of Knowledge, Tree of Life: Materials, Intimacy and Being Creole in London and Seychelles* (2019), was based on ethnographic fieldwork in both places.

Small State Studies

Half the world's sovereign states have populations of less than 5.3 million, and over 30 have populations of less than ONE million. Clearly, there is scope to consider the impact that small size and scale (of population, civil service, expertise, talent pools, ambassadorial ranks, service providers, and so on) could have on the nature of governance, politics, international relations, economic development, climate action, transportation, etc. This interdisciplinary new series closes the gap in political and social science literature by encouraging studies on the challenges facing small states, their characteristics and their strategies, thus galvanizing scholarship in a previously neglected area. It encourages comparative studies among small states, and between small states and larger states. It addresses the predicament of small size and scale as these impinge on institutional and political dimensions (such as public administration and diplomacy), and critically considers the issues and tensions arising from small but archipelagic and/or federated states.

Series editors:

Godfrey Baldacchino, University of Malta, Malta – godfrey.baldacchino@um.edu.mt
Anna-Lena Högenauer, University of Luxembourg, Luxembourg – anna-lena.hoegenauer@uni.lu
Nicos Trimikliniotis, University of Nicosia, Cyprus – trimikliniotis.n@unic.ac.cy
Roukaya Kasenally, University of Mauritius, Mauritius – roukaya@uom.ac.mu

Titles in this series include:

The Success of Small States in International Relations
Mice that Roar?
Edited by Godfrey Baldacchino

The Rotating European Union Council Presidency and Small Member States
Small States, Big Challenge
Ieva Grumbinaitė

Agency, Security and Governance of Small States
A Global Perspective
Edited by Thomas Kolnberger and Harlan Koff

The Constitutional Courts of Small Jurisdictions
Edited by Danny Pieters

Small States in EU Policy-Making
Strategies, Challenges, Opportunities
Edited by Anna-Lena Högenauer and Matúš Mišík

Challenges and Prospects for the Chagos Archipelago
Edited by Laura Jeffery, Chris Monaghan and Mairi O'Gorman

Challenges and Prospects for the Chagos Archipelago

Edited by Laura Jeffery, Chris Monaghan and Mairi O'Gorman

Routledge
Taylor & Francis Group
LONDON AND NEW YORK

First published 2025
by Routledge
4 Park Square, Milton Park, Abingdon, Oxon OX14 4RN

and by Routledge
605 Third Avenue, New York, NY 10158

Routledge is an imprint of the Taylor & Francis Group, an informa business

British Library Cataloguing-in-Publication Data
A catalogue record for this book is available from the British Library

ISBN: 978-1-032-48683-3 (hbk)
ISBN: 978-1-032-48692-5 (pbk)
ISBN: 978-1-003-39029-9 (ebk)

DOI:10.4324/9781003390299

Typeset in Times New Roman
by Deanta Global Publishing Services, Chennai, India

To all Chagossians who did not live
to see a return to their homeland

Contents

List of Figures

Contributors

Richard B. Allen works on Mauritian social and economic history and Indian Ocean and Asian colonial plantation slavery, slave trading, abolition, and indentured labour. He is author of *Slaves, Freedmen, and Indentured Laborers in Colonial Mauritius* and *European Slave Trading in the Indian Ocean, 1500-1850*, and editor of *Slavery and Bonded Labor in Asia, 1250-1900*.

Stephen Allen is Senior Lecturer in Law at Queen Mary, University of London, and a practising barrister. He has authored two monographs including *The Chagos Islanders and International Law*, and has edited several books including *Fifty Years of the British Indian Ocean Territory: Legal Perspectives*.

Priya Bahadoor has a PhD from the Université de La Réunion and is Lecturer at the University of Mauritius where she teaches Indian Ocean and International History.

Louis Olivier Bancoult was born in Peros Banhos in 1964. His family travelled to Mauritius in 1968 for medical treatment, after which they were prevented from returning to Chagos. As a founding member and subsequently longstanding chairperson of the Chagos Refugees Group (Mauritius), Olivier has led the CRG's political and legal struggles for compensation and the right to return to Chagos.

Samuel Bashfield is Senior Research Officer at ANU's National Security College, Defence Researcher at Australia India Institute, and Non-Residential Fellow at the Royal Australian Navy's Sea Power Centre. Sam's research interests include Indo-Pacific security, technology governance, and maritime security. His PhD thesis examines BIOT's Cold War history, focussing on strategy, security, and Anglo-US relations.

Owen Bowcott studied history at the University of Birmingham. In 1988 he joined *The Guardian* where he was Ireland correspondent, assistant foreign news editor, and legal affairs correspondent. Since 2021, he has been a freelance journalist. In February 2022, he was on a Mauritian government-chartered ship that sailed to the Chagos Islands.

Thomas Burri is Professor of International Law and European Law at the University of St Gallen, Switzerland. He is admitted to the Zurich bar. He co-edited *The International Court of Justice and Decolonisation: New Directions from the Chagos Advisory Opinion*.

Sue Farran is Professor of Comparative and Plural Law at Newcastle University, and AHRC-funded Research Fellow at the Foreign, Commonwealth and Development Office, providing research expertise on the Pacific islands. Sue has written several pieces on the Chagos Islands, triggered by an interest in human rights, islands, and marine protected areas.

Charles Manga Fombad is Professor of Comparative Constitutional Law and Director of the Institute for International and Comparative Law in Africa at the Faculty of Law, University of Pretoria, South Africa.

Felicity Hand is Honorary Professor in English at the Autonomous University of Barcelona. She has published articles on Indian Ocean writers including M.G. Vassanji, Abdulrazak Gurnah, Yasmin Alibhai-Brown, and Lindsey Collen.

Peter Harris is Associate Professor of Political Science at Colorado State University, where his teaching and research focus on international security and US foreign policy. He is a non-resident fellow with Defense Priorities. He holds degrees from the University of Edinburgh, SOAS University of London, and the University of Texas at Austin.

Chris Hill has an MA in Postcolonial Studies from the University of Kent. Drawing on critical race studies, Marxism, indigenous studies, and ecocriticism, his interests include race, class, and protest in Britain, the climate crisis, occupied territories, and former island colonies. He is of mixed Seychellois and British heritage, and identifies as white passing.

Marie Sabrina Jean (*née* Aristide) is a second-generation Chagossian whose father Serge Aristide was born in Peros Banhos. Sabrina was born in Mauritius in 1973. Since 2006 she has lived in the UK, where she is chair of the Chagos Refugees UK Group.

Laura Jeffery is Professor of Anthropology of Migration at the University of Edinburgh, her hometown. She has worked with the Chagossian community since 2002. She is author of *Chagos Islanders in Mauritius and the UK: Forced Displacement and Onward Migration*, and hosts the CHAGOS: Cultural Heritage Across Generations website https://chagos.online/

Satvinder S. Juss is Professor of Law at King's College London, Distinguished Global Professor of Law at Notre Dame University, and former Fellow of Emmanuel College Cambridge. He is a practising Barrister and a Master of Gray's Inn. He gave evidence to the All-Party Parliamentary Group on Democracy and the Constitution in 2023.

Thierry Mandarin has an MSc in Social Research Methods from the University of Sussex and a BSc in Social Anthropology and Sociology from the University of Roehampton, London. His MSc dissertation focuses on migration stories, impact and legacy of parents and grandparents, subsequent generations of Chagossians, and the future for the community after the Nationality Borders Act 2022. He is of Chagossian heritage and identifies as Black.

Milan J.N. Meetarbhan is Barrister and Head of Nyam Chambers in Mauritius, and holds a Doctorate in International Law from the Sorbonne. He was Ambassador and Permanent Representative of Mauritius to the UN and was part of the Mauritius delegation at the arbitration proceedings on the Mauritius v UK over the Chagos Marine Protected Area.

Chris Monaghan is Head of Law and Principal Lecturer in Law at the University of Worcester. He has interests in the Chagos Islands legal dispute, Constitutional Law, the role of Parliament, executive accountability, and the global use of impeachment.

Mairi O'Gorman is a social anthropologist who holds a PhD from the University of Edinburgh. Her doctoral thesis, *Tree of Knowledge, Tree of Life: Materials, Intimacy and Being Creole in London and Seychelles* (2019), was based on ethnographic fieldwork in both places. She is of Seychellois Creole heritage and identifies as mixed.

Esther Pujolràs-Noguer is Associate Professor in Foreign Languages and Literatures at the University of Lleida in Catalonia. Her research interests revolve around the convergence of gender and ethnicity, the representation of trauma, and transnationalism. She has published articles on Indian Ocean writers including Abdulrazak Gurnah and M.G. Vassanji.

Philippe Sands KC is Professor of Public Understanding of Law at University College London. He was President of English PEN and is a board member of the Hay Festival of Arts and Literature. He is author of several books including *The Last Colony: A Tale of Exile, Justice and Britain's Colonial Legacy*.

David Snoxell served in HM Diplomatic Service from 1969 to 2004, including as Deputy Commissioner of BIOT (1995–1997) and as High Commissioner to Mauritius (2000–2004). Since 2009 he has coordinated the Chagos Islands (BIOT) All-Party Parliamentary Group. He has written extensively on Chagos issues, advocating a negotiated settlement with Mauritius and the Chagossians.

Natasha Soobramanien is a British-Mauritian writer based in Brussels. She holds a PhD in Creative and Critical Writing from UEA for which she submitted her first novel *Genie and Paul*, a contemporary rewriting of Bernadin Henri de Saint-Pierre's colonial fantasy *Paul et Virginie*. Her second novel, *Diego Garcia*, co-authored with Luke Williams, won The Goldsmiths Prize 2022.

Saradha Soobrayen was born in London of Mauritian parentage. She is an independent researcher and creative activist. She was poet in "non-residence" with CHAGOS: Cultural Heritage Across Generations, publishing a chapbook *In Her Deepest Sleep, Madam Lisette Talate Returns To Chagos* and the poetic inquiry *Sounds Like Root Shock.* Her artwork *Chagos(nica)* toured with Guernica Remakings.

Jamie Trinidad is Fellow and Director of Studies in Law at Wolfson College, Cambridge, Fellow of the Lauterpacht Centre for International Law, and a practising barrister. He is author of *Self-Determination in Disputed Colonial Territories* and co-editor of *The International Court of Justice and Decolonisation: New Directions from the Chagos Advisory Opinion.*

David Vine is Professor of anthropology at American University (USA). David is author of three books including *Island of Shame: The Secret History of the U.S. Military on Diego Garcia.* David co-directs the *Chagos Archive* (www.chagosarchive.org) and Let Us Return USA! (www.letusreturnusa.org).

Luke Williams is from Scotland, and is Senior Lecturer in Creative Writing at Birkbeck. He studied History at Edinburgh and Creative Writing at UEA. His first novel, *The Echo Chamber,* won The Saltire Award for Best First Book. His second novel, *Diego Garcia,* co-authored with Natasha Soobramanien, won The Goldsmiths Prize 2022.

Chrisyl Wong-Hang-Sun holds an MRes in Anthropology from UCL, and works as Project Curator for the Endangered Material Knowledge Programme at the British Museum. Chrisyl is of Mauritian and third-generation Chagossian descent, and she identifies as Kreol. Her work explores anthropology of law, hope, the future, home, the Mascarene islands, migration and forced displacement, "native" anthropology, and the Nationality and Borders Act 2022.

Foreword

Olivier Bancoult

In 2023 we commemorated 50 years of deportation from our motherland Chagos Archipelago. Deportation took place firstly in 1971, when all Chagossians had to leave Diego Garcia for security because of the US military base and had to choose between Peros Banhos and Boddam Salomon, or else Seychelles or Mauritius. Most chose the first option, but a year later the same decision had to be made on Salomon and Peros. The last group of Chagossians were forcibly removed and arrived in Mauritius in a very shameful way. Chagossians were led to expect assistance, but on arrival in Mauritius the last group had to stay three days at the quay in Port Louis waiting for housing. The kind of housing they were offered was not suitable for human habitation because animals had been kept there. Eventually they were given Dockers' Flats without windows and in a very bad state.

It was very difficult for us to accept this injustice and we faced difficulties in adapting to Mauritian society because our way of life on Chagos was very different to Mauritius, not least because the kinds of jobs we did there did not exist here, and this is how our lives became a nightmare. How could we forget and stay silent? We have among us Chagossians who faced these unforgettable injuries that still affect our everyday lives. We cannot forget the way they described us as Tarzans and Man Fridays as if we were people who did not know about our rights. For many years Chagossians claimed our fundamental rights as human beings via demonstrations and hunger strikes, facing police arrest. We proceeded to the High Court in London to request judicial review of the 1971 ordinance which precluded our right to live on our birthplace. Our main focus and our motto was *Rann Nou Diego*, since Chagossians cannot accept that this is their fate, and they prefer to return to Chagos.

Our culture is precious and remarkable, and we have named community centres to commemorate Marie Charlesia Alexis and Marie Lisette Talate amongst all those women who have led our historical struggle. I would like to pay tribute to all Chagossian women together with Mauritian women's associations who have been very active. Today we are proud to be recognised as a people who have never given up, and the world has known our struggle via our continuous legal and political struggles. It's time to put an end to our suffering. Reparations should be made on behalf of all Chagossian natives. And we have the right to resettle on our own native land, including Diego Garcia.

Foreword

Philippe Sands

Challenges and Prospects for the Chagos Archipelago offers a broad and original perspective on the legal issues pertaining to the Chagos Archipelago, including human rights and other aspects of international law, constitutional matters, and domestic and international litigation. The beating heart of the book, as with the issues, turns on matters of self-determination and decolonisation, including territorial integrity and sovereignty, and the shocking mistreatment of the expelled Chagossian community. As I have described in my book *The Last Colony*, it is a tale of colonial abuse and its continuing legacy.

Laura Jeffery, Chris Monaghan, and Mairi O'Gorman have brought together a most impressive group of contributors from across the globe, bringing a range of disciplinary perspectives to the Archipelago, its history, people and environment, and legal disputes catalysed by Britain's decision – ruled to be unlawful by the International Court of Justice, the UN General Assembly, and the International Tribunal for the Law of the Sea – to detach the islands from the colony of Mauritius, back in 1965, and forcibly deport the population, an act considered by many to amount to a "crime against humanity".

The contributors include social anthropologists and academics, historians and poets, writers and lawyers, a political scientist, and two former high-ranking diplomats. Chagossians are amongst them. The approach is as balanced as it is diverse.

Charles Fombad, Satvinder Juss, Sue Farran, Jamie Trinidad, Stephen Allen, Thomas Burri, and Chris Monaghan consider the legal, human rights, and constitutional aspects of the legal dispute. An Amicus Brief on behalf of the Chagossians Committee in the Seychelles is reproduced in full, alongside an analysis that draws upon "the experience of similar situations in other African countries". The role played by the African Union is also addressed.

The history of the Chagos Archipelago and its inhabitants is addressed by Richard Allen and Priya Bahadoor, the former drawing on expertise of the slave trade in the Indian Ocean. Samuel Bashfield analyses the 1966 agreement between the United Kingdom and the United States. Former British High Commissioner David Snoxell and former Mauritian Permanent Representative to the United Nations Milan Meetarbhan offer informed observations based on first-hand experience. Owen Bowcott, who wrote for *The Guardian*, describes the voyage we took to Chagos in February 2022, with members of the Chagossian community.

The coming generation of scholars is well-represented. Chris Hill offers a fascinating review of Chagos and European concepts of Empire, commerce, and culture. Thierry Mandarin, of Chagossian heritage, considers the impact of displacement on the Chagossian community in the United Kingdom. Chrisyl Wong-Hang-Sun, also of Chagossian descent, examines the impact of the Nationality and Borders Act 2022 on older members of the Chagossian community living in Mauritius.

Poetry too plays a key role in the book. Saradha Soobrayen uses poetic form to give voice to the Chagossian community. "Their homecoming is not yet out of reach, not yet out of sight", she observes. "The Archipelago is not where one man lived but is where they all remember living. Remembering is like that". Chrisyl Wong-Hang-Sun's "Ode to Chagossian Zistwar" contains this moving passage:

Long ago we knew these waters,
Long lived our sons and our daughters.
In unison we moved to the beat of the shore,
A harmony that cannot exist anymore.

There is too an extract from *Diego Garcia* (Fitzcarraldo Editions, 2022), the fine and prize-winning novel by Natasha Soobramanien and Luke Williams. Esther Pujolràs-Noguer and Felicity Hand explore the use of creative writing to address trauma.

Laura Jeffery offers characteristically informed insights about Chagossian ethnicity and indigenous characteristics, a debate that connects with legal and political aspects. David Vine is, as always, robust and fascinatingly provocative, as is Peter Harris, who explores geo-political considerations. "What does the emergence of the 'Indo-Pacific' – the world's newest and largest megaregion – mean for the future of the Chagos Islands?", he asks.

Challenges and Prospects for the Chagos Archipelago is a most admirable, readable, and original collection. It will surely emerge as a point of reference in the next phase, as Mauritius exercises sovereignty and the Chagossians return, hopefully as first stewards of the extraordinary environment and place that is Chagos.

Indian Ocean map

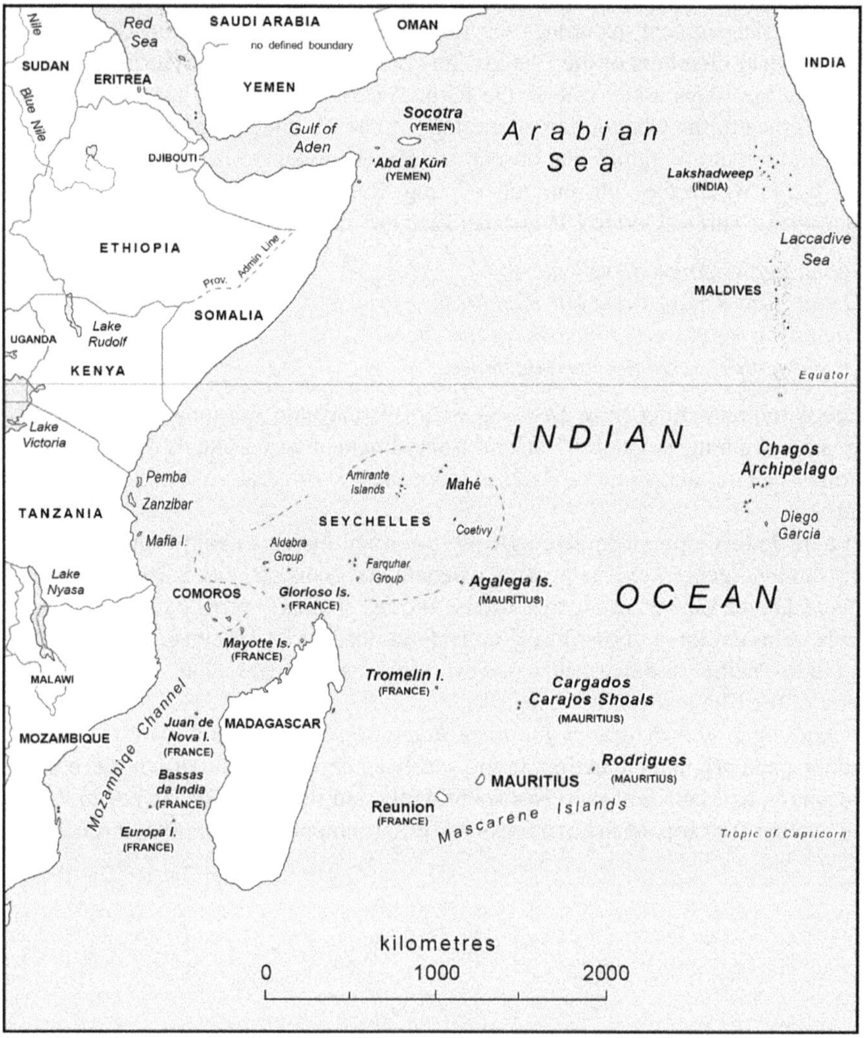

Source: Jeffery, Laura (2011) *Chagos islanders in Mauritius and the UK: Forced displacement and onward migration.* Manchester: Manchester University Press.

Chagos Archipelago map

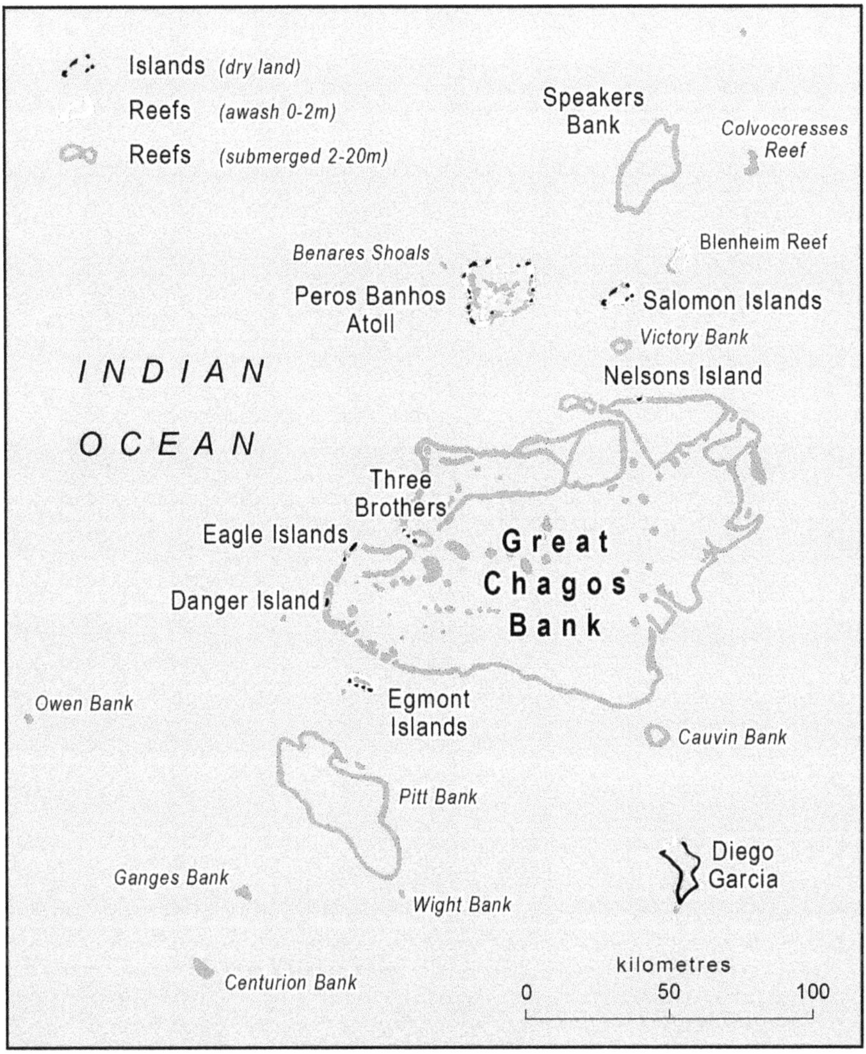

Source: Jeffery, Laura (2011) Chagos islanders in Mauritius and the UK: Forced displacement and onward migration. Manchester: Manchester University Press.

zistwar Sagosian, nu tu bizin amenn li

Chrisyl Wong-Hang-Sun

we spoke for a fleeting moment
and yet you revealed a lifetime
koz koze, blag blage[1]
these winds carry stories.

your laughter, a tale of endurance
your eyes, a testament to pain
bizin manz ar li, ki nu pu fer?[2]
for these winds carry our stories!

your words, your way with words
a foothold within my memory
standing the test of mortality
these winds - must not - carry our stories.

these winds that forced us into exile
these winds that cannot carry us home.
these winds that falsely shape our narratives,
zistwar Sagosian, nu tou bizin amenn li![3]

1 Two phrases that signify "conversing".
2 We need to get on with it, what else can we do?
3 The Chagossian history, we all need to carry it!

DOI: 10.4324/9781003390299-1

Introduction

Chris Monaghan, Laura Jeffery, and Mairi O'Gorman

Chagos Context

Challenges and Prospects for the Chagos Archipelago in the Indian Ocean brings together leading experts specialising in different aspects of the Chagos disputes to explore the origins, challenges, and prospects for the future of the Chagos Archipelago. The Chagos Archipelago was administered as a dependency of colonial Mauritius for 250 years from 1715 until 1965, when the UK Government excised the Chagos Archipelago from colonial Mauritius to create the new British Indian Ocean Territory in return for Mauritian independence in 1968. In 1966 the UK government agreed to make the largest Chagos island of Diego Garcia available to the US military for 50 years in the first instance (subsequently extended by a further 20 years to 2036). The British authorities depopulated the Chagos islands by 1973, sending the Chagos islanders to Mauritius and Seychelles. The study of Chagos is dominated by the legacy of empire and colonial expansion, the expulsion and subsequent marginalisation of the Chagossians, the long-running sovereignty dispute between the Republic of Mauritius and the UK, the US military's ongoing occupation of Diego Garcia, and debates about environmental conservation in the context of the Marine Protected Area (MPA) controversially established in 2010.

In 1972 and 1982, following protests by Chagossians in Mauritius, the UK government awarded the Mauritian government limited compensation for the resettlement of Chagos islanders, with the money belatedly disbursed to Chagos islanders in Mauritius (but not in Seychelles, where Chagos islanders have never received compensation). In 2000, the High Court in London ruled that removing the Chagos islanders from the Chagos Archipelago had been unlawful, but in 2004 the UK government used the royal prerogative of the Orders in Council to prohibit unauthorised persons from entering the territory. And the *Chagos Islanders* group litigation case progressed through the English courts in the early 2000s, but ultimately failed to secure further compensation for the displaced Chagos islanders. Meanwhile, under the British Overseas Territories Act 2002, the UK Government awarded UK citizenship to Chagos islanders and most of their second-generation descendants born outwith Chagos. Since 2002, several thousand members of the extended Chagossian community have migrated from Mauritius and Seychelles to the UK and elsewhere. However, the British Overseas Territories Act 2002 controversially did not extend citizenship either to all second-generation Chagossians

DOI: 10.4324/9781003390299-2

or to subsequent generations of Chagossians born outwith Chagos, which therefore became a focus of subsequent political activism within the extended community. Twenty years later, in the context of the UK government's concerted effort to cultivate a "hostile environment" for migrants, the otherwise hostile Nationality and Borders Act 2022 sought to address the historic injustices of the British Overseas Territories Act 2002 by extending eligibility for UK citizenship to subsequent generations of Chagossians born outwith Chagos.

Chagos has historically been dominated by a declining colonial power in collaboration with an emergent global superpower, but the agendas are increasingly being set by the Republic of Mauritius and members of the extended Chagossian community. Successive Mauritian governments have asserted Mauritian sovereign rights to the Chagos Archipelago since 1980. Mauritian governments gradually secured support to challenge the imperialist status quo, eventually rallying the international diplomatic community to support the full decolonisation of Mauritius and the return of the Chagos Archipelago to the Republic of Mauritius. Finally, in 2018 the United Nations sought an Advisory Opinion from the International Court of Justice on the Legal Consequences of the Separation of the Chagos Archipelago from Mauritius in 1965. The International Court of Justice found almost unanimously that the decolonisation of Mauritius was incomplete, and that the UK must therefore end its administration of the Chagos Archipelago. The United Nations General Assembly welcomed the Advisory Opinion and adopted a resolution calling for the complete decolonisation of Mauritius. Since 2020 the official United Nations map shows the Chagos Archipelago as Mauritian territory (and no longer as the British Indian Ocean Territory). In 2022, the Republic of Mauritius and the UK entered into negotiations regarding the status of the Chagos Archipelago.

However, these negotiations are controversial within the Chagossian community for two main reasons. Firstly, there are longstanding ideological and pragmatic disagreements between individuals and community groups based on assessments about which administration seems more or less likely to facilitate resettlement or to provide compensation. Many members of the extended Chagossian community are concerned that a future Mauritian administration would continue to prioritise economic and military interests over Chagossian resettlement. For some, including many of those Chagossians who are not also Mauritian citizens – for instance, those Chagos islanders who were displaced to Seychelles rather than to Mauritius, and those descendants born in Seychelles, the UK, or elsewhere – decolonisation looks rather like recolonisation. Secondly, it's not clear how these negotiations between states might be able to consult with and incorporate views from the Chagossian community. Despite disagreements on many topics, Chagossian groups do agree on one thing: the importance of involving Chagossians in decision-making about the future of Chagos.

The Foreign Affairs Committee's Sub-Committee on Overseas Territories launched an inquiry on the Chagos islands in late 2023, soliciting written evidence and holding an oral evidence session in early 2024. Delivering oral evidence to a Foreign Affairs Committee in January 2024, the then UK Foreign Secretary, David Cameron, declared that "it was not possible" to "relocate Chagossians back on the outer islands" and that "The absolutely crucial thing is the safety, security and long-term viability of this base [on Diego Garcia]".[1] In March 2024, the Foreign Affairs

Committee published a letter to the then Foreign Secretary which reasserts that "there is a strong moral case for resettlement", expresses scepticism about the Government's arguments that "resettlement is unsustainable", and concludes that "it is currently the UK Government, and only the UK Government, standing in the way of this taking place".[2] Meanwhile, in February 2024, the Mauritius Prime Minister's Office and the Zoological Society of London organised a workshop – attended by representatives of the Mauritian government, Chagossian groups, conservation scientists, and fisheries and shipping industries – planning for a Chagos Archipelago Marine Protected Area under Mauritian administration.

On 3 October 2024 the United Kingdom and Mauritius announced that they had reached an agreement over the Chagos Islands. The United Kingdom agreed to give Mauritius sovereignty of the Chagos Islands and in return the UK and US military base on Diego Garcia could operate initially for another 99 years. The agreement has been met with controversy, as some members of the Chagossian community are critical of the United Kingdom's failure to consult with them as part of the negotiations.

Chagos Literature

Chagos has inspired sustained engagement from researchers and others who have published extensively on Chagos (particularly but not exclusively since the London High Court judgment of 2000). This book brings together arts, humanities, and social science contributions to the study of Chagos, and correspondingly neglects scientific research on Chagos. Contributors to this book draw predominantly on the existing Chagos literature by historians, social anthropologists, political scientists, and legal scholars on the treatment and experiences of the Chagossians and on the political, diplomatic, and legal disputes.

Focusing on the role played by the US and its informal empire, David Vine's monograph *Island of Shame: The Secret History of the U.S. Military Base on Diego Garcia* (2009) provided an in-depth and provocative exposé of how the US conspired with the UK to forcibly expel the Chagos islanders from Chagos. In her monograph *Chagos islanders in Mauritius and the UK: Forced Displacement and Onward Migration* (2011), Laura Jeffery provides the most in-depth ethnographic exploration of forced displacement and onward migration within the living memory of the Chagossian community. Such anthropological perspectives demonstrate the importance of considering the implications of macro-geopolitical decisions on a small, marginalised, and forcibly displaced community. Both anthropologists' monographs were based on fieldwork during the 2000s, however, meaning that there is a need to publish updates that can draw on newly available archival material that has come to light due to international law litigation and that can address the experiences of the extended Chagossian communities in the UK in the 2010s and beyond, including following the extension of UK citizenship to subsequent generations via the Nationality and Borders Act 2022. Informed by Jeffery and Vine's extensive scholarship, social science, and arts and humanities contributors to *Challenges and Prospects for the Chagos Archipelago in the Indian Ocean* offer fresh perspectives that take the readers in new and sometimes strikingly different directions.

Stephen Allen's monograph *The Chagos Islanders and International Law* (2014) illustrates the ongoing problems arising from international law's endorsement of the territorial integrity of colonial units for the purpose of decolonisation at the expense of the countervailing claims of colonial self-determination by non-European peoples that inhabited the same colonial unit. The book uses the competing claims to the Chagos islands to demonstrate the need for a more nuanced approach to the resolution of sovereignty disputes resulting from the legacy of European colonialism. In their co-edited book *Fifty Years of the British Indian Ocean Territory* (2018), Stephen Allen and Chris Monaghan offer broad coverage of legal issues including human rights, international law, and public law. Thomas Burri and Jamie Trinidad's co-edited book *The International Court of Justice and Decolonization: New Directions from the Chagos Advisory Opinion* (2021) focuses on the International Court of Justice 2019 Advisory Opinion on the Legal Consequences of the Separation of the Chagos Archipelago from Mauritius in 1965 and the subsequent United Nations General Assembly resolution calling for the complete decolonisation of Mauritius. Most recently, Philippe Sands KC, counsel for Mauritius in its legal proceedings against the UK, has published *The Last Colony: A Tale of Exile, Justice and Britain's Colonial Legacy* (2022).

In our approach to this new edited collection of chapters on Chagos, we have been inspired by previous cross-disciplinary and cross-sector dialogues. In their co-edited book *Eviction from the Chagos Islands: Displacement and Struggle for Identity Against Two World Powers* (2011), Sandra Evers and Marry Kooy brought together experts from across and beyond the academy to demonstrate how an issue as wide-ranging as Chagos could be addressed effectively by integrating multi-disciplinary perspectives. A 2015 conference at the University of Greenwich exploring the Chagos Litigation: A Socio-Legal Dialogue similarly offered an opportunity for cross-disciplinary dialogue. However, both this 2011 book and this 2015 conference date from before any of the international law decisions, therefore necessitating updates to address subsequent challenges and prospects for the future of Chagos. Inspired by these cross-disciplinary and cross-sector dialogues, we similarly wanted in *Challenges and Prospects for the Chagos Archipelago in the Indian Ocean* to bring together the experts from diverse disciplinary perspectives and from beyond the academy.

Chagos Dialogue

Most of the chapters in this book were first brought together at a conference hosted at the University of Worcester in collaboration with the University of Edinburgh on 26 May 2023 to commemorate the 50th anniversary since the final deportation from the Chagos Archipelago. Building on the extensive literature cited above, this book makes two important contributions.

The book's first contribution relates to its timeliness. Chagos is a fast-moving topic in terms of significant developments and subsequent responses to and engagement with these developments. Contributors to this book address the implications of recent developments such as the International Court of Justice 2019 Advisory Opinion on the Legal Consequences of the Separation of the Chagos Archipelago from Mauritius in 1965, the subsequent United Nations General

Assembly resolution calling for the complete decolonisation of Mauritius, the UK Nationality and Borders Act 2022, and the ongoing negotiations between the Republic of Mauritius and the UK regarding the status of the Chagos Archipelago. Additionally, new archival evidence has come to light via international law litigation, giving rise to a clear need for reconsideration of historical issues in light of newly available archival material. *Challenges and Prospects for the Chagos Archipelago in the Indian Ocean* thus represents an opportunity to address key issues such as colonialism and the legacy of empire in the context of the political, diplomatic, legal, social, and cultural landscape of the 2020s.

The book's second contribution relates to its inclusivity. As we have shown above, the study of Chagos depends on a broad range of cross-disciplinary and cross-sector expertise and dialogue connected to the various legal disputes, the mistreatment of the Chagossians, the lived experiences and struggles of those removed from their homeland and subsequent generations, the diplomatic, military, and political considerations, and debates about environmental conservation in the context of the MPA. This book transcends disciplinary silos by incorporating chapters by experts addressing these wide-ranging debates and challenges from diverse academic perspectives. Alongside established researchers, the book incorporates early career researchers, including those of Chagossian descent, who bring fresh approaches to the study of Chagos; alongside academic researchers, it also incorporates chapters by experts working on Chagos from outwith academia, including from practitioners with longstanding professional engagement on Chagos. Most but not all of the authors are based in one or other of the three main countries implicated in Chagos: Mauritius, the UK, and the USA.

At the same time, however, we recognise the limits to timeliness and inclusivity alike. Firstly, the negotiations between Mauritius and the UK have only just reached an agreement that will see the UK give Mauritius sovereignty of the Chagos Islands, and as the chapters within this book were written before the agreement of 3 October 2024 the conclusions reached within may not withstand the test of time. And, judging from the history of political debates, legal cases, and diplomatic spats surrounding Chagos, no doubt new controversies will come to light no sooner than this book has gone to press. For example, the decision to give sovereignty to Mauritius has already been met with considerable criticism. Secondly, there are limits to the inclusivity of our decision to organise an academic conference, in the UK, and in English. And there are limits to the inclusivity of our decision – as academics – to disseminate in the form of an academic book in which chapters must be written according to academic standards. A few prospective contributors ultimately decided not to participate in the conference and/or book project for political and/or academic reasons relating to the sensitivity of the ongoing negotiations between Mauritius and the UK and/or the restrictions of academe as a medium for dissemination of material about Chagos.

Chagos Chapters

In the first chapter, "The Chagos saga: 21st century dispute about incomplete decolonisation", Milan Meetarbhan provides an extensive historical overview of the sequence of events that led to the detachment of the Chagos Archipelago and the deportation of Chagossians. The chapter describes successive judicial proceedings brought by Chagossians and their descendants, and attempts by Mauritius to assert sovereignty under international law, as a consequence of incomplete decolonisation. Richard Allen's chapter, "The Chagos Archipelago in late eighteenth- and nineteenth-century Indian Ocean world history", provides important context to the question of decolonisation through the 18th- and 19th-century history of the archipelago as a minor dependency of Mauritius. The chapter draws on Mauritian and British archival sources to situate Chagos in the Indian Ocean regional economic and social context, clarifying the links of Chagossians to other Afro-Creole people in the region, through histories of slave trading, indenture, plantation labour, and forced migration. Priya Bahadoor's chapter, "Origins, legacies, and future: the Chagossians, a population in exile", continues to trace this economic and social history into the 20th century, and the moment of detachment and deportation. This chapter charts the formation of groups like the Chagos Refugees Group (CRG), highlighting the importance of women's political action in the context of resistance, and locating the Chagossian struggle in a long and intimate material relationship with the islands.

In "Chagos: plantation or paradise? Island Edens and Indian Ocean empires, 1600–2023", Chris Hill examines the Chagos Archipelago through the language and imagery of "paradise" – an idea that informed French and British imperial expansion and colonial exploitation. Whilst Chagossians have described the archipelago in these terms, Hill argues that this framing has also been mobilised against their return, particularly through the depiction of the BIOT as "untouched" and the creation of an MPA. Sue Farran's contribution, "Human rights and the Marine Protected Area around the Chagos Archipelago", provides background to the MPA's establishment, placing it in the context of rights protection beyond marine protection alone. The Chagos Archipelago, via the MPA, is at the centre of conflicting rights claims – fishing rights, national and international security, sovereignty, the human rights of Chagossians, and the rights of nonhumans.

Charles Fombad's chapter, "Return of the Chagos Islands to Mauritius and Chagossian identity: constitutional, legal, and political perspectives", examines the implications of the return of Chagos to Mauritius, with particular attention to the current status of Chagossians under the Mauritian constitution. The chapter argues that the constitutional changes necessary to protect the rights of the Chagossians as a distinct ethnic community would have to take one of two approaches: either an "equality approach" under a general Bill of Rights, or a minority rights approach that redresses harm. In "Political and legal debates about Chagossian ethnicity and indigeneity", Laura Jeffery provides further evidence for Chagossians as an ethnic minority and indigenous people demonstrating how they meet the legislative criteria for both. However, Jeffery argues, the implications of recognition as an ethnic group and indigenous people are limited in practice, due to the power imbalances that inhere in the structures that confer this status.

Thierry Mandarin, in "Intergenerational challenges, cultural identify, and future prospects for Chagossian communities in the UK", draws on ethnographic research to reflect on the experiences of Chagossian descendants in Manchester, UK, and their feelings regarding the Nationality and Borders Act (2022). The chapter focuses both on the challenges associated with cultural trauma and on the way that these historical roots facilitate growth and hope for the future. Mandarin makes it clear that there is no one unified experience of being Chagossian, and that disagreement and conflict within the community are to be expected. In "Certainty and uncertainty: native and older generation Chagossian perspectives from Mauritius amid the UK Government's Nationality and Borders Act 2022", Chrisyl Wong-Hang-Sun considers some of the same questions, this time from the perspective of older Chagossians active with the CRG in Mauritius, who are also oriented towards future action despite past hardship and present uncertainty. Wong-Hang-Sun describes how action is produced through the Kreol concepts *lalwa* (law), *lespwar* (hope), *lavenir* (future), and *kot mo mem* (at home).

In "Voicing the trauma of the lost territory: creative writing, therapy and the Chagos Refugees Group", Esther Pujolràs-Noguer and Felicity Hand draw on a creative writing workshop they organised at the University of Mauritius, with members of the CRG. They contend that taking a literary approach to forced displacement can give a voice to the Chagossian diaspora, and position the particular plight of Chagossians in relation to other forced displacements (and forms of creative expression) across the Indian Ocean region. An excerpt from *Diego Garcia: A Novel*, by Natasha Soobramanien and Luke Williams, takes as its starting point the way that the concept of "fiction" was deployed by US and UK diplomats to expedite the deracination of the Chagossians. The book, focused on two characters who have a chance encounter with a Chagossian poet, is an attempt to reclaim fiction as a tool for liberation. In the extract, one character writes to the other about the work of Lindsey Collen, Shenaz Patel, and Saradha Soobrayen.

Chris Monaghan and Satvinder Juss, in "The British courts and the Chagos story: an exercise in colonial justice", explore the question of what justice would look like for Chagossians, and whether it has been delivered by "British" courts despite resistance from the UK government. They argue that legal action and political activism have made the voice of Chagossians audible, even as the colonial mindset of UK institutions has tried to silence it. "Stakeholders or bystanders? An attempt by Seychellois Chagossians to intervene in the International Tribunal for the Law of the Sea", by Jamie Trinidad, Stephen Allen, and Thomas Burri, is a reprint of the *Amicus Curiae* submission by Chagossian Committee Seychelles (CCS), with a contextual introduction. The CCS intervened in maritime delimitation proceedings between Mauritius and Maldives in ITLOS, emphasising the distinct rights of Chagossians as an indigenous people rather than a subset of people of Mauritius, and arguing that they have a right to be consulted over and derive benefit from use of marine spaces and resources in Chagos Archipelago.

Samuel Bashfield's chapter, "The 1966 BIOT Agreement and Polaris", examines negotiations between the UK and the US leading up to the creation of the BIOT. Drawing on archival records that set out the acquisition of the Polaris nuclear ballistic missile program, Bashfield demonstrates that it was intertwined with the BIOT agreement from the outset. The relationship between the two was concealed, allowing Britain to maintain its status as a dominant power and feeding into the other "fictions" that justified the displacement. In "The power behind the throne:

the US Government must face its responsibility for the Chagossian exile", David Vine argues that the US was the "senior partner" in this dynamic, not only first conceiving of the idea of a base, but also insisted on the expulsions, ordering and overseeing the way that they were carried out, and aiding in the coverup. The US thus outsourced the "violence of displacement", paying the UK to absorb culpability, and Vine argues that both parties should be responsible for resettlement and payment of compensation to the Chagossians. Peter Harris, in "The Indo-Pacific and the Chagos Archipelago: two logics, two futures", explores the consequences that the creation of the "Indo-Pacific" as a region has for the Chagos Archipelago. The chapter argues that its status as a product of US-China rivalry provides justification for the existence of a US military base on Diego Garcia. At the same time, the "Indo-Pacific" is supposed to be defined by adherence to rules-based international order, which is at odds with the continued occupation of the Chagos group. The political future (including sovereignty and return) of the archipelago thus depends on which idea gains ascendance.

"Flagpole fights, courtroom clashes, and coconut crabs" is an account of Owen Bowcott's journey, alongside a group of Mauritian officials, lawyers, journalists, scientists, and Chagossian exiles, from Seychelles into the BIOT in 2022. While the pretext was a survey of Blenheim Reef, the trip was also an assertion of Mauritian sovereignty, and Bowcott describes not only the tensions surrounding this but also the homecoming of the Chagossians who experienced deportation. David Snoxell's chapter, "Why has it taken 25 years for the UK to start negotiating an overall settlement on Chagos with Mauritius?", outlines the 2022 agreement between the UK and Mauritius to negotiate on sovereignty in relation to the Chagos Archipelago, aiming to come to an agreement by 2023. At the time of writing, this has still not been achieved. Snoxell gives an overview of these negotiations and the multiple factors upon which they have turned, and questions how the UK can continue to ignore the rulings of international courts and the UN, as well as world opinion.

Throughout the volume, Chrisyl Wong-Hang-Sun's poems explore her experience as a Chagossian descendent. "zistwar Sagosian, nu tu bizin amenn li" is dedicated to the memory of Mimose Furcy, activist and co-founder of the Chagos Tambour Group. "ayapana in a british plastic plant pot" tells the story of displacement through a clipping of the medicinal herb, *ayapana*, travelling across borders. "Limuria is in Our trust" speaks to the idea of "the source" that recurs in her ethnographic chapter. Finally, "Ode to Chagossian Zistwar" takes the form of a *sega* song communicated by the ancestors. Saradha Soobrayen's poems are grounded in her longstanding engagement with the displacement of the Chagos Islanders. "So immaculate – Peros Banhos, Saloman, Diego Garcia" evokes the paradisal past of the archipelago. "This poem is intuitively aware of the erasure of the Chagos Archipelago" plays with form, expressing how conversations about Chagos, especially amongst outsiders, are hampered by what remains unsaid and effaced. "UK Ambassador Lobbied Senators to Hide Diego Garcia's Role In Rendition" channels the anger of those who navigate the "fiction" that has led to the displacement of the Chagos Islanders, as they call for action to repair this harm.

Notes

1 https://committees.parliament.uk/oralevidence/14047/html/
2 https://committees.parliament.uk/publications/43824/documents/217490/default/

References

Allen, Stephen (2014) *The Chagos Islanders and International Law*. Oxford: Hart Publishing.
Allen, Stephen and Monaghan, Chris (eds.) (2018) *Fifty Years of the British Indian Ocean Territory*. Cham: Springer.
Burri, Thomas and Trinidad, Jamie (eds.) (2021) *The International Court of Justice and Decolonization: New Directions from the Chagos Advisory Opinion*. Cambridge: Cambridge University Press.
Evers, Sandra and Kooy, Marry (eds.) (2011) *Eviction from the Chagos Islands: Displacement and Struggle for Identity Against Two World Powers*. Leiden: Brill.
Jeffery, Laura (2011) *Chagos islanders in Mauritius and the UK: Forced Displacement and Onward Migration*. Manchester: Manchester University Press.
Sands, Philippe (2022) *The Last Colony: A Tale of Exile, Justice and Britain's Colonial Legacy*. London: Weidenfeld & Nicolson.
Vine, David (2009) *Island of Shame: The Secret History of the U.S. Military Base on Diego Garcia*. Princeton: Princeton University Press.

1 The Chagos Saga

21st Century Dispute about Incomplete Decolonisation

Milan Meetarbhan

Introduction

Section 111 of the Mauritian Constitution defines the territory of the Republic of Mauritius as including "the islands of Mauritius, Rodrigues, Agalega, Tromelin, Cargados Carajos and the Chagos Archipelago including Diego Garcia and any other island comprised in the State of Mauritius". These islands were all administered from Mauritius (then known as Isle de France) by the French Governor. Isle de France and the other islands were ceded to the United Kingdom, after the British conquest of 1810, under the Treaty of Paris signed in 1814.

The islands, including the Chagos Archipelago, were subsequently administered by the British Governor based in Mauritius, as "dependencies" of Mauritius. Various Ordinances made by the British Governor applied to the dependencies and reports submitted by the UK to the UN Fourth Committee mentioned these dependencies. The last pre-independence Constitution for Mauritius, adopted by the UK, provided that the territory of Mauritius includes these dependencies.

The Chagos Archipelago is about 2,200 km from mainland Mauritius, about 900 km east of Madagascar, about 1,820 km south of Seychelles, and about 2,000 km off the eastern coast of the African continent. The Archipelago consists of a number of islands and atolls. Diego Garcia, the largest island in the Chagos Archipelago, has an area of about 27 sq km.

Detachment of the Chagos Archipelago

At the height of the Cold War in the 1960s, when the Indian Ocean was considered as a major geo-strategic zone, the US sought to establish military facilities in the region (Gifford, 2018).[1]

Two other Western powers which still had colonies in the Indian Ocean had failed in their invasion in 1956 of the Suez Canal, which provided crucial access to the Indian Ocean.

The first round of formal discussions between the US and the UK on use by the US of certain British-owned islands in the Indian Ocean started in February 1964, though the issue had been canvassed earlier.

DOI: 10.4324/9781003390299-3

The US had expressed its interest in establishing military facilities on the island of Diego Garcia. The Americans wanted the territory to remain under British control so that in the event of Mauritius attaining independence the US would have security over maintenance of their presence on the islands.[2] The Archipelago was subsequently detached from Mauritius prior to the country's independence and the UK created a new colonial territory known as British Indian Ocean Territory (BIOT).

An "Agreement concerning the Availability for Defence Purposes of the British Indian Ocean Territory" was concluded between the UK and the US on 30 December 1966.

Historical Background

In September 1965, the British government held talks with leaders of political parties in Mauritius, at Lancaster House in London, on the future constitutional status of the country. A meeting was arranged in the margins of the constitutional conference between the British Prime Minister Harold Wilson and the Premier of the colonial government in Mauritius, Seewoosagur Ramgoolam, to talk about the detachment of the Chagos from the colony of Mauritius. The UK government was aware of the deep divisions in Mauritius on whether the country should become independent or not, and Ramgoolam, who led the pro-independence movement, was told that he could go home with the promise of independence if he agreed to the detachment. In a briefing paper prepared by the Colonial Office for Wilson's meeting with Ramgoolam, the British Prime Minister was advised as follows: "The object is to frighten him with hope; hope that he might get independence; fright lest he might not unless he is sensible about the detachment of the Chagos Archipelago" (Colonial Office 1965c). According to an official account of the meeting, Wilson told Ramgoolam,

> The Premier and his colleagues could return to Mauritius either with Independence or without it … Diego Garcia could either be detached by Order in Council or with the agreement of the Premier and his colleagues. The best solution of all might be Independence and detachment by agreement
> (*Record of a Conversation Between the Prime Minister and Premier of Mauritius, Sir Seewoosagur Ramgoolam, at No. 10, Downing Street at 10 A.M. on Thursday,* 1965).

Ramgoolam initially opposed the detachment and later proposed that there could instead be a long-term lease to the US. However, the Americans insisted on detachment and the British government sought to obtain the consent of the colonial ministers, though the Colonial Secretary made it clear that the UK could proceed unilaterally[3] (the UK subsequently argued before the Arbitration Tribunal that no such consent was required under UK law).[4] This was interpreted by the Mauritius Ministers as a threat by the UK to detach the Chagos Archipelago from Mauritius with or without their agreement ("*Arbitration under Annex VII of The 1982 United*

Nations Convention on the Law of The Sea, Republic of Mauritius V. United Kingdom of Great Britain and Northern Ireland", 2012, para. 330).

Ramgoolam finally gave in to British pressure, but set out the conditions under which he would grant consent. These conditions were later found by an international tribunal to have been agreed by the UK and were termed the Lancaster House Undertakings (Meetarbhan, 2015).

The Lancaster House Undertakings were as follows:"The British Government would use their good offices with the U.S. Government to ensure that the following facilities in the Chagos Archipelago would remain available to the Mauritius Government as far as practicable:

(a) Navigational and Meteorological facilities;
(b) Fishing Rights;
(c) Use of Air Strip for emergency landing and for refuelling civil planes without disembarkation of passengers."

- It was also agreed that "the benefit of any minerals or oil discovered in or near the Chagos Archipelago should revert to the Mauritius Government."
- The UK further undertook that if the need for the facilities on the islands disappeared, the islands should be **returned** to Mauritius.

The UK has since repeated, on many occasions for over four decades, that the islands will be **returned** (or "revert") to Mauritius when no longer required for defence purposes. Later the UK started using the term "ceded" rather than "returned".The British Governor of Mauritius formally conveyed the UK proposal on detachment to Mauritian Ministers on 19 July 1965. On 23 July 1965, the Governor reported to London that Ministers were seeking more time to consider the proposal. He also mentioned Ramgoolam's "dislike of detachment" (Mauritius Telegram No. 170 to the Colonial Office, 1965). On 30 July 1965, the Governor stated that Ministers considered that detachment was "unacceptable to public opinion in Mauritius".[5] The Secretary of State informed the Governor that the proposal for a lease instead of detachment was not acceptable (Colonial Office, 1965a, para. 2).

However, the formal "consent" of Mauritian Ministers to detachment was subsequently given, subject to the conditions set out at Lancaster House.

On 5 November 1965, the British Governor of Mauritius informed the Colonial Office in London that Mauritian ministers had agreed to the detachment of Chagos, on the understanding that the UK Government had agreed to the pre-conditions set at Lancaster House, and that the use of the term "in or near" the Chagos with respect to the condition relating to the benefit of any minerals or oil "means within area within which Mauritius would be able to derive benefit but for change of sovereignty".[6]

The UK government then proceeded to detach the Chagos Archipelago from the colony of Mauritius and establish a new British Indian Ocean Territory by Order in Council on 8 November 1965 (*Order 1965/1920*).

The Exchange of Notes between the UK and the USA on Availability of certain Indian Ocean Islands for Defence Purposes, of 30 December 1966, provided that the agreement was for a period of 50 years but could be extended for another 20 years. The agreement was duly extended in 2016 for a further period of 20 years (*Legal Consequences of the Separation of the Chagos Archipelago from Mauritius in 1965. Advisory opinion*, 2019, para. 151).

There was no lease agreement as such between the two countries and no provision for payment of rent. However, the US agreed to contribute up to five million pounds towards the cost of setting up the BIOT "by waiving to that extent research and development surcharges for the United Kingdom purchase of the Polaris missile system" (*Hansard: House of Commons*, 1975, cols 271–272; *The New York Times*, 1975; Waghorn, 2019; Bowcott and Rinvolucri, 2022; see also Bashfield, 2024, in this volume).

Deportation of Population

The UK had initially denied that there was a local population – except for some "Man Fridays". But the agreement between the UK and US governments provided that the UK would take any "administrative measures" necessary to ensure that the US defence needs were met, and that to this end the UK would take administrative measures that would include "resettling any inhabitants" of the islands.[7] The inhabitants of the Chagos were subsequently forcibly removed from the islands in 1971. Between 1965 and 1973 around 1,500 people whose ancestors had lived on the archipelago for two centuries were shipped to Mauritius and Seychelles.[8]

Challenge to UK Sovereignty

The Mauritian government has, over the decades following Independence, challenged the excision of the Chagos.[9] Speaking at the UN General Assembly in 1980 Prime Minister Ramgoolam recalled that Mauritius has

> reaffirmed its claim to Diego Garcia and the Prime Minister of Great Britain in a parliamentary statement has made it known that the island will revert to Mauritius when it is no longer required for the global defence of the West. Our sovereignty having been thus accepted we should go further than that and disband the British Indian Ocean territory and allow Mauritius to come into its natural heritage as before its independence. United States should make arrangements directly with Mauritius for the continued use of the island for defence purposes. And then there are the inhabitants of Diego Garcia who are domiciled in Mauritius and for whom better arrangements should be made. It must be the duty of both the United States and Great Britain to discuss with the Mauritius government how best to give satisfaction to all concerned and at the same time provide better prospects for the Islanders.
>
> (United Nations General Assembly, 1980)

In the same year, the Organisation of African Unity adopted a resolution calling for the return of the Chagos to Mauritius (Organization of African Unity, 1980; see also Organization of African Unity, 1990, Organization of African Unity, 2000; African Union, 2011). The OAU's successor, the African Union subsequently reiterated its support for Mauritius, and significantly in 2011 when Mauritius started its campaign to obtain support for a UNGA resolution seeking an advisory opinion from the ICJ, the AU not only reiterated its support for Mauritius' stance on the Chagos but also expressed support for initiatives that Mauritius may take at the UN on this matter (African Union, 2011).[10]

The challenge to the legality of the excision was based essentially on UN Resolution 1514(XV) of 14 December 1960 and UN Resolution 2066(XX) of 14 December 1965: "Question of Mauritius" and on the Right to Self-Determination under international law. In pleadings before a UNCLOS Tribunal in 2014, the UK argued that the detachment was a matter of British Constitutional Law and no consent of Mauritian Ministers was required. However, formal consent might have been sought mainly to avoid embarrassment at the UN, namely at the Committee of 24, where decolonisation was a major issue under debate since the admission of many new Member States following the "wave of change"[11] which resulted in many colonial territories acceding to independence.

After a change in government in 1982, a Mauritian parliamentary Select Committee examined the circumstances surrounding the excision of Chagos and concluded that the "consent" had been given under duress in exchange for independence and that this "cannot fall outside the most elementary definition of blackmailing" (Select Committee on the Excision of the Chagos Archipelago, 1983).

Judicial Recourse

Over the years since then, there have been two sets of judicial proceedings in relation to the Chagos issue. The first set of proceedings were cases brought by former inhabitants of the Chagos or their descendants and the second set were proceedings under international law brought or initiated by the Government of Mauritius.

Proceedings by Chagos Islanders

The former inhabitants of the Chagos and their descendants have brought a series of cases before UK courts claiming the right of return to the archipelago.

The UK adopted three immigration ordinances prohibiting the islanders' return. The Ordinance adopted in April 1971 made it unlawful, and a criminal offence, for anyone to enter or remain in the BIOT islands without a permit. The 2000 ordinance lifted the restriction for BIOT citizens entering the BIOT but entry to Diego Garcia remained subject to a permit. However, this Ordinance was repealed in 2004.

The first case brought by the islanders in 1975 was settled on payment of 4,000,000 GBP and provision of land worth GBP 1,000,000. Under the terms of the settlement, the islanders were giving up their rights to further claims. Another case brought by the islanders was struck out by the UK High Court in 2003 on the ground that further claims amounted to an abuse as the islanders had renounced their right to further claims ("*Chagos Islanders v Attorney General and HM BIOT Commissioner*", 2003).

There was another unsuccessful challenge in 2016 when the House of Lords held that in the context of the present day, rather than 1968, any right of abode on the outer islands was purely symbolic, none of the islanders having gone to live on the islands in the four-year period when this had been permitted under the ordinance then in force ("*R (on the application of Bancoult (No 2)) (Appellant) v Secretary of State for Foreign and Commonwealth Affairs (Respondent)*", 2016; Arvind, 2018; Gifford, 2018, chap. 5; Monaghan, 2018).

In 2012, the European Court of Human Rights held that a claim by the islanders was inadmissible as they were deemed to have accepted compensation following earlier litigation ("*Chagos Islanders v. the United Kingdom*", 2012).

A claim brought by the islanders before a US Court of Appeal also failed as the Court found that the claims were nonjusticiable political questions *("Olivier Bancoult et al. v. Robert S. McNamara et al'*, 2002; "*Olivier Bancoult, et al., Appellants v. Robert S. Mcnamara, et al., Appellees*", 2006).

Proceedings under International Law

The Government of Mauritius first announced consideration of a possible recourse to the International Court of Justice on the issue of Mauritian sovereignty over the Chagos in 2004. However, since the UK had, when accepting the compulsory jurisdiction of the ICJ under Article 36 of the ICJ Statute, expressed its reservation about compulsory jurisdiction of the Court over certain disputes with members of the Commonwealth, Mauritius announced that it was considering withdrawing from the Commonwealth so that it could take its dispute with the UK to the international court (*L'express*, 2004). However, shortly thereafter the UK modified its initial reservation so that henceforth the ICJ would not have compulsory jurisdiction with regard to:

> "(ii) any dispute with the government of any other country which **is or has been** a Member of the Commonwealth;"
>
> ('*Declarations recognizing the jurisdiction of the Court as compulsory: United Kingdom of Great Britain and Northern Ireland*', 2017)

As a result of this amendment to the UK declaration, the Mauritian Government could not proceed with its decision to have recourse to the ICJ.

In 2010, the Government of Mauritius decided that since bilateral talks with the UK on the issue of sovereignty would lead nowhere it would "internationalise" the dispute and seek resolution of the dispute through judicial settlement. A two-pronged approach was decided in December 2010: (1) Refer the dispute over the establishment of a Marine Protected Area around the Chagos to an arbitral tribunal and (2) initiate action on a referral of the question to the ICJ for an advisory opinion of the court.

The UK Declaration of an MPA

The British plan to declare a Marine Protected Area around the Chagos first emerged in an article published in the British media in February 2009 (Gray, 2009). The plan was opposed by the Mauritian government because the UK declaration would amount to the exercise of rights of a coastal state which the UK was not. The Mauritian view was that only Mauritius has the legitimate right to exercise the rights of a coastal state with regard to part of what was considered as Mauritian territory. The Mauritian Prime Minister, Dr Navin Ramgoolam, took up the matter with his British counterpart Gordon Brown at the Commonwealth Summit in Trinidad in 2009. Dr Ramgoolam then informed the Mauritian Parliament that he had been assured by Gordon Brown that the UK would not go ahead with the plan.

At the time, a decision of the European Court of Human Rights was expected in the case brought by the former inhabitants of the Chagos and their descendants against the British government over their right of return to the archipelago and there was widespread suspicion that the UK was attempting to pre-empt a decision of the ECHR on right of return by declaring an MPA. This would ban economic activity and thus any future right of return would be only of academic interest, as there would be no viable economic prospects for those deciding to return to the islands.[12] Documents leaked later by WIKILEAKS included a cable sent to the US embassy in London in which a Foreign Office official reportedly wrote on 15 May 2009, "Establishing a marine reserve might, indeed, as the FCO's Roberts stated, be the most effective long-term way to prevent any of the Chagos Islands' former inhabitants or their descendants from resettling in the BIOT" (*The Guardian*, 2010).[13]

In spite of the assurance which the Mauritian Prime Minister said he had obtained from his British counterpart, the British Foreign Secretary David Milliband informed the Mauritian Prime Minister, on 1 April 2010, of the UK's decision to declare the MPA. In December 2010, Mauritius filed a case before an arbitration tribunal set up under ANNEX 7 of the United Nations Convention on the Law of the Sea challenging the UK's declaration of an MPA. Mauritius submitted that:

1. The UK is not THE coastal State.
2. Mauritius is the coastal State with rights over the Chagos.
3. Independently of the issue of sovereignty, the MPA is incompatible with UNCLOS.
4. CLCS: The UK should not stop Mauritius from making submissions on the Continental Shelf to the Commission on Limitation of the Continental Shelf.

Mauritius challenged the UK appointment of Anthony Greenwood, the British Judge on the International Court of Justice, as arbitrator as the latter had maintained his links with the UK Foreign Office, but this challenge was unsuccessful (*In the Matter of an Arbitration Before An Arbitral Tribunal Constituted Under Annex Vii of the 1982 United Nations Convention on The Law of the Sea Between The Republic of Mauritius And The United Kingdom of Great Britain and Northern Ireland: Reasoned Decision On Challenge,* 2011). Following the UK's preliminary objection to the Tribunal's jurisdiction, it was decided that there would be no bifurcation and the objection would be heard along with the merits.

In its award given on 18 March 2015, the Tribunal found by a majority of three to two that it did not have jurisdiction over the claims of Mauritius regarding sovereignty and that it had to ask itself two basic questions:

1. Is the dispute primarily a matter of the interpretation and application of the term "coastal State", with the issue of sovereignty forming one aspect of a larger question?
2. Or does the dispute primarily concern sovereignty, with the UK's actions as a "coastal State" merely representing a manifestation of that dispute?

The Tribunal decided that though "in some instances a minor issue of territorial sovereignty could indeed be ancillary to a dispute concerning the interpretation or application of the Convention. That, however, is not this case" ("*Chagos Marine Protected Area Arbitration (Mauritius v. United Kingdom)*", 2015).

In relation to Mauritius's fourth submission, the Tribunal found unanimously that it had jurisdiction pursuant to Article 288(1) and Article 297(1)(c) of the United Nations Convention of the Law of the Sea to consider the compatibility of the MPA with provisions of the Convention. The Tribunal found that:

1. the UK's undertaking to ensure that fishing rights in the Chagos Archipelago would remain available to Mauritius as far as practicable is legally binding insofar as it relates to the territorial sea;
2. that the UK's undertaking to return the Chagos Archipelago to Mauritius when no longer needed for defence purposes is legally binding; and
3. that the UK's undertaking to preserve the benefit of any minerals or oil discovered in or near the Chagos Archipelago for Mauritius is legally binding.

In establishing the MPA surrounding the Chagos Archipelago the UK had breached its obligations under Articles 2(3), 56(2), and 194(4) of the Convention.[14]

However, Judges Wolfrum and Kateka (both Judges of ITLOS) stated in a Dissenting and Concurring Opinion that since characterisation of a dispute is for the Tribunal to decide, the Tribunal should have found that this is not a sovereignty dispute. "The differing views on the Coastal State are the dispute before the Tribunal and the issue of sovereignty over the Chagos Archipelago is merely an element in the reasoning of Mauritius and not to be decided by the Tribunal" (Kateka and Wolfrum, 2015).

The dissenting judges also stated that since Mauritius was a colony of the UK when the 1965 agreement was reached and the Council of Ministers of Mauritius was presided over by the then British Governor, there was a clear situation of inequality between the two sides.

> A look at the discussion between Prime Minister Harold Wilson and Premier Sir Seewoosagur Ramgoolam suggests that Wilson's threat that Ramgoolam could return home without independence amounts to duress. The Private Secretary of Wilson used the language of "frighten[ing]" the Premier "with hope".

The Colonial Secretary equally resorted to the language of intimidation. Furthermore, following the Meeting with British Prime Minister Gordon Brown there was "*a commitment which Mauritius relied upon to its detriment*".[15]

The award was the first time in over 50 years that issues over the Chagos dispute had been heard by an international Tribunal which referred to Mauritius's "reversionary interest" in the archipelago. The Tribunal had asserted the UK's legally binding obligations under the Lancaster House Undertakings and declared that Mauritius was not like "*any third State*" with respect to Chagos.

ICJ Advisory Opinion

Following the award of the Tribunal in March 2015, Mauritius resumed the campaign (already started at the UN in 2011 and later suspended so as not to prejudice the hearings before the UNCLOS tribunal) to obtain support for a UN General Assembly resolution seeking an advisory opinion on the Chagos dispute. Resolution 71/292 (United Nations General Assembly, 2017), adopted by the UN General Assembly on 22 June 2017 by 94 votes (with 15 States voting against and 65 States abstaining), requested the ICJ to render an advisory opinion on the following questions:

> (a) Was the process of decolonization of Mauritius lawfully completed when Mauritius was granted independence in 1968, following the separation of the Chagos Archipelago from Mauritius and having regard to international law, including obligations reflected in General Assembly resolutions 1514 (XV) of 14 December 1960, 2066 (XX) of 16 December 1965, 2232 (XXI) of 20 December 1966 and 2357 (XXII) of 19 December 1967?;
>
> (b) What are the consequences under international law, including obligations reflected in the above-mentioned resolutions, arising from the continued administration by the United Kingdom of Great Britain and Northern Ireland of the Chagos Archipelago, including with respect to the inability of Mauritius to implement a programme for the resettlement on the Chagos Archipelago of its nationals, in particular those of Chagossian origin?

In the course of proceedings before the ICJ, 31 States and the African Union (AU) filed written statements, and 21 States and the AU participated in oral pleadings. In its quasi-unanimous Advisory Opinion (with only the US judge dissenting)[16] delivered on 25 February 2019, the Court expressed the view that "the law on self-determination constitutes the applicable international law during the period under consideration, namely between 1965 and 1968".

> The Court considers that the peoples of non-self-governing territories are entitled to exercise their right to self-determination in relation to their territory as a whole, the integrity of which must be respected by the administering Power. It follows that any detachment by the administering Power of part of a non-self-governing territory, unless based on the freely expressed and genuine will of the people of the territory concerned, is contrary to the right to self-determination.
>
> (*Legal Consequences of the Separation of the Chagos Archipelago from Mauritius in 1965. Advisory opinion,* 2019, para. 160)

Since at the time of its detachment from Mauritius in 1965, the Chagos Archipelago was clearly an integral part of that non-self-governing territory; the Court considered that this detachment was not based on the free and genuine expression of the will of the people concerned.

> The Court concludes that, as a result of the Chagos Archipelago's unlawful detachment and its incorporation into a new colony, known as the BIOT, the process of decolonization of Mauritius was not lawfully completed when Mauritius acceded to independence in 1968.

Consequently,

> the United Kingdom's continued administration of the Chagos Archipelago constitutes a wrongful act entailing the international responsibility of that State … It is an unlawful act of a continuing character which arose as a result of the separation of the Chagos Archipelago from Mauritius.

The United Kingdom is therefore "under an obligation to bring an end to its administration of the Chagos Archipelago as rapidly as possible, thereby enabling Mauritius to complete the decolonization of its territory in a manner consistent with the right of peoples to self-determination" (Legal Consequences of the Separation of the Chagos Archipelago From Mauritius in 1965. Advisory opinion 2019, paras 177–8). The Court also expressed the view that, "all Member States are under an obligation to cooperate with the United Nations in order to complete the decolonization of Mauritius".

Some States argued before the UN General Assembly and before the ICJ that an advisory opinion could not be sought on what was essentially a bilateral dispute on sovereignty. The ICJ rejected this submission and decided that it was competent to give an opinion on this issue. The questions put to the Court in the request for an advisory opinion were "cleverly drafted"[17] so as to pre-empt the challenge to the court's jurisdiction and ensure that they raised matters of international law relating to the General Assembly's own resolutions and principles of international law.

Looking beyond the issue of the unlawful occupation of the Chagos Archipelago, the Court's acceptance of its jurisdiction in this case will be considered a significant contribution to the caselaw on advisory opinions and to the law on the right to self-determination (Guilfoyle, 2021).

Developments since the ICJ Advisory Opinion

Following the ICJ advisory opinion, UN General Assembly adopted Resolution 73/295 to give effect to the Court's Advisory Opinion on 22 May 2019 by an overwhelming vote of 116 to 6 (with 56 abstentions).[18] The UNGA Resolution 73/295:

(i) Affirmed, in accordance with the Advisory Opinion of the ICJ of 25 February 2019, that the Chagos Archipelago forms an integral part of the territory of Mauritius.
(ii) Demanded that the UK withdraw its colonial administration from the Chagos Archipelago unconditionally within a period of not more than six months.
(iii) Urged the UK to cooperate with Mauritius in facilitating the resettlement of Mauritian nationals, including those of Chagossian origin, in the Chagos Archipelago and to pose no impediment or obstacle to such resettlement.
(iv) Called upon all Member States to cooperate with the UN to ensure the completion of the decolonization process of Mauritius as rapidly as possible, and to refrain from any action that will impede or delay the completion of the process of decolonization of Mauritius.
(v) Further called upon the UN and all its specialised agencies as well as all other international, regional, and intergovernmental organisations to recognize that the Chagos Archipelago forms an integral part of the territory of Mauritius, to support the decolonization of Mauritius as rapidly as possible, and to refrain from impeding that process by recognizing, or giving effect to any measures taken by or on behalf of, the so-called "British Indian Ocean Territory".

The UK failed to withdraw its colonial administration by the deadline of 22 November 2019 set by the UNGA Resolution and this was "deplored" by the African Union on 22 November 2019.[19] The UN Secretary-General's report to the General Assembly on 18 May 2020 set out developments that have taken place since the adoption of UNGA Resolution 73/295 (United Nations Secretary-General, 2020).

However, pursuant to UNGA Resolution 73/295, the UN published a new world map in February 2020 to clearly show the Chagos Archipelago as part of the territory of the Republic of Mauritius (United Nations General Assembly, 2019).

On 24 August 2021, the 27th Universal Postal Congress adopted a resolution for the implementation of the UNGA Resolution by the Universal Postal Union (UPU) (by 77 votes in favour, six against, and 41 abstaining).

The advisory opinion of the ICJ has given rise to a scholarly debate about (a) whether what was characterised by some states as "a bilateral dispute" could have been the subject matter of an advisory opinion of the ICJ and (b) given that an advisory opinion is not binding, what the consequences are of the clear determinations on matters of law supported by 13 of the 14 Judges of the highest judicial body of the United Nations.[20] The Special Chamber of the International Tribunal on the Law of the Sea had an opportunity to address the second issue in the Mauritius v Maldives case regarding maritime delimitation ("*Dispute Concerning Delimitation of the Maritime Boundary Between Mauritius and Maldives in the Indian Ocean (Mauritius/Maldives) Preliminary Objections – Judgment*", 2021). One of the "key findings" of the Special Chamber was that

> the determinations made by the ICJ with respect to the issues of the decolonization of Mauritius in the Chagos advisory opinion have legal effect and clear implications for the legal status of the Chagos Archipelago. The United Kingdom's continued claim to sovereignty over the Chagos Archipelago is contrary to those determinations. While the process of decolonization has yet to be completed, Mauritius' sovereignty over the Chagos Archipelago can be inferred from the ICJ's determinations.
>
> (op cit 2021, para. 246)

Mauritius had argued that "the issue of sovereignty has already been resolved by the ICJ's determination that Chagos is an integral part of the territory of Mauritius, and that the UK's ongoing administration is unlawful, and must be terminated", and that there is thus no unresolved sovereignty dispute (op cit 2021, para. 239).

Mauritius had raised the ante in September 2019 when in a statement before the UN General Assembly, Mauritius stated that "The forcible eviction of the inhabitants of the Chagos Archipelago which accompanied its unlawful excision from Mauritius remains a very dark episode of human history akin to a crime against humanity" (2019).

In February 2023 in its report "'That's When the Nightmare Started': UK and US Forced Displacement of the Chagossians and Ongoing Colonial Crimes", Human Rights Watch found that the continuing forced displacement of the Chagossians, the prevention of their permanent return to their homeland, and their persecution on racial and ethnic grounds amount to crimes against humanity.[21]

More than three years after the ICJ advisory opinion and after repeated assertions that the UK had "no doubt" about its sovereignty over the Chagos, the UK announced on 3 November 2022 that it was ready to open negotiations with Mauritius on the Chagos issue. In a written statement James Cleverly the UK Foreign Secretary stated that:

> Through negotiations, taking into account relevant legal proceedings, it is our intention to secure an agreement on the basis of international law to

> resolve all outstanding issues, including those relating to the former inhabitants of the Chagos Archipelago. This will allow the UK and Mauritius, as close Commonwealth partners, to work even more closely together to tackle the regional and global security challenges that face us all. We will seek to strengthen significantly our cooperation on Indian Ocean security, maritime security and marine protection, the conservation of the environment, climate change, respect for human rights, and to tackle illegal migration, illegal fishing, drugs and arms trafficking, as well as bilateral cooperation on a range of other issues. We will work to do this in cooperation with key allies and partners in the region.
>
> (Cleverly, 2022)

The UK, which had always treated this matter as a bilateral issue, broadened the scope of the future negotiations and sought to place this in the context of "cooperation on Indian Ocean security, maritime security and marine protection, the conservation of the environment, climate change, respect for human rights, and to tackle illegal migration, illegal fishing, drugs and arms trafficking". The Foreign Secretary also stated that the UK "recognises the US's and India's interests and will keep them informed of progress" over the negotiations.

It is clear that the British government wanted to show that the announcement on negotiations was not just an about turn on the issue of sovereignty but that the talks would be about the global issues of security and cooperation in the increasingly important geostrategic region of the Indian Ocean. At the end of September 2023 there had reportedly been five rounds of negotiations between the UK and Mauritius, but there has been no official statement from the parties on progress made.

Conclusion

Twenty-three years into the 21st century the issue of decolonisation is still being discussed between a former colonial power and its erstwhile colony.

The arbitral award of the Annex 7 Tribunal and the advisory opinion of the ICJ have been widely commented upon by scholars. One author has referred to the ICJ opinion as, "a bold judgment".[22]

These are also significant in the context of small states seeking justice through legal means,

> Smaller states can and do engage in such strategic litigation against greater powers… Smaller states that resort to international litigation do not necessarily expect a decision in their favour to secure automatic compliance from the respondent. Rather, it is usually hoped that a successful judicial or arbitral outcome will provide a standard around which other states may rally in order to place diplomatic pressure on a malefactor.
>
> (Kingsbury, 2011, pp. 203, 216)

In this sense, international law and legal argument provide tools that a State may use in promoting the legitimacy of its own actions or positions, or disputing those of another (Scott, 2017; Guilfoyle, 2021). Guilfoyle goes on to argue that

> apart from being a contest of disputed sovereignty over the islands of the Chagos Archipelago and as to the legitimacy of the respective parties' positions, the Mauritius–UK dispute also became a struggle over the use of international legal process in producing and recording an authoritative history ... These two proceedings (the MPA Arbitration and the ICJ) may be read, retrospectively, as part of the one contest about the historical record and the legal significance of those events ... Taken together, these decisions have had a history-producing or history-confirming function for Mauritius.[23]

According to another commentator,

> The (ICJ) Opinion, moreover, comprises a scrupulous retelling of the political process leading to the excision of the Chagos Archipelago from Mauritius in the 1960s, and provides a cutting answer to the UNGA's questions: the process of decolonisation of Mauritius has not yet been completed, and the UK is under an obligation to bring its administration of Chagos to an end.
>
> (op cit 2021, p. 51)

Successive governments in Mauritius have, no doubt conscious of realpolitik, declared that once Mauritius can re-assert its sovereignty over the Chagos it will be prepared to negotiate an agreement with the US over the maintenance of the American base in Diego Garcia. This was stated by Prime Minister Seewoosagur Ramgoolam at the UN in 1980 and again reaffirmed in the course of proceedings before the Arbitral Tribunal and the ICJ.

Since the UK has repeatedly stated that the use of Diego Garcia was important for global security (though in the 1960s the UK only referred to the security of the "west"), and that the Archipelago will be returned to Mauritius once this is no longer required, Mauritius undertaking to maintain existing military facilities on Diego Garcia under an agreement with the US clearly shows that the continued British "occupation" of the islands is not required to meet the stated purpose of the military base.

Notes

1 "At the height of the Cold War, in the 1960s the Russians were understood to be seeking defence facilities in the Indian Ocean. Britain's power east of Suez was at the time in decline following crippling economic problems back home, and faced with the possibility that the Indian Ocean might fall under Russian influence, the US approached Britain with a proposal to develop a military facility in the Chagos Archipelago" (Gifford, 2018, p. 56).

2 For a detailed account of the chronology of events leading up to the detachment of the Chagos from Mauritius, see *Arbitration under Annex VII of The 1982 United Nations*

Convention on the Law of The Sea, Republic of Mauritius V. United Kingdom of Great Britain and Northern Ireland (2012, chap. 3).

3 The Colonial Secretary urged Mauritius Ministers to agree to the detachment of the Chagos Archipelago. The Colonial Secretary argued that "it would be possible for the British Government to detach [the Chagos Archipelago] from Mauritius by Order in Council" (*Record of a Meeting held in Lancaster House at 2.30 p.m. on Thursday 23rd September*, 1965).

4 It is understood that the UK was concerned about the adverse consequences for Britain at the United Nations, where decolonisation was a major issue in the mid-1960s.

5 As an alternative, a lease was proposed with mineral, fishing and agricultural rights maintained for Mauritius (*Record of a Meeting held in Lancaster House at 2.30 p.m. on Thursday 23rd September,* 1965).

6 On the specific issue of minerals and oil, the UK Government responded as follows: "The islands are required for defence facilities and there is no intention of permitting prospecting for minerals or oils on or near them" and that clarification sought by Mauritian Ministers did not therefore arise but that the Secretary of State "shall nevertheless give them further consideration" in view of the request (Colonial Office, 1965b).

7 "Beginning in 1967, as part of the implementation of these administrative measures, Chagossians who had left Chagos for medical treatment or regular vacations to Mauritius were prevented from returning and marooned 1,300 miles from their homes. The British also restricted the shipment of supplies that they usually sent to Chagos. By the turn of the decade, more Chagossians left the archipelago as food and medical supplies dwindled. In 1971 the U.S. military started the construction of the base on Diego Garcia and instructed British officials to complete the removals. Between 1971 and 1973, British agents forced the remaining Chagossians to board overcrowded cargo ships. They were transported to the docks in Mauritius and Seychelles and abandoned. During the deportations Chagossians witnessed British agents and U.S. soldiers collecting their pet dogs and exterminating them en masse in sealed plantation sheds. Since 1973 Chagossians have not been allowed to return to Chagos" (Vine, 2006, p. 21).

8 "The new colony had to be reported to the United Nations Decolonisation Committee. The UK informed the Committee that there were only contract labourers on the islands. It concealed the existence of a permanent population which had in fact been, settled for five generations, and was thus entitled to the 'sacred trust' of Article 73 of the Charter of the United Nations" (Gifford, 2018, n. 4).

9 Immediately after Independence, Mauritius faced serious economic challenges which had to be addressed as a top priority. In addition, with the UK entry in the then Common Market, the Commonwealth Sugar Agreement (which played a key role in the country's economy) was being terminated and Mauritius needed UK and European support to obtain a guaranteed market for its sugar which was at the time the main pillar of the economy. The Government focussed on other pressing issues.

10 The support was reiterated over the years and reaffirmed in the Solemn Declaration issued on the fiftieth Anniversary of the OAU/AU (African Union, 2016). In 2017, the AU resolved (2017) "to fully support the action initiated by the Government of the Republic of Mauritius at the level of the United Nations General Assembly with a view to ensuring the completion of the decolonization of the Republic of Mauritius and enabling the Republic of Mauritius to effectively exercise its sovereignty over the Chagos Archipelago, including Diego Garcia".

11 "The wind of change is blowing through this continent. Whether we like it or not, this growth of national consciousness is a political fact". Statement by British Prime Minister Harod Macmillan to the South African Parliament on 3 February, 1960.

12 The ECHR subsequently decided that the Claim by the slanders was inadmissible since they were deemed to have accepted compensation following earlier litigation (*Chagos Islanders v the United Kingdom (application no. 35622/04)*, 2012).

13 See Chapter 5 for further discussion of the MPA in the context of rights protection.

14 Whereas the UK had an obligation under UNCLOS to have "due regard" and to consult Mauritius but, "In stark contrast with the UK's consultations with the US to balance the MPA with US rights and interests," … "the 21 July 2009 meeting with Mauritius reminds the Tribunal of ships passing in the night, in which neither side fully engaged with the other regarding fishing rights or the proposal for the MPA" (*Chagos Marine Protected Area Arbitration (Mauritius v. United Kingdom)*, 2015, para. 526).

15 Pursuant to the principle of Estoppel under International Law, "the UK having made repeated representations in respect of undertakings over 40 years, Mauritius was entitled to rely on these representations and had in fact relied on these representations to its detriment. The UK was thus estopped from denying the binding effect of the commitments" (*Chagos Marine Protected Area Arbitration* (*Mauritius v. United Kingdom,* 2015, para. 448).

16 US Judge Donoghue's dissenting opinion focuses on the issue of the court's jurisdiction and not on the merits of the case.

17 (.,International Court of Justice (2019)., para. 183): "(5) By thirteen votes to one, is of the opinion that all Member States are under an obligation to cooperate with the United Nations in order to complete the decolonization of Mauritius".

18 Whereas the initial Resolution, 71/292, asking for an Advisory opinion had been supported by 94 States, the second resolution adopted after the Court had given its opinion was supported by 116 States.

19 The Chairperson of the African Union Commission "expresses concern over the non-withdrawal of the United Kingdom from its colonial administration of the Chagos Archipelago. The Chairperson of the Commission reiterates the support of the African Union to the Republic of Mauritius for a complete decolonization of the Chagos Archipelago, in conformity with the Constitutive Act of the African Union which defines the defence of the sovereignty, territorial integrity and independence of the Member States as one of its main objectives. He further reiterates the relevant decisions of the Assembly of Heads of State and Government of the African Union in this area, in particular Assembly/AU/Dec.747(XXXIl) on the decolonisation of the Chagos Archipelago, adopted in February 2019 in Addis Ababa, Ethiopia" (African Union, 2019).

20 See Lanzoni (2022). The author mentions the following citations: Burri and Trinidad (2021); Gaver (2021); Roeben and Jankovic (2021); Thin (2021). See also *Dispute concerning delimitation of the maritime boundary between Mauritius and Maldives in the Indian Ocean* (*Mauritius/Maldives* (2019, *cit. supra* note 8)), Separate and Dissenting Opinion of Judge *ad hoc* Oxman.

21 "The forced displacement of the Chagossians and ongoing abuses amount to crimes against humanity committed by a colonial power against an Indigenous people. UK colonial rule in the Chagos Archipelago, unlikc in most of its other colonies in Africa, did not end in the 1960s, and it has continued at extraordinary cost to the people of Chagos. This colonial rule was built on systematic racism and ethnic and racial discrimination in the treatment of the Chagossians …. The UK authorities have continued to treat the predominately African Chagossians very differently from other islanders under their rule, such as in Cyprus and the Falklands, islands which have UK military bases. The UK has tried to treat Chagos as a territory where international human rights law does not apply. And the US has continued to benefit from the operation of its geopolitically strategic military base on Diego Garcia, while refusing to take responsibility for the crimes against the Chagossians" (Baldwin, 2023).

22 "The Chagos Advisory Opinion is in many ways a bold judgment. For one, the International Court of Justice (ICJ) agreed to give advice to the UN General Assembly (UNGA) against the wishes of three permanent members of the UN Security Council, in circumstances in which it could have dodged the bullet with a reasonable degree of plausibility. It declined the invitation to characterise the request as one concerning a

bilateral territorial dispute between Mauritius and the UK, and sided, instead, with the several states who viewed decolonisation as a multilateral issue in which the UN retains a legitimate interest" (Bordin, 2021).

23 "In sum, the account of history that Mauritius succeeded in placing on the legal record had two critical elements. First, it established that, to the extent that the Mauritian pre-independence representatives acquiesced in the excision of the Chagos Archipelago, they were coerced. Secondly, Mauritius succeeded in obtaining international acknowledgement that the UK had given undertakings that: were legally binding, acknowledged certain Mauritian rights and, arguably at least, implicitly acknowledged Mauritian sovereignty. Additionally, insofar as this was a contest of legitimacy, Mauritius politically or symbolically benefitted from an authoritative determination that the excision was both unlawful and carried out in bad faith" (Guilfoyle, 2021, p. 13).

References

African Union (2011) *Resolution.* Addis Ababa, Ethiopia. Available at: http://archives.au.int/handle/123456789/351 (Accessed: 1 September 2023).

African Union (2016) *Solemn Declaration on the 50th Anniversary of the OAU/AU.* Addis Ababa, Ethiopia. Available at: http://archives.au.int/handle/123456789/320 (Accessed: 1 September 2023).

African Union (2017) *Resolution on Chagos Archipelago.* Addis Ababa, Ethiopia. Available at: https://au.int/sites/default/files/decisions/32520-sc19553_e_original_-_assembly_decisions_621-641_-_xxviii.pdf (Accessed: 1 September 2023).

African Union (2019a) 'Communiqué on the Chairperson's working visit to South Africa, African Union'. Available at: https://au.int/en/pressreleases/20191122/communique-chairpersons-working-visit-south-africa (Accessed: 1 September 2023).

African Union (2019b) 'Resolution adopted by the general assembly on 22 May 2019'. Available at: https://undocs.org/en/A/RES/73/298 (Accessed: 1 September 2023).

subje a civic ghost: Law, dominion, empire in the chagos litigation'. In *In*

Arvind, T. (2018) 'The Subject as A Civic Ghost: Law, Dominion, and Empire in the Chagos Litigation'. In S. Allen and C. Monsghan (eds.), *Fifty Years of the British Indian Ocean Territory: Legal Perspectives*. Cham. Springer., pp. 85–110.

Baldwin, C. (2023) 'That's when the nightmare started'. *Human Rights Watch* [Preprint]. Available at: https://www.hrw.org/report/2023/02/15/thats-when-nightmare-started/uk-and-us-forced-displacement-chagossians-and (Accessed: 30 November 2023).

Bordin, F.L. (2021) 'State responsibility advisory proceedings: Thoughts on judicial propriety multilateralism in the chagos opinion'. I

Bordin FL. (2021) 'State Responsibility in Advisory Proceedings: Thoughts on Judicial Propriety and Multilateralism in the Chagos Opinion. In: Burri T, Trinidad J, eds. *The International Court of Justice and Decolonisation: New Directions from the Chagos Advisory Opinion.* Cambridge: Cambridge University Press, pp. 95-116.

Bowcott, O. and Rinvolucri, B. (2022) 'Exiled Chagos Islanders return without British supervision for first time'. *The Guardian*, 8 February. Available at: https://www.theguardian.com/world/2022/feb/08/mauritian-ship-takes-scientific-team-to-contested-chagos-islands.

Burri, T. and Trinidad, J. (2021) 'Introductory note to dispute concerning the delimitation of the maritime boundary between mauritius and maldives in the Indian Ocean, preliminary objections (ITLOS)'. *International Legal Materials (ILM).* Available at: https://papers.ssrn.com/abstract=3827071 (Accessed: 30 November 2023).

Chagos Islanders v Attorney General and HM BIOT Commissioner (2003) [2003] EWHC 2222 (QB). *BAILII.* Available at: http://www.bailii.org/ew/cases/EWHC/QB/2003/2222.html (Accessed: 1 September 2023).

Chagos Islanders v the United Kingdom (application no. 35622/04) (2012) ECHR. *HUDOC.* Available at: https://hudoc.echr.coe.int/sites/eng-press/pages/search.aspx?i=003-4207010–4992253 (Accessed: 1 September 2023).

Chagos Marine Protected Area Arbitration (Mauritius v. United Kingdom) (2015) Permanent Court of Arbitration. Available at: https://pca-cpa.org/en/cases/11/ (Accessed: 1 March 2023).

Cleverly, J. (2022) 'British Indian Ocean Territory / Chagos Archipelago, Statement UIN HCWS354'. Available at: https://questions-statements.parliament.uk/written-statements/detail/2022-11-03/hcws354 (Accessed: 7 January 2023).

Colonial Office (1965a) 'Colonial Office Telegram No. 214 to Mauritius, 10 August 1965'. FO 371/184526: Annex 14.

Colonial Office (1965b) 'Colonial Office Telegram No. 298 to Mauritius, 8 November 1965'. FO 371/184529 (Annex MM-29)

Colonial Office (1965c) 'Note for the Prime Minister's Meeting with Sir Seewoosagur Ramgoolam, Premier of Mauritius, 22 September 1965'. PREM 13/3320.

Gaver, C.D. (2021) 'Dispute concerning delimitation of the maritime boundary between Mauritius and Maldives in the Indian Ocean (Mauritius/Maldives)'. *American Journal of International Law*, 115(3), pp. 519–526.

Gifford, R. (2018) 'How public law has not been able to provide the chagossians with a remedy'. . In S. Allen and C. Monsghan (eds.), *Fifty Years of the British Indian Ocean Territory: Legal Perspectives*. Cham. Springer., pp. 55–84.

Gray, S. (2009) 'Giant marine park plan for Chagos'. *The Independent*, 9 February 2009.

Guilfoyle, D. (2021) 'The Chagos Archipelago before international tribunals: Strategic litigation and the production of historical knowledge'. *Melbourne Journal of International Law*, 21(3), pp. 749–771.

Hansard: House of Commons debates (1975) 3 November, 899, 1025. Available at: https://hansard.parliament.uk/commons/1975-11-03/debates/f4d69c4b-1a1c-4d8e-b844-ff999ac01a76/HouseOfCommons (Accessed: 1 September 2023).

International Court of Justice (2017) 'Declarations recognizing the jurisdiction of the Court as compulsory: United Kingdom of Great Britain and Northern Ireland'. Available at: https://www.icj-cij.org/declarations/gb (Accessed: 1 September 2023).

International Court of Justice (2019) 'Legal Consequences of the Separation of the Chagos Archipelago from Mauritius in 1965. Advisory opinion'. Available at: https://www.icj-cij.org/public/files/case-related/169/169-20190225-01-00-EN.pdf (Accessed: 1 March 2023).

International Tribunal for the Law of the Sea (2019) 'Dispute concerning delimitation of the maritime boundary between Mauritius and Maldives in the Indian Ocean (Mauritius/Maldives)'. Available at: https://www.itlos.org/en/main/cases/list-of-cases/dispute-concerning-delimitation-of-the-maritime-boundary-between-mauritius-and-maldives-in-the-indian-ocean-mauritius/maldives/ (Accessed: 1 March 2023).

International Tribunal for the Law of the Sea (2021) 'Dispute concerning delimitation of the maritime boundary between mauritius and maldives in the Indian Ocean (Mauritius/Maldives) preliminary objections- judgment'. Available at: https://jusmundi.com/en/document/decision/en-dispute-concerning-delimitation-of-the-maritime-boundary-between-mauritius-and-maldives-in-the-indian-ocean-mauritius-maldives-judgment-preliminary-objections-thursday-28th-january-2021#decision_14650 (Accessed: 1 September 2023).

In the Matter of an Arbitration Before An Arbitral Tribunal Constituted Under Annex Vii of the 1982 United Nations Convention on The Law of the Sea Between The Republic of Mauritius And The United Kingdom of Great Britain and Northern Ireland: Reasoned Decision On Challenge (2011) 'Permanent court of arbitration'. Available at: https://pcacases.com/web/sendAttach/1792 (Accessed: 1 September 2023).

Kateka, J. and Wolfrum, R. (2015) 'Chagos marine protected area arbitration (Mauritius V. United Kingdom): Dissenting and concurring opinion'. Available at: https://pcacases.com/web/sendAttach/1570 (Accessed: 1 September 2023).

Kingsbury, B. (2011) 'International courts: Uneven judicialization in global order'. In J. Crawford and M. Koskenniemi (eds.), *Cambridge Companion to International Law*, Cambridge: Cambridge University Press pp. 11–05.

Lanzoni, N. (2022) 'The authority of icj advisory opinions as precedents: The mauritius/maldives case'. *The Italian Review of International and Comparative Law*, 2(2), pp. 296–322.

L'express, (2004) 'Cuttaree : Nous sommes choqués par la résolution britannique'. 9 July. Available at: https://lexpress.mu/node/131560 (Accessed: 1 September 2023).

Mauritius Telegram No. 170 to the Colonial Office, 23 July 1965 (1965) FO 371/184526: Annex 12.

Meetarbhan, M.J. (2015) 'Re-examining the chagos marine protected area arbitration-the lancaster house undertakings'. *Environmental Policy and Law*, 45(6), p. 248.

Memorial of the Republic of Mauritius (2012) *Arbitration under Annex VII of The 1982 United Nations Convention on the Law of The Sea, Republic of Mauritius V. United Kingdom of Great Britain and Northern Ireland,* The Hague: Permanent Court of Arbitration. Available at: https://pcacases.com/web/sendAttach/1796.

Monaghan, C. (2018) 'An imperfect legacy: The significance of the Bancoult litigation on the development of domestic constitutional jurisprudence'. . In S. Allen and C. Monsghan (eds.), *Fifty Years of the British Indian Ocean Territory: Legal Perspectives.* Cham. Springer.,pp. 111–145.

Olivier Bancoult, et al., Appellants v. Robert S. Mcnamara, et al., Appellees (2006) 'Justia'. Available at: https://law.justia.com/cases/federal/appellate-courts/F3/445/427/602650/ (Accessed: 1 September 2023).

Olivier Bancoult et al. v. Robert S. McNamara et al. (2002) 'Memorandum opinion, 01–2629 (RMU)'. *vLex.* Available at: https://case-law.vlex.com/vid/bancoult-v-mcnamara-civil-888463882 (Accessed: 1 September 2023).

Organization of African Unity (1980) *Resolution on the Diego Garcia.* Freetown, Sierra Leone. Available at: http://archives.au.int/handle/123456789/830 (Accessed: 1 September 2023).

Organization of African Unity (1990) *Declaration of the Assembly of Heads of State and Government of the Organization of African Unity on the Political and Socio-economic Situation in Africa and the Fundamental Changes Taking Place in the World.* Addis Ababa, Ethiopia. Available at: http://archives.au.int/handle/123456789/562 (Accessed: 1 September 2023).

Organization of African Unity (2000) *Decision on Chagos Archipelago.* Lome, Togo: Organization of African Unity. Available at: https://au.int/sites/default/files/decisions/9545-2000_ahg_dec_143-159_xxxvi_e.pdf (Accessed: 1 September 2023).

R (on the application of Bancoult (No 2)) (Appellant) v Secretary of State for Foreign and Commonwealth Affairs (Respondent) (2016) [2016] UKSC 35. *BAILII.* Available at: https://www.bailii.org/uk/cases/UKSC/2016/35.html (Accessed: 1 September 2023).

Record of a Conversation Between the Prime Minister and Premier of Mauritius, Sir Seewoosagur Ramgoolam, at No. 10, Downing Street at 10 A.M. on September 23, 1965 (1965) FO 371/184528.

Record of a Meeting held in Lancaster House at 2.30 p.m. on Thursday 23rd September (1965) Mauritius Defence Matters, CO 1036/1253.

Roeben, V. and Jankovic, S. (2021) 'Unpacking sovereignty and self-determination in ITLOS and the ICC: A bundle of rights?' *Ejil:Talk! Blog of the European Journal of International Law.* Available at: https://www.ejiltalk.org/unpacking-sovereignty-and-self-determination-in-itlos-and-the-icc-a-bundle-of-rights/#:~:text=International

%20institutions%2C%20such%20as%20the,the%20realm%20of%20legal%20fact (Accessed: 1 September 2023).

Scott, S.V. (2017) *International Law in World Politics: An Introduction.* Boulder: Lynne Rienner Publishers.

Select Committee on the Excision of the Chagos Archipelago (1983) *Report of the Select Committee on the Excision of the Chagos Archipelago.* Port Louis, Mauritius: Legislative Assembly.

The British Indian Ocean Territory Order 1965 (SI 1965/1920) Available at: https://vlex.co.uk/vid/british-indian-ocean-territory-812500273 (Accessed: 1 September 2023).

The Guardian (2010) 'US embassy cables: Foreign office does not regret evicting Chagos islanders'. 2 December 2010. Available at: https://www.theguardian.com/world/us-embassy-cables-documents/207149 (Accessed: 1 September 2023).

The New York Times (1975) 'U.S.-British Deal on Diego Garcia in '66 Confirmed'. 17 October. Available at: https://www.nytimes.com/1975/10/17/archives/usbritish-deal-on-diego-garcia-in-66-confirmed.html (Accessed: 1 September 2023).

Thin, S. (2021) 'The curious case of the 'legal effect' of ICJ advisory opinions in the Mauritius/Maldives maritime boundary dispute'. EJIL: Talk! Blog of the European Journal of International Law. Available at: https://www.ejiltalk.org/the-curious-case-of-the-legal-effect-of-icj-advisory-opinions-in-the-mauritius-maldives-maritime-boundary-dispute/ (Accessed: 1 September 2023).

United Nations General Assembly (1980) 'UN General Assembly, Thirty-Fifth Session'. 30th Plenary Meeting, A/35/PV.30.

United Nations General Assembly (2017) 'Request for an advisory opinion of the international court of justice on the legal consequences of the separation of the Chagos Archipelago from Mauritius in 1965: Resolution / adopted by the general assembly, Resolution A/RES/71/292'. Available at: https://digitallibrary.un.org/record/1290265?ln=en&v=pdf (Accessed: 1 September 2023).

United Nations General Assembly (2019) 'Advisory opinion of the International Court of Justice on the legal consequences of the separation of the Chagos Archipelago from Mauritius in 1965: Resolution adopted by the General Assembly, Resolution A/RES/73/295.' Available at: https://documents.un.org/doc/undoc/gen/n19/151/29/pdf/n1915129.pdf?token=jaynFOOlewho4XH6GC&fe=true (Accessed: 1 September 2023).

United Nations Secretary General (2020) 'Advisory opinion of the international court of justice on the legal consequences of the separation of the Chagos Archipelago from Mauritius in 1965: Report of the Secretary-General'. 74th session, Agenda Item 86, UN Doc A/74/834. Available at: https://digitallibrary.un.org/record/3865093?ln=en&v=pdf (Accessed: 1 September 2023).

Vine, D. (2006) 'The impoverishment of displacement: Models for documenting human rights abuses and the people of Diego Garcia'. *Human Rights Brief*, 13(2), p. 6.

Waghorn, D. (2019) 'British deal with US over Chagos Islands not its finest hour'. *Sky News*. Available at: https://news.sky.com/story/british-deal-with-us-over-chagos-islands-not-its-finest-hour-11727077 (Accessed: 1 September 2023).

2 The Chagos Archipelago in Late Eighteenth- And Nineteenth-Century Indian Ocean World History

Richard B. Allen

The Chagos Archipelago's geographical isolation, small population, economic dependence on coconuts, and status as an often-neglected dependency of Mauritius have ensured that much remains unknown about its social and economic history. Baron d'Unienville, the early nineteenth-century Mauritian colonial archivist, paid little attention to the archipelago in his classic account of Mauritius and its dependencies other than to provide brief descriptions of the physical geography, flora, and fauna of some of the archipelago's more important islands (1838, vol. 3, pp. 173–196). Modern histories of Mauritius likewise ignore the archipelago (Toussaint, 1972; Selvon, 2001; Teelock, 2009), while the accounts by Robert Scott (1961), a former British governor of Mauritius, and British diplomat Richard Edis (1983) provide limited insights into late eighteenth- and nineteenth-century Chagossian life.[1]

More recently, historian Marina Carter has contributed meaningfully to our understanding of Chagossian labour history (Wenban-Smith and Carter, 2016; Carter, 2017, pp. 213–233). As the other chapters in this book indicate, interest in the archipelago nevertheless remains focused largely on its separation from Mauritius in 1965 and designation as the British Indian Ocean Territory (BIOT) to facilitate the establishment of a US military base on Diego Garcia, the local population's displacement, and subsequent efforts to permit Chagossians to return home.

Brief accounts by missionaries, sailors, and colonial officials who visited the archipelago provide much of the information currently at our disposal about the details of late eighteenth- and nineteenth-century Chagossian life; as Marina Carter notes, relevant records in the Mauritius National Archives and the National Archives of the United Kingdom at Kew remain largely unexplored (Carter, 2022). This lack of knowledge is compounded by a failure to situate what is known about Chagossian history in more fully developed local, regional, and comparative contexts. More specifically, the archipelago's history cannot be divorced from Anglo-French competition for dominance in India and the Indian Ocean during the eighteenth century, European slave trading in the Indian Ocean during the eighteenth and early nineteenth centuries, the abolition of slavery in the British Empire in 1834, the post-emancipation diaspora of Indian and other indentured labourers throughout and beyond the colonial world between the 1830s and 1920s, and the establishment of plantation economies in Mauritius, Réunion, and the Seychelles

DOI: 10.4324/9781003390299-4

to produce tropical commodities such as cloves, coffee, indigo, and sugar for imperial and world markets.

* * * * * *

Although Maldivian, Arab, and Malay sailors probably knew about and may have visited the archipelago before European mariners learned of its existence early in the sixteenth century, its atolls remained uninhabited until 1778 when the French made the first attempt to establish a settlement on Diego Garcia against a backdrop of increasing Anglo-French competition for dominance in India and the Indian Ocean which lasted from the 1740s to the early nineteenth century. During this period, France sought to consolidate its position in the region by colonising uninhabited islands in the western Indian Ocean including Rodrigues in 1735 and the Seychelles in 1770 to prevent them from becoming British outposts. Following the British conquest of the Mascarenes in 1810, the 1814 Treaty of Paris ceded Mauritius and its dependencies including Rodrigues, the Seychelles, and the Chagos Archipelago to Britain while returning the strategically less important Ile Bourbon (Réunion) to French control.

Slave labour was crucial in these dependencies' colonisation, and the period between 1770 and the early 1830s witnessed the introduction of thousands of mostly East African and Malagasy enslaved men, women, and children into these islands. The total number of such imports cannot be determined with any certainty, but the scale of this activity is suggested by the Seychelles housing 221 slaves in 1788, a number which rose to 487 in 1791, to 1,820 in 1804, and to 3,015 in 1810 before increasing dramatically to 6,638–7,323 in 1818, after which it declined to 4,673 on the eve of slave emancipation on 1 February 1835 (Allen, 2001, p. 96; 2022b). Information about the size and composition of the early Chagossian slave population is sparse, but it indicates that the population remained small (Kuczynski, 1949, vol. 2, pp. 888–893).[2] The two British warships that destroyed the settlement on Diego Garcia in 1810 removed 134 slaves (103 men, 23 women, eight children) from the island who were sent to Colombo, Ceylon (Sri Lanka) (Carter, 2017, p. 218). Sixteen years later, the Chagossian population totalled 275 persons, 218 of whom were slaves (198 men, 17 women, 13 children) (Edis, 1983, p. 33; Wenban-Smith and Carter, 2016, p. 82). The archipelago housed 380 slaves in 1835 when slavery was abolished in Mauritius, a population that declined to 259 adult "apprentices" and 43 children in 1838. The local population remained small into the early twentieth century, increasing to some 334 souls in 1851, to 590 in 1861, to 689 in 1871, and to 1,183 in 1911 (Wenban-Smith and Carter, 2016, p. 146; Carter, 2017, pp. 220, 222–223).

Most Chagossian slaves were described as Malagasy or "Mozambican", a term used to identify persons imported into the Mascarenes not only from Portuguese-controlled ports in Mozambique such as Ibo, Inhambane, Mozambique Island, and Quelimane, but also from along the Swahili Coast, especially Kilwa and Zanzibar. Others were identified as "Creole", i.e., born in Mauritius or the archipelago. Mascarene slaves came from a global catchment area. Early nineteenth-century accounts of colonial life noted that Mauritius housed "blacks of every ethnicity": Anjouanais from the Comoros; Abyssinians from the Horn of Africa; Bambaras, Guineans, and Wolofs from West Africa; Bengalis, "Malabars", and Talingas (i.e., Telegu-speakers) from southern India; and "Malays" and Timorese from Southeast Asia (Milbert, 1812, vol. 2, p. 257; Decary, 1961, p. 17). An 1817 Mauritian slave census and contemporary accounts confirm this population's ethnic diversity. These sources reveal that Malagasy slaves originated from among 13 ethno-cultural populations on the Grand Île including the Ambanivolo, Amboalambo (Hova/Merina), Andrantsay, Antateime [*sic*], Antaisaka, Antalaotra, Antanosy, Antatsimo, Betanimena, Betsileo, Maninga [*sic*], Marvace [*sic*], and Sakalava. "Mozambicans" came from throughout eastern Africa, including as far inland as modern Malawi and eastern Zambia. The 1817 census records individuals from among 14 readily identifiable eastern African populations: the Bisa, Ekoti, Kamanga, Lolo (Lomwe), Makonde, Makua, Maravi, Mrima, Mujao (probably Yao), Ngindo, Nyambane, Nyamwezi, Sagara, and Sena. Indian slaves arrived from various ports and regions in the subcontinent including Anjengo, Bengal, Cochin, Coringa, the Coromandel and Malabar coasts, Goa, Gondelour, Karikal, Mahé, Pondichéry, and Yanam. In addition to Timorese, slaves from Bali, Java, Makassar, Nias, and Sumatra in the Indonesian archipelago also reached Mauritius, together with individuals described as Chinese (Allen, 2014, pp. 69, 73–74).

As elsewhere in the eighteenth- and early nineteenth-century European colonial world, Chagossian slaves' living and working conditions were shaped in part by racialised perceptions of the African and Asian peoples who supplied the Mascarenes with chattel labour. Contemporary observers of Mauritian life noted the purported qualities and attributes assigned to these various populations (Grant, 1801, pp. 74–77, 297–298; Milbert, 1812, vol. 1, p. 218, and vol. 2, pp. 162–174; Bernardin de St. Pierre, 1834, vol. 2, pp. 120–122; d'Unienville, 1838, vol. 1, pp. 255–258). "Mozambican" slaves were widely regarded as lacking in intelligence and best suited for physical labour, while Indian slaves were praised for their docility, grace, and intelligence, qualities which made them less suitable for hard physical labour. Malagasy slaves were widely deemed to be particularly troublesome and most likely to desert their masters. Creole slaves were castigated in turn for their laziness and love of sensual pleasures. These perceptions meant that colonists often employed Indian and "Malay" slaves as domestic servants and artisans, while employing those of African and Malagasy origin to manual labour.

The archipelago's dependence on chattel labour mirrored conditions on Réunion and Mauritius, colonised by the French in 1663 and 1721, respectively. The Mascarenes housed some 33,000 slaves by the mid-1760s, a population that increased dramatically following the advent of royal rule in 1767 and the promulgation of a decree in 1769 that opened the colony to free trade by all French nationals, a privilege extended to citizens of the United States in 1784 and all other foreign nationals in 1787. One consequence of these actions was a dramatic expansion of the slave trade to the islands. An inventory of Mascarene slaving voyages reveals that at least 571 ships reached Mauritius and Réunion with slave cargoes between 1770 and 1809, while there is evidence of another 104 probable/possible and 36 unsuccessful slaving ventures to supply the islands with chattel labour (Allen, 2014, p. 68). Census and other data suggest that this period witnessed an estimated 160,572–186,816 African, Indian, and Malagasy slave exports to the Mascarenes, 81–82% of whom (131,158–151,665) reached the islands alive. The Mascarene trade continued after the British conquest in 1810 despite the islands being subjected to the 1807 parliamentary ban on British subjects trading slaves and, following Réunion's return to French control in 1814, the abolition of the French slave trade in 1818. The number of illegal slaving voyages to Mauritius is unknown, but there is evidence of at least 212–216 such voyages to Réunion (Allen, 2014, p. 155). An estimated 123,379–144,959 African, Malagasy, and Southeast Asian slaves were exported to the Mascarenes between 1811 and the Mauritian trade's demise *circa* 1826 and the Réunionnais trade's *de facto* end in 1832–33 (Allen, 2004, p. 41). The limited information at our disposal suggests that the proportion of Malagasy slaves in the Mascarenes declined from approximately 75 to 35–40% between 1735 and 1826/7, while that of "Mozambicans" increased from 15 to 50–60% during the same period (Allen, 2004, p. 36). Scattered reports indicate that the archipelago's chattel workforce reflected this demographic trend. In 1835, for example, 54% of the 95 slaves on Mr. Ozille Majastre's establishment on Peros Banhos were listed as Mozambicans (Wenban-Smith and Carter, 2016, pp. 132–133).

Although most Chagossian slaves arrived from Mauritius, small numbers may have also arrived on slave ships that stopped occasionally at Diego Garcia to "refresh" their human cargoes and allow slaves to recover from illness and/or the other rigours that the "middle passage" from the African coast to the Mascarenes often entailed. Captains occasionally sold some of the slaves in their charge during such visits to help cover their expenses, while some slaves took advantage of such opportunities to escape. Such was the case with the 160-ton snow *La Bouffonne* which sailed from Kilwa for Mauritius on 11 October 1779 with a cargo of 195 slaves. When captain Claude Deschiens de Kulvay realised on 16 November that difficult winds and currents would keep him from reaching the Seychelles, a common "refreshment" stop for slavers sailing from the Swahili Coast, he headed for Diego Garcia where the ship arrived on 2 December. During the ship's 16-day visit, four men and a woman absconded after the ship's slaves were put ashore (MNA: OC 40/176, 3 janvier, 1780). Unfortunately, these individuals' subsequent fate remains unknown. The archipelago also functioned occasionally as a way station for slavers during the illegal slave trade era, as in 1826 when the *Chicken*, captained by a Mauritian Creole named Piveteau, called at Diego Garcia en route to Réunion from Southeast Asia with a cargo of 40 seven- and eight-year-old boys from Nias, an island off Sumatra's west coast (NAUK: CO 415/1, pp. 26-28, W.M.G. Colebrooke and W. Blair to Earl Bathurst, 21 November 1826).

Slaves were also transferred occasionally between Mauritian dependencies. Such was the case in May 1802 when *L'Aurore* carried 33 male and female slaves from Diego Garcia to the Seychelles together with approximately 200,000 lbs. of copra (MNA: F 4/1130, 21 prairial An X [10 June 1802]). That the ship also carried a large quantity of copra in its hold illustrates both the archipelago's economic dependence on coconuts and the importance of plantation agriculture in Mauritius, Réunion, and the Seychelles from the eighteenth to late twentieth century. In addition to growing the cereal grains, rice, and other foodstuffs needed to sustain local populations and provision the hundreds of ships that called at Mauritius each year between 1770 and 1810, local estates produced various export commodities. Sugar replaced coffee and cloves as the dominant export crops on Réunion in the early 1820s. Despite encouragement by Governor François Mahé de La Bourdonnais (1735–46) and his immediate successors, early attempts to turn Mauritius into a sugar colony languished. The latter part of the eighteenth century witnessed the cultivation of cloves, cotton, and indigo on the island which gave way to a renewed emphasis on sugar during the 1810s after the Haitian Revolution deprived France of its principal source of this commodity. The equalisation in 1825 of the tariffs on Mauritian and West Indian sugar entering Britain revolutionised the Mauritian sugar industry and by the early 1830s sugar dominated the island's economy (Allen, 2022c). The Seychelles exported cotton between 1802 and the early 1820s when competition from American producers spurred a move to coconut production, primarily for oil until the early twentieth century when local planters shifted to producing copra rather than oil (Allen, 2022b).

Physical geography limited plantation agriculture in the archipelago to coconuts. The first attempt to produce coconut oil dates to 1793, but British attacks and other disruptions during the French revolutionary and Napoleonic eras delayed the systematic production of this commodity until after the 1814 Treaty of Paris ceded Mauritius and its dependencies to Britain. While contemporary visitors noted workers' living and working conditions, information about the volume and value of Chagossian coconut oil production and its importance to the Mauritian economy remains limited. That Chagossian production remained modest is suggested by reports that the archipelago produced only 54,400 *veltes* (405,280 litres or 89,073 imperial gallons) of oil in 1838. Production increased as the nineteenth century progressed, reaching 188,297 gallons in 1862, and 201,164 gallons in 1889, but declined to 162,412 gallons in 1912. Information about the value of this crop during the nineteenth century is limited to the 1890s when coconut oil accounted for 94.8% of all Chagossian imports into Mauritius (Wenban-Smith and Carter, 2016, pp. 136, 261, 263).

The abolition of slavery in Mauritius in 1835 and the end of the post-emancipation "apprenticeship" system on 31 March 1839 threatened the viability of plantation workforces as most of the colony's new freedmen and -women abandoned the properties on which they had worked despite attempts to compel them to remain (Allen, 1999, pp. 105–135). The slave population's inability to supply the workforce needed by the Mauritian sugar industry's rapid expansion after 1825 prompted planters to recruit indentured or free contractual labourers from elsewhere in the Indian Ocean world to provide them with the labour they needed. Approximately 1,500 Indian and Chinese labourers recruited in Calcutta (Kolkata), Penang, and Singapore reached Mauritius in 1829 in what proved to be an unsuccessful experiment with the use of such labour (Reddi, 1984, p. 5). The impending abolition of slavery in the British Empire in the early 1830s, however, spurred renewed interest in using such labourers. The arrival of 75 indentured Indians in Mauritius on 2 November 1834 and more than 24,000 such labourers between 1835 and 1838 heralded the beginning of a global diaspora of 2.2 million African, Asian, Melanesian, and other indentured labourers throughout and beyond the colonial plantation world between the 1830s and 1920s.[3] More than 452,000 of these labourers, mostly from India but also from China, the Comoros, Madagascar, Mozambique, Southeast Asia, and Yemen, reached Mauritius where their presence transformed the island's socio-cultural and economic landscape (Northrup, 1995, pp. 159–160).

Only small numbers of these labourers reached Mauritius's dependencies. The chronic labour shortage in the Seychelles after slave emancipation was partially alleviated by the introduction between 1861 and 1875 of 2,667 "Liberated Africans", i.e., slaves removed from Arab/Swahili dhows captured by Royal Navy ships that patrolled the western Indian Ocean during the second half of the nineteenth century as part of British efforts to suppress the East African slave trade to the Persian (or Arabian) Gulf and India (Nwulia, 1981, p. 197; Carter, Govinden, and Peerthum, 2003; Hopper, 2020, pp. 271–294, especially 284–286). Many of these individuals were indentured to local planters for five years who used them to grow coconuts and manufacture coconut oil. Most of these workers refused to continue working as plantation labourers after they completed their indenture, a turn of events which prompted Seychellois planters to introduce a *moitié* (literally "half") sharecropping scheme in an attempt to secure the labour they needed (Allen, 2022b). By all accounts, only small numbers of indentured labourers reached the Chagos Archipelago. The 1850s witnessed the arrival of some Indian workers recruited illegally at Cochin on India's Malabar Coast, while 20 Malagasies were recruited in 1861 to work on the Six Islands atoll under three-year contracts. Contemporary accounts reveal that these workers were subject to considerable exploitation and maltreatment including irregular payment of wages, inadequate and erratic delivery of rations, and other forms of abuse (Carter, 2017, pp. 220–222).

* * * * * *

More than 40 years ago, sociologist Nigel Bolland argued cogently that examining developments in peripheral parts of the British Empire such as Belize can provide important insights into the nature and dynamics of the indentured labour system and the imperial system of which it was part (Bolland, 1980, 1984, 2003). The same principle applies to the Chagos Archipelago, especially in light of recent arguments that the Indian Ocean should not be viewed simply as a geographic area or cultural and economic space, but rather as a diasporic space in which communities came into existence, survived, and reproduced themselves (Walker and Slama, 2021). What we currently know about the Chagossian slave population highlights the need to appreciate that the African, Indian, and Southeast Asian slave diasporas, often overlooked in Indian Ocean history, reached into the most geographically remote corners of this oceanic world (Allen, 2020a). The 1832 and 1835 censuses of Ozille Majastre's slave workforces on Diego Garcia and Peros Banhos reveal, for example, that, in addition to Malagasies and Mozambicans, the archipelago housed at least a few of the 14,750–18,200 Indian slaves estimated to have been exported to the Mascarenes between 1770 and 1810 (Allen, 2004, p. 41; Wenban-Smith and Carter, 2016, pp. 110–111, 133).[4]

The presence of indentured Malagasies on the Six Islands in 1861 underscores the need to transcend the Indo-centrism that dominates indentured labour studies in general and Mauritian historiography in particular and pay closer attention to the African, Chinese, Javanese, Melanesian, and other labourers who also lived and worked in the nineteenth-century colonial plantation world. Equally important is the need to appreciate the ways in which these indentured labour trades were intertwined, a point underscored by Karin Speedy's research on New Caledonia in the southwest Pacific Ocean. Speedy demonstrates that Réunion played a significant role in the development of both New Caledonia's plantation sector and the so-called "blackbird" trade that funnelled more than 62,500 Melanesian workers to sugar estates in Queensland, Australia between the early 1860s and 1910 (Speedy, 2007, 2009, 2015). Unfortunately, we know little about how the indentured Malagasies who reached Mauritius and its dependencies were recruited or reached these islands. However, their presence clearly invites comparison with the *engagé* system, often viewed as the continuation of the slave trade in new garb. This system entailed the recruitment of 50,000 ostensibly liberated slaves and "free" Malagasy and Mozambican labourers to work on the French-controlled island of Mayotte in the Comoros, the island of Nosy-Bé off Madagascar's northwest coast, and Réunion between the abolition of slavery in the French Empire in 1848 and the 1880s (e.g., Renault, 1976; Fuma, 2000; Monnier, 2006).

The presence of illegally recruited Indian workers from Cochin in the archipelago reveals a hitherto unknown aspect to indentured Indian migration that bears directly on the question of whether these individuals were, as many indentured labour historians contend, little more than the helpless and hapless victims of the "new system of slavery" that emerged in the wake of British slave emancipation.[5] Their recruitment in Cochin challenges arguments that all indentured Indian labourers left the subcontinent from Calcutta, Madras (Chennai), or Bombay (Mumbai) and, moreover, points up the need to explore possible structural links between the Indian slave and indentured labour trades. The existence of such links is suggested in various ways: by Cochin exporting Indian slaves during the seventeenth and eighteenth centuries, and by the fact that the 3,100 Indian workers shipped to Réunion during the late 1820s arrived from the former French slave-trading enclaves of Pondichéry, Karikal, and Yanam. Pondichéry and Karikal likewise played a key role in the migration of at least 79,000 indentured Indians to Réunion and the French colonies of French Guiana, Guadeloupe, and Martinique in the Caribbean between 1849 and the mid-1880s (Northrup, 1995, p. 60; Weber, 2002, pp. 309–310). There is good reason accordingly to view the exportation of Indian slaves by European and indigenous merchants as establishing some of the foundations upon which the nineteenth-century Indian indentured labour trades subsequently rested (Allen, 2022a, pp. 544–545). In sum, these workers' presence in the archipelago demonstrates the need to transcend the "tyranny of the particular" that plagues modern slave, indentured, and colonial studies and situate local developments in more fully developed local, regional, pan-regional, and comparative contexts (Allen, 2020b). Doing so is essential not only to reconstructing the history of the Chagos Archipelago, but also to giving meaning to the Chagossian experience not only in the past but also in the present and the future.

Notes

1 Scott was governor of Mauritius from 1954 to 1959 while Edis served as commissioner of the BIOT from 1998 to 1991.
2 The problematic nature of these figures is indicated by reports that Diego Garcia housed 89 slaves in 1815, 126 between 1816 and 1818, 61 in 1819, 137 in 1820–21, 67 in 1822, and 132 in 1823.
3 For an overview, see Northrup (1995). On the transformations in Mauritian social and economic life, see Allen (1999, pp. 136–171)
4 In 1806, Mauritius housed 6,162 Indians who comprised 10.2% of the total chattel population (Milbert, 1812, vol. 2, p. 233bis).
5 Such arguments follow Tinker (1974).

References

Allen, R.B. (1999) *Slaves, Freedmen and Indentured Laborers in Colonial Mauritius*. Cambridge: Cambridge University Press.

Allen, R.B. (2001) 'Licentious and unbridled proceedings: The illegal slave trade to Mauritius and the Seychelles during the early nineteenth century'. *Journal of African History*, 42(1), pp. 91–116.

Allen, R.B. (2004) 'The Mascarene slave-trade and labour migration in the Indian Ocean during the eighteenth and nineteenth centuries'. In Gwyn Campbell (ed.), *The Structure of Slavery in Indian Ocean Africa and Asia*. London: Frank Cass, pp. 33–50.

Allen, R.B. (2014) *European Slave Trading in the Indian Ocean, 1500–1850*. Athens: Ohio University Press.

Allen, R.B. (2020a) 'Africans in the Indian Ocean world'. In *Oxford Research Encyclopedia of African History*. Available at: https://doi.org/10.1093/acrefore/9780190277734.013.698.

Allen, R.B. (2020b) *Slaves, Convicts, Indentured Laborers and the Tyranny of the Particular*. Joseph C. Miller Memorial Lecture 1. Berlin: EB-Verlag Dr. Brandt.

Allen, R.B. (2022a) 'Exporting the unfortunate: The European slave trade from India, 1500-1800'. *Slavery and Abolition*, 43(3), pp. 533–552.

Allen, R.B. (2022b) 'History of the Seychelles'. In *Oxford Research Encyclopedia of African History*. Available at: https://doi.org/10.1093/acrefore/ 9780190277734.013.1141.

Allen, R.B. (2022c) 'Plantation economy and slavery in the Mascarene Islands (Indian Ocean)'. In *Oxford Research Encyclopedia of African History*. Available at: https://doi.org/10.1093/acrefore/9780190277734.013.902.

Bernardin de St. Pierre, J.H. (1834) *Voyage à l'Ile de France*, 2 vols. Paris: Armand-Aubrée.

Bolland, O.N. (1980) 'Systems of domination after slavery: The control of land and labour in the British West Indies after 1838'. *Comparative Studies in Society and History*, 23(4), pp. 591–619.

Bolland, O.N. (1984) 'Reply to William A. Green's "The perils of comparative history"'. *Comparative Studies in Society and History*, 26(1), pp. 120–125.

Bolland, O.N. (2003) *Colonialism and Resistance in Belize: Essays in Historical Sociology*, 2nd rev. ed. Benque Viejo del Carmen, Belize: Cubola Productions, and Barbados, Jamaica, and Trinidad and Tobago: University of the West Indies Press.

Carter, M. (2017) 'Towards a workers' history of the Chagos Archipelago'. *Journal of the Indian Ocean Region*, 13(2), pp. 213–233.

Carter, M. (2022) 'The Chagos Archipelago'. In *Oxford Research Encyclopedia of Asian History*. Available at: https://doi.org/10.1093/acrefore/9780190277727.013.739.

Carter, M., Govinden, V. and Peerthum, S. (2003) *The Last Slaves: Liberated Africans in 19th Century Mauritius*. Port Louis, Mauritius: Centre for Research on Indian Ocean Societies.

Colebrooke, W.M.G., and W. Blair to Earl Bathurst (21 November 1826) CO 415/1, pp. 26–28. National Archives of the United Kingdom (NAUK), Kew.

Decary, R. (1961) *Les voyages du chirurgien Avine à l'île de France et dans la mer des Indes au début du XIXe siècle*. Paris: G. Durassié & Cie.

d'Unienville, B. (1838) *Statistique de l'Ile Maurice et ses dépendances, suivie d'une notice historiques sur cette Colonie et d'un Essai sur l'Ile de Madagascar*, 3 vols. Paris: Gustave Barba.

Edis, R. (1983) *Peak of Limuria: The Story of Diego Garcia and the Chagos Archipelago*. London: Bellow Publishers.

F 4/1130, 21 prairial An X (10 June 1802) Mauritius National Archives (MNA), Mauritius.

Fuma, S. (2000) 'La traite des esclaves dans le bassin du sud-ouest de l'océan Indien et la France après 1848'. In Rakoto, I. (ed.), *La route des esclaves: Système servile et traite dans l'est malgache*. Paris: L'Harmattan, pp. 247–261.

Grant, C. (1801) *The History of Mauritius, or the Isle de France, and the Neighboring Islands; From Their First Discovery to the Present Time; Composed Principally from the Papers and Memoirs of Baron Grant, Who Resided Twenty Years in the Island, By His Son, Charles Grant, Viscount de Vaux*. London: W. Bulmer & Co.

Hopper, M. (2020) 'Liberated Africans in the Indian Ocean World'. In Richard Anderson and Henry R. Lovejoy (eds.), *Liberated Africans and the Abolition of the Slave Trade, 1807–1896*. Rochester, NY: Rochester University Press, pp. 271–294.

Kuczynski, R.R. (1949) *Demographic Survey of the British Colonial Empire*, vol. 2. London: Oxford University Press.

Milbert, M.J. (1812) *Voyage pittoresque à l'Ile de France, au Cap de Bonne-Espérance et à l'Ile de Ténériffe*, 2 vols. Paris: A. Nepveu.

Monnier, J.-E. (2006) *Esclaves de la canne à sucre: Engagés et planteurs à Nossi-Bé, Madagascar, 1850–1880*. Paris: L'Harmattan.

Northrup, D. (1995) *Indentured Labor in the Age of Imperialism, 1834–1922*. Cambridge: Cambridge University Press.

Nwulia, M.D.E. (1981) *The History of Slavery in Mauritius and the Seychelles, 1810–1875*. Rutherford, NJ: Farleigh Dickinson University Press.

OC 40/176, (3 janvier 1780) Mauritius National Archives (MNA), Mauritius.

Reddi, S.J. (1984). 'The establishment of the Indian indenture system, 1834-1842'. In U. Bissoondoyal (ed.), *Indians Overseas: The Mauritian Experience*. Moka, Mauritius: Mahatma Gandhi Institute Press, pp. 1–17.

Renault, F. (1976) *Libération d'esclaves et nouvelle servitude: Les rachats de captives africains pour le compte des colonies françaises après l'abolition de l'esclavage*. Paris: Les Nouvelles Éditions Africaines.

Scott, R. (1961) *Limuria: The Lesser Dependencies of Mauritius*. London: Oxford University Press.

Selvon, S. (2001) *A Comprehensive History of Mauritius*. Port Louis, Mauritius: Mauritius Printing Specialists (Pte) Ltd.

Speedy, K. (2007) *Colons, créoles et coolies: L'immigration réunionnaise en Nouvelle-Calédonie (XIXe siècle) et le tayo de Saint-Louis*. Paris: L'Harmattan.

Speedy, K. (2009) 'Who were the Réunion "coolies" of 19th-century New Caledonia?' *Journal of Pacific History*, 44(2), pp. 123–140.

Speedy, K. (2015) 'The Sutton case: The first Franco-Australian foray into blackbirding'. *Journal of Pacific History*, 50(3), pp. 344–364.

Teelock, V. (2009) *Mauritian History: From Its Beginnings to Modern Times*. Moka, Mauritius: Mahatma Gandhi Institute Press.

Tinker, H. (1974) *A New System of Slavery: The Export of Indian Labour Overseas, 1830–1920*. London: Oxford University Press.

Toussaint, A. (1972) *Histoire des îles Mascareignes*. Paris: Berger-Levrault.

Walker, I. and Slama, M. (2021) 'The Indian Ocean as a diasporic space: A conceptual introduction'. *Journal of Indian Ocean World Studies*, 4(2), pp. 76–90.

Weber, J. (2002) 'L'émigration indienne à La Réunion: "Contraire à la morale" ou "utile à l'humanité"? (1829–1860)'. In Edmond Maestri (ed.), *Esclavage et abolitions dans l'océan Indien, 1723–1860*. Paris: L'Harmattan, pp. 309–328.

Wenban-Smith, N. and Carter, M. (2016) *Chagos: A History. Exploration, Exploitation, Expulsion*. London: Chagos Conservation Trust.

3 Origins, Legacies, and Future

The Chagossians, a Population in Exile

Priya Bahadoor

This chapter analyses the history of a small community which has positioned itself against an ex-colonial power on the international scene and had recourse to various institutions to recognise the violation of their human rights. Among the 1328 to 1522 Chagossians (Gifford and Dunne, 2014) who were forcefully exiled to Mauritius from 1965 to 1973, only around 340 were alive in 2023. There are several second- and third-generation Chagossians who live in Mauritius, Seychelles, the United Kingdom, and several other countries. Their journey, from being forcefully deported from their land of birth to being a marginalised community for decades in a country where they had to fight to keep their identity, has been an eventful one. They have lost many of their own in the different battles they had to undertake. The movement of some of the Chagossians in the United Kingdom post their legal battles constitutes another chapter in their history which is addressed in other chapters in this volume.

There are very few accounts of the lives of the first inhabitants of the Chagos Archipelago until it was illegally detached from the territory of Mauritius, in November 1965. Among them are Roger Dussercle's publications from 1934, 1935, 1936, and 1937. Roger Dussercle, who was a French Catholic priest posted to Mauritius in 1927, recorded his observation of life in the Chagos from a colonial Christian missionary perspective according to Hookoomsing (2011). There are also descriptions from early British colonial administrators like Scott. Over the years, there have been several attempts on behalf of anthropologists, historians, jurists, and journalists to provide a narrative of the past lives of the Chagossians in their native land. They have carried out extensive interviews, relying on the few publications, official accounts, and reports of the archipelago. Writing the history of the Chagossians is a complex exercise as each of their experiences has been unique. While some of them were already living in Mauritius when the news of the closure of their island was announced, others were forcefully deported to Mauritius and Seychelles. What unites them though is the fact that after 1973, none of them could return to their native land.

From their discovery in the 16th century to their colonisation by French colonists from Ile de France towards the end of the 18th century to their take over by Great Britain from 1810, the role of the Chagos Archipelago kept evolving in the eyes of the imperial powers in the Indian Ocean.

DOI: 10.4324/9781003390299-5

The different inhabitants of the Chagos Archipelago tried to exploit what the islands had to offer: salted fish, turtle shells, turtles, rope made from coconut fibre, guano, and oil (d'Unienville, 1838), which were exported to Mauritius during the different centuries. The most important product, however, was coconut oil. This is why the Chagos Archipelago was also known as the Oil Islands. The evolving balance of power in the Indian Ocean will influence the role of the Mascarene Islands as well as that of their dependencies. With the abolition of the slave trade and slavery brought about after British control of Mauritius, the population of the Chagos Archipelago kept fluctuating. Most of the ex-slaves continued to work for the same copra plantation that continued to evolve on the Chagos as free contract labourers as, unlike the case of the ex-slaves in Mauritius, there were no other occupations where they could be employed or no other place where they could live. Ex-slaves as well as Indian indentured labourers arrived from Mauritius to supplement the workers on the Chagos Archipelago during the course of the 19th century. They lived in houses provided by the plantation. Inter-marriage or cohabitation between the initial population and newly arrived indentured labourers did take place. Depending upon the requirements of work, the inhabitants had to shift to other islands of the Chagos Archipelago for months at times leaving their families behind. Their main practising religion was Catholicism, imposed during the French colonisation of the Mascarene Islands. Many indentured labourers also converted to Catholicism. The decision was taken to retain the French language, laws, and religion after the British took over Mauritius. In the year 1880, there were around 760 people living in the Chagos Archipelago.

According to Dussercle's narratives on the islands of the archipelago described by Hookoomsing (2011), there are mentions of traces of Indian practices like the *marche sur le feu* (ceremonial walk on fire practice). The ritual is organised by an Ilois sorcerer. The word *païsa* which refers to money was also present in the vocabulary of the Chagossians, and many of them wore a *tapiz* which is an amulet worn by Muslims or Hindus. All these practices attest to the *métissage* between the ex-slave community and indentured labourers as well as their descendants. Olivier Bancoult, the current President of the Chagos Refugees Group (CRG), also shares how the Chagossians have in the past undertaken rituals, which he believed were introduced on the native land by indentured labourers from India, as an attempt to cure children affected by measles.

From 1882, Diego Garcia temporarily housed a coaling station owned by the Orient Steam Navigation Company for ships from England on a long haul using the Suez Canal route to Australia. The company closed its operations in 1888 and returned the leased land back to the authorities (U.S. Institute of Peace, 2011).

The Chagos islands were not much influenced by the First World War. During the course of the Second World War, debates cropped up about the installation of a wireless to keep the islanders informed about international events. No consensus was reached as no one wanted to take the financial responsibility for its installation. The Royal Air Force started to use Diego Garcia as a base in 1941 and there was the installation of a radio in the same year. There were suggestions to administer the archipelago from Seychelles and to ship goods from Colombo. However, none of these were implemented, and Mauritius continued to administer the different islands. There is not much information on the lives of the Chagos islanders except for a few reports from visiting magistrates and missionaries. A steamer was responsible for supplying the archipelago with its essential needs three or four times yearly and would also pick up the products exported to Mauritius.

The end of the Second World War and the start of the Cold War influenced the geopolitical situation in the Indian Ocean. On one hand, the rising communist threat in China and the situation in the horn of Africa and India on the other increased the need for the United States of America to monitor the region. The British decision to depart from Aden pushed the United States of America to step in to fill in the ensuing power vacuum (Vine, 2011). The Chagossians would, unfortunately, become the silent victims of these geopolitical shifts.

In the plantations, the Chagossians worked in return for a wage. They would also receive housing, food, and land from the administration. Basic education (in the form of two schools which were run from 1951 to 1965 (Botte, 1980)) and health facilities were offered to the Chagossians.

The overpowering role of the Chagossian women can partly be explained by the fact that initially many couples did not have a civil marriage in the Chagos archipelago. Cohabitation was the preferred norm, and in the event of the man leaving the household, the children stayed with the mother. Moreover, the temporary presence of missionaries and unavailability of civil status officers did not really facilitate the procedures of marriages, religious or legal ones. Power was therefore vested in the administrator to carry out legal marriages, and he was also responsible for noting down the number of births and deaths on the islands in exchange for a salary (Hookoomsing, 2011). According to Olivier Bancoult, it was only after their forced displacement to Mauritius that the importance of a legally recognised marriage was understood.

However, during the second half of the twentieth century, many Chagossians would have to travel to Mauritius, the main administrative island, for more advanced medical treatment and for other issues. Olivier Bancoult had to travel to Mauritius along with his family for the medical treatment of his younger sister in 1968. His sister unfortunately passed away because of medical complications shortly after.

Chagossians would also travel to Mauritius at times for buying commodities not available in their archipelago. The Chagossians either had to rent a house in Port Louis or in its suburb while they waited for the departure of the ship back to the Chagos archipelago or for the duration of their medical treatment according to an interview carried out with Fernand Mandarin in 2011. Not many Mauritians knew about the existence of these inhabitants at that time. There were different companies controlling different islands in the Chagos Archipelago. However, Diego Ltd became the sole controller of Agalega and Chagos Archipelago in 1941. The company also acquired the transport line connecting the different islands (Vine, 2011). In 1962, the Seychelles-based Chagos Agalega Ltd (Vine, 2011) bought the coconut plantations from the *Société Huilière de Diego et Peros* which was a Mauritius-based company. According to the Truth and Justice Commission, the

Chagos Agalega Company controlled the Chagos Archipelago which would logically only be on lease as the dependencies of Mauritius were still crown land.

The Chagossians had developed a distinct culture of their own. What was life-like for the Chagossians who had lived there? If the songs handed down to their children are to be believed, it was quite hassle-free. They led quite a simple life, consisting of the different activities related to the copra plantation, tending to their kitchen garden, livestock (pigs and chicken), or fishing. The housing facilities belonged to the company. They would buy their rations from the company-controlled retail shop. Once or twice per year, a magistrate, a doctor, or a police officer would visit the islands. The Chagossian women would be responsible for more or less the same jobs as their male counterparts on the Chagos archipelago. The only difference is that they would work until around 11 in the morning or 12. However, the lives of the Chagossians were far from being perfect. They were provided with basic healthcare, education, housing, and pension facilities. Issues like separation from their families, extra-conjugal affairs, and voodoo have also been portrayed in the songs of the Chagossians (Jeffery, 2007).

Many of them were, nonetheless, still unprepared for some of the miseries and culture shocks that they would have to go through after their deportation from their native lands. Olivier Bancoult grew up being reminded time and again by his mother, Rita Bancoult, that food was never a problem in their native land. They never went to sleep hungry. After being uprooted from the Chagos archipelago, many of the Chagossians struggled to make ends meet. Like Olivier Bancoult's mother, many Chagossian women would have to juggle with more than one job to be able to bring food for their family. Initially, after their deportation to Mauritius, unaware of the different laws related to working conditions, many Chagossian women were exploited of as most of them were uneducated. Work-related laws and money were alien concepts for them as they were more used to the barter system on their island.

On 5 November 1965, the Chagos archipelago was detached from the territory of Mauritius to constitute, along with three other islands forming part of the colony of Seychelles, the British Indian Ocean Territory (BIOT), created by an Order in Council under Royal Prerogative in November 1965. The three islands, Desroches, Farquhar, and Aldabra, previously part of the territory of Seychelles, were returned to it in June 1976. The 1965 Order in Council made provision for the creation of the post of a Commissioner for the Territory. The Commissioner had the power for the creation of laws for the peace, order, and good governance of the territory. The decolonisation process of Mauritius gave rise to a new colony, the BIOT at the heart of the Indian Ocean (see Chapters 1 and 14 for further discussion of this process). No actor in the region protested even though the concept of the Indian Ocean as a zone of peace became quite popular during the Cold War. The concept did not result in much except some long speeches and debates as the Indian Ocean was eventually militarised by different regional and non-regional powers.

Mauritius obtained its independence on 12 March 1968, and according to Jocelyn Chan Low, the Chagos Archipelago was presented as a deal during the last

Constitutional Conference Talk between Mauritian politicians and British authorities (Chan Low, 2011). The excision of the Chagos Archipelago was thus in violation of the 1960 declaration on the granting of independence to colonial countries and peoples paragraph 6 of General Assembly Resolution 1514(XV) dated 14 December 1960 which states that "any attempt aimed at the partial or total disruption of the national and the territorial integrity of a country is incompatible with the purposes and principles of the Charter of the United Nations".

The decision was taken to relocate all the Chagossians from the different islands of the Chagos archipelago to Seychelles and Mauritius to make way for the construction of an American military base. The United States of America insisted that the island chosen for the construction of the sophisticated communications facility should be devoid of inhabitants and should not be under the sovereignty of any third-world country. The United Kingdom leased the Chagos Archipelago to the United States of America in 1966 for a 50-year period in the first instance, further renewable for a 20-year period. Their Chagossian identity of the Ilois would have to be kept hidden. As it was illegal to uproot people from their native land, the British authorities took the decision to refer to the Chagossians as seasonal workers from Mauritius and Seychelles who worked for the copra plantation on a temporary basis. The Company did, as a matter of fact, seek people from Seychelles and Mauritius as and when the need for more workers was felt. Even if the houses in which they lived until their uprooting did not belong to them, the least they were entitled to was a financial compensation and a decent housing facility in Mauritius and Seychelles.

The Chagos Agalega Company, formed in 1962, continued to exploit the coconut plantations until its closure in 1967. The British authorities then proceeded to provide a financial compensation of £660,000 to the copra exploitation company. The management of the archipelago was taken over by Moulinie & Co from Chagos Agalega Company (Vine, 2009). Copra production was run on behalf of the BIOT by Moulinie & Co on Peros Banhos until the island was closed and the remaining inhabitants were evacuated in either March or April 1973 ("*Chagos Islanders v. Attorney General and HM BIOT Commissioner*", 2003).

The Chagossians were forcibly expelled from the different islands of the Chagos archipelago from 1968 to 1973 to be deported to Mauritius and Seychelles. In the beginning, some of the inhabitants of Diego Garcia were transferred temporarily to Salomon and Peros Banhos. Those who were in Mauritius, for one reason or another (medical treatment or other reasons), were denied the return passage to the Chagos Archipelago with the excuse that their islands were closed. Section 4 of the Immigration Ordinance 1971 enacted by the BIOT Commissioner stipulated that no person was allowed to enter the BIOT or remain in the territory without a permit. Mauritius on the other hand achieved its independence on 12 March 1968. Food and medical supplies to the Chagos islands were restricted by British authorities in an attempt to coerce the Ilois to leave their islands. Previously, the ship *Mauritius* carried passengers and cargoes to and from Mauritius. However, from

July 1968, the BIOT administration secured the ship *Nordvaer* to link the BIOT with the Seychelles. The inhabitants were coerced to leave the islands of the archipelago. One of the events which marked many of the native Chagossians was the killing of the dogs in Diego Garcia. The dogs were assembled and gassed in the calorifer which was used in copra production. The inhabitants were told that they would face the same situation if they did not obey the orders to leave the Chagos Archipelago.

Once in Mauritius, the Chagossians received no help from the Mauritian government nor any financial assistance for their resettlement. Instead, they faced numerous difficulties which made their integration in Mauritian society quite difficult. Olivier Bancoult remembers how much stigma was attached to the Ilois. The term Ilois itself had a pejorative connotation in the post-independence period until lately. Rodriguans, islanders from Rodrigues island, another dependency of Mauritius, also used to come to the main administrative island in search of better job prospects. Many of them lived in the suburb of Port Louis like the Chagossians. Both groups of islanders from the dependencies of the main administrative island were not readily accepted in Mauritian society. They remained for decades as a marginalised community on the outskirts of the capital, Port Louis, most of them in grinding poverty. Many of the Chagossians lived in Roche Bois, Cassis, Salines, in the Dockers Flats, Pailles, Sainte Croix Cité La Cure, and Pointe aux Sables. Some even moved to Petite Rivière, Baie du Tombeau, Beau Bassin, and Le Hochet according to Françoise Botte, a social activist who was following their situation. Seventy-five Chagosssians had committed suicide by 1975 according to the social activist (Botte, 1980). The unusually high rate of suicides in the early years of the relocation of the Chagossians to Mauritius attests to their difficulties encountered in the multiethnic host society.

The legal battles started by the different actors of the Chagossian community have also been attempts for them to reaffirm their identity and the dignity associated with it. In the late 1970s and early 1980s, the Chagossian women undertook a series of protests and strikes to campaign for their rights. Chagossian women have been the guardians of moral standards of the Chagossian community, which was a matriarchal one. Among them were Lisette Talate and Charlesia Alexis. They received the guidance and support of politicians from Mouvement Militant Mauricien like Paul Bérenger and Kader Bhayat, from Organisation Fraternelle (Sylvio Michel and Elie Michel). They were also joined in their demonstrations by Lindsey Collen and Ragini Kistnasawmy from the Women's Liberation Movement. During an interview, Lindsey Collen, member of *LALIT*, recalls how these series of demonstrations and hunger strikes were influenced by the socio-political situation of Mauritius, namely the economic stagnation and the series of strikes which took hold of various sectors like the sugar industry, Export Processing Zone and transport. Many Chagossians worked in the docks, as helpers, or as fishermen. The Chagossian women were employed as housemaids, as machinists (in the Export Processing Zone), and in the agricultural sector. It is in this context that the Chagossians were also targeted by the various movements in place which wanted to organise, educate, and promote political awareness among workers.

In 1975, Michel Vincatassin, a native Chagossian, filed a case against Her Majesty's Government to obtain the right to return. However, he was compelled to abandon the charges before the High Court in 1982 before the settlement of his case. All this was happening in the above-mentioned context. The British government agreed to pay the second compensation to the Chagossians on the condition that Michel Vincatassin abandon his case (Vincatassin, 2011).

Eventually, negotiations between the Chagossians and the governments of Mauritius and Britain resulted in two financial compensations, the first in 1978 and the second 1982. Some of them also received compensation in terms of land. Much of the money was used by many of them to pay off debts that had been accumulated since their arrival in Mauritius. However, none of the Chagossians living in the Seychelles received these compensations. The British government had provided £650,000 to Mauritius to help in the resettlement of the Chagossians. This money was not immediately paid to the Chagossians. It was only after 6 years, in 1978, that the Mauritian government provided this money to the Chagossians. Another additional sum of £4 million was agreed to be disbursed by the British government in 1982. As part of the second payment, the Chagossians had to sign a renunciation form which enunciated that the 1982 compensation was to be the final settlement for any claims on the Chagos.

The *Ilois* Trust Fund Act 1982 was enacted by the Parliament in Mauritius on 30 July 1982 for the creation of an *Ilois* Trust Fund which would help in the payment of the compensation to the Chagossians in Mauritius.

The Chagos Refugees Group came into existence in 1983 to continue the battles started by the women in the late 1970s and 1980s to obtain the right to return to their native land (see page 8). Several other groups representing the interests of the Chagossians emerged, namely the Chagossian Social Committee or *Comité Social Chagossien* of Fernand Mandarin created in 1995, that of Allen Vincatassin before he eventually moved to the United Kingdom, and Groupe *Comité Chagossiens Seychelles* whose spokesperson is Pierre Prosper. An Interview carried out with Fernand Mandarin in the year 2011 highlighted how he had successfully represented the voice of the Chagossians at the United Nations Working Group on Indigenous Populations in 1996 with the helping hand of some Mauritians. However, the Mauritius government does not recognise the Chagossians as being an indigenous population. Recently, the representative of the Mauritian government, through a statement to the indigenous peoples' forum at the United Nations in July 2023, EMRIP (Expert Mechanism on the Rights of Indigenous Peoples), in response to the participation of the group of people representing the indigenous population of the Chagos archipelago, emphasised that there has never been an indigenous population on the Mauritian territory, including the Chagos Archipelago.

The Chagos Refugees Group obtained their first victory against the British Crown when the High Court in the United Kingdom ruled in favour of the Chagossians, declaring their expulsion from their homeland and thus the 1971 Immigration Ordinance as illegal on 3 November 2000 ("*R v Secretary of State for Foreign and Commonwealth Affairs, ex p Bancoult (No 1)*"). In 2002, the results of a feasibility study commanded by the Foreign and Commonwealth Office for the resettlement of the Chagossians were published. According to the report, the resettlement of the Chagossians would be difficult and expensive.

A second legal action was filed against the British government in 2003 for financial compensation which would be used to finance the return of the Chagossians to their homeland. The High Court pronounced itself against financial compensation but admitted that the Ilois were treated in a shameful way by the different British governments ("*Chagos Islanders v Attorney General & HM BIOT Commissioner*", 2003).

The High Court's decision was accepted and a new Immigration Ordinance was enacted according to which the Chagossians did not need an immigration permit before entering the Chagos Archipelago, except Diego Garcia. The Chagossians were therefore granted British citizenship, which consequently gave them the right of abode in the United Kingdom. Starting from 1965, the date of the creation of the British Indian Ocean Territory, the Chagossians became citizens of the United Kingdom and its colonies according to the British Nationality Act of 1948 (Allen, 2011).

An Order in Council was issued in June 2004 to prevent the return of the Chagossians to the Chagos archipelago. This was challenged through judicial review proceedings in the House of Lords in 2008 by Olivier Bancoult. However, a 3–2 majority saw the dismissal of the challenge. They also proceeded to lodge a case in the European Court of Human Rights which dismissed their application as inadmissible in December 2012 ("*Chagos Islanders v the United Kingdom*", 2012; Sand, 2015). The Chagossians have also had recourse to US federal courts which have however dismissed their action declaring the establishment of the US/UK Chagos military base in Diego Garcia a political question ("*Bancoult v. McNamara*", 2006).

In the midst of these diplomatic and legal battles, some Chagossians obtained the right to visit some of the islands of the Chagos Archipelago. In March 2006, a group of 104 Chagossians went on a four-day heritage visit to the Chagos archipelago. This visit was planned as the first of several ones to be organised by the British government with the support of the Mauritian and American governments. The Mauritian government initially agreed to collaborate with the United Kingdom for the organisation of these visits, as their sovereignty was not questioned through the action (*L'Express,* 2019). However, these limited visits highlight the disparate agendas of the governments involved.

Britain, as an ex-colonial power, tried to use environmental factors to keep the Ilois and their descendants away from the Chagos archipelago by ensuring that the islands became a restricted area. The publication of a confidential cable by WikiLeaks in 2009 came to illustrate the strength of the environmental lobby against the Chagossians' case. The engineered protection of the ecology of the Chagos Archipelago has been used as an excuse to prevent human footprints on that land (Jeffery, 2014).

The establishment of a Marine Protected Area (MPA) around the different islands of the Chagos Archipelago, except Diego Garcia, in April 2010, was a major turning point in the whole affair. Before this major unilateral decision on behalf of the United Kingdom, the Mauritian government did not provide much information about its strategy to the general public. However, the creation of the MPA pushed the Mauritian Government to adopt a more aggressive stance in the Chagos Affair. This will be highlighted through its numerous actions via the Permanent Court of Arbitration and the International Court of Justice through the United Nations in the ensuing years.

More recently, Mauritius proceeded to organise a scientific survey at Blenheim Reef in February 2022 without the permission of the United Kingdom. Acclaimed as a media stunt by many, this visit was to highlight Mauritian sovereignty over the Chagos archipelago (see Chapter 17 for Owen Bowcott's account of this trip).

On numerous occasions, the CRG has stated that their main aim was and is to obtain the right of return to the Chagos archipelago. In many places, the local people have been helping to protect and preserve their natural heritage. In the case of Chagos, not only were the natives being denied future access through this measure, they were also being kept away from any attempt for the conservation of their ancestral land.

In 2019, the International Court of Justice delivered an advisory opinion on the battle involving Mauritius and the United Kingdom. It advised the latter to put an end to its administration of the Chagos Archipelago by highlighting how the entity in question was illegally dismembered from the territory of Mauritius upon its accession to independence. A six-month deadline was provided to the UK during which it had to renounce sovereignty over the Chagos Archipelago and recognise that of Mauritius (United Nations General Assembly, 2019). The United Kingdom started negotiations with the Mauritian government in late 2022. In 2024, there are ongoing negotiations between the two governments on the issue of sovereignty. Acknowledging that the sovereignty issue concerns the governments of these two countries, Olivier Bancoult claims that the Chagossians should be involved in negotiations involving the Chagos archipelago and eventually their resettlement on their land of birth.

The forced relocation of the Chagossians from their native land destroyed their relationship with the economic, social, natural as well as cultural environments upon which their livelihood was based. As mentioned by Roos (2002), the continuity of people's traditions and practices is threatened with the loss of this relationship, putting in danger their cultural survival. Roos has also shared how the vice president of the World Council of Indigenous Peoples has illustrated the harms that result when indigenous peoples are displaced from their land. The devastating consequences were also felt by the Chagossian community which has shared a long and deep relationship with their native land. The consequences of these changing equations on the physical and cultural existence of people who have been through forced dislocation can lead to what sociologists and historians have called developmental or cultural genocide or ethnocide (Roos, 2002). Legal scholars have studied conflict-induced displacement, that is, forced dislocations of communities in conditions of armed conflict or civil strife. The Chagossians form part of the community which was displaced because of the Cold War and the changing status quo in the Indian Ocean.

The Chagossians are an ethnic community. They are the descendants of slaves from the East African coast and Madagascar as well as descendants of indentured labourers from India. With time they came to develop their own culture and their lives revolved around the plantation economy that emerged after more than one and a half centuries. Even though the forced dislocation of the Chagossians was not done with the intent of exterminating the group, many of them lost their lives because of the psychological trauma of being displaced from their land of birth, and difficulties encountered in trying to adapt to the social, economic, and natural environment in Mauritius.

There are currently around 340 native Chagossians residing in Mauritius and 130 in the UK according to Olivier Bancoult. The role of all Members of Parliament in Mauritius is to represent the interests of their voters. Geographically, most of the Chagossians have been living in the regions found on the outskirts of the capital city, Port Louis. Since their arrival, they had the support of different organisations and political groups in the 1970s and 1980s, which have helped the Chagossian community in different ways, be it through their education or sensitisation programmes for the working class in Mauritius. Olivier Bancoult highlights the support of the different Prime Ministers of Mauritius, more specifically at the beginning of the legal battles. According to Philippe Sands (2022), the Chagossians were the ones who initiated the battle. Eventually, they obtained the support of different actors or governments.

In the Mauritian context, the Chagossians can be classified as a minority group due to the fact that they come from a specific geographical region, the Chagos Archipelago. Forced displacement does engender some sort of loss of cultural knowledge. The Chagossians have, for decades, tried to survive by facing the harsh conditions in Mauritius. They had to put in extra effort to try to preserve their culture. They have tried their best to transmit their culture to their future generations. However, there are several factors which at times hinder this process of transmission and are thus responsible for alienating many young Chagossians from the practice. For example, the *sega tambour Chagos*, one of the cultural practices of the Chagossians, has been included in the list of intangible cultural heritage in need of urgent safeguarding by UNESCO in 2019. Vina Ballgobin (2014) in her article "Le patrimoine musical de la République de Maurice: L'archipel des Chagos (1900–1950)" has mentioned how the Chagossians had specific songs for different milestones in life, be it birth, baptism ceremony, wedding, or new year festivities. Many elements of their culture are at times hard to preserve because these have evolved in a specific geographical context, that is, the Chagos Archipelago. Devoid of this particular element, cultural practices will naturally change. During his interview, the president of the CRG highlights how once in Mauritius Chagossians did not have to be taught fishing as it was a basic survival practice learnt by everyone since their childhood in their native land. Olivier Bancoult believes that a community without culture is like a tree without roots. Likewise, there are many aspects of their culture that are in need of preservation.

Conclusion

This paper has been an attempt to retrace the past and present of the Chagossians currently living in Mauritius. Many of them are now living in the United Kingdom as a consequence of their legal battles. The different struggles of the Chagos Refugees Group have led their adherents to adopt a particular narrative to demonstrate a united front in the face of the ongoing moral, legal, and political procedures. With time, the Chagos Refugees Group has become the platform representing the majority of the Chagossians currently living in Mauritius.

The plantation economy of copra, built on slave and indentured labour, disappeared during the Cold War to make place for the construction of an American military base. The identity of the descendants of slaves has been responsible for the exile of the Chagossians from their native land. They believe that they have been the victims of the racist treatment of British authorities during the 1960s and 1970s. Their legal battle against the United Kingdom and moral battle on the international scene to obtain recognition as a community born on the Chagos have lasted for almost 50 years. The General Assembly of the United Nations has recognised the illegal detachment of the Chagos Archipelago from the territory of Mauritius on the eve of its independence. The challenges that they faced for their survival, for the continuation of the practice of their culture and for the safeguarding of their identity, that of an Ilois have been numerous. Their experiences in Mauritius have taught them resilience and they have managed to preserve part of their culture in the face of the violent uprooting. They possessed no substantial material wealth, but their most valued dream since their illegal expulsion, at least of those born on the Chagos archipelago, is to obtain the right to return home and to eventually be buried next to their ancestors, on their native land.

To make right the wrongdoings of USA and UK authorities would imply acknowledgement of the violation of human rights, which have been recognised by competent international institutions. The Chagossians will not be reunited with siblings or parents lost due to extreme poverty and sadness (*sagrin*) of having been illegally exiled from their native land, but acceptance of those crimes by the responsible authorities would be a first. The Chagossian should receive adequate institutional support to try to overcome the trauma of displacement, decades of misery and exclusion that some of them have faced and eventually compensation. They have obtained partial recognition as their identity as natives, born on the islands of the Chagos Archipelago, has been acknowledged legally. However, their right to return to the Chagos Archipelago is still being debated over. They have yet to be taken on board the different negotiation processes between the two sovereign governments involved in the whole Chagos affair. The president of the Chagos Refugees Group believes that their return to their native land is imminent. However, he believes that the Chagos should not fall under the control of the Outer Islands Development Corporation as they should be able to enjoy a degree of sovereignty and freedom after all the past struggles.

References

Allen. S. (2011) Responsibility And Redress: The Chagossian Litigationin The English Courts. In Evers, S. and Kooy, M. (eds.) *Eviction from the Chagos Islands: Displacement and Struggle for Identity against Two World Powers*. Leiden: Brill, pp. 127–152.

Ballgobin, D.V. (2014) 'Le patrimoine musical de la République de Maurice: L'archipel des Chagos(1900–1950)'. *Revue Historique de l'océan Indien*, 11, pp. 600–615.

Botte, Françoise (1980) *The "Ilois" Community and the "Ilois" Women.* Mauritius: University of Mauritius. Unpublished Ms.

Chagos Islanders v Attorney General and HM BIOT Commissioner (2003) [2003] EWHC 2222 (QB). *BAILII*. Available at: http://www.bailii.org/ew/cases/EWHC/QB/2003/2222 .html (Accessed: 1 September 2023).

Chagos Islanders v the United Kingdom (application no. 35622/04) (2012) ECHR. *HUDOC.* Available at: https://hudoc.echr.coe.int/sites/eng-press/pages/search.aspx?i =003-4207010-4992253 (Accessed: 1 September 2023).

Chan Low, J. (2011). The Making of the Chagos Affair: Myths and Reality. In Evers, S. and Kooy, M. (eds.) *Eviction from the Chagos Islands: Displacement and Struggle for Identity against Two World Powers*. Leiden: Brill, pp. 61–79.

d'Unienville, B. (1938) *Statistique de l'Ile Maurice et ses dépendances, suivie d'une notice historiques sur cette Colonie et d'un Essai sur l'Ile de Madagascar*, 3 vols. Paris: Gustave Barba.

Gifford, R. and R. Dunne (2014) 'A Dispossessed People: the Depopulation of the Chagos Archipelago 1965–1973'. *Population, Space and Place,* 20(1), pp. 37–49.

Hookoomsing, V (2011). "Native Ilois of Chagos": Excerpts from the Narratives of Dussercle (1933-36). In Evers, S. and Kooy, M. (eds.) *Eviction from the Chagos Islands: Displacement and Struggle for Identity against Two World Powers*. Leiden: Brill, pp. 41–58.

Jeffery, L. (2007) 'How a plantation became a paradise: changing representations of the homeland among the displaced Chagos islanders'. *Journal of the Royal Anthropological Institute*, 13(4), pp. 951–968.

Lexpress (2019) 'Voyage sur l'archipel des Chagos: un planning suivi depuis deux ans'. Available at https://lexpress.mu/article/354070/voyage-sur-larchipel-chagos-un -planning-suivi-depuis-deux-ans (Accessed: 1 September 2023).

Bancoult v. McNamara (2006) 'Olivier Bancoult, et al., Appellants v. Robert S. Mcnamara, et al., Appellees, 445 F.3d 427 (D.C. Cir. 2006)'. Available at: https://law.justia.com/ cases/federal/appellate-courts/F3/445/427/602650/ (Accessed: 1 September 2023).

R v Secretary of State for Foreign and Commonwealth Affairs, ex p Bancoult (No 1) (2000) [2000] EWHC Admin 413

Roos, S.R. (2002) 'Development genocide and ethnocide: Does international law curtail development- induced displacement through the prohibition of genocide and ethnocide?' *Human Rights Brief*, 9(3), p. 4.

Sand, P.H. (2015) 'Stephen Allen. *The Chagos Islanders and international law*'. *European Journal of International Law*, 26(2), pp. 573–578.

Sands, P. (2022) *The Last Colony: A Tale of Exile, Justice and Britain's Colonial Legacy*. London: Weidenfeld and Nicolson.

UNESCO (2019) 'Decision of the intergovernmental committee: 14.COM 10.a.3'. *Bogota*. Available at: https://ich.unesco.org/en/Decisions/14.COM/10.a.3 (Accessed: 1 September 2023).

United Nations General Assembly (2019) 'General assembly welcomes international court of justice opinion on Chagos Archipelago, adopts text calling for mauritius' complete decolonization, GA/12146'. Available at: https://press.un.org/en/2019/ga12146.doc.htm (Accessed: 1 September 2023).

U.S. Institute of Peace (2011) 'Report of the truth and justice commission, volume 1'. Available at: https://www.usip.org/sites/default/files/ROL/TJC_Vol1.pdf (Accessed: 1 September 2023).

Vincatassin, A. (2011) Negotiating Life in Mauritius and the UK. In Evers, S. and Kooy, M. (eds.) *Eviction from the Chagos Islands: Displacement and Struggle for Identity against Two World Powers*. Leiden: Brill, pp. 125-125.

Vine, D. (2009) *Island of Shame: The Secret History of the U.S. Military Base on Diego Garcia*. Princeton: Princeton University Press.

Vine, D. (2011) From the Birth of the Ilois to the "Footprint of Freedom": A History of Chagos and the Chagossians. In Evers, S. and Kooy, M. (eds.) *Eviction from the Chagos Islands: Displacement and Struggle for Identity against Two World Powers*. Leiden: Brill, 11–36.

So immaculate – Peros Banhos, Saloman, Diego Garcia

Bien Prop – Peros Banhos, Saloman, Diego

Saradha Soobrayen

The Archipelago will be mapped with such precision, such smoke
and mirrors while the Chagos children cling to the margins of sleep.

They will be hurrying slowly, unaware of the will of the west,
unaware of the milk from the eyes of the coconut, seeping.

Their houses will not be made of wood but small hands of air,
a "floating population", a thumbprint on a door will cease to exist.

The pregnant goat yawns, and the hen scrapes a ditch to bed down.
A fiction will unfold while a boy scratches his name on a rock.

They will not be told why. The copra worker's tools will lie limp
and dull. The mainland winding down for the rest of its natural life.

They will not be told when. Washing will be left hanging.
The crops and herbs unpicked. Parts of the forest will remain.

The shed will catch the last whimpers of dogs, rounded and gassed.
Their *sagren* will begin. The graves of ancestors will not be tended.

Women will be sent on bogus trips to Port Louis. As the home ship
is finally docked they will be told that their islands have been sold.

DOI: 10.4324/9781003390299-6

4 Chagos: Plantation or Paradise?

Island Edens and Indian Ocean Empires, 1600–2023

Chris Hill

Before the results of the first "Bancoult" trial graced the headlines of major media outlets in late 2000, the story of the Chagos Archipelago might have seemed doomed to remain but an obscure footnote in the grand palimpsest of European imperial history; the cynical exile of its people at the supposed height of the decolonial moment but one of Britain's many unresolved colonial legacies. Due to the tireless efforts of the Chagossian diaspora and their supporters both in and outside the courts, the shameful history of the British Indian Ocean Territory is today known the world over – recorded in a wide array of mediums from public trial records, documentaries, literary fiction and graphic novels to poetry, interviews, and academic works. While the events surrounding and following the establishment of the British Indian Ocean Territory (BIOT) in 1965 are therefore well-understood, historian Marina Carter has observed that the colonial history of Chagos from the eighteenth to mid-twentieth centuries remains "comparatively neglected". Due to this state of affairs, contemporary understandings of this period have typically drawn from the accounts of the Chagossian diaspora themselves in depicting life on Chagos prior to exile – reflected in the common motif of a "paradise lost" presented throughout both popular and scholarly works. The use of such iconography in relation to Chagos' colonial past has however courted debate within both public and scholarly spheres.

In *Chagos: A History*, the first major effort to redress the neglect of this chapter of the islands' history, Carter and collaborator Nigel Wenban-Smith observe that, due to the absence of white settlers and the low value and task basis of copra production, the Chagos islands were administratively neglected by imperial governors between the eighteenth and mid-twentieth centuries, seeing the Chagossians ancestors enjoy a relatively idyllic quality of life relative to that of a typical plantation society in this period. Laura Jeffery has demonstrated how this state of affairs saw the emergence of a unique cultural identity in Chagos, similar yet distinct from neighbouring Creole cultures in Mauritius and the Seychelles (Jeffery, 2011). In this context, Steffen Johannessen has defended the use of such iconography as reflective of the community's common Christian heritage and "hellish" experience of life-exile; accounts of life on Mauritius running counter to the typical assumed narrative of decolonisation, which saw newly independent peoples supposedly gain a better quality of life than under colonial rule (2015, pp. 201–202). Moreover, as reflected by the Chagos Refugees Group's 2008 "Back to Paradise" Campaign,

DOI: 10.4324/9781003390299-7

such motifs have been mobilised to not only reflect on the past, but mobilise the exiled communities towards the future goal of return (Johannessen, 2015, p. 150). Reflecting on the manner in which inter-state sovereignty disputes and British claims to historical ownership have marginalised Chagossians from both the events and recounting of their own history, use of paradise iconography can be seen to comprise a culturally specific register for the community to relate their history on their own terms.

On the other side of this debate, Carter has argued that the use of such iconography ultimately misrepresents the true lived experience of the Chagossians' ancestors, a sensibility shared by voices within the community itself, who have critiqued the politically motivated nature of such portrayals. This point speaks to Carter's awareness of the broader resonance of paradise iconography within the context of colonial and postcolonial history. Emerging most prominently in European writing of the imperial period, tropes of paradise were typically mobilised to fetishise the lush, abundant environments of the colonial tropics as an empty "terra nullius" with lucrative bounties ripe for the taking – becoming a highly resonant signifier for the imperial ideologies of capitalistic extraction and militaristic domination throughout the age of imperialism. Moreover, what Paradise scholar Sherae Deckard terms the "discourse" of imperial paradise can be seen to continually underpin Western representations and understandings of the postcolonial world, most visible in the threefold mantra of sun, sea, and sand widely employed by the luxury tourism industry to both commodify and conceal the diverse histories of the postcolonial tropics. For Carter and collaborator Nigel Wenban-Smith, the use of paradise tropes ostensibly risks omitting the true facts of Chagos' little-known colonial history, a state of affairs their 2016 work *Chagos: A History* seeks to redress. While showing how Chagos' state of isolation would condition an ostensibly paradisical state of existence in one sense, this isolation would also allow Chagos' resident planting companies to exploit the basic human rights of their workers beyond the purview of colonial governance (Wenban-Smith and Carter, 2016, p. 252).

The spread of these arguments ultimately reflects the extremely portable nature of paradise, which Deckard understands as "value-laden discourse that alters according to whomever is estimating its value". The "double valence" of such discourse, Deckard explains, performs both utopian and ideological functions – at once a vessel for Chagossian longing for homeland, while simultaneously an ideological symbol of western desire concealing the true impact of imperialist extraction and conflict. To reconcile Chagossian cultural depictions of paradise with the factual, archival history which those such as Carter present, we must understand how the history of Chagos has itself been informed and shaped by imperial desires for paradise. Charting a course across the Chagossian history of the early, high, late, and post-colonial periods, this chapter demonstrates how the entwinement of paradise discourse with imperial ideologies of extraction would see tropical island colonies in particular transform to both reflect and support the repressed longings of western power throughout different world orders – from the plantations of the early and high imperial to the floating fortresses, tourist paradises, and conservationist Edens of the postcolonial. Ultimately, it demonstrates how paradise discourse comprises a highly constructive lens through which to not only understand the nature of the Chagos Archipelago's current exploitation as a military base, but provide a critical lens to organise resistance to its occupation.

Finding Paradise: Old World Edens and the Age of Exploration, 1500–1800

While the Chagos Archipelago was first discovered by sailors of the Portuguese (or Iberian) empire in their pioneering Indian Ocean expeditions of the early sixteenth century, the islands were avoided for the following three centuries due to the dangerous surrounding waters of the intertropical convergence zone (Carter and Wenban Smith, 2016, pp. 13–16). Indeed, more lucrative opportunities lay in the ocean's western region, which led knowledge of the group to fade until rediscovered by French and British sailors in the mid-eighteenth century (Carter and Wenban Smith, 2016, p. 21). While producing a clear account of the factors at play in the early exploration of Chagos, Carter and Wenban Smith fail to appreciate the structural nature of imperialist maritime economics, and the significance of its interactions with those of local Muslim cultures. While Eurocentric models of history typically champion the great innovation of European sailors in early forms of maritime commerce, historian Edward Alpers argues that the arrival of Europeans to the Indian Ocean World ultimately did little to change the historic patterns of the Indian oceanic economy (2014, p. 79). Following Vasco De Gama's 1502 landing in India, the Portuguese, Dutch, French, and British empires would merely adopt patterns of profit practised by local Islamic sailors long before their arrival, seeing practices such as maritime taxation, plunder, and spice trading routes between Asia and India form the common imperial praxis for these powers between the sixteenth and eighteenth centuries. Perhaps the one form of European innovation would come in the arrival of a novel, state-sponsored form of state-maritime warfare, structured around the naval fortification of coastlines and islands along the line of Indigenous monsoon trade routes; a strategy bringing great success to the Portuguese in their sixteenth century war with the local Ottoman empire (2014, pp. 79–81).

Observing how such strategies formed a common imperial praxis between the respective powers of the early and high imperial ages, Alejandro Colás and Liam Campling show how the historically terrestrial power relations of medieval Europe would be mapped onto the new terrain of vast oceanic space, each power struggling to claim the few precious spots of land as vessels from which to project their claim to oceanic sovereignty. Tropical islands thereby morph into critical strategic objects of imperial political economy throughout the age of imperialism, serving as simple settlements and fortresses to sustain the long, dangerous voyages between continental operations and safely convey luxury goods back to European markets (Campling and Colás, 2021, pp. 136–140). To expand on the description provided by Carter and Wenban-Smith, the imperial exploitation of the Indian Ocean World thereby followed a distinct logic responding to both the historic and contemporaneous dynamics of oceanic commerce, and the reliance on such logic irrevocably conditioned the avoidance of Chagos from the sixteenth to eighteenth centuries. Moreover, while acknowledging the appeal of more lucrative trading opportunities in the western ocean, *Chagos: A History* also neglects to understand the history of this appeal; one marking the interpolation of paradise discourse with imperial ideologies of oceanic exploitation.

Particularly, the period of the eleventh to fourteenth century, when the Italian Maritime Republics of Venice, Genoa, and Pisa enacted the initial model of maritime empire practised by the early modern powers two centuries hence. Peter Frankopan argues that due to their early naval dominance of the Mediterranean, these Republics would facilitate the shipping demands of the Catholic First Crusade's conquest of the Islamic Holy Land, seeing them receive privileged footholds in key Levantine economic centres which they would use to monopolise trade in the exotic goods produced throughout the east (2015, pp. 134–135). Due to the great appeal of such goods (particularly spices) among the wealthy European aristocracy, the Republics amassed great wealth and power between the twelfth and fourteenth centuries until the fall of Constantinople in 1453. Under the governance of the insurgent Ottoman Empire, this marked the closure of their treasured Mediterranean route due to heavy import taxes. In the subsequent Age of Exploration, Britain, France, Spain, Portugal, and the Netherlands entered a chapter of intense naval exploration, colonisation, and naval conflict to gain their own monopolies over eastern spice trading (2015, p. 140).

Due to the earlier contact between Europe and the eastern Levant, early imperial sailors particularly focused on establishing a route to the Indian Ocean World. While inspiring Vasco De Gama to sail south to circumnavigate the South African Cape in 1497, Christopher Columbus would in turn sail west in search of a different route to India, discovering instead the tropical climes of the Caribbean and Americas, famously mislabelled as the West Indies. In the writings of Columbus, we find not only the earliest interpolation of the discourse of paradise with imperial obsession with spice wealth, but perhaps the most resonant evocation of tropical islands as the object of imperial paradisical desire. Deckard shows that upon his landing in present-day Bahamas in 1492, Columbus reported his believed discovery of not only a land of exotic riches, but the Biblical Garden of Eden – reflecting how the motivations of early imperialists were not merely economic, but profoundly religious in nature (2010, pp. 7–8). Steven Darian has argued that, due to the cultural insularity of the preceding medieval Dark Ages, early European exploration was underpinned by a persisting equivalence between religious doctrine and established material fact. Merchant explorers of the feudal European monarchies sought not only the exotic luxuries of the Indian Ocean World, but the literal Christian Garden of Eden, described by the Hebrew Old Testament as lying in the distant East. While the scientific advancements of the late Renaissance would lay the groundwork for the rational world order of the eighteenth-century Enlightenment, it would also serve to broaden religious belief in terrestrial paradises along the fault lines carved by luxury trade routes. Lost classical epics such as the Greek Alexander Romance sensationalised Alexander's own search for Eden in the Mughal Indian subcontinent, and grew in popular consumption, seeing early imperial explorers adopt an Orientalist obsession with India as the site of mythical religious paradises (Darian, 2001, pp. 93–94).

Moreover, while the sixteenth to eighteenth centuries saw early imperial claimants to Indian Ocean hegemony concentrate their focus on India as the primary vessel of economic and cultural riches, the sixteenth century would also see tropical islands emerge as a highly resonant trope for imperial paradisical fantasies. This is presented famously in works such as Dante Alighieri's fourteenth-century *Purgatorio*, which situated the promise of spiritual salvation within the topology of tropical islands, to Thomas More's 1516 work *Utopia*, a tale of the eponymous isle's exploitation by European colonists (Grove, 1996, pp. 84–85). Besides the common praxis of spice trading and naval fortification, early imperial powers entwined classical figurations of paradise discourse into their epistemic appraisal of the Indian Ocean World, a fact we can moreover demonstrate by returning to the little-documented early encounters of the Iberians with the Chagos Archipelago. Where the Catholic First Crusade sought to claim Jerusalem for the spiritual deliverance of Christian Europeans, Giuseppe Marcocci demonstrates that, looking to the Indian Ocean World, the Portuguese-Ottoman war followed a similar logic some five centuries hence, seeing Iberians' imperial expansion justified as a "just war" to rescue the predominantly Muslim "infidels" of the Indian Ocean World from Ottoman rule (Marcocci, 2022, p. 679). Historians including George van Driem have suggested that the naming of Chagos as the "Bassas de Chagas" refers to the five wounds of Christ's crucifixion, a reading arguably inciting the islands' characterisation as a cultural object of early imperialists war against Islam in the predominantly Muslim Ocean (van Driem, 2021, p. 239). Moreover, reflecting on how a century of anti-Islamic conquest was justified as an act of charitable enlightenment, the naming of sites such as Chagos in religious terms ultimately reflects what Deckard terms the "double valence" of paradise discourse in the imperial age – the resonant spectre of religious paradise both motivating and justifying imperial exploitation while concealing the material realities of imperial violence (2010, p. 3).

It is critical to remember how the rapid colonisation of the Atlantic, Pacific, and Indian Ocean worlds would comprise not merely an economic, but cultural expansion of European Christian values. The entwinement of these is perhaps best reflected in the words of famed Christian missionary and colonial explorer David Livingstone, who, as Fidelis Nkomazana documents, rationalised imperial commercial exploitation throughout the sixteenth and eighteenth centuries as the benevolent extension of Christian civilisation to the Indigenous occupants of the colonial world in the late nineteenth century (1998, pp. 44–45). Therefore, we might consider how from its earliest beginnings, the history of the Chagos Archipelago was constituted within the terms of religious paradise, which recontextualises the Chagossians' own contemporary invocations of paradise discourse as speaking back to the Christian colonisation of the Indian Ocean World. While the Chagos Archipelago remained neglected for much of the seventeenth and eighteenth centuries, the nineteenth to mid-twentieth centuries saw the exploitation of Chagos continue under new terms.

Building Paradise: New World Edens and Imperial Ecology, 1800–1965

While informing the earliest encounters with the island group in a broader way, the nineteenth to twentieth centuries would see the discourse of paradise inform the history of Chagos in the most fundamental sense. Carter and Wenban-Smith show that, in the decades following the French occupation of Bourbon, Mauritius, and the Seychelles between 1643 and 1770, the Chagos Archipelago became locked in a climactic struggle for control of the Mascarene region between the navies of Napoleonic France and the British East India Company (29). The islands' strategic value was reappraised in a range of surveys conducted by both empires in subsequent decades. Observing that both French and British expeditions to the archipelago demonstrated its limited ecological capacity for the cultivation of cash crops such as sugar or spices, the authors argue that the divergent economic models of these rival powers reached different conclusions on the islands' strategic potential. Britain's overwhelming focus on spice exports from its interests in the Indian Subcontinent meant the islands were appraised in purely militaristic terms, seeking to protect its precious passage to India from French Mascarene hegemony. Due to the French empire's distinct focus on expanding their burgeoning settler colonies throughout their Mascarenes possessions, Mauritian officials thereby appraised Chagos' great potential for the production of copra oil, a widely used basic good within the local Mascarene economy (Wenban-Smith and Carter, 2016, pp. 29–30). Tor Sellstrom observes that from its settlement in 1715, the French isle of Mauritius became a veritable department of imperial France, with considerable investments in its military, commercial, political, and social infrastructure emerging as France's most critical Indian Ocean possession, in no small part due to its highly lucrative exports of its sugar plantations (2015, p. 13).

As discussed earlier, Carter and Wenban-Smith observe that due to the comparatively low yield and value of copra exports and its marked absence of a white settled population, the Chagos Archipelago subsequently languished in a state of historical isolation marked by longstanding administrative neglect by local Mauritian officials and its disconnection from the broader networks of imperial commerce (2016, p. 252). From its settlement in the early eighteenth century to the closure of its plantations in the early 1960s, this isolation conditioned a slower, more peaceable pace of life in Chagos compared to the intensity of French and British Mauritius' sugar plantations. Reflecting on the decline of Chagos' plantation society through the early to mid-twentieth century, the authors observe that Chagos resident planting companies would "cynically exploit" Chagos' distance from authority to sustain the exploitative and unproductive management of their operations (2016, p. vii). In the wake of Indian Ocean industrialisation during the British Century of 1815–1914, Chagos' production increasingly fell behind that of rival copra producers, implicitly informing the dissolution of Chagos' plantations in the context of the BIOT's 1965 establishment (2016, p. 252).

While presenting a compelling account of how the logic of imperial spice trading informed the tragic events of the contemporary Chagos Affair, *Chagos: A History* neglects to appreciate the persisting relevance of paradise mythology to this second chapter of Chagos' history; demonstrable by looking to the evolution of imperial paradise discourse throughout the eighteenth to mid-twentieth century "high imperial" period. Carter observes that, due to the gradual decline of religious order and parallel rise of the rational sciences within the context of the European Enlightenment, prior scholars of paradise studies famously declared the "death" of paradise as a culturally significant metaphor within the broad palimpsest of post-Enlightenment history (2017, p. 1). Due however to the demonstrated entwinement of paradise mythology within the early expansion of the European empire in the sixteenth and seventeenth centuries, Deckard argues that the terms of imperial paradise discourse ultimately transformed to accommodate the new longings and anxieties of the high imperial period (2010, pp. 2–3). Environmental historian Robert Grove provides a critical broader context to the divergent strategies of the French and British empires, demonstrating how the evolution of imperial paradise discourse once more emerged from the exploitation of tropical islands, the most resonant vessels of imperial paradise mythology. Observing how Indigenous and imperial rivalries threatened the production and circulation of luxury goods on continental colonies like India or the Americas, Grove suggests that the tropical islands were increasingly appraised as more easily defendable sites of resource production, a sensibility informing the more archipelagic approach of the Dutch and French empires within their Indian Ocean campaigns (1996, pp. 28–30). Grove suggests that as the first major landfalls of the Age of Sail, tropical islands would come to form not only critical military footholds for the circulation and protection of luxury trade, but a metaphor for the hope and promise of the imperial New World. The vast and seemingly limitless resource potential of continental India, Africa, and the Americas became mapped onto enclosed and "knowable" space of the island (1996, pp. 120–122).

While the Dutch Empire settled Mauritius in 1638 in an attempt to establish sugar plantations and expand the reach of its burgeoning maritime empire, the exploitation of the islands' resources for trade and shipbuilding would have a devastating impact on its sensitive tropical ecology. A period of extensive deforestation and soil erosion caused disease and starvation to beset the Dutch's Mauritian settlement, pushing them to abandon their colony by 1710. Following similar experiences in the British and French Caribbean, Grove observes that the Dutch, French, and British empires patronised new scientific institutions dedicated to the study of tropical ecology to address the new ecological threat to their imperial hegemony (1996, p. 135). Once more, these experiences signalled not merely economic, but profoundly cultural transformations within the structure of imperial world reason. While the pervadingly religious worldview of seventeenth-century imperialists saw the resonant spectre of the imperial "New World" reflect a belief in the limitless, God-given bounties of the natural world, the environmental wasting of the colonial tropics, and subsequent study of tropical ecology, however, impressed upon Europeans their increased capacity to alter environments. This stimulated a radical evolution of an ontological relationship with the natural world, perhaps most resonantly evoked in the work of British enlightenment philosopher John Locke. In his championing of the new project of agricultural improvement and enclosure, Locke rationalises the bounties of the natural world as extending not from God, but the civilising force of European man as his chosen agent. Ellen Meiksins-Wood suggests that such discourse was mobilised in the colonial context to justify the widespread land grabs committed throughout the preceding century in terms of environmental stewardship, presenting European man as the global agent of environmental improvement and Indigenous residents as backward, destructive agents of environmental wasting (2002, pp. 104–105).

While the spread of ecological reason established agrarian and industrial capitalism throughout eighteenth- and nineteenth-century England, Grove observes that the discourse of political humanism espoused by the 1789 French Revolution saw the French embed the earliest forms of modern conservation policy, particularly in their overwhelming preoccupation with its Mauritian Ile de France. While a critical object of French political economy from its settlement in 1715, subsequent decades saw Mauritius take on an immense cultural importance to imperial France, chiefly due to establishment of the islands' own "Jardin du Roi" by Pierre Poivre. Grove observes how Poivre applied the Renaissance principles of Locke's French parallel, famed Enlightenment philosopher Jean-Jacques Rousseau, in envisioning the Ile de France as not only a site of great commercial importance, but that of a new social utopia, reflecting the great legacy of Moore's *Utopia* several centuries hence. Poivre's appointment in Mauritius was approved on the condition of sustaining the capitalistic productivity of the Ile De France's critical sugar plantations within the logic of merchant capitalist exploitation. However, Poivre's ecological policies were moreover directed towards addressing what he perceived as the increasing corruption of French Renaissance values within the increasingly capitalistic nature of the French imperial order (Grove, 1996, pp. 160–165).

The immense cultural resonance of Mauritius as a distinctly ecological Eden concealed, through the double valence of paradise discourse, the material exploitation of slave and indentured labour, the true producers of Mauritian bounties. If Mauritius can be seen to represent European man's mastery of the natural world within the discourse of New World paradise, the Chagos Archipelago instead embodies the infernal, hellish wastelands of the colonial world sat far beyond the purview of imperial ecological improvement. This characterisation is best demonstrated in one of the few literary representations of Chagos during the imperial age, J.A. Thompson's *Only the Sun Remembers* (1950). Following the outbreak of the Second World War, Thompson was stationed on Chagos for a period due to its use as a remote military outpost of the Western allies. Compared to more developed and vibrant spheres of the industrialised colonial world, Thompson characterises Chagos as a barren, lawless wasteland, the "end of the world" and civilisation, invoking hellish iconography which ultimately serves to represent Chagos' portrayal within the terms of paradise discourse (1950, p. 151). If colonies like Mauritius serve to justify European imperial rule as a reflection of their capacity to construct an Edenic paradise, Thompson's representation of Chagos represents what Deckard terms the infernal, hellish shadow of the "anti-paradise", a vessel for the repressed anxieties and failures of European imperial praxis (2010, p. 3).

Thompson's portrayal of Chagos aligns well with perhaps the most resonant example of the imperial anti-paradise, the Dutch Congo of Joseph Conrad's *Heart of Darkness* (2007; first published in 1899). Deckard sees Conrad's novel as a disparaging reflection on the project of imperial rational "progress", characterising the colonial world as a land not of utopian possibilities, but one presenting the dystopic ruin and death of European civilisation (2010, p. 91). The entwined cultural representations of Mauritian paradise and Chagossian anti-paradise at the culmination of the high imperial age moreover serve to foreshadow how imperial notions of utopian progress and dystopian collapse would intensify within the increasingly globalised vantage of postimperial world order. Reflecting on the transformative capacity of paradise mythology to express the longings and anxieties of imperial reason, from its religious to economic to ecological contexts, the discourse of paradise is perhaps most relevant to the exploitation of Chagos in the postcolonial era, specifically looking to its use as a critical US military base and equally significant environmental conservation zone.

Protecting Paradise: Postimperial Edens and the War on Climate, 1965–2023

The "British Century" of 1814–1915 broadly refers to the period of Britain's supreme imperial dominance of the high seas, formalised in the 1814 Vienna settlement which saw Britain's rivals present no further challenge to British hegemony in exchange for protection from piracy and plunder. This agreement, for Campling and Colás, would present the first modern iteration of "open sea" oceanic governance, stimulating the unhindered movement of "free trade" between the colonial and European world. Due to Britain's early industrialisation, its supreme naval power, and early discovery of oil and steam power, the era of Pax Britannia would fundamentally remap the dynamics of Indian Ocean imperial commerce (Campling and Colás, 2021, pp. 57–58). Tor Sellstrom observes that while Indian Ocean trade would broadly follow the historic patterns established by Islamic sailors prior to the sixteenth-century arrival of European sailors, the construction of the Suez Canal in 1869 would mark the first major divergence from these patterns. This signalled the evolution of the Indian Ocean from an "Islamic sea" to a "English Lake", a shift in focus from luxury tropical goods to the new critical commodities of coal, oil, and gas that would ultimately recircuit imperial trade patterns away from the Mascarenes towards Suez and the Persian Gulf (Sellstrom, 2015, p. 14). Following this shift, the economies of small, isolated colonies such as Mauritius or Chagos suffered great economic instability throughout the nineteenth and early twentieth centuries (Sellstrom, 2015, p. 17).

Following its independence from Great Britain in 1971, this instability would compel the isle of Mauritius to embrace luxury tourism as the main driver of its post-independence economy under the auspices of UN sustainable development. This subjected the island to the industrial "resortification" impacting similar places throughout the postcolonial tropics, and the Chagos Archipelago's aforementioned isolation from the broader networks of imperial governance saw its post-imperial exploitation follow an altogether different logic. Ultimately, the infamous terms of the US Strategic Island Concept saw the USA investigate possibilities of establishing an overseas military base within the Mascarene region in the wake of the UN-sanctioned decolonisation of the European empire (Campling and Colás, 2021, p. 67). Speaking to the broader context of the concept, Colás and Campling observe that following a period of unprecedented geopolitical stability, the culmination of the Second World War reverted the Indian Ocean into a theatre of great power conflict in much the same manner as it had prior to the British Century, recapitulated within the terms of the Cold War. Recognising the growing threat of the USSR to capitalist production in the wake of British decolonisation, the US would embrace its self-imposed mission as a global peacekeeper for the capitalist west, reflected within the discourse of the 1947 Truman Doctrine, the American equivalent to the British Pax Britannica (Campling and Colás, 2021, pp. 63–64).

Where the Mascarene isles of Mauritius and Seychelles would be deemed unsuitable for occupation due to the threat of political resistance from their local colonised populations, the Chagos Archipelago's distinct state of economic and administrative isolation became the most viable candidate for a US overseas military installation. For Colás and Campling, the subsequent use of the US-British "Camp Freedom" within the Cold War and the twenty-first century War on Terror reflects Chagos' status as a "quintessential product of a post-war American maritime order" (Campling and Colás, 2021, 67). Chagos became a state of "indirect imperialism", which more broadly exploits the persisting wealth divides of the Global North and South to transcend the political sovereignty of other isolated states such as Guam – the Pacific Ocean counterpart of the BIOT base (Campling and Colás, 2021). The use of Chagos and Guam as critical vessels of the US imperial military-industrial complex ultimately reflects how long after the decline of the European empire, tropical islands have remained critical objects of political economy, transforming in line with the utopian projections of post-imperial world order. In line with the changing nature of imperial desire for order and control, the discourse of paradise arguably remains critical to understanding the distinctly ideological nature of such exploitation. Reflecting on the discursive implications of the BIOT's "Camp Freedom", the Chagos Archipelago can today be seen as a vessel for US desires for global domination, the utopian discourse of global peacekeeping concealing the repressed, dystopic impact of military industrialisation upon the peoples inhabiting such installations. Moreover, where the widespread land grabs of the colonial era would be justified in line with European anxieties of environmental decline, Robert Marzec observes how the US military-industrial complex would similarly exploit the public anxieties of the Cold War Red Scare and rampant hysteria of the War on Terror. The all-too-real threat of global cataclysm is weaponised in the post-nuclear, post 9/11 era to sustain the neo-imperial governance of the world at large (Marzec, 2015, p. 3).

The British century would see ecological science entwine closely with imperial economic praxis, with advancements in botanical science, aerial mapping, and the modelling of natural "ecosystems" significantly informing the exploitation of natural resources and division and territorial boundaries throughout the "high" imperial age (Anker, 2002, pp. 84–85). Such developments would critically lay the groundwork for the evolution of island's political economy in the nuclear postimperial age, in which Marzec observes this alliance would take on new disturbing qualities. The natural world would increasingly be viewed not merely as a vessel for capitalist exploitation, but as a weapon to be utilised in increasingly global conflicts. Following the development of atomic weaponry by the close of the Second World War, the increasingly grandiose dystopian projections of global power would subject various remote sites to the devastating impacts of nuclear testing, for our purposes, best reflected by the US nuclear tests in Bikini Atoll. Reflecting on how the geographic isolation of tropical islands would condition their unique strategic value for postimperial power, the USA would detonate 24 weapons between 1946 and 1958, in one case wiping one island from the world map completely. Reflecting on how local approval for these tests would be gained under the vague premise of global salvation, this example serves to reflect how utopian, paradisical discourse of global peacekeeping would see the peoples of the Global South continue to pay the price of such grandiose fantasies (Marzec, 2015, pp. 40–43).

Where the BIOT base can be seen to thereby reflect the paradisical longings of global order, the history of Chagos' Marine Protective Area can be similarly understood in terms of postimperial paradise discourse. Charles Sheppard and Mark Seaward characterise early conservation efforts on the Chagos Archipelago as a critical step towards protecting and replenishing the ecological sustainability of the Indian Ocean, particularly following the devastation of El Nino and depletion of oceanic resources through globalised neoliberal capitalism (Sheppard & Seaward, 1999, pp. 1–2). Since the establishment of the Chagos MPA in 2010, Laura Jeffery has shown that the Chagos Conservation Trust has continually argued against the repopulation of Chagos as a threat to the precious ecological functions which Sheppard and Seaward had described (2013, pp. 310–311). Due to the common interests of the CCT and US military in keeping Chagos beyond the purview of both capitalist development and its exiled indigenous population, the management of the MPA reflects the disturbing entwinement of militarised climate science in the contemporary world. This state of affairs moreover echoes an earlier case in which ecological rights would supersede those of the Chagossian people. While we have seen how Chagos would ultimately emerge as the most viable site for sustaining British-US military hegemony over the Indian Ocean due to the fact of its historical-political insularity, the island of Aldabra would initially appear the most viable candidate for the US's concept of an Indian Ocean floating fortress.

While enjoying similar strategic positioning to its Mascarene counterparts, Aldabra's marked lack of settled population would engender its high appeal within the logic of the proposal. The planned use of Aldabra would fail in part due to mounting protest within the international scientific community, which sought to protect the islands' rare and endangered Giant Aldabra Tortoises from western interference (Stoddart and Savy, 1983, p. 184). In the contemporary moment, these factors present the cynical manner in which the ecological rights of tortoises would appear to have superseded the human rights of the Chagossian people within the twisted logic of neoliberal geopolitics. Within the discourse of paradise, we might consider how the Edenic, utopian discourse of the Chagos MPA project serves to materially respond to the dystopic, hellish possibilities of the Climate Crisis by exploiting the modern occupation of Chagos. Marzec observes that while global climate control remains a heavily politicised subject within the hallways of world politics, the global climate is increasingly rationalised within the securitised terms of US global peacekeeping, exploiting mass hysteria surrounding environmental collapse to pursue its new "War on Climate" (2015). In this sense, the epistemic implications of the Chagos MPA serve as a disturbing prophecy for the future of the Global South. Within this context, Marzec observes installations such as the Chagos MPA as reflective of the re-colonisation of the Global South as the "ground zero" of the US "War on Climate; an uncanny recapitulation of the eugenically inspired land grabs of the colonial period, which similarly disposed of Indigenous rights on the grounds of environmental stewardship. Ultimately, the CCT's description of the Chagos MPA as a "rare haven of glob[al] importan[ce]" can be seen to reflect ecological terms of paradise discourse, inviting its characterisation as a Edenic Indian Ocean Ark for the salvation of oceanic species, exploiting contemporary anxieties of environmental collapse to conceal the imperial nature of Chagos' occupation, marginalising and concealing the Chagossian people as the perpetual victims of imperial longings for order (Chagos Conservation Trust, no date).

Acknowledgements

With thanks to Kaori Nagai, Matt Whittle, Bashir Abu Manneh, and Laura Jeffery whose mentorship, encouragement, and faith have proved invaluable to me and this project.

References

Alpers, E.A. (2014) *The Indian Ocean in World History*. Oxford: Oxford University Press.
Anker, P. (2002) *Imperial Ecology: Environmental Order in the British Empire, 1895–1945*. Cambridge, MA: Harvard University Press.
Campling, L. and Colás, A. (2021) *Capitalism and the Sea: The Maritime Factor in the Making of the Modern World*. London: Verso Books.
Carter, M. (2017) 'Towards a workers' history of the Chagos archipelago'. *Journal of the Indian Ocean Region*, 13(2), pp. 213–233.
Carter, M. and Wenban-Smith, N. (2016) *Chagos, A History: Exploration, Expolitation, Expulsion*. Sandy: Chagos Conservation Trust.
Chagos Conservation Trust (no date) 'The Chagos conservation trust's strategic plan, 2023-2028'. Available at: https://chagos-trust.org/Chagos_strategy1-3.jpg.pdf (Accessed: 1 January 2024)
Conrad, J. (2007) Heart of Darkness. London: Penguin Classics. (First published 1899)
Darian, S.G. (2001) *The Ganges in Myth and History*. Motilal Banarsidass Publ.
Deckard, S. (2010) *Paradise Discourse, Imperialism, and Globalization: Exploiting Eden*. London: Routledge.
van Driem, G.L. (2021) *Ethnolinguistic Prehistory: The Peopling of the World from the Perspective of Language, Genes and Material Culture*. Leiden: Brill.
Frankopan, P. (2015) *The Silk Roads: A New History of the World*. London: Vintage.

Grove, R.H. (1996) *Green Imperialism: Colonial Expansion, Tropical Island Edens and the Origins of Environmentalism, 1600–1860*. Cambridge: Cambridge University Press.
Jeffery, L. (2011) *Chagos Islanders in Mauritius and the UK: Forced Displacement and Onward Migration*. Manchester: Manchester University Press.
Jeffery, L. (2013) '"We are the true guardians of the environment": Human-environment relations and debates about the future of the Chagos Archipelago'. *Journal of the Royal Anthropological Institute*, 19(2), pp. 300–318.
Johannessen, S.F. (2015) 'Sacralising the contested-the Chagossian diaspora and their first pilgrimage to the homeland'. PhD Thesis, Martin-Luther-University Halle-Wittenberg.
Marcocci, G. (2022) 'Iberian theories of empire in the sixteenth and seventeenth centuries'. *Journal of the History of Ideas*, 83(4), pp. 671–683.
Marzec, R.P. (2015) *Militarizing the Environment: Climate Change and the Security State*. Minneapolis: University of Minnesota Press.
[Preprint] Nkomazana, F. (1998) 'Livingstone's ideas of Christianity, commerce and civilization'. *Pula: Botswana Journal of African Studies*, 1(12), pp. 1 & 2.
Sellstrom, T. (2015)*Africa in the Indian Ocean: Islands in Ebb and Flow*. Leiden: Brill.
Sheppard, R.C. and Seaward, M.R.D. (1999) *The Ecology of the Chagos Archipelago*. Otley: Linnean Society Occasional Publications.
Stoddart, D. and Savy, S. (1983) 'Aldabra: Island of giant tortoises'. *Ambio*, 12(3/4) pp. 180–185.
Thompson, J.A. (1950) *Only the Sun Remembers*. London: Andrew Dakers.
Wenban-Smith, N. and Carter, M. (2016) *Chagos: A History. Exploration, Exploitation, Expulsion*. Sandy: Chagos Conservation Trust.
Wood, E.M. (2002) *The Origin of Capitalism: A Longer View*. London: Verso Books.

5 Human Rights and the Marine Protected Area around the Chagos Archipelago

Sue Farran

Introduction

The removal of Chagossians from their homes in the Chagos archipelago in the period 1965–1973 has given rise to a plethora of human rights challenges.[1] These have been considered in the domestic courts of the United Kingdom and the European Court of Human Rights in Strasbourg ("*Chagos Islanders v. the United Kingdom*", 2012).[2] Rights related matters have been heard at the international level at the International Court of Justice (ICJ, 2019) and the Arbitral Tribunal constituted under the United Nations Convention on the Law of the Sea ("*Chagos Marine Protected Area Arbitration (Mauritius v. United Kingdom)*", 2015). The United Nations General Assembly has also been involved, resolving to seek an ICJ opinion (United Nations General Assembly 2017b), and subsequently adopting that opinion of the ICJ (United Nations General Assembly, 2019). Many of the rights issues raised have focussed on individual rights under the European Convention on Human Rights and its Protocols, notably those of Article 8 and Article 1 of Protocol 1, whether the Convention applied to the British Indian Ocean Territory under Article 56 and various procedural issues raised under judicial review.

This chapter does not seek to rehearse the cases that have been pleaded which have been extensively commented on by many,[3] but rather to step back and reflect on the potential tensions between different rights' claims going forward, foregrounding the significance of the Marine Protected Area (MPA) declared around the islands to a wide range of human rights not only of Chagossians but also others.[4] To do this, this contribution first briefly provides a background to the establishment of the marine protected area. Secondly, it places this within a wider context of marine protection and the potential use of marine protection for other forms of rights protection, including national and international security. Thirdly, the chapter turns to the conflicting rights' claims raised by the protection of marine resources, which invariably means some kind of limitation on marine resource extraction, especially when viewed from the perspective of not only commercial fishing fleets but also indigenous or local fishers who rely on the ocean to provide food security and sustain modest livelihoods. Decisions relating to fishing rights and negotiations to return the sovereignty of the islands to Mauritius throw these issues into sharp focus. Finally, the retention or abandonment of an MPA around the islands is relevant not only to the viability of Chagossians returning to live on the islands and the rights which they may hope to enjoy but also the more tenuous rights of others.

DOI: 10.4324/9781003390299-8

The Marine Protected Area

The Marine Protected Area (MPA) around the islands of the Chagos Archipelago was created in 2010 by way of declaration by the British Indian Ocean Territories Commissioner. It covers 640,000 km^2 and is one of the world's largest MPAs as well as one of the most diverse with over 800 species of fish, including 50 different types of sharks, and significant coral reefs as well as deep sea plains, seamounts, and limestone platforms (Chagos Conservation Trust, 2023). The declaration of the MPA was challenged in the English courts in *Bancoult No 3* ("*R (Bancoult) v Secretary of State for Foreign and Commonwealth Affairs*", 2018) on the grounds that it had been established for improper purposes – namely to prevent resettlement of Chagos islanders – as suggested by a leaked cable recording a meeting between US and UK officials. Much of the court's time in *Bancoult No 3* was taken up in deciding whether the cable was admissible as evidence or was protected by the inviolability of diplomatic communications. Having decided that it was admissible, the majority of the court held that even if it had been considered by the court of first instance the decision that the MPA had not been actuated for an improper motive stood ("*R (Bancoult) v Secretary of State for Foreign and Commonwealth Affairs*", 2018; Allen, 2018).

However, the declaration of the MPA triggered the initiation by Mauritius of proceedings against the United Kingdom under Article 287 and Annex VII, Article 1, of UNCLOS due to the impact on its fishing rights (Farran, 2018). The Permanent Court of Arbitration found the UK in breach of a number of articles of UNCLOS and that the declaration of the MPA was "not in accordance with the provisions of the convention" (Samaranayake, 2020). The future existence of the MPA is therefore in question.

The International Significance of Marine Protection

Protection of Marine Resources

Targets for the protection of the oceans and their resources stem from the World Summit on Sustainable Development and the Convention on Biological Diversity (CBD) (Farran, 2021, p. 161). In 2010 the international community agreed on a ten-year plan for protecting and conserving nature, which included 20 targets. Aitchi target 11, under Strategic Goal C for example, aimed "to improve the status of biodiversity by safeguarding ecosystems species and genetic diversity", and sought the protection of at least 17% of terrestrial and inland water, and 10% of coastal and marine areas, by 2020. In 2016 the World Conservation Congress suggested 30%, and this is a figure taken up by the UK government in its ambition to achieve 30% by 2030 through its leadership of a Global Network Alliance (UK Government, 2020). By the end of 2020, it was clear that most targets agreed in 2010 had not been reached. In Montreal, the 15th Conference of the Parties to the CBD, held in late 2022, adopted the Kunming-Montreal Global Biodiversity Framework which included 23 new targets including protection of 30% of the lands, oceans, coastal areas, and inland waters of the world (Target 3). The Declaration of the MPA around the Chagos archipelago is one of several measures taken, not only by the United Kingdom but also others, to meet these targets.

Prior to the declaration of the MPA, there had been conservation measures introduced in the archipelago. Several of the islands (of which there are around 60 in total) had been declared nature reserves and part of Diego Garcia was made a restricted area in 1994.[5] The Ramsar Wetlands Convention was extended to the islands by the UK in 1998, and in 2001 a designated site on Diego Garcia included all of the lagoon waters there and part of the territorial sea (UNESCO, 1971).[6] In 2003 an extensive Environment Protection and Preservation Zone (EPPZ) was declared over the underwater coral reefs of the Great Chagos Bank. This extended from the territorial waters to the 200 nautical mile limit. The subsequent MPA fell within this EPPZ.

The drivers behind the creation of an MPA were primarily national and international conservation and environmental organisations and charities that had lobbied for the creation of a large-scale marine reserve around the islands. In 2007 the Chagos Environment Network led by the Chagos Conservation Trust and the Pew Environment Group lobbied the United Kingdom Foreign and Commonwealth Office to hold a public consultation on establishing an MPA around the islands. This was held in late 2009. Two key points were advocated: (1) an MPA would make a "significant contribution to the wider biological productivity of the Indian Ocean", and (2) it would have "no direct immediate impact" on the inhabitants of the islands (Dunne *et al.*, 2014, p. 81).

However, others have argued that the scientific rationale for creating this large no-take area was weak, not least because the most overfished area was around the military base at Diego Garcia, which was excluded from the area covered by the MPA (Dunne *et al.*, 2014). There were, moreover, fishing regulations in place, including an effective licensing system.[7] As Appleby (2015, p. 531) wrote, "It is unlikely that there was even a need in law to designate the MPA to justify the Director's decision not to issue fishing licences". It has also been pointed out that while the MPA may have been significant for the protection of species with low mobility: sharks and coral fish, it is questionable whether it has successfully protected more migratory fish such as tuna, or simply shifted unsustainable fishing to the margins of the MPA. It was also argued that at the outset the data on fisheries stocks in the archipelago was generally poor (Sheppard, 2010),[8] so that it was difficult to forecast with any certainty whether an MPA would be beneficial. Without data benchmarks, it is difficult to determine if the MPA has been justified on marine biodiversity conservation grounds.

Safeguarding a Free and Open Ocean

The United Nations Charter states in Article 1 that the purposes of the United Nations include: "To maintain international peace and security …". Mindful of the terrible damage caused by two World Wars and the subsequent tensions raised by the Cold War, in 1971 the United Nations urged member states to regard the Indian Ocean as a "zone of peace" (Misra, 1977; United Nations General Assembly, 1971,

1972). Given the relations between the West and Russia at the time, there were challenges, particularly once the United Kingdom announced its intention to withdraw its presence from east of Suez in the 1960s (Hornat, 2016, p. 434). The US saw its key role in the Indian Ocean as a protector of the sea lines of communication against possible Russian interference. The construction of a naval base on the centrally located Diego Garcia was key to this.

Despite the ending of the Cold War, one of the arguments raised by the UK has been that it will return the islands to Mauritius when they are no longer needed for defence purposes, suggesting that this point has not yet been reached. The US, unsurprisingly, has supported the UK on this. The alliance rests on a bilateral US-UK agreement made in 1966 on the "Availability for Defence Purposes of the British Indian Ocean Territory" (Sand, 2013, p. 127). US military installations and activities on Diego Garcia have expanded over the years, including the use of the base for rendition flights, the docking and maintenance of nuclear submarines, and the storage of anti-personnel mines on freight vessels in the Diego Garcia lagoon (Sand, 2013, pp. 129–131).

Even without considerations of military defence, the Indian Ocean is of considerable importance as discussed by Harris in this collection (see also Pascu, 2011). It is an area of geo-strategic competition with China, India, and the United States seeking to assert influence through investment in trade and trading routes and security frameworks.

The United States, Australia, Japan, and the United Kingdom also seek to secure their maritime interests in the region through asserting their own interpretations of a free and open Indo-Pacific. In a 2009 Australian Defence White Paper, it was noted that "over the period to 2030, the Indian Ocean will join the Pacific Ocean in terms of its centrality to our maritime strategy and defence planning" (Green and Shearer, 2012, p. 175). The US, which has traditionally looked towards the Northwest Pacific Ocean, has recently adopted an Indo-Pacific strategy.[9] Erickson et al have described the focus on the Indian Ocean as a ""center of gravity"" shift from the Euro-Atlantic to the Asia Pacific" (2010). It is clear, therefore, that the international waters around the Chagos Islands have increased in security importance in line with the heightened geo-political competition.

Fishing Rights

In 1965, when the United Kingdom detached the Chagos Archipelago from Mauritius – prior to the independence of Mauritius, the traditional fishing rights of Mauritius, "to fish the internal waters and the territorial sea" (Dunne *et al.*, 2014, p. 84), were preserved, and these rights were protected in the 1971 and 1984 British Indian Ocean Territory (BIOT) Fishery Ordinances.[10] Even when a Fisheries Conservation and Management Zone was introduced in 1991, Mauritius-registered fishing licenced vessels were permitted to continue fishing. The declaration of the MPA put an end to this despite the UK government itself indicating that the mean catch of fish was some 200 tonnes per year in the period 1977–2009, "well below the estimated maximum sustainable yield of the time" (Archer-Rand *et al.*, 2018, p. 3).

As indicated above, the drive to declare MPAs originated in targets agreed under the 1992 Convention on Biodiversity (CBD). However, this Convention also stresses the importance of recognising the importance of indigenous communities. The Preamble recognises

> the close and traditional dependence of many indigenous and local communities embodying traditional lifestyles on biological resources, and the desirability of sharing equitably benefits arising from the traditional use of traditional knowledge, innovations and practices relevant to the conservation of biological diversity and the sustainable use of its components.

Article 8(j) echoes this, stating:

> Subject to its national legislation, respect, preserve and maintain knowledge, innovations and practices of indigenous and local communities embodying traditional lifestyles relevant for the conservation and sustainable use of biological diversity and promote their wider application with the approval and involvement of the holders of such knowledge, innovations and practices and encourage the equitable sharing of the benefits arising from the utilization of such knowledge, innovations and practices

and Article 10 (c) states that each contracting party shall (as far as possible) "protect and encourage customary use of biological resources in accordance with traditional cultural practices that are compatible with conservation or sustainable use requirements". The importance of taking into account indigenous livelihoods, the connection of indigenous people with the resources or the oceans, and the value of integrating indigenous people into management frameworks is self-evident.

This is reinforced in the targets agreed under the 2022 Kunming-Montreal Global Diversity Framework (GBF) which explicitly refers to the importance of "recognising indigenous and traditional territories and practices" in implementing measures to effectively conserve and manage at least 30% of the world's lands, inland waters, coastal areas, and oceans (United Nations, 2022).

The CBD also affirms in its Preamble that "the conservation of biological diversity is a common concern of humankind" indicating thereby that this is not simply a matter of individual rights, while reference to "indigenous and local communities" also suggests that collective interests are at stake here. Unfortunately, however, the CBD, which was ratified by the United Kingdom in 1994, has not been extended to BIOT and so does not apply to the Chagos Archipelago.[11] This is despite the rhetoric of the British government in terms of its 30 × 30 goal for ocean protection, its Blue Belt initiative which aims to create a Blue Belt of ocean protection around the 14 UK Overseas Territories and its positioning as an environmental steward and champion of measures to address climate change, all of which appear to align with many of the goals under the Convention. Indeed, in its arguments put before the UNCLOS Arbitral Tribunal, the UK stated: "We are committed to furthering biodiversity of the oceans, and we believe that one significant way of doing this is through the establishment of marine protected areas" ("*Chagos Marine Protected Area Arbitration (Mauritius v. United Kingdom)*", 2015, para. 290). From a CBD perspective however, the UK is not legally bound to observe the provisions relating to indigenous people and local communities.

Retaining or Abandoning the Marine Protected Area: The Impact on Chagossians

In November 2022, the UK's Foreign Secretary announced in Parliament that the UK and Mauritius had decided to begin negotiations on the exercise of sovereignty over the British Indian Ocean Territory (BIOT) Chagos Archipelago (Cleverly, 2022). If the MPA remains in place, the impact of its retention would depend on the form that this took and whether Chagossians would be involved in the management of the MPA or not. At present, the MPA is managed under an interim BIOT Conservation Management Framework established in 2014 by the BIOT Administration. In 2018 this produced a Conservation Management Plan intended to run through to the end of 2023. Despite there being no formalised observer programme, only one fisheries patrol vessel and an acknowledged risk of illegal fishing (Archer-Rand *et al.*, 2018, p. 3), the UK government claims that the marine environment "is managed to the highest international standards, with effectively regulated marine activities underpinned by robust science" (Archer-Rand *et al.*, 2018, p. 4).

A more equitable arrangement and one that would provide more opportunity to returning Chagossians to exercise greater control over the resources of the islands would be a re-negotiated model of management as suggested by Lobo (2016). This could draw on comparative models (Lobo suggests the Papahãnaumokuãkea Marine National Monument in Hawai'i) which regulate fishing on a permit basis with criteria which can be adjusted to meet social, economic, and ecological circumstances under a multi-level collaborative governance framework. Above all the "fortress conservation" thinking behind the MPA which promotes the removal/relocation/exclusion of indigenous fishers and people needs to be abandoned.

Even if a revised management model was negotiated, a fully protected area with a no-take policy would deny Chagossians and others the opportunity to gain a livelihood from the catch and commercial sale of fish and other marine resources. While an allowance might be made for resident Chagossians to catch enough to feed themselves (as happens with other MPAs, such as the Hawai'i model), this would effectively apply a brake on commercial activity, however modest, and therefore opportunities to earn income for other necessities. It might, of course, be argued that any returning Chagossians could be employed to assist in the management of the MPA, but this would in effect make them labourers on their own islands, returning them, at least on the face of it to the position many of their ancestors were in when first brought to the islands.

If the MPA was retained but became a mixed zones Area – with some commercial fishing permitted either of certain species or in certain areas, there is the question of who would benefit? The Arbitral ruling on fishing rights found that Mauritius had been wrongly denied fishing rights, not Chagossians per se, holding "that fishing rights would remain available to Mauritius as far as practicable" ("*Chagos Marine Protected Area Arbitration (Mauritius v. United Kingdom)*", 2015). While some Chagossians might be employed in the Mauritius fishing industry, it seems unlikely that they would benefit other than through continued employment. By and large, Chagossians living in Mauritius and in Seychelles have not been well treated (Gifford and Dunne, 2014), and it seems doubtful (without further financial assistance targeted specifically at Chagossian fishers) that this concession would be hugely beneficial.

Although there are initiatives to support small-scale semi-commercial fishing boats (see e.g. initiatives supported by the EU under an EU-Mauritius agreement 2017–2021), those most likely to benefit from extended fishing rights into any formerly protected waters of the archipelago are likely to be EU vessels fishing for tuna – the EU has a Fisheries Partnership with Mauritius for 4,000 tonnes of tuna and tuna-like species per annum,[12] Japan – which has a base in Mauritius for fishing in the Indian Ocean, and China whose distant water fleet has around 17,000 fishing vessels registered in China, and a further 1,000 or so registered elsewhere under flags of convenience (Kanodia, 2022).

Abandonment of the MPA would also jeopardise other activities. As indicated while MPAs are primarily intended to protect marine resources, and therefore legitimise activities that seek to prevent illegal fishing, dumping at sea, and other actions that damage the marine environment, they also provide a reason for patrolling protected areas. If, under any plans to return sovereignty of the islands to Mauritius, the military base on Diego Garcia is maintained – and Mauritius has indicated that it would allow this, the retention of the MPA permits this type of surveillance to continue. The current agreement is due to expire in 2036. If the United States agreed to relinquish its lease over Diego Garcia – an option canvassed by Harris (2023), the rights of Chagossians to return might be enhanced. However, an enlarged Mauritius – expanded to include the archipelago and its resource-rich seas, would be vulnerable to overtures from a number of competing players. It is also questionable whether Mauritius would be sufficiently equipped to counter the ocean-based problems of illegal, unregulated, and unreported (IUU) fishing,[13] people and drugs trafficking – including by fishing vessels, and piracy.

Conclusion

The MPA around the Chagos Archipelago has been described as "fortress conservation" (De Santo, Jones, and Miller, 2011; Lobo, 2016), an example of "greening imperialism" (Sand, 2012) and "environmental imperialism" (Sand, 2010), in other words using the MPA as a tool to defeat the individual rights of Chagossians to (1) return to the islands and (2) enjoy the economic rights necessary for viable livelihoods. But perhaps from a "rights" perspective, the argument is not straightforward. There are the individual human rights argued in the cases that have come before the courts; there are – if one accepts Chagossians/Ilois as indigenous peoples – the collective rights of Chagossians;[14] there are the rights of all to the heritage of mankind via the global commons and more abstractly a healthy planet; and – if one takes matters a step further as some have advocated – rights of nature, such as the living organisms of the oceans (Viaene, 2022), which, as suggested by Sheppard (2010, p. 1900), suffer the "tragedy of the commons". There are also the rights of all people to a safe and secure world order, free from the attacks of terrorists, and for many the importance of upholding the international legal order – although interpretations of this may vary. As the quotations above demonstrate, these rights' discourses can be manipulated but their co-existence also raises the question of priorities or the hierarchy of rights. As individuals, we are familiar with having our individual rights constrained by considerations of public good or national security. Increasingly the damage to the environment means that we are also becoming familiar with our freedoms being curtailed by broader considerations of environmental harm, including our individual and collective responsibilities for contributing to or assisting to reduce climate change. Indigenous people are caught up in this despite having contributed least to the Anthropocene. Agendas focussing on interventions that claim to be of universal benefit (an environmental universalism), verge on the neocolonial (Simpson 2020) and fail to acknowledge the inequalities of impact or to take into consideration indigenous perspectives. This assumption of a shared mission is evident in developments such as the Stockholm Declaration and Plan of Action (1972), the Rio Declaration (1992), the United Nations Framework Convention on Climate Change, and the Paris Agreement (2015a).[15] Concern for the oceans and life below water finds international support in the agreed Sustainable Development Goals,[16] which refers to the "planet", "the world", and "people" – rather than individuals or different "peoples", and in the recently agreed convention on Marine Biodiversity Areas Beyond National Jurisdiction (BBNJ) to advance the governance of marine areas beyond national jurisdiction in order to promote the conservation and sustainable use of marine biodiversity (United Nations General Assembly, 2017a). Saving the planet therefore is not the same as striving towards environmental justice. Although these developments may be seen as little more than a shift to increasingly abstract universal ideals which are unlikely to benefit displaced and impoverished peoples, such as the Chagossians, there may be a glimmer of hope. In July 2022, the United Nations General Assembly declared that everyone has a right to a healthy environment (United Nations General Assembly, 2022). Although not binding on UN members, there is optimism that this first step will influence UN member states to give practical meaning to the right and perhaps lead to reconceptualising of human rights (Cima, 2022). In any reconceptualisation, however, there are likely to be winners and losers especially where there are power imbalances. In the case of the MPA around the Chagos Archipelago, the combined voices and reach of scientists, environmental groups, conservation societies, and defence analysts may well drown out those of Chagossians. Humankind might benefit, Chagossians may not.

Notes

1 See e.g.: "*R (Bancoult) v. Secretary of State for Foreign and Commonwealth Office (No 1)'* (2000); "*Chagos Islanders v Attorney General and HM BIOT Commissioner*" (2003); "*R (Bancoult) v. Secretary of State For Foreign and Commonwealth Affairs (No 2)*" (2008); *"R (Bancoult) v Secretary of State for Foreign and Commonwealth Affairs (No 3)*" (2018); "*R (Hoareau and Bancoult) v Secretary of State for Foreign and Commonwealth Affairs*" (2020).

2 There has also been litigation in the United States in 2006 (Sand, 2015). For detail see Sand (2013, p. 133, note 52).

3 See for example on the ICJ opinion Rrecaj (2020); Hilpold (2022); and more broadly Burri and Trinidad (2021) and Allen (2014). On the human rights aspects, see Sand (2013). On the wider picture, see Evers and Kooy (2011), Allen and Monaghan (2018).

4 I use the term Chagossians as a collective but the term *Ilois* or Chagos Islanders is also sometimes used. Essentially these are people whom themselves, or their ancestors, regard the islands in the Chagos Archipelago as their indigenous homelands. Some are in Mauritius, some in Seychelles, some in the United Kingdom, and others elsewhere.

5 The British government advice to visitors states: "The following islands are Strict Nature Reserves. It is an offence to approach within three nautical miles, land on or anchor at Great Chagos Bank: a. The Three Brothers and Resurgent Islands (6°09'-4S 71°31'-4E). b. Eagle Island (6°12'-0S 71°19'-0E) and Cow Island (6°14'-1S 71°17'-7E). c. Danger Island (6°23'-3S 71°14'-4E) and the drying coral reef (6°27'-3S 71°14'-5E). d. Nelson's Island (5°40'-9S 72°19'-0E). Or to enter the following area within the Peros Banhos Atoll: All territorial sea, internal water, land and inter-tidal of Peros Banhos (5°20'-5S 71°51'-0E) to the east of a line between the eastern extremities of Moresby Island and Fouquet Island and extended on the same azimuth to the territorial sea limit." (BIOT administration, 2024, p. 7).

6 The Convention entered into force in the United Kingdom of Great Britain and Northern Ireland on 5 May 1976. The United Kingdom currently has 175 sites designated as Wetlands of International Importance.

7 For example, the 1971 Fishery Limits Ordinance – Ordinance No 2 1971, replaced in 1984, and the 1991 (Conservation and Management) Ordinance. Exemptions were made for those lawfully on the islands (i.e., military and other personnel attached to the military base) and visiting yachts.

8 Including the distance that migratory species travel.

9 See for example the Press Release by the White House, "Fact Sheet: Indo-Pacific Strategy of the United States" (2022).

10 The laws of the BIOT are made by the Commissioner of BIOT primarily by way of Ordinances and Statutory Instruments. The power to do so derives from the British Indian Ocean Territory Order 1965 (an Order in Council) and the British Indian Ocean Territory (Constitution) Order 2004.

11 A number of other international treaties and conventions either directly conferring rights or protecting the environment have not been extended to BIOT – see Sand (2010). The United States has not ratified the CBD.

12 This was originally agreed in 2014, with the details established in a Protocol in 2017 to run until late 2021 then extended for six months by an Exchange of Letters pending the negotiation of a new agreement. The Indian Ocean is the largest source of tuna catches for the EU.

13 China was the top offender of IUU fishing in 2019 and 2021 (Kanodia, 2022), but the EU has also been accused of over-fishing, especially yellow-fin tuna (McVeigh, 2021).

14 There is no consensus on this. The UK government refers to Chagossians as former "residents" of the British Indian Ocean; others refer to them as "the indigenous inhabitants of the Chagos Islands" (Grandison, Kadaba, and Woo, 2012), "the indigenous people of the Chagos Archipelago" (Allen, 2008).

15 The Paris Agreement emerged from COP21 in 2015 and was signed and ratified by 187 parties.

16 This United Nations summit concluded with a declaration of 17 sustainable development goals (SDGs) and 169 targets. Goal 13 "Take urgent action to combat climate change and its impacts" and Goal 14 "conserve and sustainably use the oceans, seas and marine resources for sustainable development" are particularly relevant in the context of the MPA (United Nations, 2015b).

References

Allen, S. (2008) 'International law and the resettlement of the (outer) Chagos Islands'. *Human Rights Law Review*, 8(4), pp. 683–702.

Allen, S. (2014) *The Chagos Islanders and International Law*. Oxford: Hart.

Allen, S. (2018) 'R (on the application of Bancoult No 3) v. Secretary of State for Foreign and Commonwealth Affairs (UK Sup. Ct.)'. *International Legal Materials*, 57(4), pp. 671–707.

Allen, S. and Monaghan, C. (2018) *Fifty Years of the British Indian Ocean Territory*. Cham: Springer.

Appleby, T. (2015) 'The Chagos marine protected arbitration—a battle of four losers?'. *Journal of Environmental Law*, 27(3), pp. 529–540.

Archer-Rand, S., Hardman, E., Collins, M. and Deary, A. (2018) *Blue Belt Overseas Territory Work Plan: British Indian Ocean Territory*. Marine Management Organisation; Centre for Environment Fisheries & Agriculture; UK Government. Available at: https://assets.publishing.service.gov.uk/media/5f56247ce90e07099624f031/002_Blue_Belt_work_plan_-_British_Indian_Ocean_Territory__BIOT_.pdf (Accessed: 1 September 2023).

BIOT administration (2024) 'British Indian Ocean Territory Guidance for Yachts'. Available at: https://www.biot.gov.io/wp-content/uploads/20240531-BIOT-Guidance-For-Yachts-1.pdf.

Burri, T. and Trinidad, J. (2021) *The International Court of Justice and Decolonisation: New Directions from the Chagos Advisory Opinion*. Cambridge: Cambridge University Press.

Chagos Conservation Trust (2023) 'Overview'. Available at: https://chagos-trust.org/chagos/overview (Accessed: 8 January 2024).

Chagos Islanders v Attorney General and HM BIOT Commissioner (2003) [2003] EWHC 2222 (QB). *BAILII*. Available at: http://www.bailii.org/ew/cases/EWHC/QB/2003/2222.html (Accessed: 1 September 2023).

Chagos Islanders v the United Kingdom (application no. 35622/04) (2012) ECHR. *HUDOC*. Available at: https://hudoc.echr.coe.int/sites/eng-press/pages/search.aspx?i=003-4207010–4992253 (Accessed: 1 September 2023).

Chagos Marine Protected Area Arbitration (Mauritius v. United Kingdom) (2015) Permanent Court of Arbitration. Available at: https://pca-cpa.org/en/cases/11/ (Accessed: 1 March 2023).

Cima, E. (2022) 'The right to a healthy environment: Reconceptualizing human rights in the face of climate change'. *Review of European, Comparative & International Environmental Law*, 31(1), pp. 38–49.

Cleverly, J. (2022) 'British Indian Ocean Territory / Chagos Archipelago, Statement UIN HCWS354'. Available at: https://questions-statements.parliament.uk/written-statements/detail/2022-11-03/hcws354 (Accessed: 7 January 2024).

De Santo, E.M., Jones, P.J. and Miller, A. (2011) 'Fortress conservation at sea: A commentary on the Chagos marine protected area'. *Marine Policy*, 35(2), pp. 258–260.

Dunne, R.P. *et al.* (2014) 'The creation of the Chagos marine protected area: A fisheries perspective☆'. *Advances in Marine Biology*, 69, pp. 79–127.

Erickson, A.S., Walter III, L.C. and Mikolay, J.D. (2010) 'Diego Garcia and the United States' emerging Indian Ocean strategy'. *Asian Security*, 6(3), pp. 214–237.
Evers, S. and Kooy, M. (2011) *Eviction from the Chagos Islands: Displacement and Struggle for Identity against Two World Powers*. Leiden: Brill.
Farran, S. (2018) 'Chagos and the ICJ–The marine protected area [the advisory opinion of the international court of justice on the chagos archipelago: An anticipatory analysis (Part I, II & III)]'. *Questions of International Law Zoom-out* [Preprint] **55**: 71-84.
Farran, S. (2021) 'The Chagos marine protected area'. In T. Burri and J. Trinidad (eds.), *The International Court of Justice and Chagos Islands*. Cambridge: Cambridge University Press, pp.159–186.
Ghosh, P. (2020) 'India's Indian Ocean region strategy'. *Journal of Indo-Pacific Affairs* [Preprint]. Available at: https://www.airuniversity.af.edu/JIPA/Display/Article/2331112/Indias-indian-ocean-region-strategy/ (Accessed: 2 January 2024).
Gifford, R. and Dunne, R.P. (2014) 'A dispossessed people: The depopulation of the Chagos Archipelago 1965–1973'. *Population, Space and Place*, 20(1), pp. 37–49.
Grandison, C., Kadaba, S.N. and Woo, A. (2012) 'Stealing the islands of Chagos: Another forgotten story of colonial injustice'. *Human Rights Brief*, 20, pp. 37–43.
Green, M.J. and Shearer, A. (2012) 'Defining US Indian ocean strategy'. *The Washington Quarterly*, 35(2), pp. 175–189.
Harris, P. (2023) 'The Chagos dispute: Where right makes might'. *Third World Quarterly*, 44(2), pp. 395–404.
Hilpold, P. (2022) ''Humanizing 'the law of self-determination–the Chagos Island case'. *Nordic Journal of International Law*, 91(2), pp. 189–215.
Hornat, J. (2016) 'The power triangle in the Indian Ocean: China, India and the United States'. *Cambridge Review of International Affairs*, 29(2), pp. 425–443.
International Court of Justice (2019) 'Legal consequences of the separation of the Chagos archipelago from mauritius in 1965. Advisory opinion'. Available at: https://www.icj-cij.org/public/files/case-related/169/169-20190225-01-00-EN.pdf (Accessed: 1 March 2023).
Kanodia, H. (2022) 'IUU fishing in the Indian Ocean: A security threat'. *The Diplomat*, 9 June. Available at: https://diplomatist.com/2022/06/09/lets-catch-the-big-fish/ (Accessed: 8 September 2023).
Lobo, J. (2016) 'The Chagos marine protected area: A whole kettle of fish'. *Queen Mary Human Rights Law Review*, 3(1), pp. 10–32.
McVeigh, K. (2021) 'EU accused of "neocolonial" plundering of tuna in the Indian Ocean', *The Guardian*, 5 March. Available at: https://www.theguardian.com/enviornment/2021/mar/05/eu-accused-of-neocolonial-plundering-of-tuna-in-indian-ocean (Accessed: 8 January 2024).
Misra, K.P. (1977) 'Indian Ocean as a zone of peace: The concept and the alternatives'. *Indian Quarterly*, 33(1), pp 19–32.
Pascu, M.L. (2011) 'The geo-strategic importance of the Indian Ocean in the context of the world oil crisis'. *Bulletin of the Transilvania University of Brasov. Economic Sciences. Series V*, 4(53)(1), p. 221–226.
R (Bancoult) v. Secretary of State for Foreign and Commonwealth Office (No 1) (2000) [2000] EWHC 413 (Admin). *BAILII.* Available at: http://www.bailii.org/ew/cases/EWHC/Admin/2000/413.html (Accessed: 8 September 2023).
R (Bancoult (No 2)) v. Secretary of State For Foreign and Commonwealth Affairs (2008). [2008] UKHL 61. *BAILII.* Available at: https://www.bailii.org/cgi-bin/format.cgi?doc=/uk/cases/UKHL/2008/61.html (Accessed: 8 September 2023).
R (Bancoult (No 3)) v Secretary of State for Foreign and Commonwealth Affairs (2018) [2018] UKSC 3. *BAILII.* Available at: http://www.bailii.org/uk/cases/UKSC/2018/3.html. (Accessed: 8 January 2023).
R (Hoareau and Bancoult) v Secretary of State for Foreign and Commonwealth Affairs (2020) [2020] EWCA Civ 1010. *BAILII.* Available at: http://www.bailii.org/ew/cases/EWCA/Civ/2020/1010.html. (Accessed: 8 September 2023).

Rrecaj, B.T. (2020) 'Legal Consequences of The Separation of the Chagos Archipelago from Mauritius in 1965 (ICJ Advisory Opinion, 25 February 2019, General List No. 169)'. *Utrecht Journal of International & European Law*, 35, p. 50–55.

Samaranayake, N. (2020) 'The Chagos Archipelago dispute: Law, diplomacy and military basing'. *Lawfare*, 6 October. Available at: https://www.lawfareblog.com/chagos-archipelago-dispute-law-diplomacy-and-military-basing (Accessed: 28 December 2022).

Sand, P.H. (2010) 'The Chagos archipelago – footprint of empire, or world heritage?' *Environmental Policy and Law*, 40, p. 232.

Sand, P.H. (2012) '"Marine protected areas" off UK overseas territories: Comparing the South Orkneys Shelf and the Chagos Archipelago'. *The Geographical Journal*, 178(3), pp. 201–207.

Sand, P.H. (2013) 'The Chagos Archipelago cases: Nature conservation between human rights and power politics'. *Global Community Yearbook International Law Jurisprudence*, 26, pp. 125–149.

Sand, P.H. (2015) 'Stephen Allen. *The Chagos Islanders and international law*'. *European Journal of International Law*, 26(2), pp. 573–578.

Sheppard, C. (2010) 'Marine protected areas and pelagic fishing: The case of the Chagos Archipelago'. *Marine Pollution Bulletin*, 60(11), pp. 1899–1901.

Simpson, M. (2020) 'The Anthropocene as colonial discourse'. *EPD: Society and Space*, 38(1), pp. 53–71.

The White House (2022) 'FACT SHEET: Indo-pacific strategy of the United States'. Available at: https://www.whitehouse.gov/briefing-room/speeches-remarks/2022/02/11/fact-sheet-indo-pacific-strategy-of-the-united-states/ (Accessed: 8 January 2024).

UK Government (2020) 'Global Ocean alliance: 30by30 initiative'. *Gov.uk*. Available at: https://www.gov.uk/government/topical-events/global-ocean-alliance-30by30-initiative (Accessed: 8 January 2024).

UNESCO (1971) 'Convention on wetlands of international importance especially as waterfowl habitat'. Available at: https://www.ramsar.org/sites/default/files/documents/library/current_convention_text_e.pdf.

United Nations (1972) 'Declaration of the United Nations conference on the human environment, A/CONF.48/14/Rev.1'. Available at: https://digitallibrary.un.org/record/523249?ln=en&v=pdf (Accessed: 8 January 2024).

United Nations (1992) 'Rio Declaration on environment and development, A/CONF.151/26/Rev 1(Vol I)/Corr.1'. Available at: https://digitallibrary.un.org/record/165795?ln=en&v=pdf (Accessed: 8 January 2024).

United Nations (2015a) 'Paris agreement'. Available at: https://digitallibrary.un.org/record/827098?ln=en (Accessed: 8 January 2024).

United Nations (2015b) Transforming our world: The 2030 agenda for sustainable development, A/RES/20/1'. Available at: https://digitallibrary.un.org/record/1654217?ln=en&v=pdf (Accessed: 8 January 2024).

United Nations General Assembly (2019) 'General assembly welcomes international court of justice opinion on Chagos Archipelago, adopts text calling for mauritius' complete decolonization (GA/12146)'. *United Nations Meetings Coverage and Press Releases*. Available at: https://press.un.org/en/2019/ga12146.doc.htm (Accessed: 1 March 2023).

United Nations (2022) 'Press release: Nations adopt four goals, 23 targets for 2030 in landmark UN biodiversity agreement'. 19 December. Available at: https://www.un.org/sustainabledevelopment/blog/2022/12/press-release-nations-adopt-four-goals-23-targets-for-2030-in-landmark-un-biodiversity-agreement/ (Accessed: 6 January 2024).

United Nations General Assembly (1971) 'Declaration of the Indian Ocean as a zone of peace, A/RES/2832 (XXVI)'. Available at: https://digitallibrary.un.org/record/192075?ln=en&v=pdf (Accessed: 8 January 2024).

United Nations General Assembly (1972) ‘Declaration of the Indian Ocean as a zone of peace, A/RES/2992 (XXVII)’. Available at: https://digitallibrary.un.org/record/191429?v=pdf (Accessed: 8 January 2024).
United Nations General Assembly (2017a) ‘International legally binding instrument under the United Nations Convention on the Law of the Sea on the conservation and sustainable use of marine biological diversity of areas beyond national jurisdiction, A/RES/72/249’. Available at: https://digitallibrary.un.org/record/1468985?ln=en&v=pdf (Accessed: 8 January 2024).
United Nations General Assembly (2017b) ‘Request for advisory opinion transmitted to the Court pursuant to General Assembly resolution 71/292 (A/71/L.73) of 22 June 2017: Legal consequences of the separation of the Chagos Archipelago from Mauritius in 1965’. Available at: https://www.icj-cij.org/sites/default/files/case-related/169/169-20170623-REQ-01-00-EN.pdf (Accessed: 8 January 2024).
United Nations General Assembly (2019) ‘General assembly welcomes international court of justice opinion on Chagos Archipelago, adopts text calling for mauritius’ complete decolonization, GA/12146’. Available at: https://press.un.org/en/2019/ga12146.doc.htm (Accessed: 1 September 2024).
United Nations General Assembly (2022) ‘The human right to a clean, healthy and sustainable environment, A/RES/76/300’. Available at: https://digitallibrary.un.org/record/3983329/files/A_RES_76_300-EN.pdf?ln=en (Accessed: 8 January 2024).
Viaene, L. (2022) ‘Can rights of nature save Us from the anthropocene catastrophe? Some critical reflections from the field’. *Asian Journal of Law and Society*, 9(2), pp. 187–206.

6 Return of the Chagos Islands to Mauritius and Chagossian Identity

Constitutional, Legal, and Political Perspectives

Charles M Fombad

Introduction

Three significant interventions by a number of international institutions have virtually settled the question of permanent sovereignty over the Chagos Archipelago in favour of Mauritius. The first of these was the *Chagos Marine Protected Area Arbitration Award* case ("*Mauritius v. United Kingdom*", 2015) on 18 March 2015. The Tribunal, constituted under Annex VII of the United Nations Convention on the Law of the Sea, found that the Marine Protected Area (MPA) declared by Britain on 1 April 2010 disregarded Mauritius' rights, rendering it unlawful indirectly.[1]

The second was the request made on 23 June 2017 by the United Nations General Assembly (UNGA) to the International Court of Justice (ICJ) for an advisory opinion clarifying the legal status of the Chagos Island Archipelago.[2] The case turned on whether Britain had violated the 1960 United Nations Declaration on Independence. The ICJ was of the opinion that the process of decolonisation of Mauritius was not lawfully completed at independence and that the Chagos Archipelago was clearly an integral part of Mauritius and could not have been dismembered. It declared that Britain was under an obligation to end its administration of the Archipelago as rapidly as possible ("*Legal Consequences of the Separation of the Chagos Archipelago from Mauritius in 1965. Advisory opinion*", 2019, pp. 46–48, 170–178). In May 2019, the UNGA supported a motion endorsing the advisory opinion and setting a six-month deadline for the Chagos Archipelago to be reunified with Mauritius (United Nations General Assembly, 2019). That deadline set by the UN has since elapsed. A third intervention occurred when, in February 2021, the International Tribunal for the Law of the Sea (ITLOS) reaffirmed the advisory opinion when dealing with a dispute over the Maldives and Mauritius' maritime boundary.[3]

If history is anything to go by, the British will delay the return of the Chagos Island to Mauritius for as long as they can. Eventually though, they will depart but what will they leave behind? In a number of African countries, such as Cameroon and Botswana, the precipitated British departure has, at least in the former case, left an enduring legacy of marginalisation, oppression, and conflict for the minority anglophone community that the British left in the lurch in 1961.[4] Will they do better and try to undo more than a half century of harm they have done and negotiate an arrangement that will ensure that the Chagossians are recognised

DOI: 10.4324/9781003390299-9

and protected in a new constitutional arrangement that will restore their dignity before they leave? In the case of the Chagos Islands, the situation is even more complicated as it involves American occupation even though the administration remains British and the return of the Chagos Islands to Mauritius will demand that both leave the territory. As a result of British colonialism, the Chagossians are effectively refugees wherever they are today, and even within Mauritius, they are a specially oppressed group living on the margins of society. The present out-dated Mauritian Constitution will need to be amended to address the special civil, political, economic, social, and cultural needs of the Chagossians. Whilst primary responsibility for such changes lies with the Mauritians, the British have, at least, a moral obligation to use this opportunity to influence these changes in a manner that will rectify some of the harm they have needlessly caused to the Chagossians in the last 50 years. However, the British, whenever approached by the Mauritian authorities in terms of owning up to their responsibilities and the harm caused to Chagossians, have always brushed the issue aside.

The African Union (AU),[5] which has played a critical role in drawing the world's attention to the Chagos issue (and has been supportive of Mauritian claims – see African Union, (2018)), also needs to play a role in the final arrangements needed to facilitate the re-unification of the Chagos within Mauritius in a manner that will prevent any future conflicts. There is a need for the AU and the international organisations trying to put pressure on the British to leave to ensure that the interests of the Chagossians are recognised and protected in the re-unification arrangements. This will also achieve the implementation of one of the goals enshrined in Agenda 2063 which aims at the complete decolonisation of the continent.

Drawing from the experience of similar situations in other African countries, this chapter suggests some of the important constitutional and other legal measures that need to be adopted to enable a harmonious reintegration of the Chagos Islands within Mauritius. The objective of the chapter is to draw attention to the fact that there is potential for future internal conflicts within Mauritius unless a carefully crafted constitutional arrangement forms the basis for the return of the Chagos Island to Mauritius.

The discussion focuses on two main issues. Firstly Chagossian identity and its possible implications on re-unification. Secondly, the constitutional options on the reunification of the Chagos Islands with the rest of Mauritius. The chapter ends with some concluding remarks. The crux of the matter is that it is necessary to ensure that British colonisation is not replaced by Mauritian colonisation.

Chagossian Identity and Its Possible Implications on Reunification

Chagossian Identity in Mauritian Society Generally

We need to look at the Chagossian legal identity in the broader context of Mauritian society, bearing in mind that the two polities have been separated for at least 58 years. From this perspective, two things are worth noting.

The first is the population dynamics of the two polities. According to a Worldometer March 2023 estimate, the population of Mauritius is 1,277,400, with a population growth rate of 0.4% (Worldometer, 2023). The country is a multi-ethnic polity that consists of 67% Indo-Pakistani, 27.4% Creole (that is mixed Caucasian, Indo-Pakistani, and Africans), 3% Chinese, and 2.6% others. By contrast, it is difficult to say how many Chagossians there are today. The population of Chagossians in 1965, just before the forced displacement began, was estimated to be between 1,500 and 1,750 (Human Rights Watch, 2023). It is difficult to estimate how many are now living in exile, particularly in the three main countries to which they were forcibly moved; that is Britain, Mauritius, and the Seychelles. If we assume the same annual population growth rate of 0.4% for a population of 1750 (using the upper limit) from 1965, then the population of Chagossians will today probably have increased by 508 to make it around 2258. This will make the Chagossian population only about 0.18% of the total Mauritian population. The Chagossian community is also equally mixed. Although for most of its history the Chagossian Islands were a dependency of Mauritius, except as noted above during the last 58 years, the people mostly have an African ancestry. They are said to come from Madagascar, Mozambique, and other African countries, with a few having Indian and Malay ancestry (see Chapter 2 for further discussion of Chagossian African ancestry).

The second point to note concerns debates amongst many of the researchers, scholars, international organisations, as well as international NGOs who have written on the topic about whether the Chagossians qualify under numerous UN and AU instruments to be classified as "a people", "indigenous people", or a minority entitled to special protection and a right to self-determination (Demšar *et al.*, 2018; Gundowry, 2018; Human Rights Watch, 2023). Whether or not one agrees with any of these descriptions, what is however clear is that many analysts agree that the Chagossians, irrespective of where they are, as a group possess and manifest distinct common cultural and linguistic characteristics that distinguish them from other peoples in Mauritius and the Seychelles. There is also some evidence that in spite of being in exile, the Chagossians self-identify as a distinct community (Bhatt, 2019; Human Rights Watch, 2023). Through a number of organisations and advocacy groups they have also kept alive their oral history, songs, and food. Even though the Chagossians speak the same Creole language spoken by the Creole community in Mauritius, the vocabulary and pronunciation are slightly different from the Creole spoken in Mauritius (Walker, 1986, pp. 15–17). The situation of the Chagossians is similar to Rodriguans, Rodrigues being another island of Mauritius but people having their own distinct cultures and way of life.

Chagossian Identity under Mauritian Law

The legal status of the Chagossians in today's Mauritian society is critical to their future. The main legal instrument defining this is the Constitution (1968). Section 3(4) of the First Schedule to the Constitution divides the population into communities. It states as follows:

> For the purposes of this Schedule, the population of Mauritius shall be regarded as including a Hindu community, a Muslim community and a Sino-Mauritian community; and every person who does not appear, from his way of life, to belong to one or other of those 3 communities shall be regarded as belonging to the General Population, which shall itself be regarded as a fourth community.

The Constitution therefore classifies the diverse ethnic groups in Mauritius into four categories, the largest being Hindus, which make up 49% of the population, followed by Muslims (17%), Sino-Mauritians (about 1–2%), and a category referred to as "General Population" (32%). This general population category consists mainly of people of French origin and those of African descent, the latter being commonly referred to as Creoles. As a result of this classification, most Mauritians identify primarily with their ethnic community or with the sub-group, in the case of the Chagossians, of one of the main communities (Carroll and Carroll, 2000).

Most of the Chagossians belong to the Creole ethnic group who are primarily of African ancestry and whose ancestors were forcibly uprooted and later mixed with those from other ethnic groups. The Afro-Creoles in Mauritius have throughout been marginalised and their situation has been worsened by the political and social dominance of the Indo-Mauritians leading to the label of Mauritius as "little India" (Boswell, 2006; Eisenlohr, 2006; Jeffery, 2011). The Afro-Creole community as a whole have been systematically subjected to discrimination and racism as well as associated with negative stereotypes leading to such social, economic, and political exclusion that the expression "Malaise Creole" (that is, "Creole ailment") was coined to express the gravity of the injustices they have been subjected to.[6] Because the Chagossians in Mauritius were settled in the most deprived areas (namely Baie du Tonbeau, Cassis, and Roches Bois, which are considered deeply impoverished townships close to the city centre), their living conditions have been described as extremely harsh caused by poverty and discrimination not only by the non-Creole community but also by the Mauritian Creoles (Madeley, 1982, p. 54; Vine, 2011). As a result of this, Chagossians have experienced double discrimination first as Afro-Creoles and secondly as Chagossians. They are referred to as "*zilwa*", a pejorative term used to describe any person behaving in an anti-social or immoral way (Jeffery and Vine, 2011). Ian Walker, writing in 1986, noted that children of native Chagossian islanders who were born in Mauritius were classified as *Ilois* because of their circumstances known by other people or because their behaviour was indicative of their Ilois upbringing and added that the Chagossians are considered an "unwanted group", in Mauritius (Walker, 1986, p. 35). They have struggled between different self-identifications: Ilois or Chagossian; Mauritian; Creole; and British. The conflictual sense of belongingness does not only limit itself to the generations which were forced to leave the Chagos Islands but continues across generations. According to Johannessen, many Chagossians have never wanted to identify themselves as Mauritians because they consider the Mauritian government, especially the then Prime

Minister Sir Seewoosagur Ramgoolam, had "sold" the Chagos in order to obtain the independence of Mauritius from the British government (in Gundowry, 2018, p. 35). Chagossians often feel that they have been the "collateral damage" figuratively in Mauritius's quest for independence. Numerous Chagossian organisations with the assistance of several international NGOs have helped to bring the plight of the Chagossians to the attention of the international community, especially the African Union and the United Nations Working Group on Indigenous Peoples in Geneva (Gundowry, 2018, pp. 36–42).

Identity Issues and Reunification Implications

Britain has already missed several deadlines that required it to hand over the control of the Chagos Island Archipelago to the control of Mauritius. Although since November 2022 the British government had announced that it was starting negotiations with Mauritius to discuss the future of the islands, little appears to have happened. There is little transparency about the negotiations and only a vague suggestion that the Chagossian people will be effectively and meaningfully consulted. From the preceding discussions, there are a number of practical and legal problems with the present approach.

Firstly, the Mauritian government in a letter to Human Rights Watch in January 2023 is alleged to have indicated that all individuals of Chagossian origin will be allowed to resettle in the Chagos Archipelago in accordance with the laws of Mauritius (Human Rights Watch, 2023, p. 59). It is also said that the Prime Minister, Pravind Kumar Jugnauth, had in March 2022 indicated that Mauritius will continue to lease Diego Garcia (the main island in the Chagos Archipelago) to the US for its military base (Human Rights Watch, 2023). It is not clear to what extent the Chagossian communities in Mauritius, the Seychelles, Britain, and elsewhere were consulted before such decisions were taken. This is bound to raise eyebrows and remind Chagossians and their supporters of what happened in 1965 when the Chagos island was "sold" to the British.[7]

Secondly, considering the insignificant percentage of the general population that the Chagossians make of the overall population and the marginalisation and discrimination that they have been subjected to in Mauritius, there is really little chance that the government will seriously take their genuine interest into account during the discussions with Britain. If the plight of the minority anglophone community in Cameroon is anything to go by (as per footnote 4), it is unlikely that the British will bother about the interest of the Chagossians and try to use this opportunity to undo the half a century of injustice they have inflicted on them. Thirdly, the absence of Chagossians as part of the discussions on the future of their formal reintegration poses a real danger that their interest will come secondary to the interests of the British and Mauritian governments, if at all this will be a matter that the two parties will consider. Their interest will best be protected if there is a discussion in which they are part and in which their interest is formally recognised and protected in the constitution.

Constitutional Options on Reunification

The main contention here is that in the light of the marginalisation, discrimination, and other injustices that the Chagossians have been subjected to, only a new constitutional dispensation in which their minority status is recognised and protected can give them a sense of genuine belonging to Mauritius. There are two possible options; one under which reliance will be placed on the anti-discrimination provisions in the present constitution and another under which the constitution is amended to specifically entrench minority rights provisions to protect them. Before considering these two options, we will start by examining the position of Chagossians under the present Constitution (1968).

The Status of Chagossians under the Present Constitution

Besides section 3(4) of the First Schedule to the Constitution that categorises the Mauritian ethnic population into four communities, one of which can be taken to refer to the Chagossian people, there is only one express reference to the Chagos Archipelago. This appears in the interpretation section, which, in section 111(1), defines "Mauritius" to include, inter alia:

> the islands of Mauritius, Rodrigues, Agalega, Tromelin, Cargados Carajos and the Chagos Archipelago, including Diego Garcia and any other island comprised in the State of Mauritius.

This particular part of the Constitution was introduced through a constitutional amendment in 1991 (before Mauritius became a Republic in 1992) and supersedes the original definition of Mauritius in the 1968 independence Constitution (granted by Britain). In the earlier Constitution, Mauritius was defined to only include the territories which immediately before 12 March 1968 constituted the colony of Mauritius. As the Chagos Archipelago had been excised by Britain in 1965, the British made it clear that "immediately before March 1968" would not apply to Chagos Archipelago as part of the colony of Mauritius.

As a result of the 1991 constitutional amendment, the civil and political rights enshrined in the Bill of Rights in the Constitution became automatically applicable to Chagossians. This was followed by the adoption of the Chagossian Welfare Fund Act (No. 21 of 1999). This was set up under the aegis of the Prime Minister's office, the Chagossian Welfare Fund to, inter alia, advance and promote the welfare of members of the Chagossian community and their descendants, develop programmes and projects for their total integration into Mauritius. The Fund is also required to maintain community centres and other community facilities vested in it for the benefit of members of the Chagossian community and other descendants. Representatives of the Chagossian community form part of the Board of the Chagossian Welfare Fund and are elected by members of the Chagossian community. The management of other islands such as Rodrigues and Agalega also falls under the same office.

There is also the issue of stateless Chagossians who live in Mauritius today. This category has resulted from the disparity in dates of recognition and conferral of citizenship contained in the relevant legislation in Britain and Mauritius. The eviction of the Chagossians started in 1965 and ended in 1973. While Mauritian legislation provides that anyone born on the islands before 8 November 1965 is a Mauritian, Britain for its part provides that anyone born after April 1969 but before January 1983 is a British citizen. As a result, individuals who were born on Diego Garcia during that time are neither covered by the Mauritian Constitution nor the British legislation. The effect is therefore that people born after 8 November 1965 and before April 1969 are stateless persons as they are neither Mauritians nor British. Unless there is a constitutional amendment to deal with this and other issues that may arise as a result of the reunification of the Chagos Archipelago with Mauritius, this category of Chagossians will remain stateless. As indicated above, this and other related issues can be addressed either in the context of an amended Bill of Rights that provides for equality of treatment and prohibits discrimination (the equality approach) or specific provisions that recognize and protect the Chagossians as a minority group (the minority rights approach).[8] Explicit constitutional provisions are a critical part of any credible and effective institutional framework for recognising and protecting the rights of the Chagossians because this will form the basis for shaping the content of any subsequent legislation to deal with the Chagossian community and their special needs.

Protecting Chagossians under a General Bill of Rights in the Constitution

The first approach to recognizing and protecting the rights of Chagossians after the formal reintegration of those presently within and outside Mauritius is to rely on the provisions of Chapter 2 of the Constitution which protect fundamental rights and freedoms of the individual. Two main provisions in this section provide, what is usually referred to as the equality approach to protecting minorities, such as the Chagossians. The first of this is section 3, which contains a general equality clause that guarantees equality for all regardless of race, place of origin, political opinions, colour, creed, or sex, but subject to respect for, inter alia, the rights and freedoms of others and for the public interest. The second provision dealing with this is section 16. It prohibits the making of any law that is discriminatory either of itself or in its effect. "Discriminatory" is defined in section 16(3) as affording different treatment to different persons attributable wholly or mainly to their respective descriptions by race, caste, place of origin, political opinions, colour, creed, or sex whereby persons of one such description are subjected to disabilities or restrictions to which persons of another such description are not made subject or are accorded privileges or advantages that are not accorded to persons of another such description. However, this is qualified to allow for special treatment that will not qualify as discrimination in certain specified situations.[9] Will this broadly worded general equality provision suffice in protecting Chagossians after reunification?

Firstly, in spite of the existence of these equality provisions, the Chagossians have, as we have seen, suffered from diverse forms of discrimination and marginalisation. It is not likely that this will change. Secondly, both provisions mainly provide for formal equality, which basically means that all Mauritians must be treated the same way. However, there is an attempt in some of the subsections of section 16 to provide for substantive, real, or full equality. This provides, for example, in section 16(4) (aa), that "a minimum number of candidates for election to local authorities to be of a particular sex, with a view to ensuring adequate representation of each sex on a local authority".

In the light of numerous challenges that the Chagossians presently face, the general protection provided by the present human rights provisions is unlikely to help them overcome the numerous impediments that have limited their equal access to employment, public services, and effective participation in economic, social, and cultural life as well as in public affairs. A better option is to introduce special minority rights protection provisions in the constitution.

Protecting the Chagossians through a Minority Rights Protection Provision in the Constitution

The amendment of the Mauritian Constitution to introduce a minority rights provision is an exceptional measure that is bound to be controversial. Without the need to go into the copious literature on minority rights, which have highlighted the difficulties of defining the concept, it will suffice to suggest that the Chagossians can be classified, even under the present constitutional dispensation, as an ethnic minority deserving of recognition and protection. Most of the studies that have been carried out to underscore their plight show that they meet all the basic requirements to be classified as an ethnic minority, viz.;

i) They constitute an ethnic and linguistic community within Mauritius and in those other countries where they are. Chagossians as a group possess common cultural and linguistic characteristics distinct from that of any other peoples in Mauritius and the Seychelles.
ii) They are in a non-dominant position in these countries.
iii) They are made up of individuals who possess a sense of belonging to that group.
iv) They are determined to preserve and develop their distinct ethnic identity.
v) They have for more than half a century been discriminated against and marginalised on the grounds of their ethnicity and language in the communities where they find themselves.

The recognition and protection of the minority rights of the Chagossian peoples must be seen as an integral part of their fundamental human rights. This will require an amendment of the Mauritian Constitution to ensure that it preserves their identity and guarantees their equality with other communities in the country and in this way restore their dignity and fundamental human rights. There is a need to constitutionally entrench these rights in a manner that will ensure that the dominant majority in the country cannot use their majority to arbitrarily amend the constitution to remove the protective provisions. This will require not only goodwill on the part of the Mauritian and British governments but some creative constitutional engineering. The fact that the Chagossian community is fairly small and is only one of the several other ethnic groups in the country will make this task complicated unless there is a buy-in and understanding from the other communities.

The key elements of constitutional provisions to protect the Chagossian community should consist of provisions which:

i) Provide for some form of regional autonomy. This must be crafted in a manner that factors in the small population of the Chagossians and their limited economic and manpower resources.
ii) Protect the distinct language and culture of the people.
iii) Provide a mechanism for ensuring the representation of Chagossians at all levels of government.

Conclusion

It is indisputable that by the time the British excised the Chagossian Archipelago from the rest of Mauritius, the former was an integral part of the latter. However, we cannot ignore the fundamental changes that have taken place during the last 58 years of their separation and simply assume that a simple reunification of the two is sufficient to undo the injustices of what happened in the past. A reunification of the two communities will not only close the last chapter of the European colonisation in Africa but also emphasise the moral obligation the international community has to ensure that this is properly done. The British abandoned their former trust territory of Southern Cameroon in another reunification arrangement in which the latter now face the real prospects of losing their separate and distinct legal and linguistic identity as a result of the machinations of another dominant community courtesy of French assistance and continuous support. The hope is that the British will not do the same to the Chagossians.

Notes

1 The Tribunal unanimously found that, as a result of undertakings given by the United Kingdom in 1965 and repeated thereafter, Mauritius holds legally binding rights to fish in the waters surrounding the Chagos Archipelago, to the eventual return of the Chagos Archipelago to Mauritius when no longer needed for defence purposes, and to the preservation of the benefit of any minerals or oil discovered in or near the Chagos Archipelago pending its eventual return.

2 The main issue was formulated thus: Was the process of decolonization of Mauritius lawfully completed when Mauritius was granted independence in 1968, following the separation of the Chagos Archipelago from Mauritius and having regard to international law, including obligations reflected in General Assembly resolutions 1514 (XV) of 14 December 1960, 2066 (XX) of 16 December 1965, 2232 (XXI) of 20 December 1966 and 2357 (XXII) of 19 December 1967? (ICJ, 2019).

3 As to the Chagos advisory opinion, the Special Chamber finds that "[t]he determinations made by the ICJ with respect to the issues of the decolonization of Mauritius in the Chagos advisory opinion have legal effect and clear implications for the legal status of the Chagos Archipelago" and that "[t]he United Kingdom's continued claim to sovereignty over the Chagos Archipelago is contrary to those determinations". The

Special Chamber also finds that, "[w]hile the process of decolonization has yet to be completed, Mauritius' sovereignty over the Chagos Archipelago can be inferred from the ICJ's determinations" (ITLOS, 2019, para. 246).

4 The Chagossians need to learn from the way the British handled the re-unification of the former British Cameroons (1916–1961) with the former French Cameroun (1916–1960). During the discussions leading to the reunification of the two communities in 1961, whereas French constitutional law experts took part and ensured an arrangement that favoured the majority French-speaking community, the British virtually abandoned the minority English-speaking community to their own devices. The sham federal arrangement that was virtually imposed on the anglophone minority paved the way for their progressive assimilation and marginalisation. The civil conflict that has been going on since 2016 is a direct result of the marginalisation and discrimination that the anglophone community has been subject to as a result of the unfavourable terms that formed the basis of the re-unification and the absence of British advisers to assist the anglophone minority. See generally Ngoh (2011) and Susungi (1991).

5 The African Union has been strongly supporting the Mauritian claims – see African Union (2018).

6 According to Gundowry, this was coined by a Catholic priest, Father Roger Cerveux (2018, p. 32).

7 It should also be noted that the Mauritius government has made a secret deal with the Indian government to build a base on one of its remote islands, Agalega, without consulting its estimated 300 inhabitants. The islanders now fear for their future (Ritzen, 2020).

8 For a discussion of these approaches, see Henrard (2010) and Gilbert (2013).

9 See section 16(4)–(6), which for example allow for the requirement of a minimum number of candidates to be of a certain sex, and the flexibility in criteria for the appointment to certain positions.

References

African Union (2018) 'The African Union, in its effort to ensure the decolonization of the Chagos Archipelago, takes part in the oral hearing before the International Court of Justice'. 3 September. Available at: https://au.int/en/pressreleases/20180903/african-union-its-effort-ensure-decolonization-chagos-archipelago-takes-part.

Bhatt, K. (2019) 'A post-colonial legal approach to the Chagos case and the (dis) application of land rights norms'. *International Journal of Law in Context*, 15(1), pp. 1–19.

Boswell, R. (2006) *Le malaise créole: ethnic identity in Mauritius*. Oxford: Berghahn Books.

Carroll, B.W. and Carroll, T. (2000) 'Trouble in paradise: Ethnic conflict in Mauritius'. *Journal of Commonwealth & Comparative Politics*, 38(2), pp. 25–50.

Chagos Marine Protected Area Arbitration (Mauritius v. United Kingdom) (2015) Permanent Court of Arbitration. Available at: https://pca-cpa.org/en/cases/11/ (Accessed: 1 March 2023).

Demšar, U. *et al.* (2018) 'The destiny of the Chagos Islands and its people'. Available at: https://www.pf.uni-lj.si/media/memorandum.concerning.legal.consequences.of.the.separation.of.the.chagos.archipelago.from.mauritius.in.1965_1.pdf.

Eisenlohr, P. (2006) *Little India: Diaspora, Time, and Ethnolinguistic Belonging in Hindu Mauritius*. Berkeley: University of California Press.

Gilbert, J. (2013) 'Constitutionalism, ethnicity and minority rights in Africa: A legal appraisal from the great lakes region'. *International Journal of Constitutional Law*, 11(2), pp. 414–437.

Gundowry, M.S. (2018) *Acculturation of Young Mauritian people of Chagossian Origin in the UK: Negotiating Living in the Host Society*. Brighton: University of Brighton.

Henrard, K. (2010) 'Minorities in Africa and the right to equality and non-discrimination'. In S. Dersso (ed.), *Perspectives on Minority and Indigenous Peoples Rights in Africa.* Pretoria: Pretoria University Law Press, pp. 207–252.

Human Rights Watch (2023) '"That's when the nightmare started" UK and US forced displacement of the chagossians and ongoing colonial crimes'. Available at: https://www.hrw.org/report/2023/02/15/thats-when-nightmare-started/uk-and-us-forced-displacement-chagossians-and (Accessed: 1 March 2023).

International Court of Justice, (2019) 'Legal consequences of the separation of the Chagos archipelago from Mauritius in 1965. Advisory opinion'. Available at: https://www.icj-cij.org/public/files/case-related/169/169-20190225-01-00-EN.pdf (Accessed: 1 March 2023).

International Tribunal for the Law of the Sea (2019) 'Dispute concerning delimitation of the maritime boundary between Mauritius and Maldives in the Indian Ocean (Mauritius/Maldives)'. Available at: https://www.itlos.org/en/main/cases/list-of-cases/dispute-concerning-delimitation-of-the-maritime-boundary-between-mauritius-and-maldives-in-the-indian-ocean-mauritius/maldives/ (Accessed: 1 March 2023).

Jeffery, L. (2011) *Chagos Islanders in Mauritius and the UK: Forced Displacement and Onward Migration.* Manchester: Manchester University Press.

Jeffery, L. and Vine, D. (2011) 'Sorrow, sadness, and impoverishment: The lives of Chagossians in Mauritius'. In S. Evers and M. Kooy (eds.), *Eviction from the Chagos Islands: Displacement and Struggle for Identity against two World Powers.* Leiden: Brill, pp. 83–102.

Madeley, J. (1982) *Diego Garcia: A Contrast to the Falklands.* 54. London: Minority Rights Group.

Ngoh, V.J. (2011) *The Untold Story of Cameroon Reunification: 1955–1961.* Limbe: Presprint PLC.

Ritzen, Y. (2020) 'Agaléga, a secret base, and India's claim to power'. *Al Jazeera Media Network.* Available at: https://interactive.aljazeera.com/aje/2021/island-of-secrets/index.html (Accessed: 1 March 2023).

Susungi, N.N. (1991) *The Crisis of Unity and Democracy in Cameroon: Can a Country which Has Pronounced Itself Dead be Saved by Democracy?* Self-published: N.N. Susungi.

'The Constitution of the Republic of Mauritius' (1968) Available at: https://mauritiusassembly.govmu.org/mauritiusassembly/index.php/the-constitution/ (Accessed: 1 March 2023).

United Nations (2019) 'General assembly welcomes international court of justice opinion on Chagos Archipelago, adopts text calling for mauritius' complete decolonization (GA/12146)' *United Nations Meetings Coverage and Press Releases.* Available at: https://press.un.org/en/2019/ga12146.doc.htm (Accessed: 1 March 2023).

Vine, D. (2011) 'Chagossians twice forgotten: Exile in the seychelles'. In S. Evers and M. Kooy (eds.), *Eviction from the Chagos Islands: Displacement and Struggle for Identity against two World Powers.* Leiden: Brill, pp. 105–124.

Walker, I. (1986) *Zaffer Pe Sanze: Ethnic Identity and Social Change among the Ilois in Mauritius.* Mauritius: KMLI.

Worldometer (2023) 'Mauritius population (live)'. Available at: https://www.worldometers.info/world-population/mauritius-population/ (Accessed: 1 March 2023).

7 Political and Legal Debates about Chagossian Ethnicity and Indigeneity

Laura Jeffery

Introduction

The Chagos Archipelago was unpopulated prior to European expansion in the Indian Ocean from the late eighteenth century onwards, whereupon it was administered as a dependency of colonial Mauritius. French and later British colonists populated the islands, first with enslaved labourers, mostly from East Africa and Madagascar via Mauritius, and later with contract workers, mostly from India via Mauritius (Wenban-Smith and Carter, 2016). Throughout the settled history of the Chagos islands, coconut plantations were the economic base and main source of employment. Also known as the Oil Islands, they relied almost entirely on the production of copra (dried coconut flesh) exported for the extraction of coconut oil that was refined for energy and used in the production of soap (among other products) in Mauritius and beyond. The population of Chagos rose steadily throughout the nineteenth century and hovered around a thousand people over the first half of the twentieth century (Gifford and Dunne, 2014, pp. 39–40). In 1965, as part of negotiations leading to Mauritian independence in 1968, the UK government excised the Chagos Archipelago from colonial Mauritius to form part of the new British Indian Ocean Territory (BIOT). The UK government orchestrated the depopulation of the Chagos Archipelago: first by preventing the return of islanders who had gone on trips to Mauritius and Seychelles, and later by restricting supplies, winding down work on the coconut plantations, and finally coercing the remaining islanders onto crowded ships. By 1973, between 1328 and 1522 Chagos islanders had been relocated to Mauritius, and 232 to Seychelles (Gifford and Dunne, 2014, p. 46).

In 1966 – in anticipation of the depopulation of the Chagos islands – two British diplomats exchanged comments in what has become an infamous piece of correspondence. A diplomatic cable sent on behalf of the Permanent Under-Secretary of the Foreign and Commonwealth Office Paul Gore-Booth articulated that "there will be no indigenous population" on the Chagos islands (Greenhill, 1966). Underneath, the then head of the Colonial Office Dennis Greenhill responded that the Chagos islands were inhabited by "some few Tarzans or Men Fridays whose origins are obscure" (Greenhill, 1966). Such racist depictions of the Chagos islanders chimed with the UK Foreign Office legal advisor Anthony Aust's advice to classify the Chagos islanders as "only a floating population" of "labourers and their families" ("*R (Bancoult) v. Secretary of State for Foreign and Commonwealth Office*", 2000,

DOI: 10.4324/9781003390299-10

para. 18). Nearly two centuries after the Chagos Islands were first settled, Aust advised the UK government "to maintain the fiction that the inhabitants of Chagos are not a permanent or semi-permanent population" ("*R (Bancoult) v. Secretary of State for Foreign and Commonwealth Office*", 2000, para. 18). Suggesting that the inhabitants of the Chagos islands had only limited connections to the Chagos Archipelago set the scene for the longstanding argument that their removal from the Chagos Islands would not constitute dislocation from a homeland. By contrast, a recent Human Rights Watch report argues that

> the Chagossians have been severely deprived of their rights by intentional acts because of their race and ethnicity ... not only in the manner of their expulsion from Chagos, but in the institutional and systematic way that UK authorities continue to treat the Chagossians, as people whose rights, especially the right to return, need not be respected.
>
> (Human Rights Watch, 2023, p. 8)

Concepts such as "ethnic group" and "indigenous people" have a long, complicated, and contested history in anthropology. On the one hand, American anthropologists in the early twentieth century sought to document indigenous kinship systems, clan organisation, oral traditions, and material cultures as part of a concerted effort to valorise and safeguard indigenous cultures at risk of loss due to colonial dispossession, displacement, and massacre. On the other hand, the discipline of anthropology itself was a product of European colonialism, and the "Savage slot" and the preoccupation of "salvage anthropology" with impending "extinction" reproduced colonial ideologies of cultural immutability and assimilation and colonial concerns about racial purity and miscegenation (Trouillot, 2003). Subsequent generations of anthropologists have critiqued the risks of the strategic essentialism necessitated by attempts to homogenise internally diverse putative collectives of people into often racialised categories such as "ethnic group" or "indigenous people". The anthropologist Susan Ellison notes that

> the category [of indigeneity] itself is not inherently liberating; it may be deployed toward violent and exclusionary ends or may become a trap for those who organize around it by pressuring them to narrow their self-presentation to fit public consumption and governmental expectations of premodern primitives.
>
> (Ellison, 2018, p. 2)

As the legal scholar Kinnari Bhatt put it, "we find in the Chagos case first-hand evidence of just how the Indigenous label might be racialised when connected to ethnicity and culture" (Bhatt, 2019, p. 10).

Nevertheless, lawyers commonly solicit anthropological expertise in legal cases in which the establishment that a group of claimants do or do not constitute an "ethnic group" or an "indigenous people" may have material consequences (Clifford, 1988). Thus anthropologists may find themselves wrestling with tensions between scholarly critique and political necessity in "post"-colonial contexts. Indeed, this chapter draws on an expert report I prepared for Leigh Day on behalf of their client Solange Hoareau, one of the two Chagossian claimants in *R (Hoareau and Bancoult) v Secretary of State for Foreign and Commonwealth Affairs*" (2020), in which I was instructed to set out facts and matters which are relevant to whether the Chagossians meet the definition of an ethnic group set out on pages 561–564 in the judgment of Lord Fraser in "Mandla (Sewa Singh) v Dowell Lee" (1982). In that case, the legal team representing the UK Secretary of State of Foreign and Commonwealth Affairs questioned whether the Chagossians constitute an ethnic group, although the judgment notes that, following some debate, "For the purpose of the present proceedings only, it is conceded on behalf of the Defendant that Chagossians form an ethnic group within the meaning of the Equality Act" ("*R (Hoareau and Bancoult) v Secretary of State for Foreign and Commonwealth Affairs*", 2020, para. 152). Alert to anthropological critiques of the risks of strategic essentialism, this chapter traces how the concepts of ethnicity and indigeneity are produced, deployed, and contested, and it concludes with a consideration of the potential political, legal, and economic implications for Chagossians of recognition as an "ethnic group" and/or an "indigenous people".

Ethnicity

For precedence on ethnicity and racial discrimination, the English law courts frequently cite the "*Mandla (Sewa Singh) v Dowell Lee*" (1982) judgment in which Lord Fraser found that Sikhs are an ethnic group under the provisions of the Race Relations Act 1976. Lord Fraser's judgment provides a widely cited guidance that

> For a group to constitute an ethnic group in the sense of the Act of 1976, it must, in my opinion, regard itself and be regarded by others, as a distinct community by virtue of certain characteristics. Some of these characteristics are essential; others are not essential, but one or more of them will commonly be found and will help to distinguish the group from the surrounding community.

Fraser identifies "essential" characteristics as: first "a long-shared history of which the group is conscious as distinguishing it from other groups, and the memory of which it keeps alive", and second "a cultural tradition of its own, including family and social customs and manners, often but not necessarily associated with religious observance". Fraser lists "commonly" found characteristics as: third, "either a common geographical origin, or descent from a small number of common ancestors"; fourth "a common language, not necessarily peculiar to the group"; fifth, "a common literature peculiar to the group"; sixth "a common religion different from that of neighbouring groups or from the general community surrounding it; and seventh "being a minority or being an oppressed or a dominant group within a larger community, for example a conquered people".

This implies that Fraser considered it possible actually to *become* an "ethnic group" in part through processes such as being conquered and oppressed, and by extension potentially through processes such as forced displacement and dispossession. Fraser concluded that "the word 'ethnic' in the 1976 Act should be construed relatively widely, in ... a broad, cultural/historic sense": in other words,

> a group is identifiable in terms of its ethnic origins if it is a segment of the population distinguished from others by a sufficient combination of shared customs, beliefs, traditions and characteristics derived from a common or presumed common past, even if not drawn from what in biological terms is a common racial stock. It is that combination which gives them an historically determined social identity in their own eyes and in the eyes of those outside the group. They have a distinct social identity based not simply on group cohesion and solidarity but also on their belief as to their historical antecedents.

The following subsections examine the evidence and practices highlighted by Chagossians and their supporters in their attempts to demonstrate how Chagossians meet these "essential" and "commonly" found criteria.

Historical Consciousness

Lord Fraser's first essential characteristic is "a long shared history of which the group is conscious as distinguishing it from other groups, and the memory of which it keeps alive". Colonists developed coconut plantations on several other Outer Islands in the Colony of Mauritius including Seychelles and Agalega islands, but the shared history and aftermath of forced displacement of the Chagos islanders from the Chagos Archipelago distinguishes the Chagossian community from other island groups. This is not merely the commonality of a complaint about past treatment, but rather a shared history of forced displacement with direct and ongoing repercussions: dislocation, impoverishment, and marginalisation. The dispersed Chagossian community in Mauritius, Seychelles, and the UK seeks to keep this shared history alive through oral traditions of autobiographical storytelling and song lyrics in which the shared history is narrativised as follows. Firstly, they reflect on collective experiences of the forced displacement itself (Jeffery, 2011, pp. 64–67). Secondly, they draw direct comparisons between the lifestyle they enjoyed on the Chagos Archipelago and the harsh living conditions that confronted them on arrival in Mauritius and Seychelles (Jeffery, 2011, pp. 67–68). Thirdly, they connect shared experiences of dislocation and marginalisation to an ongoing desire to return to the Chagos Archipelago (Jeffery, 2011, pp. 68–71).

Cultural traditions

Lord Fraser's second essential characteristic is having "a cultural tradition of its own, including family and social customs and manners, often but not necessarily associated with religious observance". *Sega* is a syncretic Indian Ocean musical genre that emerged on the colonial plantations through encounters between enslaved labourers with diverse ancestral origins, who played music, danced, and sang lamentation and protest songs to resist their everyday hardship and domination. The word *sega* likely derives from the Mozambican *tschiéga* and the Madagascan *chéga* (Dussercle, 1937, p. 50). The Mauritian Government has successfully nominated a series of musical genres to the UNESCO Representative List of the Intangible Cultural Heritage of Humanity: traditional Mauritian *sega tipik* was inscribed in 2014 (UNESCO, 2022a), Bhojpuri *geet gawai* folk song was inscribed in 2016 (UNESCO, 2022b), and *sega tambour* from the Outer Island of Rodrigues was inscribed in 2017 (UNESCO, 2022c). Chagossian *sega* music is routinely distinguished from Mauritian and other Indian Ocean *sega* music through reference to differences in costume, dance, instrumentation, and tempo (Jeffery, 2011, pp. 64, 87–88). The Mauritian Government successfully nominated *sega tambour Chagos* to be inscribed on the UNESCO List of World Intangible Cultural Heritage in Need of Urgent Safeguarding in 2019 (UNESCO, 2022d). Thus the Mauritian Government and UNESCO recognised that the Chagossian community has "a cultural tradition of its own" in that Chagossian *sega* music is distinct from the *sega* music of the main island of Mauritius and the Outer Island of Rodrigues.

Common Descent

Lord Fraser's third relevant characteristic is sharing "either a common geographical origin, or descent from a small number of common ancestors". The Chagos Archipelago was unpopulated prior to European colonial expansion in the Indian Ocean from the late eighteenth century onwards, whereupon it was populated in much the same way as the other Mauritius islands: i.e. with enslaved labourers (mostly from East Africa and Madagascar) and later with contract workers (mostly from India). The ancestors of the first Chagos islanders thus had geographical origins in Africa and India; Chagos islanders and their descendants clearly have "a common geographical origin" in the Chagos Archipelago. Kinship has received limited attention in anthropological or historical research on the Chagossian community. However, in the early 2000s, the Chagos Refugees Group solicited demographic information from Chagos islanders and their second-generation descendants as part of a process to register them as prospective claimants in the *Chagos Islanders* compensation case (*"Chagos Islanders v Attorney General and HM BIOT Commissioner*", 2003). The data gathered in these registration forms on Chagos islanders' parents and grandparents strongly suggest that Chagossians do indeed share "descent from a small number of common ancestors".

Common Language

Lord Fraser's fourth relevant characteristic is "a common language, not necessarily peculiar to the group" in the sense that the Chagos islanders both have a common language (Kreol) and developed distinctive vocabulary and pronunciation that distinguishes Chagossian from other Indian Ocean Kreol languages. The Kreol languages of the Indian Ocean derive primarily from French but also incorporate words from other languages. The Kreol languages of Seychelles, Mauritius, Rodrigues, and Chagos share a grammatical structure and are mutually intelligible while each being distinctive in terms of specific vocabularies and differences in pronunciation (Walker, 1986, p. 16). Reflecting the "omnipresence of the coconut" in Chagossian material culture, the anthropologist Iain Walker noted that

> One distinctive feature of the Ilois Kreol is the extensive vocabulary pertaining to the coconut palm and the copra industry, reflecting the importance of the coconut to the islanders in daily life: classification of the various parts of the coconut palm was extensive and specific, the subtleties of which would be lost on a Mauritian.
>
> (Walker, 1986, p. 11)

Such distinctiveness is reflected in the second edition of the eminent Mauritian linguist Arnaud Carpooran's *Diksioner Morisien* (Mauritian dictionary), published in 2011, which contains *Enn esantiyon vokabiler spesifikman sagosien* (A sample of specifically Chagossian vocabulary) (Carpooran, 2011, pp. 1123–1126). The Chagossian section of the Mauritian Dictionary evinces that the Chagos islanders had developed distinctive vocabulary relating to social and environmental aspects of the Chagos Archipelago including: employment in the coconut industry such as plantation work (*labati*) and dehusking work (*pliser*); coconut tools such as spike (*pike*), mallet (*mayos*), and deshelling knife (*kouto-dekoke*); coconut handicrafts such as coconut leaf basket (*kapas*) and coconut broom (*zig*); marine and terrestrial flora and fauna such as coconut crab (*sipay*) and germinating coconut (*zerm-koko*); cuisine such as brews (*baka*, *kalou*, and *rannmafann*), stews (*seraz* and *kangay*), and coconut cakes (*matouftwa* and *mouf*); spiritual beliefs outwith Roman Catholicism such as the funerary rite (*aniwawa*) and supernatural children (*zanfan bengne*); and the stringed musical instrument (*zez*). The Chagossian section of the Mauritian dictionary also evinces some differences in pronunciation such as *douri* instead of *diri* (from the French *du riz*, rice) and *tann* instead of *tantinn* (from the French *tante*, aunt).

Common Orature

Lord Fraser's fifth relevant characteristic is "a common literature peculiar to the group". Chagos islanders were already marginalised in relation to access to education in Chagos Archipelago (Botte, 1980, p. 29), a situation that has persisted in Mauritius and Seychelles due to structural disadvantages such as the concentration of Chagossians in neighbourhoods far from good schools and the challenges for impoverished families of accessing even "free" schooling (Dræbel, 1997, chap. 2). A very small proportion of the extended Chagossian community has attended further or higher education in Mauritius or Seychelles. Since 2002, when the British Overseas Territories Act granted UK citizenship to Chagos islanders and most of their second-generation descendants, many Chagossians have migrated onwards to the UK in search of better education and employment prospects, as reflected in Sylvia Gundowry's research with young people of Chagossian origin attending secondary school, college, or university in the UK (Gundowry, 2018). Increased engagement in formal education is a gradual process, and as such, it is not surprising that Chagossians have not developed their own written literature.

In this context, a postcolonial, anthropological critique of the colonialist, ethnocentric valorisation of written literature demands consideration instead of the prevalence or otherwise of oral traditions (or "orature"). Chagossians have strong and distinctive oral traditions in the forms of performance storytelling and song lyrics, both of which tend to be characterised by autobiographical accounts, comedic double entendre, and collective historical consciousness. The main themes running through recordings of *sega* songs that were originally composed on Chagos include: colonial violence, work and separation from loved ones, sexual exploitation and sexual politics, religious practices, and self-referential reflections on the joys of *sega* itself. Chagossian *sega* songs composed outwith Chagos, meanwhile, add themes such as: recollections of the displacement, experiences of ongoing dislocation from the homeland, and calls for community mobilisation for the right of return (Jeffery, 2011). Through these song lyrics, Chagos islanders have articulated local histories of enslavement in the eighteenth and nineteenth centuries alongside an attempt to keep alive their memories of (ongoing) colonial occupation and the forced displacement, which is by now only just still within living memory.

Distinctive Religion

Lord Fraser's sixth relevant characteristic is having "a common religion different from that of neighbouring groups or from the general community surrounding it". Although its inhabitants were nominally Roman Catholic, the colonial administrators did not prioritise religious adherence: the Chagos Archipelago did not have a resident priest; an itinerant priest visited annually to perform important ceremonies such as baptisms, christenings, and weddings (Dussercle, 1934, p. 10). In the absence of a resident priest, Chagos islanders developed a matrifocal system characterised by female-headed households and a relative instability of sexual relationships, akin to the matrifocal system amongst Creoles in Seychelles (Benedict and Benedict, 1982). Matrifocality amongst Chagossians persisted to a considerable degree in Seychelles and Mauritius alike (Botte, 1980, pp. 60–61). In between the Roman Catholic priest's annual visits, administrators conducted weekly services (Descroizilles and Mülnier, 1999, p. 26). In common with other colonial plantation societies, however, Christianity coexisted with other spiritual beliefs and practices on the Chagos Archipelago, resulting in a distinctive syncretic belief system. Not surprisingly, given the need to deal with the dead in the absence of Catholic priests, these rituals concentrate around death (Walker, 1986, p. 16). The Chagossian funerary rite *aniwawa*, thought to be of African or Malagasy origin, aims to release the *nam* (the spirit of the deceased person, from the French *l'âme*, spirit) from the earthly world and into the spirit world in order to avoid becoming a *jab* (a spirit who remains stuck in purgatory, from the French *diable*, devil) (Botte, 1980, pp. 12–14). The anthropologist Steffen Johannessen recorded that these funerary rites were still being performed in Mauritius in 2006 (Johannessen 2011, pp. 208–215).

Oppressed Minority

Lord Fraser's seventh relevant characteristic is "being a minority or being an oppressed … group within a larger community". In his ethnographic monograph on ethnicity in Mauritius, the anthropologist Thomas Hylland Eriksen devised an ethnic taxonomy drawing on ethnic classification schemes outlined to him by Mauritians (Eriksen, 1998, p. 51). He divided Mauritians into Hindu (the majority), Muslim, Sino-Mauritian, and the (predominantly Catholic) so-called General Population, which he subdivided into Franco-Mauritian and Creole. Creole is further subdivided into Coloured and Other, which is further subdivided into *Kreol*, Rodriguais, *Ilois*, and Mixed. Thus, in Mauritius the *Ilois* (i.e. Chagossians) tend to be categorised as a minority group within the larger Creole community, which is itself a minority group within wider Mauritian society. Mauritius and Seychelles are both characterised by the socio-economic marginalisation of Black "Afro-Creoles" in general and of Chagossians in particular.

Social scientists, government officials, and journalists have documented how the already marginal Chagos islanders were further impoverished by their forced displacement, suffering an array of economic, social, cultural, physical, and psychological harms. Displaced islanders lost their land, houses, and other property; their jobs; their access to shared resources such as fish and seafood, coconut palms and other edible plants, and animals; and their access to common property such as the sea, beaches, and ancestral graveyards. Social networks, village ties, and cultural practices of sharing and socialising were ruptured through the dispersal of the community in Mauritius and Seychelles. Islanders' mental and physical health suffered from the stressful and traumatic experiences of displacement, relocation, and dislocation from a society where they and their ancestors had lived and worked for several generations.

When the Chagos islanders disembarked in Mauritius or Seychelles, they lacked contacts, education, training, and experience relevant to the local job markets. Particularly in the decades immediately following their arrival in Mauritius and Seychelles, Chagos islanders were oppressed by ethnic discrimination which was manifest in myriad ways including being called derogatory names reflecting assumptions that they were uneducated, uncivilised, lazy: *Ilwa* or *Ilois* (islander, from the French *îlot*) in Mauritius (Carpooran, 2011, p. 421) and *Anara* [a word whose provenance and precise meaning are unclear] in Seychelles (Gillieaux, 2017, p. 47). Together these factors negatively impacted their ability to find adequate housing and jobs in Mauritius (see Jeffery and Vine, 2011) and in Seychelles (see Vine, 2011). Chagossian families have consequently suffered disproportionately from the concomitants of unemployment, underemployment, and poor housing in disadvantaged neighbourhoods: low levels of educational achievement and high rates of poverty, physical and psychological ill-health, teenage and unplanned pregnancy, alcohol and drug addiction, prostitution, gambling, and crime.

Such traumatic experiences may have led directly to disproportionately high rates of suicide, miscarriage, and deaths attributable to poverty and exposure to and susceptibility to diseases that were not common in Chagos (such as influenza and diphtheria). According to John Madeley's Minority Rights Group report (Madeley, 1982, pp. 5–6), there was a significant number of deaths within a year of arrival in Mauritius, including suicide and extreme poverty, and by 1975 "at least 1 in 40 had died of starvation and disease". A Comité Ilois Organisation Fraternelle survey concluded that "The causes mostly are unhappiness, non-adaption of Ilois within the social framework of Mauritius, extreme poverty, particularly lack of food, house, jobs" (quoted in Madeley, 1982, p. 6) Chagos islanders' repeated descriptions of their lives in terms of *sagrin, tristes*, and *mizer* – sorrow, sadness, and impoverishment – thus capture their material, social, and psychological suffering as a result of their forced displacement and dislocation (Jeffery and Vine, 2011). Members of the Chagossian community commonly self-identify as an uprooted people [*enn lepep derasine*] living in exile [*exil*] from its natal homeland [*later natal*].

Indigeneity

Successive Mauritian and UK governments have relied on a restricted definition of indigeneity to claim that the Chagos islanders are not indigenous to the Chagos Archipelago. In recent years, representatives of both governments have continued to argue that the Chagossians are not an indigenous people because human population on the Chagos Archipelago was only because of colonial settlement there, and the Chagos islanders therefore lack continuity with any pre-colonial settlement, which both governments assume to be a prerequisite for recognition as an indigenous people. This argument was evident in the material prepared on behalf of the UK government in "*R (Hoareau and Bancoult) v Secretary of State for Foreign and Commonwealth Affairs*" (2020). More recently, in July 2023, a representative of the Mauritius permanent mission to the UN asserted at a meeting of the UN Human Rights Council on the Rights of Indigenous Peoples that

> there has never been an indigenous population on the entire Mauritian territory, which includes the Chagos Archipelago. Mauritius is a multiracial and multicultural country populated by people whose ancestors came from Africa, Asia, and Europe, and where all the people enjoy the same right.
>
> (UN Web TV, 2023)

The UN Working Group on Indigenous Populations, established in 1982, did indeed initially conceive of indigenous populations as those "having a historical continuity with pre-invasion and pre-colonial societies that developed on their territories" (APF and OHCHR, 2013). This definition excluded many parts of the world, including the south-western Indian Ocean, where there were no precolonial populations and where colonists populated the islands initially with enslaved labourers from Africa and later with indentured labourers from Asia (Bhatt, 2019).

However, over the subsequent decades, the UN Working Group on Indigenous Populations developed a more inclusive and nuanced understanding of the factors relevant to the establishment of indigeneity. By the time of the UN Declaration on the Rights of Indigenous Peoples in 2007 (OHCHR, 2007), the UN Working Group sought not to provide a "comprehensive" or "precise" definition but rather to "ensure that there is a room for the reasonable evolution and regional specificity of the concept of 'indigenous' in practice" (APF and OHCHR, 2013). It listed the following factors as relevant to understanding the concept of indigeneity: first, "Priority in time, with respect to the occupation and use of a specific territory"; second, "The voluntary perpetuation of cultural distinctiveness, which may include the aspects of language, social organization, religion and spiritual values, modes of production, laws and institutions"; third, "Self-identification, as well as recognition by other groups, or by State authorities, as a distinct collectivity"; and fourth, "An experience of subjugation, marginalization, dispossession, exclusion or discrimination, whether or not these conditions persist". This contingent and relational concept of indigeneity includes those who have the earliest claim to a territory, whether or not this predated colonial settlement, and incorporates cultural distinctiveness, self-identification as a group, identification by others as a group, and experience of discrimination (Allen, 2007). The previous section of this chapter already discussed cultural distinctiveness, self-identification, and marginalisation with regard to ethnicity; this section therefore focuses on priority in time and on recognition by others.

In Mauritius, the Ilois Trust Fund Act 1982 evinces that the *Ilois* (islander) community was an identifiable entity by the early 1980s; identity cards issued on or prior to 14 May 1984 identified the holder as *Ilois*, and "the Ilois community" was allocated "Ilois Community Centres" and "other community facilities". However, the collective noun *Ilois* is imprecise – potentially signifying islanders from any small island – and was already racialised and pejorative by the 1980s (Walker, 1986, p. 16). During the 1990s, the Chagossian Social Committee popularised the more collective noun Chagossian, which signified a connection to the specific territory of the Chagos Archipelago (Jeffery, 2011, pp. 78–80). The Chagossian Social Committee leader Fernand Mandarin also attended the 1997 meeting of the UN Working Group on Indigenous Peoples (Jeffery, 2011, pp. 51–52). In the Ilois Welfare Fund (Amendment) Bill 2011, the Mauritian government noted that:

> The object of this Bill is to amend the Ilois Welfare Fund Act by deleting the word "Ilois", wherever it appears, and replacing it by the word "Chagossian" to make more precise reference to the place of origin of the Chagossian community.

"Self-identification, as well as recognition by other groups … as a distinct collectivity" was evident at an international conference in 2022, in which the Pretoria/Tshwane Declaration on the Chagos Question agreed by participants – including representatives of Chagossian groups based in Mauritius, Seychelles, and the UK alongside scholars from South Africa and beyond – opened by "Noting that the Chagossians are an Indigenous People of the Chagos Islands as per the definition of the United Nations Declaration on Indigenous People 2007".

In line with the updated and more inclusive understanding of indigeneity, several judges in the English courts have described the Chagossians as an indigenous people. Even before the UN Declaration on the Rights of Indigenous Peoples (in 2007), Lord Justice Laws had concluded (in 2000) that the Chagos islanders "were an indigenous people: they were born there, as were one or both of their parents, in many cases one or more of their grandparents, in some cases (it is said) one or more of their great-grandparents" ("*R v Secretary of State for Foreign and Commonwealth Office, ex p Bancoult*", 2000, para. 1). In a minority opinion written in 2008, Lord Bingham of Cornhill and Lord Mance questioned whether the royal prerogative could legitimately be "exercised to exile an indigenous population from its homeland" in a colonial territory ("*R v Secretary of State for Foreign and Commonwealth Affairs, ex p Bancoult*", 2008, para. 70).

Recognition of indigeneity would imply the potential for application of indigenous-specific rights under international law. Indeed, in the ongoing "*Dispute Concerning Delimitation of the Maritime Boundary Between Mauritius and Maldives in the Indian Ocean*", an *Amicus Curiae* submitted to a Special Chamber of the International Tribunal for the Law of the Sea on behalf of the Chagossian Committee Seychelles argues that as an indigenous people, the Chagossians have indigenous-specific rights under international law (Trinidad, Allen, and Burri, 2022, para. 25). In particular, the *Amicus Curiae* notes that indigenous people have the right to self-determination in the form of consultation and participation in decision-making processes that concern them; the right to use, manage, and conserve natural resources (terrestrial and marine alike); the right to share in any economic and other benefits resulting from natural resource exploitation (terrestrial and marine alike); and the right to redress, including restitution when they have lost access against their will to those lands, territories, and resources that they had traditionally used (Trinidad, Allen, and Burri, 2022, paras 26–29). In 2022, the Pretoria/Tshwane Declaration on the Chagos Question similarly declared that "Chagossians have a fundamental human right to return to the Chagos Archipelago to visit or resettle there as they desire" and that "Chagossians have an inalienable right to self-determination". And in 2023, the UK-based Chagossian Voices sent delegations to the UN Permanent Forum on Indigenous Issues and to a meeting of the UN Human Rights Council on the Rights of Indigenous Peoples, where they noted that "Chagossians and other indigenous groups have been excluded from negotiations between nation-states about the sovereignty of their indigenous territories" and called for "mechanisms embedded in all the decision-making processes which safeguard indigenous rights" (UN Web TV, 2023).

Conclusion

Alert to anthropological critiques of the risks of strategic essentialism, this chapter has traced how concepts such as ethnicity and indigeneity are produced, deployed, and contested. First, in relation to ethnicity, this chapter has illustrated arguments made by and on behalf of the Chagossian community that the Chagossians meet the criteria for recognition as an ethnic group because they share historical consciousness, cultural traditions, common descent, common language, common orature, and distinctive religion, and they are an oppressed minority within a larger community. Second, in relation to indigeneity, this chapter notes that successive Mauritian and UK governments continue to rely on an outdated and restricted definition of indigeneity that has been superseded by the UN Working Group on Indigenous People's more contingent and relational understanding. The Chagossians and their supporters would argue that the Chagossians clearly have the earliest claim to a territory and meet the other criteria of cultural distinctiveness, self-identification as a group, identification by others as a group, and experience of discrimination. Indeed, several judges in the English courts had already accepted the Chagossians as an indigenous people.

This chapter has also unpacked the potential political, legal, and economic implications of establishing ethnicity and indigeneity. Human Rights Watch concluded recently that the "colonial rule was built on systematic racism and ethnic and racial discrimination in the treatment of the Chagossians" (Human Rights Watch, 2023, p. 2) and that the "forced displacement of the Chagossians and ongoing abuses amount to crimes against humanity committed by a colonial power against an Indigenous people" (Human Rights Watch, 2023, p.2). The Human Rights Watch report calls on the UK government to hold "a full and independent public inquiry into the crimes and violations committed against the Chagossians, and in particular the specific acts of racism shown by officials at the highest levels of the UK government" (Human Rights Watch, 2023, p. 99) and on the UN to establish "an international inquiry to investigate systematic discrimination and repression based on race, ethnicity, or national origin, including the group identity of the Chagossians" (Human Rights Watch, 2023, p. 102). Recognition as indigenous people should imply that they hold rights – under international law – to self-determination, natural resource management, economic benefits, and redress including restitution.

Despite relatively successfully jumping through these political and legal hoops, however, to a large extent the difference it makes is limited by their lack of application in practice: "rights" matter in the abstract, but even when legal judgments have been in favour of the Chagossian cause, Chagossians have not necessarily benefited. For instance, in relation to sovereignty (and, by extension, self-determination), Mauritius (and the UK) can choose to consult Chagossians (and other stakeholders), but only representatives of the two states can participate in the bilateral negotiations. Thus there is a tension in the global political order: non-state actors can assert ethnic and indigenous identity, and can substantiate claims to having been subjected to systematic racism and ethnic discrimination, but cannot actually access the attendant human and indigenous rights if and when doing so would undermine state claims. Regardless of the success or otherwise of attempts to establish politically or in law that the Chagossians are an "ethnic group" or an "indigenous people" who have been subjected to systematic racism and ethnic discrimination, the potential political, legal, and economic implications are limited in practice when power imbalances remain unaddressed, attendant rights remain unacknowledged, and material needs remain unmet.

Acknowledgements

I am grateful for insightful comments from Rebecca Rotter and Mairi O'Gorman.

References

Allen, S. (2007) *The Chagos Islanders and International Law*. Oxford: Hart.

APF and OHCHR (2013) 'The United Nations declaration on the rights of indigenous peoples: A manual for national human rights institutions'. Available at: https://www.ohchr.org/sites/default/files/Documents/Issues/IPeoples/UNDRIPManualForNHRIs.pdf

Benedict, B. and Benedict, M. (1982) *Men, Women, and Money in Seychelles*. London: University of California Press.

Bhatt, K. (2019) 'A post-colonial legal approach to the Chagos case and the (dis) application of land rights norms'. *International Journal of Law in Context*, 15(1), pp. 1–19.

Botte, F. (1980) 'The "Ilois" community and the "Ilois" women'. Unpublished thesis. University of Mauritius.

Carpooran, A. (2011) *Diksioner Morisien: Premie diksioner kreol monoleng. Deziem edision*. Mauritius: Éditions Le Printemps.

Chagos Islanders v Attorney General and HM BIOT Commissioner (2003) [2003] EWHC 2222 (QB). *BAILII*. Available at: http://www.bailii.org/ew/cases/EWHC/QB/2003/2222.html (Accessed: 1 September 2023).

Clifford, J. (1988) *The Predicament of Culture: Twentieth-century Ethnography, Literature, and Art*. Cambridge: Harvard University Press.

Descroizilles, M. and Mülnier, A. (1999) *Bor'endan bor'déhor*. Mauritius: Éditions de l'Océan Indien.

Dræbel, T. (1997) *Evaluation des besoins sociaux de la communauté déplacée de l'Archipel de Chagos. Volet Un: Santé et Education*. Mauritius: Ministry of Social Security and National Solidarity.

Dussercle, R. (1934) *Archipel de Chagos en mission 10 Novembre 1933 – 11 Janvier 1934*. Mauritius: The General Printing & Stationery Cy. Ltd.

Dussercle, R. (1937) *Dans les "Ziles là-Haut"*. Mauritius: The General Printing & Stationery Cy. Ltd.

Ellison, S. (2018) 'Indigeneity in anthropology'. In H. Callan and S. Coleman (eds.), *The International Encyclopedia of Anthropology*. Hoboken: Wiley.

Eriksen, T.H. (1998) *Common Denominators: Ethnicity, Nation-Building and Compromise in Mauritius*. Oxford: Berg.

Gifford, R. and Dunne, R.P. (2014) 'A dispossessed people: The depopulation of the Chagos Archipelago 1965–1973'. *Population, Space and Place*, 20(1), pp. 37–49.

Gillieaux, C. (2017) *Diksyonner Trileng: Kreol Seselwa, Francais, English. Liv 1: A-L*. Seychelles: Pangaea.

Greenhill, D.A. (1966) 'File: Diplomatic cable signed by D.A. Greenhill, dated August 24, 1966.jpg'. Available at: https://commons.wikimedia.org/wiki/File:Diplomatic_Cable_signed_by_D.A._Greenhill,_dated_August_24,_1966.jpg

Gundowry, M.S. (2018) *Acculturation of Young Mauritian People of Chagossian Origin in the UK: Negotiating Living in the Host Society*. University of Brighton.

Human Rights Watch (2023) '"That's when the nightmare started": UK and US forced displacement of the chagossians and ongoing colonial crimes'. Available at: https://www.hrw.org/sites/default/files/media_2023/04/chagos0223web.pdf

Jeffery, L. (2011) *Chagos Islanders in Mauritius and the UK: Forced Displacement and Onward Migration*. Manchester: Manchester University Press.

Jeffery, L. and Vine, D. (2011) 'Sorrow, sadness, and impoverishment: The lives of Chagossians in Mauritius'. In S. Evers and M. Kooy (eds.), *Eviction from the Chagos Islands: Displacement and Struggle for Identity against two World Powers*. Leiden: Brill, pp. 83–102.

Johannessen, S. (2011) 'Cleaning for the dead: The chagossian pilgrimage to their homeland'. In S. Evers and M. Kooy (eds.), *Eviction from the Chagos Islands: Displacement and Struggle for Identity against two World Powers*. Leiden: Brill, pp. 183–215.

Madeley, J. (1982) *Diego Garcia: A Contrast to the Falklands*. Minority Rights Group, 54. London: Minority Rights Group.

Mandla (Sewa Singh) v Dowell Lee (1982) 'UKHL, case 7'. *BAILI*. Available at: https://www.bailii.org/uk/cases/UKHL/1982/7.html (Accessed: 8 September 2023).

OHCHR (2007) 'UN declaration on the rights of indigenous peoples'. Available at: https://www.ohchr.org/sites/default/files/Documents/Publications/Declaration_indigenous_en.pdf

R (Bancoult) v. Secretary of State for Foreign and Commonwealth Office (No 1) (2000) [2000] EWHC 413 (Admin). *BAILII*. Available at: http://www.bailii.org/ew/cases/EWHC/Admin/2000/413.html (Accessed: 8 September 2023).

R (Bancoult) v. Secretary of State For Foreign and Commonwealth Affairs (No 2) (2008) [2008] UKHL 61. *BAILII*. Available at: https://www.bailii.org/cgi-bin/format.cgi?doc=/uk/cases/UKHL/2008/61.html (Accessed: 8 September 2023).

R (Hoareau and Bancoult) v Secretary of State for Foreign and Commonwealth Affairs (2020) [2020] EWCA Civ 1010. *BAILII*. Available at: http://www.bailii.org/ew/cases/EWCA/Civ/2020/1010.html (Accessed: 8 September 2023).

Trinidad, J., Allen, S. and Burri, T. (2022) *Amicus Curiae Submissions by the Chagossian Committee Seychelles in the Dispute concerning Delimitation of the Maritime Boundary between Mauritius and Maldives,* 18 February 2022. Available at: https://ssrn.com/abstract=4038071 or http://dx.doi.org/10.2139/ssrn.4038071

Trouillot, M. (2003) *Global Transformations: Anthropology and the Modern World*. New York: Palgrave Macmillan.

UNESCO (2022a) 'UNESCO - Bhojpuri folk songs in Mauritius, Geet-Gawai'. Available at: https://ich.unesco.org/en/RL/bhojpuri-folk-songs-in-mauritius-geet-gawai-01178 (Accessed: 8 September 2023).

UNESCO (2022b) 'UNESCO - Sega tambour Chagos'. Available at: https://ich.unesco.org/en/USL/sega-tambour-chagos-01490 (Accessed: 8 September 2023).

UNESCO (2022c) 'UNESCO - Sega tambour of rodrigues Island'. Available at: https://ich.unesco.org/en/RL/sega-tambour-of-rodrigues-island-01257 (Accessed: 8 September 2023).

UNESCO (2022d) 'UNESCO - Traditional Mauritian Sega'. Available at: https://ich.unesco.org/en/RL/traditional-mauritian-sega-01003 (Accessed: 8 September 2023).

UN Web TV (2023) 8th *Meeting, 16*th *Session of Expert Mechanism on the Rights of Indigenous Peoples*. Geneva: United Nations Human Rights Council. Available at: https://media.un.org/en/asset/k1m/k1mnlypgyo (Accessed: 8 September 2023).

Vine, D. (2011) 'Chagossians twice forgotten: Exile in the Seychelles'. In S. Evers and M. Kooy (eds.), *Eviction from the Chagos Islands: Displacement and Struggle for Identity against two World Powers*. Leiden: Brill, pp. 105–124.

Walker, I. (1986) *Zaffer Pe Sanze: Ethnic Identity and Social Change among the Ilois in Mauritius*. Mauritius: KMLI.

Wenban-Smith, N. and Carter, M. (2016) *Chagos: A History. Exploration, Exploitation, Expulsion*. Sandy: Chagos Conservation Trust.

8 Intergenerational Challenges, Cultural Identity, and Future Prospects for Chagossian Communities in the UK

Thierry Mandarin

Introduction

The starting point of this research was an awareness that the Chagossian community in the UK have experienced emotions of displacement, cultural loss, and overall desynchronisation of identity, especially with previous findings that they do not see themselves as "fully British" (Jeffery, 2011, p. 34). This chapter explores three central themes, which are all interlinked; environments and challenges; roots and growth, and lastly, an insight into future prospects for the Chagossian community.

The community overall has faced a number of challenges, in different environments, time periods, and geographies over the past 60–70 years. Perspective or philosophy obtained from parents and grandparents towards tradition, heritage, and cultural identity is one of contemporary hardship, but historic beauty. In other words, prior generations that lived on the islands lived peacefully on paradise, but their children and grandchildren in Mauritius and the UK have to live in poverty, displacement, and marginalisation – an intergenerational image which is painted clearly of *how happy we were back then, but look what's around us now.* Prior research and findings support this hypothesis and have been thoroughly carried out on migration, identity, displacement, and children living in Crawley, UK (Jeffery, 2010a, 2010b, 2011; Gundowry, 2018); however, no study exists that attempts to show if or whether the following generations of Chagossians have transformed this cultural trauma – collective and individual – into growth, independence, education, and employment opportunity. Lastly, insight into the impact of the Nationality and Borders Act of 2022 will also be explored as it has now opened the possibility for a lost generation of Chagossians citizenship in the UK.

The findings in this chapter draw on material gathered from ethnographic interviews with Chagossian research participants in Wythenshawe, Manchester in July 2022. Manchester was chosen as a field site for two reasons: it had previously been unexplored by academics in this space, and it allowed me, as a Crawley-based Chagossian researcher, to move away from "home territory" to explore the unknown (one of the best things about anthropology!). My positionality was clearly significant in this case; whilst I have rarely been involved with Chagossian culture and politics, I was open to adapting the epistemologies of seeing challenges in an alternative light, which was dormant. The use of ethnography was more naturalistic and fitting – "building, expressing and tracking the subjective meaning from the

DOI: 10.4324/9781003390299-11

researcher involved that befits the intertwined complexity of the topic" (Reeves, 2010, p. 315). At the same time, the "personal" nature of ethnographic findings for an insider-researcher could potentially be a draining activity fraught with ethical, emotional, and macro-political challenges which may force some findings harder to replicate for other researchers (Chavez, 2008, p. 478; Reeves, 2010; Webb, 2021). In contrast to the way ethnography was deployed at its inception – studying the "other" from an objective perspective – this methodology, findings, and chapter offer a classified insight into identity, thoughts on sensitive topics, and perception of the future. Ethnography and insider-positionality then, when dealt with honesty, respectfulness, courage, and reflexibility, impact the researcher's "ability to pro-activity reflect, analyse and self-critically vocalise" reflections (MacFarlane, 2008, p. 125).

Considering my own positionality, working on a project associated with cultural trauma, it was important for me to approach potential participants ethically and transparently (Wellington *et al.*, 2005). I drew on existing networks, as well as the online Chagossian leaders, to reach out to community groups in Manchester. The leaders of Instagram pages such as "*chagossiansofmanchester*" and "British Indian Ocean Territory Citizens Group" on Facebook, as well as existing acquaintances, were approached as "mediators" (Kristensen and Ravn, 2015) with knowledge of a large population of potential participants in Manchester (Wejnert and Heckathorn, 2008). Interviews were carried out in a mixture of Kreol and English.

In summary, this chapter attempts to comprehend if or whether generations of Chagossians have transformed cultural and individual trauma into growth, independence, education, and free thought.

Environment and Challenges

Figure 8.1 illustrates how the historical and contemporary intergenerational challenges in the Chagossian community can be grouped as follows: collective cultural trauma; identity and belonging; generational consciousness. Although they are all linked, elements like conflict and leadership in the wider Chagossian community or the access to resources found in Manchester are new concepts still unexplored in academic literature.

Reading the chart from top to bottom effectively highlights the relationship between past, present, and future that will be apparent throughout this chapter; but more importantly, how an environment like Manchester has benefited members of the Chagossian community by offering what previous environments could not. This raises several questions: what differentiates Manchester as an environment from Crawley? How do fragmented communities thrive and rebuild after decades of cultural trauma? What does this tell us about the Chagossian community across the UK?

Manchester was chosen as a field site because it served as unexplored territory for myself and researchers previously, but also with inside perspective that many Chagossians/Mauritians migrated from Crawley to Manchester in search of a better

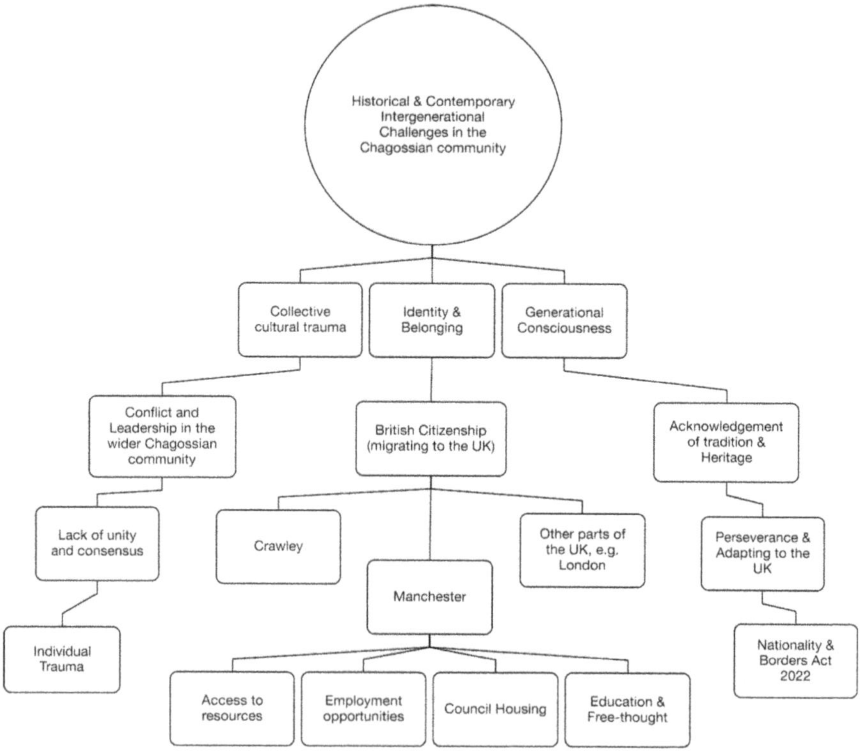

Figure 8.1 Mind Map of Historical and Contemporary Intergenerational Challenges for the Chagossian Community.
Source: Original Creation

quality of life. Crawley, being my hometown, sits 28 miles south of London but 18 miles north of Brighton & Hove; meaning that opportunities have tended to be extremely limited to Gatwick Airport, cleaning roles or generally minimum wage roles, unless one is able to work in London or Brighton. Considering these were the available jobs in the town for individuals with no formal qualifications or recognised skillsets, they were filled quickly. I was directly impacted by having brothers and sisters who arrived in the UK between 18 and 24 years old and had no choice but to start contributing to rent and bills. Engulfed by shame and refusal to return to Mauritius, they associated the UK with work and stress, never realising the rights, advantages, education, and traditions present in the country. Laura Jeffery (2011, p. 34) brilliantly explored some of this and effectively displayed that Chagossians in the UK did not believe they were "fully British". This was explained by one participant in the study:

> ...we have a British passport, but we did not have the opportunities, so we suffered mentally, psychologically, and emotionally as well. I was thinking to myself – "why did I come here for?

In the study, one participant spoke through their experience of moving to the UK in 2003 with two things: a British passport as the key to entering the country, and the thought of a better future. The expectation of access to resources immediately was met with extreme disappointment in Heathrow, London, and Gatwick, London. This left many Chagossians to become dependent on "leaders" in the Chagossian community to speak on their behalf or help them with personal, employment, or financial matters, which was not the rose-tinted vision they had of the UK. Whilst existing research findings fail to address why this generation moved away from Crawley, a participant offered deeper insight into the comparison between Crawley and Mauritius, where everyone knows each other and the negative stereotypes, rumours, and jealousy were attached to the location. Environment, location, and the challenges they provide are key elements for the community. Based on this, Manchester was chosen for work opportunities, difference in lifestyle, and a true "new start" for many.

Employment opportunities in Manchester were rich in the early 2000s and had recently become a point of interest for students around the world to become graduates in a progressing city. For instance, another participant arrived in the UK to study at the school of art, and quickly found that whilst Manchester had wider cultural challenges such as lack of representation, the development of the city pushed for people of all backgrounds to learn and develop skills that were deemed attractive: which brought resources such as council housing, community safety, and incentive for educational development. Whilst Chagossians were more fascinated with getting established in employment and doing right per their grandparents and parents, their children/new generation/participants of recent years have prioritised education and developing their skills. Over time, the mindset and mentality towards the UK, in general, changed towards the acknowledgement of priorities, and what they could or couldn't do.

One participant, who arrived in 2002, expressed that multiple factors stunted their own personal growth and purpose upon arriving in the UK, but also that the differences in environments encouraged ambition, growth, and personal image:

> INTERVIEWER: What overall challenges did you find growing or simply living in the UK?
>
> PARTICIPANT: "I wish I knew my rights more … by not knowing my rights – it made me a bit late that it took me about 5 years to start understanding what I can do and what I can't do".

There are multiple intertwined concepts here concerning environment and challenges – notably education, self-image, and rights. Literature and historical accounts from researchers, social workers, and investigative journalists indicate that the Chagossians were in exceedingly poor living conditions and unemployment in Mauritius. These disadvantages in Mauritian society were topped with cultural racism and discrimination – associated with derogatory terms like laziness. Negative stereotypes and marginalisation were defined concepts placed onto the wider community when they first arrived and continued to live in Mauritius – a sense of consciousness passed down. Being conscious of this, people confided in community leaders and elders and were likely encouraged to apply for manual and mostly nonverbal communication roles such as cleaning and baggage handling when they first arrived in the UK. People did not think independently or utilise their skillsets from Mauritius (such as carpentry), but prioritised providing for those in Mauritius instead – potentially due to a language barrier or self-limitation as a by-product of cultural shock or peer pressure. Another participant realised that there was more than working to provide for those back home and eventually enlisted in the military. They listed Manchester as the key catalyst for thinking differently – free of judgement. Interestingly, their experience in the military later stimulated autonomy, discipline, education, and skills – proving to themselves that they *could* do more than the negative stereotypes they likely dealt with in Mauritius.

According to the participants, Manchester was described as more advantageous than Crawley because of the access to resources and sense of liberation from negative consciousness – it was aligned with growth, progression, and independence. For example, two participants outline that "Manchester is all about progress" because of the opportunities for housing, employment, cheaper food, and resources. This potentially affected or slightly shocked the Chagossian community as they had their own council houses, difference in employment opportunities, and the necessity for learning different skills and qualifications – all elements of what was proposed for British citizens. Hence, whilst Jeffery (2011) identifies that Chagossians did not feel fully British, my analysis and findings emphasise that it depends heavily on the environment, access to resources, and overall acceptance. Wythenshawe, to my realisation, was in poverty and located close to Manchester Airport. Members of the community were grateful for what they had and mentioned a sense of togetherness.

When participants did identify challenges, they were not derived from the environment itself but the mental and psychological limitations that the community placed on themselves – fear of venturing out, and disappointing family members/elders. The mid-generation of Chagossians, aged between 31 and 40 years, felt unable to pursue their wants, but have begun to pass on elements of individuality, responsibility, and pressure for the children to be well-educated, focus on what they want, and help reshape the foundations of what it means to be Chagossians today. Fear can be identified as an effect of generational consciousness and self-image – based on cultural trauma. Ultimately, it reminds the mid-generation of their struggles in Mauritius and their parents' life stories – holding overwhelming responsibility of setting up their life and others around them. This expands upon and moves beyond the literature of cultural trauma; it highlights that Chagossians today have a level of unspoken pressure to illustrate to their community that they are growing in the UK. Many return to Mauritius on short holidays to illustrate wealth and progression. The generational consciousness and cultural trauma were subconscious concepts that threatened their ability to think and view the social world positively but, under the right circumstances and environment in Manchester, were motivated to move beyond.

Roots and Growth

Whilst *Environment and Challenges* answers the question of how generational consciousness was passed down to Chagossian descendants, this section provides insight into whether Chagossians still feel connected to their roots. It is important to acknowledge that the intergenerational challenge (the way Chagossians see themselves today) is the weight of cultural trauma passed down from their predecessors – resulting in mental and psychological limitations being placed on themselves. Two linked recurring themes were "heritage and tradition" along with "collective cultural trauma".

The impact of Chagossian parents was heavily emphasised by participants. This factor, as well as the connection with the wider Chagossian community, offers insight into cultural identity on an individual and collective level. The word "roots" also appeared frequently in responses. The word follows a concept previously explored by Laura Jeffery, known as *déraciné* (uprooting), reflecting how the Chagossians across the islands were forcefully uprooted from the Chagos Archipelago. The use of roots suggests that participants acknowledge where they started from, or where generations before them started – but it is also their duty to keep growing. These roots can be understood as elements of what Chagos was like, both as a culture and as a people. A range of participants emphasised that passing life stories, knowledge, and traditional food or drinks is a way to "grow" these roots. Maintaining and taking care of it every day is minimal but accumulates over the years – building fruits of identity for the future generation of Chagossians. One theme from my ethnographic fieldnotes suggests that UK-born, Mauritian-Chagossian-descendant children speak very good Kreol, and were in touch with Mauritian food, music, and even news. Another participant detected that the fourth generation of Chagossians will start families in the UK – hence, it is the responsibility of parents today to explore roots, as many of the grandparents and parents who provided information for them may have already passed away. Keeping in touch with what makes one Chagossian can be found in the music, food, and language but more importantly – a sense of strong community. Cultural identity here can be seen as a plant: acknowledged and planted from young, and throughout life experiences, stories, and interaction with the wider community – it grows. As one participant phrased it, "Where your belly button cut, this is where you belong". In this analogy, your belly button acts as the seed – stamped from birth and a physical and spiritual gift from your parents and grandparents. Whilst feeling this way about their Chagossian identity, a participant proudly labelled themselves as a "British citizen" as an accomplishment of their parents and grandparents.

The phenomena of passing knowledge and stories through generations is at the core of what keeps the Chagossian community alive, but for the past 20–30 years, there has been a delay in speaking about trauma. Another participant elaborates that mental health and trauma were not heavily discussed when they were children, as they held negative connotations with illness. This means that the mid-generation grew up "craving" an understanding of how to grow spiritually and why more information about the islands was not passed down. Contrastingly, one participant, as a university graduate, elaborated that although tradition must be acknowledged, it must also eventually be re-adapted, re-explored, and grow with the different individual experiences, rather than a collective. This suggests that cultural identity itself can be malleable and distinctive but only if the generational consciousness is recognised. Mental growth and transformation in Manchester, therefore, could potentially be linked with the spiritual growth and acknowledgement of the generational consciousness that the community shares, found in education.

Education, according to several participants, forms a sense of individuality and confidence in recognising knowledge themselves. For example, one of the main reasons why one participant was connected to their Chagossian roots was due to the Black Lives Matter movement in mid-2020 as well as exposure to anti-racist ideologies. They explained that this acted as a form of encouragement towards the exploration of roots and heritage. Here, the acknowledgement of differences, struggles, and history with marginalisation, colonialism, and the contributions to systematic racism allowed them to grasp identity more carefully, especially towards the community. This suggests that the young generation has a broad understanding of the potential challenges to their cultural identity; it is not just cultural loss or trauma but in a broader sense they are also affected by institutional racism.

Comparatively, whilst the older generations understand their cultural trauma as a linear thing, as factors or things happening to them, the younger generation of graduates understand and connect with others who share similar backgrounds, acting in strength in numbers. Education here appears to provide a sense of free thought and choice.

Regarding the narrative of the community from previous literature, Manchester has treated Chagossians with respect, and quick access to resources, such as housing, employment, and education and subsequently, offered an open space for Chagossians to think freely.

Insight into Future Prospects for the Chagossian Community

The future prospects of the Chagossian community are linked to how it is constituted as one among many ethnic communities in Manchester. The politics of the past were characterised by participants as divisive, but participants were hopeful for future unity. The Nationality and Borders Act of 2022 was particularly instrumental in this sense of a shared future.

One key point of discussion about the Manchester community was that there were different established ethnic communities in the area, such as Jamaican, Pakistani, and Bangladeshi, all with their own shops and way of life. One participant contended that the Chagossian identity and community in relation to Britishness did not feel "established" enough – which plays into their perception of identity, potentially as a by-product of the lack of agreement in the community. However different, people of Bangladeshi origin could always revisit the country of their descendants, whereas the Chagossians in this case could not, and are forced to create a concept of community from their grandparents/parents. As perfectly exemplified by Baumann (1996, p. 17), "community and culture are two terms which mutually reinforce one another, which impacts ethnic identity, nature and then eventually culture". If that very community is fragmented from within, it creates multiple concepts of what being "Chagossian" should be. The findings here suggest that the participants of Chagossian descent perceive that not only are they different from other migrants (Jeffery, 2011), but they are also potentially envious of nearby communities who have successfully integrated into British society. The influence of internal Chagossian politics is a significant cause for this divisive mindset/mentality amongst the community today, a previously unexplored topic in academia. One participant underlined their frustrations with the wider community, especially concerning leadership, identity, and dominant ideologies:

> PARTICIPANT: "…I followed Fernand Mandarin, Olivier Bancoult and Allen … and then by the end of the day – the Chagossian politics became very dirty. I just pulled away from it all. They don't come together enough and the opinions of one are always misread by another".

Significantly, one participant has listed three of the major Chagossian leaders over the past 20 years, notably Olivier Bancoult, who has been interviewed and the subject of research by previous anthropologists. The findings above suggest that the politics associated with the community have become muddled as different leaders in the community have all attempted to deal with cultural trauma, identity, and belonging and generational consciousness in their own way, with their own following. Consequently, they segregate, marginalise, and often displace the very community they are attempting to heal after generations. This topic has not previously been made apparent to outsiders looking in, as it could build the image that the Chagossian community is a multi-faceted and fragmented collective who disagree amongst themselves.

Lack of consensus was not found in Manchester but amongst the wider community. It was an apparent thorn in the side of the community, decreasing the strength of communication amongst each member. A participant continued to explore this concept in further detail mentioning there could be up to 11 sub-groups amongst the wider group and that the "dirtiness" is exploited by charismatic leaders, who were educated or could voice their opinion with confidence. This hints at an earlier explored concept of why individuals came to Manchester in the first place – to grasp their future with their own hands.

What does this tell us about the potential factors impacting the growth of the Chagossian community across the UK or even globally? Findings suggest that as the elder generation began to pass away, leaders of the community have effectively fragmented individuals around the globe encompassing "tainted" knowledge and political stances on how to deal with the trauma itself. This could have potentially perpetuated marginalisation itself, and may be why many have struggled to cope with the idea of British citizenship.

Further exploration of this significant topic should be explored in more detail. It could potentially explain the lack of growth, cultural loss, and identity and why the majority of the Chagossian community remains hard to reach today as their opinions will lure other individuals from different stances. Lack of confidence in the community is also linked.

Individuals' perceptions of the future of the community, the attitudes, and the requirements for the community to truly transform beyond collective cultural trauma suggested cause for optimism.

> PARTICIPANT: "...we need to be together as one. We cannot continue to be divided like that. The world is watching us".

One participant gave the most contributions regarding the future of the Chagossian community overall. They suggested that to be taken seriously across the UK, Mauritius, Seychelles, and other countries, they need to unite. I propose that to be taken seriously, Chagossian leaders must push generations of ego aside, pull all different leaders with platforms and viewpoints, and create an open space for democracy and well-educated Chagossians to lead an effective council to represent multiple perspectives.

The majority of the participants expressed that the Nationality and Borders Act of 2022 enforces unification and consensus amongst the Chagossian community. The Nationality and Borders Act of 2022 states that a person may only acquire British Nationality if they can illustrate that they are a direct descendant of a person who was a citizen of the UK and Colonies by virtue of birth. This proves significant for the descendants who have never been a British Dependent Territories citizen. Henceforth, the participants are enforcing the need for lost family members in Mauritius and Seychelles to join their family in the UK. One participant expresses that future citizens "deserve" to be here because of the cruelties and suffering that the community have experienced, because otherwise they would all be equal in the Chagos Archipelago or Mauritius. Manchester, as suggested, has big opportunities waiting if future migrants are willing to work hard and shift their mentality from follower to leader, not of the community – but themselves. To choose what they want, not what others want of them. Conversely, one participant feared the repercussions of the Nationality and Borders Act of 2022 may lead to more suffering than benefits in the UK due to the current political stance of the UK treating migrants, especially the recent controversial Rwanda Policy of 2022.

The overall community perception of the Nationality and Borders Act of 2022 is generally positive as it encompasses seeing the community getting bigger. Throughout the interview, multiple participants attempted to offer advice to the younger generation who are attempting to visit Manchester or the UK for the first time. Participants have also hinted at the idea of a programme to help the Chagossian youth to maintain discipline due to previous poor mentalities shown in this study alone. Chagossians in Manchester have high expectations for the Nationality and Borders Act of 2022 as it may offer more educated individuals to come into the UK to uphold leadership positions in society to represent and acknowledge their struggles for the past 40–50 years. Nonetheless, this suggests that the concept of perseverance is required from all because it was significantly different to the life they led in Mauritius. There are language barriers. There are other challenges faced in the UK. Adapting to the different environments is another repeated advice set by the participant, as many have gone through the rigorous process before in 2002, and they have now established their experiences. Becoming a British citizen, in this fashion, is a lived experience-, but the goal here is to maintain one's core belief in bettering oneself and those around one.

Conclusion

In summary, this chapter sought to question the contemporary challenges of Chagossians in Manchester, to shift the dominant paradigm away from cultural trauma toward growth and transformation.

The history of the Chagossians, being uprooted from their home in the Chagos Archipelago, and the displacement to Mauritius where they suffered for more than 50 years, have been the subject of a discrete body of literature. This chapter makes a further intervention: suggesting that this history has given rise to intergenerational challenges that still impact Chagossian descendants today – collective cultural trauma, identity and belonging, and generational consciousness. All my interlocutors carried these three challenges in their daily lives. The goal, therefore, was to acknowledge, recognise, and make connections between history and lineage; contemporary challenges faced in Manchester and their perceptions of the future. To obtain such detailed and intertwined answers surrounding their experiences and stimuli – I adopted a miner ethnographic, interpretive, and qualitative approach with semi-structured interviews. Aims, objectives, and methodology were determined and justified by previous anthropologists such as Laura Jeffery, and the real contribution was my ability to discourse ongoing challenges from an insider-positionality perspective. This led to sensitive research questions, access, and even sampling capabilities. Discourse analysis was favoured for my subjective and objective relationship with the study, providing socio-cultural contexts and meaning beyond the text.

The chapter focussed on three topics which included the intergenerational challenges listed: the environment of Manchester and its challenges; legacies left behind by Chagossian parents and grandparents plus the connection with Chagossian tradition and roots; and the future of the Chagossian community. While there were methodological constraints to my fieldwork, which was part of a small-scale research project, the findings represent a shift in emphasis and focus towards a more future-oriented perspective of the community.

In 2002, some Chagossians (first and second generations) were granted British citizenship to live and work in the UK. However, when they all arrived, most found that Crawley was like Mauritius as negative stereotypes, rumours of how well they were doing, and jealousy were still amongst the community. Effectively, it was an existing Mauritius community in Crawley, behaving like back home. Consequently, Manchester was chosen for work opportunities but a fresh start for many. The Manchester community – although in poverty in Wythenshawe, has survived physically but continues to thrive mentally due to overall access to resources, respect, and acknowledgement of lineage.

The environment in Manchester had no formal challenges per se. It was described as more advantageous by participants, notably quicker access to resources that later aligned with growth, progression, and independence. Whilst individuals were more focused on employment in the early 2000s, university participants have prioritised education due to responsibility, encouragement, and pressure from parents. Over time, it was identified that the challenges holding the Chagossians back from growth and transformation were individuality, discipline, and the ability to think for oneself. Findings show that the environment itself pushed towards growth but mental and psychological limitations the older Chagossian generations placed on younger generations kept them fearful of venturing out in anticipation of disappointing elders and family members. These intergenerational challenges are the weight of cultural trauma, identity and belonging, and generational consciousness passed down from their parents and grandparents – resulting in mental and psychological limitations.

Two recurring themes present in my analysis were "heritage and tradition" alongside "collective cultural trauma", with a potential relationship between the two. Participants in Manchester offered a new perspective on "roots" and identity – which can be understood as a seed granted at birth. The acknowledgement of the history of the Chagossians plants the seed, and throughout life experiences, interactions, and stories, it grows into confidence, passion, and perseverance. Manchester offers the right environment to plant, water, and photosynthesise the plant in this analogy. Hence, although they are living and surviving physically, individuals in Manchester have shown that they are thriving mentally due to access to resources (specifically education), respect, and acknowledgement of lineage.

Another key finding suggests as the elder generations begin to pass away, leaders of the community have fragmented the concept of identity amongst individuals of the community, upholding "tainted" political stances as a way of dealing with the collective cultural trauma. The influence of internal Chagossian politics has previously been unexplored in academia. One participant outlined that there could be up to 11 leaders within the wider Chagossian community – which makes consensus, growth, and transformation difficult across the board.

The future of the Chagossians, according to the findings, looks bright as many participants anticipate people in the community to become more active. Younger people are now encouraged and possess high expectations of becoming leaders, subsequently, helping the generations before them in employment, education, and voicing everyday issues.

References

Baumann, G. (1996) *Contesting Culture: Discourses of Identity in Multi-ethnic London*. New York: Cambridge University Press.

Chavez, C. (2008) 'Conceptualising from the inside: Advantages, complications and demands on insider positionality'. *The Qualitative Report*, 13(3), pp. 474–494.

Gundowry, M.S. (2018) 'Acculturation of young Mauritian people of Chagossian origin in the UK: Negotiating living in the host society.' Doctor of Philosophy Thesis, submitted to the University of Brighton. Available at: https://cris.brighton.ac.uk/ws/portalfiles/portal/6459574/MARIA_SYLVIA_GUNDOWRY.pdf#page44 (Accessed: 30 July 2022).

Jeffery, L. (2010a) 'Forced displacement, onward migration and reformulations of "Home" by chagossians in Crawley, UK'. *Journal of Ethnic and Migration Studies*, 36(7), pp. 1099–1117.

Jeffery, L. (2010b) 'Creole Festivals and Afro-Creole Cosmopolitanisms in Mauritius'. *Social Anthropology*, 18(4), pp. 425–432.

Jeffery, L. (2011) 'Unusual immigrants', or, Chagos Islanders and their confrontations with British citizenship'. *Anthropology in Action,* 18(2), pp. 33–44.

Kristensen, G.K. & Ravn, M.N. (2015) 'The voice heard and the voices silenced: recruitment processes in qualitative interview studies'. *Qualitative Research,* 15(6), pp. 722–737.

MacFarlane, B. (2008) *Research With Integrity: The Ethics of Academic Enquiry*. London: Taylor & Taylor Group.

Nationality and Borders Act 2022. Available at: https://bills.parliament.uk/bills/3023

Reeves, C.L. (2010) 'A difficult negotiation: Fieldwork relations with gatekeepers'. *Qualitative Research,* 10 (3), pp. 315–331.

Webb, R. (2021) 'Confronting ethical issues in social research [PowerPoint]. 502X8: *Research design and ethics'*. Available at: https://canvas.sussex.ac.uk/courses/11698/pages/week-4?module_item_id=821345.

Wejnert, C. and Heckathorn, D.D. (2008) 'Web-based network sampling: Effiency and efficacy of respondent-driven sampling for online research'. *Sociological Methods & Research,* 37(1), pp. 105–134.

Wellington, J.J., Bathmaker, A., Hunt, C., McGulloch, G. and Sikes, P. (2005) *Succeeding with Your Doctorate.* London: Sage.

ayapana in a british plastic plant pot

Chrisyl Wong-Hang-Sun

small clipping
plastic bag
twelve-hour flight
perhaps he is trying to reclaim his land?
budding adolescence
unknown territory
one year of survival
he nurtures you the way you nurtured his ancestors.
marcescent leaves
hostile climate
second winter
he cannot rejoice under the sun and dance with his daughters.
confined roots
inadaptable land
death signals life
it is time for him to return to his homeland.

DOI: 10.4324/9781003390299-12

9 Certainty and Uncertainty

Native and Older Generation Chagossian Perspectives from Mauritius amid the UK Government's *Nationality and Borders Act 2022*

Chrisyl Wong-Hang-Sun

My first day volunteering at the Chagos Refugee Group [CRG/*sant Chagos* hereafter] was prophetic. Even though anthropologists try to stay away from them, first impressions count, and in ethnography, they can sometimes be indicative of what is to come. Bonding over the bus delays on my way to the CRG, I conversed with a middle-aged *Kreol*[1] woman. She was curious about my accent, so I expressed I was born in England, and had come to Mauritius to learn about my Mauritian and Chagossian heritage. She confidently replied, "*to pe rod to ben rasin, to pe retourn ver la surs*" [you're looking for your roots, you're returning to the source]. Continuing our conversation, I shared that I was travelling to research and volunteer at the CRG, to understand how Chagossians think and feel towards the *lalwa* [law] that will give all descendants British citizenship. Familiar with the Chagossian history, she shared: "Young people can study in the UK. Here in Mauritius, they do not have the same opportunities. There they can make a *lavenir* [future]".

After 30 minutes of conversing, the bus finally arrived. The woman instructed the bus conductor to inform me when the bus reaches "*sant Chagos*" [referring to the CRG, which translates to "Chagos centre"]. Once there, Bibi, the main administrator of *sant Chagos*, greets me at the gate. Glimpses of *lespwar* [hope] illuminate the building: a poster detailing Nelson Mandela's life journey, Martin Luther King's "I have a dream speech", and a map of Diego Garcia beautifully painted onto a goatskin ravanne.[2] Bibi brings me a comforting tea made with sugar and condensed milk – I immediately feel at ease. Later, she invites me to a peachy-orange room, centred with four Chagossian volunteers of the native and older generation, sharing a meal together. Partaking in this meal, *mo ti santi moi kot mo mem* [I felt myself at home]. These words and phrases in *Kreol* that I experienced during my first day echoed continuously throughout my fieldwork in Mauritius. As I recreate my experience with Chagossians mainly of *sant Chagos*, these themes will feature throughout this chapter.

After being forcibly and illegally displaced by the British government between 1968 and 1973 (Figure 9.1), Chagossians have resisted and advocated against their displacement through women-led hunger strikes (see Chapter 3), numerous protests, and Chagossian songwriting (Jeffery, 2011a). Located in Pointe-aux-Sables, a small coastal village close to the capital of Port Louis, *sant Chagos* was inaugurated as a space for the Chagossian diaspora to gather, learn together, and raise awareness for their right to return to their islands (Figure 9.2). Spearheaded by

DOI: 10.4324/9781003390299-13

Figure 9.1 A Painting by Chagossian Artist, Clement Siatous, Depicting the Last Stage of Displacement.

Source: Photograph by the author.

Olivier Bancoult, *sant Chagos* has been involved in numerous legal court cases and hearings as they continue the fight to return to their homeland, and regain their communal, familial, and tranquil way of life (see Chapter 1). This journey has been characterised by extensive periods of waiting, uncertainty, and yet, hope.

The *Nationality and Borders Act 2022* (NaBA) is an important and recent legal update to the Chagossian case study, where Section 3 of the Act allows British citizenship for people who are a direct descendant of a person who was born in the Chagos before 8 November 1965. Applicants over the age of 18 must make their application up to five years from the Act's commencement, whilst applicants under the age of 18 of the commencement date have until the age of 23 to apply. The applications for citizenship opened on 23 November 2022.

Considering the extensive history, this chapter explores how Chagossians in Mauritius, particularly those involved with the CRG, perceive the NaBA: What are the immediate effects of the Act? Are they interested in migrating to the UK? How do they think the Act will affect their communal and familial relations? What do they think about law more generally? Finally, do they still have hope to return home?

As a researcher of both Mauritian and Chagossian descent, whose parents emigrated from Mauritius seeking a "better life", my positionality (Rosaldo, 1989) both influenced my research questions and facilitated my integration into the CRG.

Figure 9.2 Outside of Sant Chagos.

Source: Photograph by the author.

I had not known my Chagossian grandfather before his death, and with my mother passing at my tender age of 15, I was left with many questions about my Chagossian heritage. In this sense, returning to Mauritius was both a personal and professional endeavour (Narayan, 1993, p. 681). Many of my interlocutors expressed pride in my research interests and my ability to converse in *Kreol* as a young Chagossian. It proved particularly empowering for the native/older generation of Chagossians, some of whom are concerned that the younger generation of Chagossians will "forget" their *rasin* [roots]. It is here, in recognition of this hybridity (Narayan, 1993), that I embody a decolonial methodology of working *with* the diaspora that I identify with (Smith, 2012).

As part of my fieldwork at *sant Chagos*, I assisted in the organisation of events commemorating 50 years since the last deportation boat, as well as helping to edit letters and posters in English. There were a few days when members of the wider diaspora came together to help clear out the offices, re-paint the interior and exterior walls, and tend to the gardens. On such days, I also helped, by cleaning and cooking lunch-time meals. At the end of my field days, I took comprehensive notes of my fieldsite, noting aspects such as the space, actors involved, activities, and temporality (Spradley, 1980, p. 78). I also made note of and photographed any "salient episodes" or spaces that I found of particular interest (Wolfinger, 2002, p. 89). I

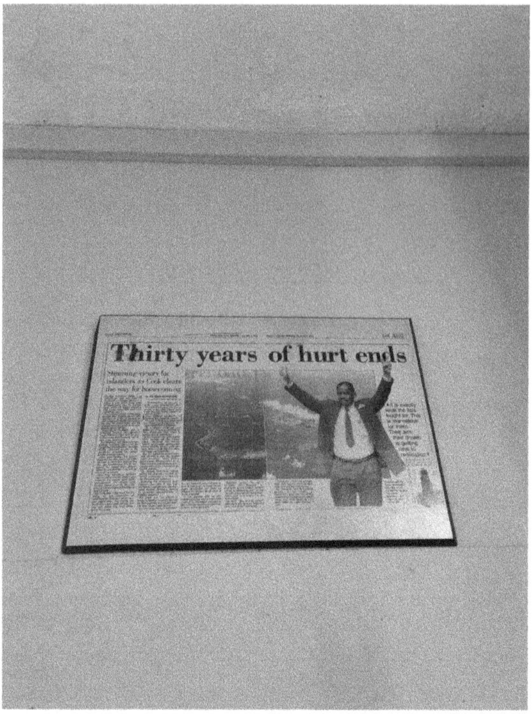

Figure 9.3 Postered onto a wall in *Sant Chagos* is a newspaper article about the court case Olivier Bancoult won against the UK Government in 2000. The High Court ruled that the displacement was illegal, and that Chagossians could return to all Chagos Islands except for Diego Garcia.

Source: Photograph by the author.

regularly ate with the other volunteers and members of the community within the main room, and it is within these settings that I informally interviewed seven people who volunteered regularly and occasionally; five who were native to the Chagos, one who was a Chagossian descendant, and one of Mauritian descent.[3] I also interviewed one middle-aged Chagossian descendant who was not part of the CRG. The voice-recorded interviews were semi-structured and conducted in Mauritian *Kreol*, with a set of questions based on themes that were deductive as part of my research design, and inductive, emerging saliently through interactions with members of *sant Chagos*. I followed this structure with all my interlocutors, whilst also allowing space to explore topics and conversations that I did not foresee. As I looked to understanding and defining key *Kreol* terms relative to the experiences of *sant Chagos* members, this inevitably shaped the interactions of my research.

Although there are various Chagossian organisations/groups in Mauritius, the UK, and the Seychelles, my research is located mainly within *sant Chagos*, as the CRG has been and remains a key organisation in the legal fight to return home[4] (Figure 9.3). For this reason, my research cannot account for the views of the entire

Chagossian diaspora. I situate my discussion with the native/older community of *sant Chagos*, whilst recognising the space for further research from the wider diaspora, exploring how the Act will continue to affect generations over the decades to come.

I begin by exploring an understanding of *lalwa* [law], particularly considering the recent NaBA. I then explore what *lespwar* [hope] is and how it is exercised in the fight to return home. Finally, I question the prospect of migrating to the UK by providing insight into the *Kreol*/French term "lavenir", and dialogue with what "at home" [*kot mo mem*] is for the Chagossian community that works at *sant Chagos.* Exploring these four main phrases, the running theme that emerged throughout my research was certainty. I argue the members of *sant Chagos* are certain in themselves and their legal right to return home, and thus, this hope is located on a direct linear trajectory towards the fixed goal of regaining the Chagos. Through this analysis, I reveal the uncertainty the diaspora feels towards the Act, the British government, and the idea of *lavenir* in the UK. I also demonstrate how the native and older generation of Chagossians feel at home in Mauritius, and particularly within the CRG, as opposed to the UK, by translating "home" as the ability to feel at home in oneself, characterised by certain factors that allow Chagossians to dwell in a manner that stays true to the embodied memory of their homeland (Figure 9.3).

Lalwa

To understand how "law" is understood in the context of Chagossian legal battles and related legislations (particularly the NaBA), I follow Pirie who argues that as anthropologists, we must seek to understand the "nature of law" for the people we research with, thus moving away from its western universality as a "category of the English-speaking world" (2013, pp. 4–5). I draw too on the words of an interlocutor at *sant Chagos,* Christophe, who described law as "certain" and textual in nature; to *derasin* [uproot] the Chagossians, the British had to go against "the laws that they themselves had created".

Grasping the concept of certainty to which Christophe refers requires an understanding of the relationship between Magna Carta and the "rule of law". As a reason for taking the British government to court, Olivier Bancoult referred to the illegality of exile found in the Magna Carta.[5] The Magna Carta forms the basis of the British constitution and is the foundation of what is exercised as the "rule of law" in Western democratic societies (Elkins, Ginsburg, and Melton, 2016, p. 1; Fernández-Villaverde, 2016, p. 2). "Rule of law" cannot easily be defined, but Tamanaha (2004) conceptualises it through a "thin description" of guidance in how people in a society should live, and a "thick description" encompassing respect for human rights and liberties. Fundamental to this understanding is the assertion that within the "rule of law", no one can be above the law (Dicey, 1897). Whilst anthropologists have questioned the use of the "rule of law" within society (Mattei and Nadar, 2008; Pirie, 2021), it remains true that in the Chagossian context "rule of law" is nonetheless an insightful and useful analytical category. The notion of the rule of law as a basis for counterhegemonic practice (see Cheesman, 2018;

Sapignoli, 2018) is particularly resonant. "*Lalwa*" translates to both "law" and "rules" in *Kreol*. The members of *sant Chagos* are advocating for their legal right to return as a people who have been illegally displaced by the British, utilising the underlying certainty of the "rule of law", and its validity in the eyes of the British and international legal community to resist Britain's hegemony. They are thus in a position to criticise the UK's inability to follow the rule of the Magna Carta.

This concept of certainty in the law was complicated in the case of the NaBA. One interlocutor, Bibi, distinguished between the "law of man", used by the British in a self-serving way, and the "law of justice", which would allow Chagossians to return to their homeland. The concept of certainty was underlined, while this law itself was conceptualised as spurious.

Chagossian artist, Clement Siatous, directly expressed that the NaBA was "not a law". As a people native to the Chagos, Clement recognises that through the formation of the "BIOT", all Chagossians should have "received the British passport".[6] His words point to a level of uncertainty in the integrity of the Act, as the UK has only just changed its position on whether Chagossian descendants can acquire British citizenship, 55 years after Mauritius gained independence. The "law of man" is thus based on fluid and malleable positions.

Bibi believes that the Act was swiftly ushered in response to Mauritius formally challenging the British occupation of the Chagos: the British government has "shown Mauritius that they can also do something … they have just passed a law, but they haven't studied for this law". She then explained that the British government should have conducted a study *with* the diaspora to understand how families feel towards a proposed law, and whether they agree with it. Her words point to a recognition that law must be rooted in the knowledge of the people it seeks to support. Her words also demonstrate uncertainty in the Act. If, as she explains, the law of justice is the right to return home, law should not reflect the geopolitical actions of a nation-state, but rather, should reflect the human rights and liberties that are fundamental to the rules of English law. Law, as Chagossians relay, must be certain and reliable, paving the way for justice. The NaBA, a "law of man", is thus plagued by uncertainty, and does not serve justice for their illegal displacement. As law is justice, the NaBA cannot be conceived as law for some members of *sant Chagos*.

The uncertainty surrounding the act was further brought to my attention in conversation with both Olivier, leader of the CRG, and Antoinette, an occasional volunteer of *sant Chagos*. Olivier felt that this "law" was a way to "divide and rule", and that its impact on future Chagossian generations would be to make them "forget the past". He asked, "Will the youth return to the source?" Antoinette echoed the same idea that the British were encouraging the young to "forget", stating that "they are trying to keep them preoccupied". Both native Chagossians, Olivier and Antoinette are concerned by the physical and metaphysical divide that this Act creates between the native generation that want to return home and the younger generation that are looking for a better life in the UK.

Further, the route to citizenship is limited to Chagossian descendants only, which does not include any Mauritian spouses. Migration to the UK through the NaBA poses a continuation of the familial separation that took place after the British Overseas Territories Act (2002; BOTA hereafter)[7] (Jeffery, 2011b, pp. 37–39). Christina, a Chagossian descendent who at the time of my fieldwork was preparing to migrate to the UK once her application had been approved, shared concern that spouses who are eligible to gain citizenship could be unfaithful to partners left behind in Mauritius.

The divisiveness expressed is not solely found between generational and familial relations. For as Bibi highlighted, it also echoes across the entire diaspora: "Each person is understanding it in their own way, and not everyone is speaking with one voice, one word. There are multiple voices causing conflict, division, disintegrating the community". She then stated: the "English like it when we have these divisions", which evokes scepticism that the Act may be a British tactic to weaken the Chagossian collective resistance of their displacement. *Sant Chagos* has elicited international support for their cause by highlighting the collectivity of life in the Chagos (Jeffery, 2011a, pp. 70–71). A people described as very familial, consistently helping one another, and living in unison (Jeffery, 2011a, pp. 65–66), the divisiveness poses a threat not just to their movement, but to their communal and familial way of life that plays a large role in their identity.

Amongst all this insight, perhaps the most disheartening revelation was the concern that the Act could create an opportunity for "another displacement". As Christina explained: "You [British government] deported them from Chagos. Threw them into a country [Mauritius], alone, without a house or anything. Now you are telling them to come to England. It's like you are uprooting them again".

With the expected migration of many Chagossians, Bibi also echoed a concern of "another displacement". She predicts that the older generation of Chagossians will struggle to adjust to the UK, just as they struggled to adjust when they were displaced to Mauritius. From both Bibi's and Christina's accounts, we see a vicious circle of continuing displacement provoked by the NaBA. This sets the case for quite the opposite of justice for the Chagossian displacement. With the absence of justice, this Act leaves space to speculate the intentions of the British government. By this same token, the uncertainty of the Act reinforces the community volunteers' certainty in the law of justice, as they continue to legally battle for their right to return to their native homeland.

Lespwar

When I asked Olivier what he thought of the NaBA, he explained:

> You cannot say to me to go to England. England is not my birthplace … How can it be permitted that other people can live on my land, but I cannot live on my own land? I am continuing to fight.

Indeed, in any discussion of the NaBA, native Chagossians almost always responded with a hope of returning home – the Act itself does not serve the momentum to regain the Chagos. It is here that I explore what hope is and the role it plays for Chagossians, arguing that it is rooted in a certainty of Chagossian self-knowledge.

This hope can be explained as the momentum towards the attainable end goal of returning home, expressed through what I call "insistent practice".

I begin with Miyazaki's notion of *hope as a method* for generating self-knowledge (2004). Miyazaki's fieldwork with the displaced Suvavou argues that hope is not just a method for engaging with the world (Bloch, 1986, 1998), but a method for both generating and encouraging the formation and pursuit of self-knowledge (2004). By petitioning an inquiry into their landownership, the Suvavou aim to determine their self-knowledge. Here, Miyazaki highlights the inextricable relationship of "indeterminacy as a condition for the possibility of hope" (2004, p. 71). Inspired by Bloch who argues hope is an indeterminate "future-orientated direction" (1998, p. 340), Bryant and Knight challenge the relationship between hope and indeterminacy by arguing that "hope is not always solely an indeterminate affective attachment to a potential future" (2019, p. 139). The words of Marie, below, echo Bryant and Knight's contention that hope is a momentum that bridges indeterminate possibility with determinate actualisation (2019, pp. 136–139). Conceptualising this notion of hope as "futural momentum" (2019, p. 142), Bryant and Knight argue that hope "emerges collectively in its various forms [optimistic, pessimistic, filled with certainty, filled with yearning] when people mobilise to push potential into the future actual" (2019, p. 142). Hope in this regard is the teleological momentum towards a future end goal (2019, pp. 139–142).

Almost all Chagossians I connected with communicated a secure and confident hope in the end goal of regaining their homeland. Marie, a middle-aged Chagossian descendant who volunteered daily, expressed her hope in a compelling tone, sharing that it came from "within" her. She then shed light on her native parents, hoping one day to "recover" their birthplace. The term "recover" can be defined as regaining something that has been lost, which denotes a sense of knowing that comes from certainty. When we declare something as lost or stolen, we articulate what we know of that thing (a description of some sort) and evoke a sense of yearning to regain it. We hope to find that which we know is ours. Despite not being born on the Chagos, Marie's hope to return[8] to her parent's birthplace is rooted in the certainty of her identity as a Chagossian descendant, whose parents were wrongfully displaced from their homeland.

Olivier too expressed a hope to return to his native homeland which, in his words, comes from his "own determination". Determination is the momentum towards a fixed end goal. The act of determining is agentive as it involves action that contributes to something viewed as definite. In determination, there is no space for doubt – Olivier is sure of his birthplace. Certainty here is a definite state of being. Again here, hope demonstrates the certainty of Chagossian self-knowledge. It is the futural momentum towards the end goal of returning to the land that they rightfully know is theirs.

How is the momentum, the movement, towards this goal actioned? In addition to the notion of hope as "futural momentum", I draw on the concept of "situational waiting" (Dwyer, 2009) to explore how Chagossians move towards regaining their homeland through their active and performative waiting as insistent practice. As Dwyer writes, situational waiting is "of the world"; it is "fully embedded in time, engaged and never passive" (2009, pp. 20–21), and because of this, I argue that it evokes certainty. Existential waiting, however, is embodied, passive, plagued with uncertainty, and is "removed from time", yet "endlessly consuming" (2009, p. 21). For Chagossians, what transforms existential waiting into situational waiting is the certainty that they have of themselves, exercised by the practices in *sant Chagos*.

Hope has also been described in the ethnographic literature as a form of work (Pedersen, 2012), and as form of practice (Hauer, Østergaard Nielsen, and Niewöhner, 2018). The active and insistent engagement of Chagossian volunteers demonstrates the inextricable relationship between hope, self-knowledge, and work/practice. *Sant Chagos* is a base for the diaspora to practice their right to return home by gathering frequently, organising events that elicit support in Mauritius and worldwide, and to engage with wider international legal proceedings. As a daily volunteer, Marie's waiting to return is driven by the hope from "within" her. Her waiting is agentive, engaged, and therefore, "embedded in time" (Dwyer, 2009, pp. 20–21), as she moves towards returning to her parent's birthplace. This hope is not uncertain, it is active in certainty. Her active practice is situated on a linear trajectory toward the end goal of regaining the homeland (cf. Bryant and Knight, 2019).

At the time of my research, the volunteers were preparing various events to commemorate 50 years since the last deportation boat. Each day, volunteers would come together at lunch to share a meal, discussing demonstrations, events, and publicity. Each person engaged in a defined role and action that contributed to the insistent momentum. As Bibi expressed to me, "for me, I don't get paid. But I have a joy for it. I do everything. Sometimes I get tired, but I keep going. I keep moving".

"Moving" is key here. Insistence is movement, and movement is active. To halt the movement is to accept that they are not returning home. To remain passive and stagnant is to accept living in Mauritius and the UK as all that could be. The way in which the members come together and move towards the future goal is a testament to the certainty of their homeland. For many people within the native and older generation of Chagossians, no other possibility is as important as the goal of returning home.

The other aspect that lays testament to hope as the momentum towards home is the Chagossian diaspora's insistent practice of their Catholic faith. In the main meeting room of *sant Chagos*, pictures displaying members of the community meeting the Pope adorn the walls. Conversing as we were re-painting these walls, Christophe expressed that his hope to return home came from: "God. My thoughts are in God". Like Haugen who argues that the hopeful practice of Pentecostalism is a method that provides "material optimism and promises of instant blessings" towards undocumented Nigerian migrants who live uncertain lives in China (2017, p. 110), Chagossian Catholic faith also serves as a method of hope towards their journey of returning home.

Biblical theology was a prominent idiom for support and solidarity within the momentum of volunteers. Erick, a Mauritian volunteer, and advisor to Olivier, expressed a resemblance between the Chagossian exile and the Biblical exile of the Israelites. "Moses didn't know how to speak; it was Aaron who spoke. So, I

Figure 9.4 Taken from the Chagossian Mass. Image Depicts an Altar with Chagossian Flag, Ravanne, Woven Palm Leaf Baskets, Coconuts.

Source: Photograph by the author.

remember when Olivier couldn't speak, I would always back him from behind", he expressed.

As Catholicism was the main religious belief practised on the Chagos (Jeffery, 2011a, pp. 97–98), the expression of faith has strong ties with Chagossian sense of cultural identity. The main event to commemorate 50 years from the last displacement boat was a mass that was held in a large cathedral in Port Louis, which was televised, attracting journalists from across the Indian Ocean. The mass was adorned with Chagossian cultural emblems: the Chagossian flag, woven palm leaf baskets, paintings of Chagossian livelihood, a *ravanne,* and coconuts (Figure 9.4) – insistent testaments to the irrefutable relationship between Chagossian material self-knowledge and their faith to return home. Pleased to hear the Cardinal's support for the Chagossian cause, Bibi expressed that her faith in God provides "strength", enabling her to continue fighting. Further, the support of key Catholic figures such as the Cardinal of Mauritius and Pope Francis evokes a sense of religious certainty and solidarity for their cause.

In cyclical fashion then, hope is rooted in the certainty of their right to return home, actioned, and expressed by the momentum of insistent practice. This in turn reinforces people's self-knowledge, propelling them through the linear trajectory of hope, with a fixed goal of returning home in place.

Lavenir

"*Lavi dans Moris byen dificil*" [life in Mauritius is very difficult] is a phrase I was constantly told. From market vendors to volunteers at *sant Chagos*, the financial struggle and prospects for young people, particularly *Kreol* Mauritians, are concerning. Despite being a multi-ethnic population from South Asia, East Africa, Europe, and China, there exists an ethnic hierarchy, where afro-Mauritians and Chagossians struggle at the bottom (Eriksen, 1998; Jeffery, 2010, p. 1102). Historically, these forms of ethnic categorisation and valorisation are found in the "social, political, and economic dominance of Indo-Mauritians", marginalising *Kreol* people (Jeffery, 2011a, p. 25). Boswell terms this as "*le malaise Creole*", which is the structural violence afro-Mauritians face, indicated through poverty, crime, drug abuse, and poor education and employment prospects (2006, pp. 77–78). At the turn of the Covid-19 pandemic (see UNDP Mauritius, 2021; Ranzani and Kern, 2022), the situation worsened significantly. Illustrating this, Erick explained that Chagossian children struggle extensively to obtain employment, despite higher education qualifications. "We look at faces", he said. "In school, if the teachers see you have a red string in your arm [referring to Hindu students], you will pass. Chagossian children are living as if they don't have papers".

Frequently, the older volunteers at *sant Chagos* expressed that the NaBA would be good for the younger generation to make a *lavenir* and receive a good education, evoking the possibilities of a better life. *Lavenir* can be translated as "the future" in both French and *Kreol*, and "prospects" in *Kreol* (*Lalit*, 2015).[9] However, this understanding is incomplete in relation to the recent context of Chagossian migration from Mauritius. Although the term points to prospects and opportunities that exist in the future, it encompasses an agentive role in the present, inspired by experiences in the past, that lead to [un]certain prospects of what the future could be.

The history of *l'avenir*[10] within ethnographic literature appears in Bourdieu's work with the Algerian Kabyle, for whom it was the "experienced forthcoming", characterised by an organic unity between the past, the present, and future (1963, p. 61). With a certain image in mind of the past, Kabyle farmers worked within the present to reduce a future of "innumerable possibilities" (1963, p. 69). The Kabyle peasant was consistently working, but never with haste; action is prolonged (1963, p. 58). As Bourdieu concluded, the Kabyle lifestyle was characterized by a "courtesy of a man of leisure", with "the same indifference to time" (1963, p. 57).

This has some relevance for the *Kreol* understanding of *lavenir*. Christina, a Chagossian descendant who will migrate for the *lavenir* of her daughter, defined the term as a "work" of the present, impacted by the "choices of the past", that "make" the future. For Christina, as for the Kabyle, the present calls for an agentive role that stems from an understanding learnt in the past, which moves towards possibilities of the future. The aspect, however, that differs from Bourdieu's understanding of *l'avenir* is the type of future that is being worked towards. As he described it, the future was certain for the Kabyle, who worked in a manner that lessened the number of possibilities (1963, p. 69). For Christina, she is working towards giving her child as many prospects and "opportunities" as possible, prospects she describes as unavailable in Mauritius.

As such, for my Chagossian interlocutors, the purpose of *lavenir* is not to reduce possibility, but to open the prospect of various possibilities and opportunities to build a life. Thus, *lavenir* can be understood as the process of "making a life for oneself". I return to a point I made earlier, that for my Chagossian interlocutors, hope is a futural momentum, on a linear trajectory towards a specific goal in mind: returning to the Chagos. This hope is situated in the certainty that the Chagossians have of themselves. By contrast, *lavenir* is not simply a linear trajectory toward "the future'; it is a labyrinth of possibilities and outcomes.

As I asked Christina whether she was excited to migrate to the UK, I was met with an anxious response. "I don't know" repeatedly shaped every expression: uncertainties about how "life will be there", whether she could be "happy" there, whether it will be "worthwhile", whether her documents will be accepted by the UK Home Office, and the possibility of her daughter encountering racism in the UK. In this complicated movement, a direct linear trajectory of one fixed goal is almost impossible; there are too many uncertainties. Christina will need to source employment, a place to stay, and then, of course, there is the task of adjusting to the British pace of life. It is the insecurity that comes with a vast array of prospects in the UK that further propels the uncertainty of the NaBA for some Chagossians migrating to the UK.

Such uncertainties are rooted in the certainty of lived experience, for, as Erick explained, Chagossians who emigrated to the UK in 2002 had trouble adapting to the individualistic and demanding 40-hour work week, and subsequently fell into the temptation of addiction to alcohol/drugs to cope. Similarly, Antoinette's son who emigrated in 2002 found himself isolated, without employment or community, became homeless, and was later imprisoned. Her son's harrowing experience demonstrates the effects of alienation felt by those who migrate and try to integrate into western society.

To make a *lavenir* is to make a life for oneself, a life that is not certain. This uncertainty makes the option of having strong hope for the future quite unachievable. For as I concluded earlier, for the Chagossian members of *sant Chagos*, to hope is to be certain in self-knowledge. It is a gamble to leave everything you have ever known behind, to try to assimilate in an entire new world. The uncertainty and anxiety that I experienced conversing with Christina, Erick, and Antoinette serves as a painful reminder to the extent of suffering that the Chagossians endure trying to make a life for themselves in exile. Bibi's daughter, who also emigrated for *lavenir* in the UK, expressed that she missed her family and her Chagossian network, and aspires to return to Mauritius to retire. Here, the opportunity to come to the UK is a chapter in passing. In truth, many of my interlocutors cannot identify with the NaBA because it does not reflect who they are, their connection to their homeland, and it does not serve the greater futural momentum of returning home.

Kot mo mem

As a diaspora connected to the Chagos, Mauritius, the Seychelles, and the UK, Chagossians find themselves amidst the complex host and home dichotomy of not just two locations, but four. Jeffery's extensive research with the Chagossian diaspora across the UK, Mauritius, and the Seychelles demonstrates the implausibility of identifying a single location of "home" for the extended Chagossian diaspora, and instead, she engages with the strategies (such as songwriting) Chagossians use to make a home for themselves in the world (2011a, p. 8). Indeed, cultural, material, and spatial homemaking have continuously been recognised as a vital tool for displaced and diasporic communities to create a sense of home and connection in the host land (Jansen, 2008; Jeffery, 2011a; Lenhard and Samanani, 2019). But to what extent can homemaking be likened to the homeland? Further, can homemaking allow a person to feel at home in themselves?

Throughout I have made mention of *sant Chagos*, and this final section makes its significance explicit through an engagement with the meaning of several *Kreol* terms. Drawing on the *Kreol* expression for "home", I argue that "home" for the Chagossians at *sant Chagos* is the ability to *feel* at home in oneself, and link this to Heidegger's conception of "dwelling" (2012[1951]). For the Chagossian diaspora in Mauritius, "home" is characterised by certain factors attainable in Mauritius and the Chagos that allow for the ability to dwell as Chagossians. For this reason, the experience of feeling at home in oneself cannot be made in the UK; it is more a life [*lavenir*], centred in career and educational prospects that has the possibility of being made.

"*Sant Chagos*" translates to the "Chagos centre". My experience of the centre was characterised by immense feelings of warmth, community, and belonging. As a Chagossian descendant who had limited knowledge and experience of her *rasin* [roots], my interlocutors quickly helped me to feel at home during my time at *sant Chagos*. In fact, the extent I felt at home encouraged me to question whether members also felt this way. "I feel myself as if I am home", Marie replied. She detailed that "it was like that in the Chagos", the way in which all Chagossians come together and meet "family". Bibi, who also volunteered daily, similarly expressed that every time she walks into *sant Chagos*, she felt herself "entering home". Her and Marie habitually share Chagossian food, and have their friends visit often to speak and "recount" stories of the Chagos. The centre then acts as a space for the native diaspora to be together in a way that was distinct from their life back home in the Chagos.

In Mauritian/Chagossian *Kreol*, the word for "home"/"house" is *lakaz*, but when referring to feeling at home in a sentence, we either say *kot mwa* ("at me") or *kot mo mem* ("at me myself"). This directly translates to "at me myself". The meaning of the phrase points to the idea of "home" as intertwined with one's sense of self. To feel at home, one's home must align with who and how they are.

As human beings, Heidegger argues that we are dwellers (2012[1951], p. 247). That is, mortals on earth that cultivate and construct to dwell. He follows that the true capacity for dwelling resides in the presence of peace, that is, "to remain at

Figure 9.5 Gardens at Sant Chagos, Where Food and Medicinal Herbs that Were Consumed on the Islands Are Grown.

Source: Photograph by the author.

peace within the free, the preserve, the free sphere that safeguards each thing in its essence" (2012[1951]). Dwelling can only truly take place in a building (both the verb and noun) that preserves and cultivates the aspects that distinguish a person or group and sets a space for them to exist as they are.

Sant Chagos is a building, yes, but it is the collective action and agency of the community members that cultivate the space as a space to dwell in a manner native to Chagos. Their cultural practice is characterised by commensality, community, and sharing (Jeffery, 2011a). It is this cultivation that in turn reinforces their self-knowledge. "We live how we used to on the Chagos", Antoinette explained. "We all come together to give a hand. Whatever we have, we share".

On a particular field day, many Chagossians gathered to repaint the walls, tend to the gardens (Figure 9.5), and clean the interior of *sant Chagos*. Joyous conversations and contagious laughter engulfed the atmosphere. Christophe taught me how to grate coconuts using tools and techniques that were used on the Chagos (Figure 9.6), and a native Chagossian woman taught me how to make *Seraz,* a Chagossian dish of meat slow cooked in coconut milk, served with rice (Figure 9.7). The natives embody what it means to be Chagossian: they carry their islands, their home, through their interactions with one another. So, when Marie

Figure 9.6 Rap Koko (Chagossian Tool to Grate Coconuts).

Source: Photograph by the author.

and Bibi expressed that they felt *kot mo mem* at *sant Chagos*, I truly understood. *Sant Chagos* [Chagos centre] is the centre of what it means to be Chagossian; it reflects the broader communitarianism that was central to life in the Chagos. Clement Siatous recalled living in the Chagos as a "full harmony", without the need for a police force. Whilst Olivier expressed a cultural unity: "The people who went fishing wouldn't just go fishing for themselves, they would look for others too. We lived as one family. We had our culture, on Saturdays we danced Sega". If home is characterised by the ability to feel at home in oneself, such factors need to be met for Chagossians to feel at home.

As I highlighted earlier, many Chagossians expressed a lack of enthusiasm for migrating to the UK. Christina expressed disgust at the small, stacked housing, in comparison to the large, spatial houses, with land to grow produce in Mauritius. Antoinette explained, "I don't like their weather. I won't feel myself *kot mo mem* [home]", as the main reason why she would not migrate. Having visited the UK before, Clement expressed that the cold weather is hard to adapt to, and that the "heavy" atmosphere of the UK made it quite difficult for him to paint. And Bibi reiterated the difficulty to meet with other Chagossian families due to the centrality of work and individualism that pervades life in the West, directly contrasting the collective action of *sant Chagos*. With the cold climate and lack of sunshine,

Figure 9.7 Chagossian *Seraz.*

Source: Photograph by the author.

the individualistic work-life, and the lack of space and land, the native and older Chagossian diaspora would be unable to feel at home themselves.

During my conversation with Christina, every moment she mentioned the arduous task of looking for a place to stay, she referred to it as looking for a "lodgment" [accommodation]. A *lavenir* in the UK is seen as accommodation, a momentary movement that one must do for one's future. But not a place to dwell. For home is a secure way of being for Chagossians, and as the members have described, it is located in a certain place, time, and space, with certain characteristics that evoke a sense of unity and belonging. In *Kreol*, "at home" is the ability to feel at home in oneself, which is fairly achievable in Mauritius, and particularly within *sant Chagos*, but less so within the UK.

Conclusion

I recall a distinct day of my fieldwork where Olivier expressed: "I am proud of you for returning and learning Kreol. You must be proud to call yourself Chagossian". I immediately became teary. Being raised in England, I missed out on many cultural, communal, and family experiences. My sense of self felt empty. But the peace I experienced connecting with both Chagossians and Mauritians in Mauritius allowed me to come *home to myself*.

I began with a discussion of law, demonstrating that the Chagossians of *sant Chagos* have certainty in the law of justice. They believe in its counterhegemonic potential to achieve the justice of their right to return home. The NaBA, on the other hand, is a "law of man", containing British hidden agendas, and is perceived by some as "another displacement". It evokes uncertainty and, thus, cannot be conceptualised in the same way as "law of justice". My interlocutors' hope to regain their homeland is rooted in the certainty of themselves, as native Chagossians. Chagossians express their hope through the momentum of insistent volunteering, religious, and material practice; movements that take place on a direct linear trajectory towards the sole fixed goal of returning to their homeland.

Amongst the conversations of *lespwar* [hope] and *lalwa* [law], the word *lavenir* and the phrase *kot mo mem* echoed continuously throughout my fieldwork. As I continued to develop my *Kreol*, an understanding of the terms *lavenir,* as "making a life for oneself", and "at home", as "a place one can feel at home within oneself" emerged. Here, making a life in the UK through the NaBA is uncertain. It is seen as a journey towards a life that is away from being at home in themselves. It is an uncomfortable, but obligatory chapter in passing, which does not contribute to the greater futural momentum of returning home. For the ability to feel at home in oneself is possible only when certain factors native to the Chagossian way of life are met.

Sant Chagos is a home for the Chagossian diaspora. It is a centre of what it means to be Chagossian: a space to dwell, to be at home in themselves. The space allows Chagossians to practice their self-knowledge as they legally battle, in the movement of hope, towards the goal of returning home. The British government illegally stripped my people of our land, our home, and our livelihood and continue to block our right to return[11]. And yet, the knowledge of who we are remains steadfast. Being native to, and descendants of, our homeland is the certainty of our perpetual lived experience – something the British government could never take away from us.

Acknowledgements

This chapter is dedicated to my mother, Christine Suzanne Wong-Hang-Sun, who passed away when I was 15 years old, and my grandfather, Roger Ancrasamy, who passed away before I was born. The memories of my mother and stories of my grandfather drive my momentum to continue to *return to the source* and learn more about what it means to be Kreol. The ethnographic research for this chapter was conducted in 2023, for the thesis requirement of my MRes Anthropology degree at UCL. I would like to thank Professor Charles Stewart for his guidance and support with my research, Professor Laura Jeffery for this opportunity, and Dr Mairi O'Gorman and Dr Caroline Osella for editorial support with this chapter.

Notes

1 "*Kreol*" is a racialised category signifying Mauritians that look more "African" in their appearance, and/or are mixed with the other ethnic groups in Mauritius, particularly including African descent (Vaughan, 2005; Eriksen, 2007, p. 157).
2 Percussion instrument of the Mascarene/Chagos Islands.
3 All names excluding Olivier Bancoult and Clement Siatous (with their permission) have been pseudonymised.
4 The CRG and Olivier Bancoult have been involved in many of the cases brought against the United Kingdom regarding the expulsion from Chagos (see also Chapter 3, p. 7). For an overview of these, see Chapter 1.
5 In reference to clauses 39 and 40 in the 1215 charter, and clause 29 in the 1297 statute of the Magna Carta. These clauses remain today in English law, stating: "NO Freeman shall be taken or imprisoned, or be disseised of his Freehold, or Liberties, or free Customs, or be outlawed, or exiled, or any other wise destroyed; nor will We not pass upon him, nor condemn him, but by lawful judgment of his Peers, or by the Law of the land. We will sell to no man, we will not deny or defer to any man either Justice or Right".
6 A useful case study that some of my interlocutors use to highlight this injustice is to compare their treatment by the British government to that of the Falklanders, who were given British Citizenship in 1983, after the 1982 Falklands War.
7 In 2002, Britain announced the BOTA, giving citizenship to native Chagossians born before 1965, and their children. This excluded grandchildren, Mauritian partners, and the children whose mothers had given birth in Mauritius, resulting in the separation of many families (Jeffery, 2011b, pp. 37–39).
8 There have been numerous debates on the idea of "return" for second- and third-generation descendants, particularly the idea of an "ontological paradox" of returning to a land that one was not born in (Kılınç, 2022, p. 285). It is here that I would like to highlight that the certainty of hope to return that I have discussed demonstrates that "return" is based on the lived experience, and cultural and insistent practices of being Chagossian. For the case of Marie, whose parents were illegally displaced from the Chagos, I do not wish to delve into questions of "return" that question the autonomy and validity of her words and lived experience.
9 Sourced from the *Lalit* online dictionary. *Lalit* is a left-wing political organisation in Mauritius that historically has supported the Chagossian cause. The party has successively fought to introduce Mauritian *Kreol* into schools in 2011.
10 "*L'avenir*" is spelt with an apostrophe in French, and without in *Kreol*.
11 Here, I am referring to the *British Indian Ocean Territory (Constitution) Order 2004*, which bars Chagossians from ever returning to the Chagos Archipelago; the illegal MPA around the Chagos that was established in 2010 which would restrict Chagossians from fishing if they were granted return, and Britain's blatant disregard to the 2016 ICJ Advisory Opinion on the Chagos, which stated that the Chagos islands must be returned to Mauritius, to allow for Chagossian resettlement.

References

Bloch, E. (1986) *The Principle of Hope*. Translated by N. Plaice, S. Plaice, and P. Knight. P. London: Blackwell.

Bloch. E. (1998) *Literary Essays.* Translated by A. Joron et al. Stanford, CA: Stanford University Press.

Boswell, R. (2006) *Le Malaise Creole: Ethnic Identity in Mauritius.* New York: Berghahn Books.

Bourdieu, P. (1963) 'The attitude of the Algerian peasant toward time'. In J.A. Pitt-Rivers (ed.), *Mediterranean Countrymen: Essays in the Social Anthropology of the Mediterranean*. Paris: Mouton, pp. 55–72.

Bryant, R. and Knight, D.M. (2019) *The Anthropology of the Future*. Cambridge: Cambridge University Press.

Cheesman, N. (2018) 'Rule-of-law ethnography'. *Annual Review of Law and Social Science*, 14(1), pp. 167–184. Available at: https://www.annualreviews.org/doi/10.1146/annurev-lawsocsci-101317–030900 (Accessed: 10 March 2024).

Dicey, A.V. (1897) *Introduction to the Study of the Law of the Constitution*. London: Macmillan and Co.

Dwyer, P. (2009) 'Worlds of waiting'. In G. Hage (ed.), *Waiting*. Carlton, Victoria: Melbourne University Publishing, pp. 15–26.

Elkins, Z., Ginsburg, T. and Melton, J. (2016) 'On the influence of Magna Carta and other cultural relics'. *International Review of Law and Economics*, 47, pp. 473–9. DOI: 10.1016/j.irle.2016.05.004

Eriksen, T. H. (1998) *Common Denominators: Ethnicity, Nation-building and Compromise in Mauritius*. Oxford: Berghahn.

Eriksen, T.H. (2007) 'Creolization in anthropological theory and in mauritius'. In C. Stewart (ed.), *Creolization: History, Ethnography, Theory*. Walnut Creek: Taylor & Francis Group, pp. 153–177.

Fernández-Villaverde, J. (2016) 'Magna Carta, the rule of law, and the limits on government'. *International Review of Law and Economics*, 47, pp. 22–28. DOI: 10.1016/j.irle.2016.05.006

Hauer, J., Østergaard Nielsen, J. and Niewöhner, J. (2018) 'Landscapes of hoping: Urban expansion and emerging futures in ouagadougou, Burkina Faso'. *Anthropological Theory*, 18(1), pp. 59–80. DOI: 10.1177/1463499617747176

Haugen, H. Ø. (2017) 'Prospective moments, eternal salvation: The production of hope in Nigerian pentecostal churches in China'. In N. Kleist and D. Thorsen (eds.), *Hope and Uncertainty in Contemporary African Migration*. New York: Routledge. pp. 94–112.

Heidegger, M (2012[1951]) 'Building dwelling thinking'. In B.G. Chang and G.C. Butchart (eds.), *Philosophy of Communication*. Cambridge, MA: The MIT Press, pp. 245–256.

Jansen, S. (2008) 'Troubled locations: Return, the life course and transformations of "home" in Bosnia and Herzegovina'. In S. Jansen and S. Löfving (eds.), *Struggles for Home: Violence, Hope and the Movement of People*. Oxford: Berghahn, pp. 43–64.

Jeffery, L. (2010) 'Forced displacement, onward migration and reformulations of "home" by chagossians in Crawley, UK'. *Journal of Ethnic and Migration Studies*, 36(7), pp. 1099–1117. DOI: 10.1080/13691830903517511

Jeffery, L. (2011a) *Chagos Islanders in Mauritius and the UK: Forced Displacement and Onward Migration*. Manchester: Manchester University Press.

Jeffery, L. (2011b) '"Unusual immigrants", or Chagos Islanders and their confrontations with British citizenship'. *Anthropology in Action*, 18(2), pp. 33–44.

Kılınç, N. (2022) 'Revisiting Second-Generation Return Migration to the Ancestral Homeland'. In King, R. and Kuschminder, K. (eds.) *Handbook of Return Migration*. Cheltenham, Gloucestershire: Edward Elgar Publishing Limited, pp. 283–298.

Lalit (2015) 'Dictionary'. Available at: https://www.lalitmauritius.org/en/dictionary.html?letter=l (Accessed: 10 March 2024).

Lenhard, J. and Samanani, F. (2019) *Home: Ethnographic Encounters*. London: Taylor and Francis.

Mattei, U. and Nader, L. (2008) *Plunder: When the Rule of Law is Illegal*. Oxford: Blackwell Publishing.

Miyazaki, H. (2004) *The Method of Hope: Anthropology, Philosophy and Fijian Knowledge*. Stanford, CA: Stanford University Press.

Narayan, K. (1993) 'How native is a "native" anthropologist?'. *American Anthropologist*, 95(3), pp. 671–686.
Pedersen, M.A. (2012) 'A day in the cadillac: The work of hope in Urban Mongolia'. *Social Analysis*, 56(2), pp. 136–151.
Pirie, F. (2013) *The Anthropology of Law*. Oxford: Oxford University Press.
Pirie, F. (2021) *The Rule of Laws: A 4000-year Quest to Order the World.* London: Profile Books.
Ranzani, M. and Kern, A. (2022) 'The impact of COVID-19 on labour markets and living standards in Mauritius'. *The Economic and Labour Relations Review*, 33(4), pp. 806–828.
Rosaldo, R. (1989) *Culture & Truth: The Remaking of Social Analysis.* Boston, MA: Beacon Press.
Sapignoli, M. (2018) *Hunting Justice: Displacement, Law, and Activism in the Kalahari.* Cambridge: Cambridge University Press.
Smith, L.T. (2012) *Decolonizing Methodologies: Research and Indigenous Peoples*. (2nd ed.). London: Zed Books.
Spradley, J.P. (1980) *Participant Observation.* New York: Holt, Rinehart &Winston.
Tamanaha, B.Z. (2004) *On the Rule of Law: History, Politics, Theory*. Cambridge: Cambridge University Press.
UNDP Mauritius (2021) 'Socio-economic impact assessment of covid-19 in Mauritius'. Available at: https://www.undp.org/africa/publications/socio-economic-impact-assessment-covid-19-mauritius (Accessed: 10 March 2024).
Vaughan, M. (2005) *Creating the Creole Island: Slavery in Eighteenth-Century Mauritius*. Durham: Duke University Press.
Wolfinger, N.H. (2002) 'On writing fieldnotes: Collection strategies and background expectancies'. *Qualitative Research*, 2(1), pp. 85–93.

Legislation

British Overseas Territories Act 2002, c. 8. Available at: https://www.legislation.gov.uk/ukpga/2002/8/contents (Accessed: 10 March 2024).
Nationality and Borders Act 2022, c. 36. Available at: https://www.legislation.gov.uk/ukpga/2022/36/section/3/enacted (Accessed: 10 March 2024).

Limuria is in Our trust

Chrisyl Wong-Hang-Sun

O, Limuria[1]
Reduced to an inanimate theory
A speculation, a conspiracy, a distant memory
But We know.
          We know.
                We know.

La surs is calling Us home
And We are waiting
For the moment she will arise

O, great Limuria
For centuries you lay beneath the modern surface
Silenced and erased by western imperialism
But We know.
          We know.
                We know.

The truth to Our being
La surs is calling Us home
Et a la surs Nu pu returne[2]

1 This poem is an act of resistance against two injustices: firstly, against the BIOT coat of arms that states in Latin that Limuria is in Britain's trust, and secondly, against Mr Justice Ouseley's 2003 ruling against a case by Chagos islanders for further compensation, based on the 'unreliable' testimonies that were given using collective language such as 'We' and 'Us', rather than from individual experience. *Chagos Islanders v Attorney General and HM BIOT Commissioners* [2003] EWHC QB 2222
Jeffery, L. (2011). *Chagos Islanders in Mauritius and the UK: Forced Displacement and Onward Migration*. Manchester: Manchester University Press, pp.72-73.

2 And to the source We will return.

DOI: 10.4324/9781003390299-14

10 Voicing the Trauma of the Lost Territory

Creative Writing, Therapy, and the Chagos Refugees Group

Esther Pujolràs-Noguer and Felicity Hand

In *The Literature of the Indian Diaspora. Theorizing the Diasporic Imaginary*, Vijay Mishra, echoing Tolstoy's Anna Karenina, offers us a compelling opening line: "All diasporas are unhappy, but every diaspora is unhappy in its own way" (Mishra 2007, p. 1). Taking Mishra's statement as our starting point we thus pose the following question: what are the specific characteristics of the Chagos Islanders' forced displacement that articulate their distinct unhappiness? Despite the silencing mechanisms exerted by the perpetrators of the Chagos Islanders' forced displacement, namely the UK and the US, the Chagossians have managed to incorporate, and thus articulate, their distinct diasporic unhappiness through sega music and dance. As a form of material culture specific to the Chagos Islands, sega evolves into a site of archipelagic memory in its role as preserver and disseminator of the people's *sagren* (sadness in Mauritian Kreol). The diasporic imaginary Mishra delineates in his book is the resultant of the study of works of literature written by well-known, published authors such as V.S. Naipaul, Salman Rushdie, Bharati Mukherjee, Rohinton Mistry, David Dabydeen, and Hanif Kureishi. Their diasporic unhappiness Mishra inscribes within the literature of trauma studies and so demonstrates how their literary performances are ways to "work through" the trauma of displacement and thus liberate them from a meaningless repetition – "acting out" – of the traumatic episode (LaCapra, 2001). The displacement to which the Chagos Islanders were subjected is fundamentally different to those experienced by the abovementioned authors for one significant reason: the possibility and materiality of return, which features the works analysed by Mishra, are denied to the Chagos Islanders who are literally banned from their homes. Their homeland, so to speak, has been irretrievably lost. Their experience of dislocation is framed around what we call "the myth of the empty territory" (Pujolràs-Noguer and Hand, 2021), in which their present reality is powerfully conditioned by an elusive myth of return. Another crucial aspect differentiates the Chagos Islanders' experience of displacement to that of Mishra's authors, namely, the very fact that they are not authors themselves and, therefore, their literary presence has always been mediated by a third party, the author that writes about them (Benson, 1989; Bigaignon, 2011; Grosset, 2021; van Haltern, 2014–5; Patel, 2005). Aware of the particularities of the Chagos Islanders' experience of displacement but nonetheless assured of the therapeutic properties of creative writing workshops, we organised a creative writing

DOI: 10.4324/9781003390299-15

workshop, *Myth and Memory. Fighting Cultural Injustice*, in August 2019 at the University of Mauritius with members of the Chagos Refugees Group of Port Louis. Our experience with creative writing has shown us that creative writing workshops generate a space wherein traumatic experiences can be, in LaCapra's terminology, *worked through* since participants are able to voice their suffering in a meaningful manner. In other words, creative writing workshops are not solely aimed at training future professional writers but, more significantly, they have proved to be effective tools to help individuals to face, reflect upon, and, ultimately, assuage the anxiety attached to their displacement angst.

The impelling collective intensity of the Chagossians' remembrances, on the one hand, and the intricate network of imperialistic lines of operation that the Chagossian case elicits, on the other, make the Chagos Islanders' trauma of displacement a plight that can be analysed under the lens of Michael Rothberg's multidirectional memory (2009). Hence, Rothberg's multidirectional memory alongside Marianne Hirsch's concept of postmemory (1992, 2019) instructed the design – choice, presentation, and handling of material – of the creative writing workshop. Rothberg's concept of multidirectional memory envisions remembrance acts as "knots of memory" (Rothberg, 2010, p. 3), as a recipient of multiple articulations of trauma that connects histories temporally and geographically distant. As the title of Rothberg's book points out, *Multidirectional Memory: Remembering the Holocaust in the Age of Decolonization*, the two historical episodes that he connects are the Holocaust and the decolonisation movements that took place after World War II. As he contends, decolonisation revived memories of the Holocaust that functioned at a multidirectional level. What he qualifies as memory's multidirectionality is the "convoluted, sometimes historically unjustified, back-and-forth movement of seemingly distant collective memories in and out of public consciousness" (Rothberg, 2009, p. 17). This will be particularly evident in the choice of literary texts that form the basis of our material for the creative writing workshop. These texts reflect traumas geographically and historically distant from the Chagos Islanders' banishment but which nonetheless the participants in the workshop felt very close to their own experiences. In this sense, the Chagos Islanders' displacement must be located within a shared network of dispersals engineered by colonialism to preserve Western territorial control. The collective memory that this displacement forged within the Chagossian community is entangled with Hirsch's concept of postmemory. Akin to LaCapra's notion of intergenerational trauma, Hirsch's postmemory encapsulates the traumatised memories that assail descendants of conflict survivors that have not experienced the tragedy themselves. This is an inherited trauma; a trauma that the parents pass on to their children and, in turn, this becomes the basis for their Chagossian sense of identity.

Through a description of our creative writing workshop we aim to disclose the peculiarities of the unhappiness of the Chagossian diaspora through the actual, unmediated voices of the Chagossians. Ultimately, we would like to demonstrate how a literary approach can contribute originally to the study of the history of forced displacement of the Chagos Islanders. The intimate relationship between history and trauma expressed in Caruth's (1996) and LaCapra's (2001) works is further noted by Mishra who defends that "history cannot be written without trauma (both on the level of the individual and the group)" (Mishra, 2007, p. 118), but he convincingly asserts that trauma, despite its historical core, cannot be articulated through historical discourse because trauma "disrupts the linear flow of historical narrative" (Mishra, 2007, p. 118), but literature can. Without undermining historical narrative, the creative writing workshop we organised allowed the participants to delve into the intricacies, individual and communal, of their traumatic experience of loss, in both its geographical and psychological dimension. Thus, we conclude, literature equipped them with the tools to reflect upon and own the history of their displacement. However, and bearing in mind Rothberg's assertion that "the truths of memory are often in tension with the truths of history" (2009, p. 14), we would like to insist on the fact that the ultimate objective of this creative writing workshop was not to determine historical truths, but rather, to build up a space in which a shared memory[1] of the tragedy of the Chagos Islands is expressed.

In reference to the particular colonialist streak of the Chagossian displacement, we would like to quote Craps when he notes how many of the founding texts of the field of trauma studies

> tend to ignore traumatic experiences and histories of currently subordinate groups both inside and outside Western society, and/or to take for granted the universal validity of definitions of trauma and recovery that have developed out of the history of Western modernity.
>
> (2010, p. 53)

He notes that "traumas [...] tend to be collective experiences, whereas the study of trauma has traditionally focused on individual distress" (2010, p. 55). While Astrid Erll acknowledges that "*memory work* is for many historical, political and ethical reasons an important activity" (2011, p. 4; emphasis in original), she suggests that "we have now arrived at a point of saturation with 'memory'. Instead of continuing to deal with the past, [...] we should start looking at the present and future" (2011, p. 5). We argue that for some cultural groups, this point of saturation has never been achieved. The focus of our current research – the Chagossian community – has never been in the spotlight as far as vindications are concerned. Ecologists seem to have ignored the outrageous eco-injustice brought about by the forced deportment of the inhabitant of the islands to make space for the American military base on Diego Garcia as opposed to the Aldabra Atoll, 1,150 kilometres south-east of Mahé, the largest of the Seychelles islands, which had been the Americans' first choice. Aldabra is the breeding ground of rare giant turtles, which conservationists campaigned to protect so the United States military finally decided on the less controversial solution: Diego Garcia (Bragard, 2008, p. 134; Johannessen, 2018, p. 283). There is a certain irony in the desire to protect an endangered species of non-human animals while the livelihood of a group of two thousand human animals is disregarded completely.

Many are the implicated subjects (Rothberg, 2019) that configure the historical narrative of the displacement of the Chagos Islanders. Ranging from the British and

Americans' colonialist interventions and the complicity of the Mauritian Government in the negotiations of their imminent independence to the alleged environmentalist justifications used to prohibit the Chagossians' return to their homelands, an elaborated web of violence emerges that unsettles the binaries victim-perpetrator. That is why the category "beneficiary", different from that of the accomplice or direct participant, which Rothberg introduces in his study on implicated subjects is of utmost importance here. As he puts it, "the beneficiary profits from the historical suffering of others as well as from contemporary inequality in an age of global, neoliberal capitalism" (Rothberg, 2019, p. 14). We contend that the Chagos Islanders' case, far from being an isolated tragedy affecting a few individuals, is imbricated in a global history of colonialism which turns us all into implicated subjects insofar as we are agents in the neoliberal capitalist structure that defines the twenty-first century.

Writing the Chagossian Ecotragedy

The Chagossians' experience of dislocation is clearly framed around our myth of the empty territory (see Chapter 4) in which their present reality is powerfully conditioned by an elusive myth of return. As mentioned before, although Chagossians have encountered in sega music and dance a means to express their *sagren*, as far as written accounts are concerned, their sadness has been appropriated by authors who, after Spivak's fashion (1988), speak *for* them. To elucidate whether, in the context of the Chagos Islands, the subaltern can successfully speak for her/himself rather than being spoken for is not the aim of this chapter, and yet this was one of the crucial concerns we had that moved us to organise a creative writing workshop wherein Chagossian voices, unmediated and unfiltered by the narration of third parties, could be heard and written down. However, we believe it is worth examining how these narrative interventions function in order to establish the manner through which the Chagossian community has been defined from the outside and, in turn, how Chagossians themselves reflect upon the ecotragedy that stands at the core of their *sagren.* So, in the following section, we briefly comment on a selection of creative writing that focuses on the Chagossian community before we move on to describe the creative writing workshop that we organised in an attempt to prove that the subaltern, when placed in a caring space that prioritises her/his life experiences, can indeed speak.

Starting with the oldest, Peter Benson's *A Lesser Dependency* (1989) focuses on a family, husband, wife, son, and daughter, living harmoniously on Diego Garcia, whose lives are torn apart when they are forced to abandon their home and their familiar surroundings. Benson describes in painstaking detail the alienation the characters suffer and their daily struggle to keep alive in an inhospitable Mauritius. Guy-Sylvio Bigaignon's 2011 novel *Out of the Cyclone* is set in the 1950s before the forced exodus of the people from the islands so his novel paints an idyllic island even though two murders are committed. Only one section of the novel is actually set in the Chagos. Valerie van Haltern's trilogy *Song of Chagos* (2014a, 2014b, 2015) features a large number of Chagossian characters who are forced to adapt to their new circumstances with varying degrees of success.

Before we mention the two more recent novels, we also would like to briefly discuss the work of two better-known writers who have also played their part in making the Chagossian tragedy more visible. Written in French, Shenaz Patel's *Le silence des Chagos* (2005) traces the poignant despair of three characters based on real-life Chagossians: Charlesia, Raymonde, and Désiré. Charlesia is forced to remain in Mauritius with her husband and six children in 1967 when the family had travelled there to seek medical treatment not available on the islands. Raymonde gives birth to Désiré on board the *Nordvaer* in 1973 on its final trip deporting Chagossians from their homeland. The novel narrates the trauma of loss and the coming to terms with the impossibility of return. Through her three main figures, Patel highlights the drama of the two thousand Chagos inhabitants forced to leave "the soil and sand they had been living on for decades" (Bragard, 2008, p.133). *Le silence des Chagos* gives a voice to so many people who, like Charlesia, were repeatedly told that "the islands are closed" (Patel, 2005, p. 31).[2] On the other hand, Lindsey Collen who is well known as being a member of *Lalit* (struggle), a radical left-wing organisation that has fought tirelessly for the demilitarisation of Diego Garcia,[3] features a sole Chagossian character in her 2001 novel *Mutiny*. In this novel about a prison mutiny planned to coincide with the eye of an approaching cyclone, she relies on a recurrent trope in her work, that of the cyclone as an equaliser, the means to bring about social upheaval so that radical economic changes can take place in society (Hand, 2010, pp. 120–122). Her Chagossian character, Mama Gracienne, plays a decisive role in the plot as she brings a vital message to Juna Bhim, the narrator of the novel, but Collen does not use her as a representative of the Chagossian struggle as her purpose in the novel is to eschew any ethnically related identity politics surrounding the detachment of the Chagos from Mauritius. Collen's inclusion of a Chagossian woman, or *Ilwa* (Islander) as they were somewhat derogatively called before 1980, serves as a recognition of the marginalisation of this community. Mama Gracienne's intense *sagren* (sadness in Mauritian Kreol) is a reminder of the plight of the abandoned Chagossians: "*The Islands are in my heart and head and eyes and ears and understanding, and I am in them*. I've got nothing left" (Collen, 2002, p. 258; italics in original). *Mutiny* focuses on a social rebellion and what is of interest for this chapter is the use of the cyclone to indicate "social uncertainty" and the need to be prepared for it by developing "strategies of resilience" (Ravi, 2017, p. 29), the same resilience amply demonstrated by the Chagossians in their battle against the ravages of environmental injustice.

Environmental issues, such as climate change, are articulated in literature on the Chagossian tragedy through the juxtapositioning of the calm, idyllic lifestyle experienced by the people before the dramatic upheaval so powerfully captured in Book I of van Haltern's trilogy *Song of Chagos* (2014a) with the precarious, deprived existence of the Chagossians in Mauritius. Much of the literature featuring the Chagossian experience reveals an underlying text. In contrast to the idyllic lifestyle cherished by the first-generation Chagossians, day-to-day existence in Mauritius after the 1970s is likened to a permanent cyclone, tossing the people around making it impossible for them to grow any new roots. Johannessen observes how in their public discourse on their sense of belonging and exile the Chagossians frequently refer to their sense of *derasine* (uprootedness) (Johannessen, 2018, p. 274). In Book II of van Haltern's trilogy, the west coast of Mauritius, the one furthest away from the Chagos Islands, is the least hospitable side of the country and where "[c]yclones hit the homeless in their slums harder than they hit anywhere else. They hit that debris of humanity sheltered in the flimsiest buildings near the west coast" (2014b, p. 164). In the Chagossian context, these consequences reflect both their new life in Mauritius and the irreparable harm being done to the coral reefs especially around Diego Garcia.

> "Talk about craziness", Victor adds, "They're blasting away a lot of ground, making a big runway for planes, a turning basin for nuclear subs. I hear big aircraft carriers come and go. Everything seems to be changing there".
>
> (van Halten, 2015, p. 120).

Novels featuring a Chagossian element, however fleeting, cannot avoid a nostalgic turn but underneath the pain of deportation and the prohibition of a legal recuperation of the homeland there lies the added complication of the Marine Protected Area and the suggestion that a return of the people would somehow harm the environment and provoke more climatic change on an already delicate ecosystem.

Myths of a lost paradise notwithstanding, Chagossians have fought to promote and preserve their culture through highlighting various elements of material culture, as commented on before (see Chapters 8 and 9). Remembering and writing about their experiences works as a great therapy for building up self-esteem as a people and for claiming a space in the Indian Ocean imaginary. Aware of the primordial role played by sega music and dance in the life of Chagossians, these literary works incorporate sega in their narrations and clearly position this artistic manifestation as a direct connection with the homeland. In many senses, sega was "the occasion for entire island communities to gather" (Vine, 2011, p. 30), so the exiled Chagossians look at these elements as part of their heritage (Jeffery, 2007; Boswell, 2017).

Home constitutes a site that is gradually eroding as it edges away out of reach so the islands become a site of desire, of painful longing that gnaws away despite the awareness of the practical impossibility of ever returning to the islands. The collective memory of the Chagossians will and must feed on the powerful emotions that sega inspires in them and continue to make their voices and their story heard.

> The time will come when there are no more living voices to tell the story, when only the canvas of the artist and the notes of the musician will live to play back the hours of the long sea journey.
>
> (Van Halten, 2014b, p. 25)

The trilogy *Song of Chagos* together with Bigaignon's *Out of the Cyclone* and Benson's *A Lesser Dependency* all contribute in different ways to keeping the tragedy of the Chagossians in the public eye. By focussing on the social harmony and community spirit that knitted the people together and the utter degradation that they suffer when in exile, the stories of the characters in these novels continue to resonate and raise questions about the ecological and social dilemmas that can and should be reconciled. More recently Florian Grosset has published a graphic non-fiction book compellingly entitled *The Chagos Betrayal: How Britain Robbed an Island and Made Its People Disappear* (2021). The discursive power of the book lies in Grosset's vivid and emotive illustrations which give voice to the tragedy of the islanders.

Likewise, *Diego Garcia* (2021) a novel co-authored by Natasha Soobramanien and Luke Williams poses the all-important question of who has the right to tell a story that is not actually theirs to tell, which constituted our need to organise a creative writing workshop so the Chagossians themselves could tell their own stories.

Figure 10.1 Images from Page 23: Abandoning Their Whole Lives.

Source: Florian Grosset, The Chagos Betrayal: How Britain Robbed an Island and Made Its People Disappear (2021)

Figure 10.2 Images from Page 94: Humanitarian Visits.

Source: Florian Grosset, The Chagos Betrayal: How Britain Robbed an Island and Made Its People Disappear (2021)

The Workshop: Hearing the Chagossians' Own Stories

The workshop we organised lasted for three very intensive days as in such a short time we were able to accomplish two vital goals. First and foremost, the men and women who attended understood that their culture was being valued by people from outside their community. Secondly, their memories would be published online and thus become visible to a potential worldwide audience.[4] In short, they were ensured that their life stories were meaningful and valuable. As we mentioned earlier, the objective was to create a space for them to grow emotionally and explain their feelings without the constraints of academic research and, therefore, the workshop was not aimed at discerning veracities from falsities.

The methodology we employed to conduct the workshop was geared by the capacity of literature to foment empathy (see Chapter 11). As literature teachers, we

Figure 10.3 Images from Page 98: The Marine Reserve – A Ploy to Keep the Chagossians Out.

Source: Florian Grosset, The Chagos Betrayal: How Britain Robbed an Island and Made Its People Disappear (2021)

have witnessed the power of literary aesthetics to engage students emotionally and ethically with the representation of reality exposed in written and/or visual texts. Although we were aware of the fact that our participants were not students of literature and that some of them could barely read or write, we nonetheless used a literary aesthetics approach in our sessions. We were extremely sensitive towards the fact that some of the participants were among the original deportees who had limited literacy and so, we adapted conscientiously the texts to this reality, often shortening them and accompanying them with visual material that helped to convey the message in an uncomplicated manner – we used PowerPoint presentations that included short texts and images. We believe it is important to emphasise that limited literacy does not in the least impair cognitive richness and aesthetic sensitivity and, as a matter of fact, the older members of the group were the most articulate in recounting their life experiences. The moment they sensed that their life stories were treasured, they generously shared their experiences with us. What is more, in a conjoined communal effort, their stories were actually written down by the younger participants.

The three sessions were structured around the following themes: (1) Names and Homes; (2) Land, Sea, Borders, Travels, Exile; and, finally, (3) Remembrances, History Box. As can be elucidated from the titles of each session, the themes touched upon crucial aspects of the Chagossians' traumatic experiences. Each session was carefully crafted to motivate them to work through their traumas (LaCapra, 2001, pp. 21–22) so as to reflect on their suffering and thus enable them to act upon these traumatic events productively. We usually started with a seemingly innocent questionnaire to gradually motion them towards the core of the traumatic event via a literary text that exposed some issues concurrent with the Chagossian experience of displacement.

The very simple question "What is your name?" functions as a stepping stone to reach more intimate information about oneself when this question is placed alongside two related questions: "Who gave you your name and why" and "Where and when were you born?" Thus, in this first session, we managed to unite "names" with "home" since behind each name there is surely a family story about genealogical continuation or discontinuation tightly linked with a sense of "home". This was illustrated through a passage from the novel *Love Marriage* by the Canadian-Sri-Lankan author V.V. Ganeshananthan in which the narrator, Yalini, reflects upon her name. Born in Canada to Sri Lankan parents, her name is an attempt on the part of their parents to alleviate the disturbing pain of displacement they must endure in Toronto. Their daughter's name becomes their permanent attachment to their homeland.

> My parents named me Yalini, after the part of their home that they loved the most. It is a Tamil name, with a Tamil home: a name that means, in part, Jaffna, Sri Lanka, the place from which they came.
>
> (Ganeshananthan, 2009, p. 21).

The idea behind posing "names" and "home" as our first topics was clearly to question to what extent the Chagossians could regard Mauritius as their home bearing in mind the initial – and perhaps continued – rejection of the exiles as undesirable migrants. To enhance the fragmented identity they had to face in Mauritius, they were confronted with a passage from Sandra Cisneros' *The House on Mango Street* (1983) in which the protagonist, Esperanza, must wrestle between the Spanish she speaks at home with her family – the parents are from Mexico – and the English she speaks at school since she lives in the US. The protagonist of Cisneros' novel must negotiate her hybrid identity, her cultural roots spreading across the US and Mexico, and her untranslatable Spanish name, a constant reminder of her Mexican ancestry. Via the fictional character of Esperanza, our participants pondered on their own hybridity and what they envisioned as their true home. Whereas the older participants did not recognise Mauritius as "home", the younger participants deployed a closer Mauritian affiliation. To finish the session with an optimistic note, we resorted to a section from Grace Nichols' poem "Wherever I hang" in which she unabashedly affirms that "Wherever I hang me knickers – that's my home" (1998, p. 3) thus exhibiting "home" as a fluctuating and adjustable concept whose stability is contingent upon geopolitical sensibilities.

The second session opened with images of the 2015 refugee crisis. Shameful pictures of people fleeing poverty, religious, and/or political persecution captured the attention of the older participants who relived their own unceremonious banishment from the Chagos Islands. Vivid moments of deportation scenes were recreated by those participants who experienced the traumatic homeland displacement first-hand. Two episodes recalled by Yaya, one of the oldest participants, have been selected to reproduce that fateful moment since, we believe, they are rueful testimonies of the cruelty of humankind in the face of power relations. The first one relates to the anguish she – and they all – felt when all of their dogs were gassed before their very eyes and thought that their children would be next in line. That is the moment, she conceded, when they understood that they had to agree to leave, otherwise their children would be killed. The second episode is particularly alluring in its combination of domesticity and forced displacement. Just the day before, the laundry had been done and the clothes lay spread out on stones to let the sun dry them; it was while on board the ship that took them to Mauritius that she suddenly remembered about the clothes and realised then how they would remain there for ever, lying in the sun, forgotten and abandoned, a reflection of their own fate. And yet, the Chagos Islands would perennially remain with them, their children, and their grandchildren. This is what the poem "Voyager Dust" by Syrian-American Mohja Kahf (2003) showed them, how "voyagers" always "carry it on their shoulders, / the dusting of the sky they left behind" (p. 1). As the American-transplanted Mohja Kahf realises, the voyager's dust that impregnated her mother's scarves is now on her shoulders too, a poetic recognition of inter-generational communion. This poem illustrated a more optimistic expression of postmemory, somehow counteracting the usual sadness that envelops Hirsch's concept.

While preparing this session, we knew we had to be extremely tactful in the way we presented the material and how we could manage the posterior discussion. The reason for this is the knowledge that the Chagossians, as mentioned before and unlike other displaced individuals, cannot return to their islands because of the presence of the American military base. It is true that a select group of Chagossians, among them some of our participants, was permitted to visit the island in 2006 but that was regarded as a pilgrimage and were not allowed to take anything from the islands, not even sand from the beach.[5]

Gisele, one of the participants who went on this pilgrimage, shared with us how distressed she was before the sight of her parents' neglected grave which was located next to the immaculately tended grave of a dog that had belonged to one of the Americans living in the military base. The right to mourn your loved ones is not equally granted to all human beings, as Judith Butler insidiously observes in *Precarious Life* (2006) and the Chagos Islanders' experience of exclusion crudely testifies to. It is painfully obvious that racism and colonialism determine the value of human beings – the special treatment that the inhabitants of the Falklands/Malvinas received during and after the conflict with Argentina in the 1980s leaves no doubt about a continuing hierarchy of human worth. The literary materials we used in the workshop were carefully selected to mirror these blatant inequalities. Both archipelagos are in – from a Global North perspective – remote areas but their histories are in no way similar. Whiteness clearly lay behind the visceral reaction by Margaret Thatcher's government to assert the Britishness of the Falklands and, what was even more important, the inhabitants of the South Atlantic islands were considered to be "our kith and kin" (Mercau, 2019) unlike the Chagossians, who were regarded as little more than "Man Fridays" (Evans and Norton-Taylor, 2010).

A passage from Abdulrazak Gurnah's 2001 novel *By the Sea* was the starting point for our third session which was devoted to remembrances. In this extract, the protagonist, 62-year-old Saleh Omar, is humiliated by the customs officer at Gatwick airport who, in a theatrically exaggerated manner, displays the meagre contents of his suitcase and confiscates the only valuable possession he took with him from Zanzibar: a small casquet containing the perfume *ud-al-qamari*. As it is, *ud-al-qamari* is his emotional link with his homeland, which he is obliged to leave for fear of his life. When Kevin Edelman, the customs officer at Gatwick, dispossesses Saleh Omar from his precious object, this is felt as a theft, as an illegal act sanctioned by the law, and this is exactly the way that our participants interpreted the scene and connected it with the theft of the Chagos Islands. We think it is worth reproducing the whole passage:

> "What's this?" he asked, then carefully sniffed the open casket. It was hardly necessary, as the little room had filled with glorious perfume as soon as he opened the box. [...] So I didn't tell him that it was ud-al-qamari of the best quality, all that remained of a consignment I had acquired more than thirty years ago, and which I could not bear to leave behind when I set out on this journey into a new life. When I looked up again I saw that he would steal it from me. Ud-al-qamari: its fragrance comes back to me at odd times, unexpectedly, like a fragment of a voice or the memory of my beloved's arm on my neck.
>
> (Gurnah, 2001, p. 13–14)

The historical, emotional, and cultural import attached to the wooden casquet of *ud-al-qamari* led us to request the participants to bring any objects that they regarded as part of their history to form part of what we called the history box. The rationale behind this exercise was that these objects could be placed within a box and could be sent to outer space as an example of their culture so if any being opened the box they would have an idea of what this culture meant for humanity. Among the objects that the participants chose for the history box were sand and shells from the islands, conscientiously preserved by the older members of the group, which they had collected on the pilgrimage trip mentioned above deliberately contravening the regulations enforced by the administrative organs that authorised the pilgrimage. The younger members of the group suggested putting a fishing rod in the box as a reminder of the profession of many of the inhabitants of the islands. The *bomme* and the *zeze*, musical instruments used in *sega* singing and dancing, were also considered to represent their culture and the inclusion of a *piké*, a tool used to cut up coconuts, indicated the widespread use of the fruit in their cuisine as well as a tribute to the major export and source of livelihood of the archipelago.

The ultimate aim of this creative writing workshop was to grant *visibility* to the Chagossian fight for identity and recognition. Moreover, as is often the case, ultimate aims are forged within a poignant desire to express that which lies beyond expression because, as Gisele, one of the participants in the workshop revealed in a terrifyingly genuine declaration of emotional incapacity, "It hurts". In this simple albeit not simplistic "It hurts" resided the essence of a successful creative writing methodology: to create a space wherein participants whose existence is enveloped by the persistent and overwhelming shadow of trauma can find a way to articulate their frustrations, their desires, their longings, and, above all, their stubbornly human claim to existence. In an act of exceptional generosity, Monette thanked us for helping them verbalise emotions that were kept inside themselves because they were too harrowing to be let out and shared with others. As far as we are concerned, and in what attempts to be an act of profound admiration, we would like to conclude this chapter by overtly thanking all the participants in the workshop and, above all, for giving us an invaluable lesson in human dignity.

Notes

1 We understand "shared memory" in a multidirectional sense. This means that although a shared memory "integrates and calibrates the different perspectives of those who remember the episode … into one version" (Rothberg, 2009, p. 15), we are also aware of the potential pitfalls that may result from a unique mnemonic version.
2 In Kreol in the original "Zil inn fermé".
3 See *Lalit* (2002).
4 The participants in the workshop expressed their consent to have their names appear on the blog, which indicates their eagerness for their stories to be heard and read as authentic. See Pujolràs-Noguer & Hand 2019.
5 Needless to say, and as the objects they brought to our last session testified to, they disobeyed and took with them sand and conch shells they picked up from the beach.

References

Benson, P. (1989) *A Lesser Dependency*. London: Alma Books.
Bigaignon, G.S. (2011) *Out of the Cyclone*. Port Louis: Elp Publications.
Boswell, R. (2017) '*Sega* as voice-work in the Indian Ocean region'. *Journal of the Indian Ocean Region*, 13(1), pp. 92–110.
Bragard, V. (2008) 'Murmuring vessels: Relocating chagossian memory and testimony in Shenaz Patel's *Le Silence des Chagos*, 'L'ici et l'ailleurs': Postcolonial literatures of the francophone Indian Ocean'. *e-France : an on-line Journal of French Studies*, 2 , pp. 132–147.
Butler, J. (2006) *Precarious Life*. London: Verso.
Caruth, C. (1996) *Unclaimed Experience: Trauma, Narrative and History*. Baltimore: Johns Hopkins University Press.
Cisneros, S. (1983) *The House on Mango Street*. New York: Vintage.
Collen, L. (2002) *Mutiny*. London: Bloomsbury.

Craps, S. (2010) 'Wor(l)ds of grief: Traumatic memory and literary witnessing in cross-cultural perspective'. *Textual Practice*, 24(1), pp. 51–68.
Erll, A. (2011) 'Travelling memory'. *Parallax*, 17(4), pp. 4–18.
Evans, R. and Norton-Taylor, R. (2010) 'WikiLeaks: Foreign office accused of misleading public over Diego Garcia'. *The Guardian*, 3 December 2010. Available at https://www.theguardian.com/politics/2010/dec/03/wikileaks-cables-diego-garcia-uk (Accessed: 1 September 2023).
Ganeshananthan, V.V. (2009) *Love Marriage.* W&N.
Grosset, F. (2021) *The Chagos Betrayal: How Britain Robbed an Island and Made Its People Disappear*. Oxford: Myriad Editions.
Gurnah, A. (2001) *By the Sea.* Bloomsbury.
Hand, F. (2010) *The Subversion of Class and Gender Roles in the Novels of Lindsey Collen.* Lampeter, UK: Edwin Mellen Press.
Hirsch, M. (1992) 'Family pictures: Maus, mourning, and post-memory'. *Discourse*, 15(2), pp. 3–29.
Hirsch, M. (2019) 'Connective arts of postmemory'. *Analecta Politica*, 9(16), pp. 171–176.
Jeffery, L. (2007) 'How a plantation became paradise: Changing representations of the homeland among displaced Chagos Islanders'. *Journal of the Royal Anthropological Institute* 13/4 pp. 951–968.
Johannessen, S.F. (2018) 'Dis/entangled hubs: Connectivity and disconnections in the Chagos Archipelago'. In Burkhard Schnepel and Edward A. Alpers (eds.), *Connectivity in Motion. Island Hubs in the Indian Ocean World.* London: Palgrave Macmillan, pp 259–287.
Kahf, M. (2003) *E-mails from Scheherazad.* Gainesville: University Press of Florida.
LaCapra, D. (2001) *Writing History, Writing Trauma.* Baltimore: Johns Hopkins University Press.
Lalit (ed.). (2002) *Diego Garcia in Times of Globalization.* Port Louis: Ledikasyon Pu Travayer.
Mishra, V. (2007) *Literature of the Indian Diaspora: Theorizing the Diasporic Imaginary.* London: Routledge, .
Mercau, E. (2019) *The Falklands War. An Imperial History.* Cambridge: Cambridge University Press.
Nichols, G. (1998) 'Wherever I hang'. *Kunapipi*, 20(1) p. 3.
Patel, S. (2005) *Le silence des Chagos.* Paris: Éditions de L'Olivier.
Pujolràs-Noguer, E. and Hand, F. (2019) 'When the Island was sold : Memory, resilience and survival among the Chagossians'. Available at: https://ddd.uab.cat/record/258819 (Accessed: 1 September 2023).
Pujolràs-Noguer, E. and Hand, F. (2021) 'The myth of the empty territory: The tragedy of the Chagos Islanders'. *Revista Canaria de Estudios Ingleses*, 82, pp. 155–172.
Ravi, S. (2017) 'Tropical cyclones in Mauritian literature'. In Anne Collett, Russell McDougall, and Sue Thomas (eds.), *Tracking the Literature of Tropical Weather.* Basingstoke: Palgrave Macmillan, pp. 25–44.
Rothberg, M. (2009) *Multidirectional Memory: Remembering the Holocaust in the Age of Decolonization.* Stanford, CA: Stanford University Press.
Rothberg, M. (2010) 'Between memory and memory: From Lieux de mémoire to Noeuds de mémoire'. *Yale French Studies,* 118/119, pp. 3–12.
Rothberg, M. (2019) *The Implicated Subject. Beyond Victims and Perpetrators.* Stanford, CA: Stanford University Press.
Spivak, G. (1988) 'Can the subaltern speak?' In Cary Nelson and Lawrence Grossberg (eds.), *Marxism and the Interpretation of Culture*. Urbana: University of Illinois Press, pp. 271–313.
van Haltern, V. (2014a) *Song of Chagos Book I Hearts in Exile.* Livermore, CA: WingSpan Press. Kindle edition.

van Haltern, V. (2014b) *Song of Chagos. Book II Hunger and Heroes. Songs Across the Sea.* Livermore, CA: WingSpan Press.

van Haltern, V. (2015) *Song of Chagos Book III Hardship to Harmony, Hands United.* Livermore, CA: WingSpan Press.

Vine, D. (2011) 'From the birth of the *Ilois* to the "footprint of freedom": A history of Chagos and the Chagossians'. In Sandra J.T.M. Evers and Marry Kooy (eds.), *Eviction from the Chagos Islands: Displacement and Struggle for Identity against Two World Powers*. Leiden: Brill, pp. 11–36.

This poem is intuitively aware of the erasure of the Chagos Archipelago…

Saradha Soobrayen

This poem is intuitively aware of the erasure of the Chagos Archipelago
at the 2022 University of Mauritius/Kings College/Witwatersrand conference,
Archipelagic Memories: 'Intersecting Geographies, Histories and Disciplines':

*"We had to face some major complications recently as we were directed by
government authorities that no presentations or conversations about Chagos,
Diego Garcia, or British sovereignty in the Indian Ocean shall take place,*

This poem is intuitively aware that *British sovereignty* rather than Mauritius
decolonisation begs the question which authority issued the directive
and which government wishes to control the Chagos narrative and to what end?

*"…no presentations or conversations about Chagos, Diego Garcia, or British
sovereignty in the Indian Ocean shall take place, seeing that the dispute over
the Chagos Islands remains a highly sensitive and controversial issue in Mauritius."*

This poem is sensing that it is a far more sensitive issue for the British
and US Governments who illegally occupy the Chagos Archipelago and
who operate a military base on Diego Garcia contrary to international law.

*We have already been in touch with the delegates whose presentations
is (sic) more directly related to the Chagos question, but we must also ask
everybody to avoid any reference to these issues during the panel sessions.*

This poem is sensing the nervousness of the scribe in the grammatical error: *is*.
Who are…who were the delegates *whose presentations were more directly related
to the Chagos question* and in which far off universe have they been exiled to?

*Please rest assured that academic freedom and research integrity remain central
concerns for us.* This poem is intuitively aware that Chagossian freedom and integrity
existed before they were theorised and referenced. Chagossian concerns are not at rest.

*We are committed to our conference as a space for sharing multiple dimensions
of our work and our explorations into 'archipelagic memory', whether
formally or informally, and are deeply apologetic about this delicate situation.*

DOI: 10.4324/9781003390299-16

This poem is sharing the multiple dimensions of Chagossian archipelagic memories;
the upfront Trump-Modi defence pact giving India military access to Diego Garcia,
and the secretive Mauritian and Indian pact militarising the geography of North Agaléga,

whether formally or informally this poem is based on sense and intuition, on facts
and a deep feeling of refusal to accept the ongoing erasure of the Chagos Archipelago.
This poem is deeply apologetic to the Chagossian community about this delicate situation.

11 "Notes for an Essay: On a Literature of Solidarity" from *Diego Garcia, A Novel*

Natasha Soobramanien and Luke Williams

The following is an excerpt from *Diego Garcia, A Novel*. This book is our attempt to circulate and highlight the story of the Chagossian people's continuing political struggle for the right to return to their homeland. We chose to write a novel rather than a non-fiction work because of the way that the very concept of fiction was instrumentalised in a geopolitical context to expedite the deracination. The word "fiction" was cited by US and UK diplomats in the very specific lie used to allay UN concerns about British and American plans to forcibly displace the inhabitants of the Chagos Islands to secure the site for a US military base: the fiction that the Chagossian Islanders were not a settled people, but an itinerant population. The book is, in part, an attempt to reclaim fiction as a tool for questioning power and reimagining other, liberatory possibilities.

In the novel, two writer friends, Damaris and Oliver Pablo, develop an obsession with this history and the urge to write about it after a chance meeting with a poet of Chagossian heritage who calls himself "Diego". Diego has named himself after Diego Garcia, the island from which his mother, now dead, and her community were forcibly removed, alongside the inhabitants of all the other islands of the Chagos Archipelago.

Like Damaris and Oliver Pablo, we realised the only way we could tell this story was by writing it together. In *Diego Garcia* we propose a kind of intersubjectivity, inscribed through our construction of a grammatical subject that shifts between she, he, and we – an attempt to speak with the collective core of Chagossian resistance. In writing this book, we wanted to take on the labour of circulating the Chagossians' story without speaking for, or over, the community. We drew on extant testimony from legal depositions, documentaries, interviews, sega lyrics, and other texts, using strategies such as quotation and transcription to amplify the voices of Chagossian protest. We also looked to other writers who have written, with great care and honesty, in solidarity with the Chagossian community, through their fiction and poetry.

In this extract, Damaris writes to Oliver Pablo about the work of Lindsey Collen, Shenaz Patel, and Saradha Soobrayen.

DOI: 10.4324/9781003390299-17

To: Oliver Pablo Herzberg
From: Damaris Caleemootoo
Subject: Judge Gaja's question
(Notes for an essay: On a literature of solidarity)
Date: 13 January 2021

Dearest Oliver,

Thank you for the birthday present/card (so clearly one of your books! That you have written in it as though it were a card! So YOU!). It just arrived.

I love it. And the promise of a letter to follow made my heart sing.

I'll wait. I have so many *fucking questions* but I'll wait.

I saw *Who Touched Me* in rile* the amazing bookshop here, but I bought *Ban in Banlieu* instead.

I don't know Wu Tsang's work but I want to explore it now – *Wildness* sounds amazing. And I loved this: 'she experiments with how to be accountable to the communities that she documents'.

I only know Moten's collaborations in terms of his conversations, but not this one. Thank you.

And I love the look of this text: how it is performing friendship and thinking together.

'Wu Tsang's works explore hidden histories, marginalized narratives, *and the act of performing itself*'. I am reading through – around? Within? – Daniel's Fred Moten books – so it's hard not to read Daniel's death in terms of performance: performance or non-performance though? I still don't know.

I ask myself sometimes, Where is Daniel's privilege now?

+++++

my *half century* wow. And still not a *grown-up*.

Are *you* grown up now? Is that why you don't write? Does it make you suffer?

Are you and Diego somewhere together? I am a bit obsessed with that – whether you found each other.

Remember that bit in *Chagos ou la mémoire des îles* where the Chagossian pilgrims on the *Mauritius Trochetia* arriving in DG are briefed by some English Navy prick who sets out the terms of the 'visit' –

Photography is not allowed, 'it's a *sensitive* island'.

He says: 'We're all *grown-ups*.'

What did he mean by 'grown-ups'??

Fully interpellated subjects?

A 'grown-up' knows the difference between fact and fiction.

There's something particular about the use of fiction and narrative as a strategy by the UK government in the story of the Chagossians' deracination that I still can't believe

e.g. that FCO memo headed 'maintaining the fiction' – from the John Pilger documentary – cynically stating the intention to misrepresent the Chagossians as itinerant workers instead of a *people.*

You see I'm trying to write an essay, and I wanted to think it through with you…

It's enough to feel you're reading at least: your reader's voice in my head as I write.

This all began because I finally read *Le silence des Chagos* by Shenaz Patel.

Someone in the book reminded me of Diego, one of the three people featured, and to whom the book is dedicated:

À Charlesia, Raymonde et Désiré, qui m'ont confié leur histoire. À tous les Chagossiens, déracinés et deportés de leur île, au profit du "monde libre"…

I feel in *Le silence des Chagos* that Patel herself is playing with the UK and US government's instrumentalizing of fiction and narrative – highlighting it through her novelization of her interlocutors' lived experience.

Sorry, this is not a letter perhaps.

Do you remember John Douglas Miller's article about Guibert's photographs of Foucault in *Tinted Window*? That beautiful letter of Foucault's he republished?

That was a letter! So not a letter but notes for an essay then I guess.

+++

Notes for an Essay

Magic

I have a photo of you on my wall. It's the one I made you pose for, the restaging of the Guibert photograph of Foucault in his robe. Dina asked who you were. I said I didn't know.

She comes up here to read with me sometimes. It's made me think back to the books I loved as a kid. I don't care how much fuckin "magic" is in a book, if it doesn't attempt to reimagine the structures of our world but with every word enforces them, it's about as magic as a breezeblock.

Empathy v Solidarity

What I notice about the most amazing children's literature is there is not much of what gets called "empathy" in it. "Empathy" in literature – litfic I should say – is an impoverished thing: centring your understanding as a reader and a writer of "the other".

But then there's Elena Ferrante, making a performance of how little she understands her characters or they one another, or themselves.

Chris Kraus's luminous consideration of Simone Weil's radical empathy in *Aliens and Anorexia.*

Octavia Butler's worldmaking empathy: her "sharers", her *ooloi* (I just finished *Dawn*).

What does a fiction of solidarity look like? I guess this is Patel's project in *Le silence des Chagos.* I am trying to think/feel through this for an essay – about three writers from outside the Chagossian community who have written about the Chagossian people's forced exile. Patel, Lindsey Collen, and Saradha Soobrayen.

Maybe translation is one of the purest forms of writing as solidarity. Spivak and her translations of Mahasweta Devi.

Solidarity requires us to get over ourselves. Outside ourselves.

I can't talk to anyone the way I talk to you. It's unnerving you not talking back. Is that how it was all that time ago? Me talking at/over you?

Pronouns have been preoccupying me; prepositions too.

I need to go now, though, sorry. Souad and Dina are coming for dinner.

Version/Hag

They've gone. It was lovely. We danced. Dina was DJ, playing her gloriously terrible autotune faves.

Dina used to turn her nose up at my cooking until I started cooking Mauritian food for her. She loves it! Especially *ladob poul*, which I cooked tonight. I never cooked that for you, obvs.

Dina pointed out to me that my hair is falling out. She said it like she was being helpful. Thanks Dina!

I've been going through the menopause, perimenopause, symptoms are peaking now – hot flushes – covid false alarms – which I don't mind, like flashbacks to the 90s and coming up on an e.

I can't wait to be a Hag. Like Ariana Reines says about Duras (and "Sucking" is the model for my structure here, I see now – so maybe what I'm thinking about here in the end is just *good* writing vs *bad* writing…).

I go to Tai Chi now like Gom and all my great-aunties. In lockdown I saw a group practising in the park and I remembered Hong Kong.

Listening/Voice

It's crazy now to think how many times I tried and failed to read *Le silence des Chagos* – the fear of my French failing me, the fear of mistranslating Patel, if only to myself. But now I live in a Francophone place. *Je me débrouille...*

The book draws on Patel's journalistic background. She tells the story of the Chagossian community exiled to Mauritius through the experiences of three people she came to know – Charlesia, Raymonde, and Désiré – their stories shared with Patel in conversations spanning a number of years.

There is something powerful in the force of narrative fiction combined with testimony – it's fiction in the sense that Patel uses the techniques of a novelist to tell a true story, to *inhabit it* as a writer. Interesting to consider it alongside Svetlana Alexievich's project of testimony, her *novels in voices.*

Patel is drawing on the feelings of Charlesia, Raymonde and Désiré as well as their stories. A different strategy to Alexievich's. But both feel like radical acts of listening.

Charlesia Alexis's Voice

Charlesia in the book is the activist and singer Charlesia Alexis who died in 2012: she was in Daëron's film and of course we have read about her in countless legal documents, research papers, etc. She was one of the elders who took part in the original women's protests and hunger strikes and was a founder member of the Chagos Refugees Group in Mauritius.

I'm listening to her album on Spotify now: *La voix des Chagos*. Chagossian sega.

Charlesia Alexis's voice is incredible, raw, like a voice sounds when someone has cried so much they can't cry any longer – or like she *refuses* to. Patel writes *voix de cendre et de sel*. You can *feel* it. And the sound of the tambour, how the fingers play on it, a kind of knocking, or rapping, like on a door, no, perhaps more the tapping you would do on wood to replicate hard raindrops as sound effects for a story. But more rhythmic. A sort of shuffling of the fingers. It's mesmerising. And on one track in particular, "Wiyem alé" – elemental.

Patel writes about this song in her novel, written by Charlesia and her group for a fellow musician who has died, a tambourier, Wiyem. So this instrument is the song's heartbeat.

Testimony and Fiction

Do you remember watching *Chagos ou la mémoire des îles* with Heather and Morgan at Cove Park? Charlesia Alexis is one of the members of the Chagos Refugee Group who came to London in 2003 to testify in the High Court. But I have since discovered that for complex funding reasons Michel Daëron made another film covering that same period, *Il était une île, Diego Garcia*, focusing on this court case.

After the judge rules against the Chagos Refugee Group members there's a scene in their b'n'b in London where they read out reports of the case from the papers. Some of these reports highlight derogatory remarks made by Judge Ouseley about Charlesia Alexis, who is then seen blaming herself for the outcome of the case. I went and found Judge Ouseley's 300-page summary online. He's highly critical of the credibility of the Chagossian witnesses, but is particularly contemptuous of Charlesia Alexis, accusing her of lying.

In the film the Chagossians' lawyer Robin Mardemootoo says:

> Amongst the archives in London we found many things we didn't know existed. Because around 1997–98, certain documents were declassified, came into the public domain and became available to anyone. Hence the wonderful exchange – today I can say "wonderful" – between the British Minister of Foreign Affairs and the American Minister of Foreign Affairs where the American writes: "Nowadays, with all the independence debates taking place in the United Nations, it must remain secret. We must create a fiction that lets it be known that these islands were always uninhabited."
>
> Three weeks later, the British replies: "I would go further, not only must we create a fiction, but we must maintain that fiction. We must engage a political plan to this end."

Point of View

In Patel's book, it's from the POV of Charlesia Alexis that the story of the forced displacement is introduced. Charlesia Alexis was one of the Chagossian people who went to Mauritius on routine business (medical care for her husband) and was suddenly prevented from returning – told *Zil inn fermé*. How can you close an island? Like a factory shut down.

Charlesia Alexis returns to the docks again and again to ask about her passage home and is always turned away. Six years later, in 1973, she is once again on the docks when she sees the *Nordvaer*. The passengers are being escorted off by soldiers, among them a woman she recognises from home. That is when she realises that she will never be able to return.

How Patel tells the story through the specific perspectives of the individuals she writes about but also, how she allows these individuals to *see* one another. In Charlesia seeing Raymonde come off the boat, in Désiré seeing Charlesia at the port, there is an affirmation of Charlesia, Raymond, and Désiré's recognition of one another as people from the same community who understand one another's experiences as only *they* can, a move by Patel that at once acknowledges her power as the story's writer to *mediate* this story, but at the same time, *refuses this power*, giving it up to the people she's writing about. *With.*

Boat

An incredible section which could only happen in a novel.

It features Désiré, nicknamed *Nordvaer* since he is born on the ship that has taken the last of the Chagossians still living on the islands into their forced exile.

Because of his birth at sea and the way the registration is fucked up by careless administrators, he lacks valid ID papers.

> *Désiré ne savait plus où il en était. Mauricien? Il avait toujours vécu ici, mais n'en avait pas la nationalité. Seychellois? Il n'avait jamais vu ce pays. Britannique? On voudrait encore moins de lui là-bas. Chagossien? Il ne connaissait pas ces îles où il aurait dû voir le jour. Son lieu de naissance était un bateau, qui avait disparu.*

In trying to sort out his identity papers he ends up writing to the national library of Norway, where the ship was originally in service. He receives some newspaper cuttings about the ship.

What follows is a trippy sequence, a dream, where the boat's "life", and its role in the deracination, is imagined in close third person, which could also be read as Désiré's perspective, given the ambiguity of the ship's masculine gender (afterwards we read that: *Toute la nuit, ce bateau a parlé dans sa tête*).

The story of the dogs' extermination is recounted as something the boat "hears" one of the passengers confessing. The boat "witnesses" the suffering of the Chagossians, and is haunted by it:

> *Ils resonnent en lui, les cris silencieux que ces hommes et ces femmes ont étouffés au fond de leur gorge, tellement fort qu'ils ont coulés de leurs yeux en longues trainées salées. C'est ce jour-là qu'il a commencé à rouiller de l'intérieur.*
>
> *They resounded in [it/him?], the silent screams those men and women had stifled deep in their throats, so powerful these had leaked from their eyes in long, salty streaks. It was on that day that [he/it] had begun to rust from the inside.*

The ship, an object, shows more feeling – more empathy – than the "humans" who executed this deracination.

In a beautiful review of the book, the writer Ariel Saramandi tells us that Patel first wrote about Chagos as a journalist, "but she always felt like it wasn't enough. 'I wanted to give flesh and voice to their story, tell it from the inside.'"

From the *inside*. So perhaps solidarity is to write from the *inside*. Back to prepositions again … Trinh T. Minh-ha, and "*speaking nearby*". From an interview with Minh-ha: "Nothing is given in the process of understanding the 'social' of our daily lives. So every single work I come up with is yet another attempt to inscribe this constant flow from the inside out and outside in."

NB "nearby", not "beside". The difference between solidarity and empathy.

Concrete

Reading the book made me think of Diego, and of Daniel. I thought of Diego when Désiré tries and fails to get a bank account so he can get paid for his two days' labour on a building site, the episode that leads to his trying to sort out his paperwork.

And I thought about Daniel when I read about Désiré's brutal experience on the construction site –

> *Tout ce gris refermait d'un coup sur lui. La tour, déjà haute, obstruait le ciel, le ferraille hérissait le béton froid, la poussière de ciment fardait indistinctement l'herbe rare et les cheveux des hommes. ... La poussière de ciment lui collait au corps, son acidité lui rongeait la peau. La grisaille asphyxiait ses muscles et sa volonté.*

What Daniel wrote about the concrete dust of London:

> *Liquid concrete seeps through the synapses and it doesn't just make it hard to think – it hurts. Concrete is killing the planet, I read. Of course it is. What would be the smallest possible degree of concrete and would it fit in a brain cell. There's no doubt; my brain cells have toxins of all kinds in them, concrete dust too I'm sure. Can we at least form a community around this. Toxic Brain Anonymous, in which we can cry and look at pictures of each other as smiling children. Remind each other that there was a time when we were not really thinking all that clearly and it was ok.*

In *Chagos ou la mémoire des îles* the pain of seeing the Chagossian elders setting foot on Diego Garcia for the first time since the expulsion, falling to their knees and kissing the ground – concrete.

In/visible

At the end of the book, after Charlesia has told Désiré the full story of the deracination, the struggle to return, and the story of life on Chagos before the British forced them to leave, Désiré asks Charlesia if it was really as wonderful in Chagos as everyone remembers. Charlesia tells him, *C'est comme ça dans notre souvenir. Et le souvenir, c'est tout ce qu'il nous reste.*

The book ends on a really beautiful formulation about remembrance.

You will be able to read it now, thanks to Jeffrey Zuckerman's translation. Or you could let me read it to you one day. I could translate it for you.

Patel's *book* is an act of remembrance.

I think that too of Clément Siatous' paintings.

Memory as resistance. Resisting erasure. I saw Clément Siatous in an interview online. He was being filmed painting. He said, in Mauritian Kreol, When I'm painting like this, I am *there.*

I go back to Daëron's film, to Rosmond Saminaden's question, why the deportation was *at night.* And the only possible answer he can find: so that the island would no longer be visible to the Chagossians. But this is what Clément Siatous does: *he makes the islands visible.*

But I haven't even reached Collen and Soobrayen yet. Tomorrow?

"Tomorrow"

In fact it's two days now, sorry.

I had to go to the commune to fetch my new residence/ID card, to allow me the right to stay.

To collect this you go to guichet 12 from 8 to 12 pm. I went yesterday but forgot a particular piece of paper. So I had to go back again.

Souad and Dina have a parrot that matches their sofa, down to an exact match in colour/shape of the orange splodge on each cheek. Whenever they let it out of its cage, which they do every day, it likes to sit on the top of their fridge and nibble the edges of the important papers for appointments etc. that Souad has attached there with magnets. The effect is quite artistic.

Learning to Read Lindsey Collen

In the same way it took me a while to read *Le silence des Chagos*, it took me a while to learn how to read Lindsay Collen's writing. I changed, or the world did. There was something I struggled to connect to it, an energy that disturbed me, but which I now find exhilarating. Writing as an intense kind of speaking. (Reading Mahasweta Devi helped.)

Mutiny

Collen's novel *Mutiny* features a Chagossian character, Mama Gracienne, although the story of the Chagossian exile is not centred in the novel, but connected to a wider narrative: the state's monopoly on violence.

It's set in 1998 in a jail cell of the women's maximum security prison on the main island of Mauritius, in the few days before a powerful cyclone is due to pass over the area. The narrator, Juna, is a computer expert imprisoned on the charge of "allegation", a fiction. She shares a cell with the young Leila, banged up for causing an "effusion of blood" – aka punching a policeman. They are joined by Mama Gracienne, a Chagossian elder, in for "confession" – accused of murdering her daughter.

As they wait for the cyclone to hit, they swap stories of their "crimes" and share recipes for the dishes they most crave – (including *bred sonz*, my mother's favourite) and Juna lets them in on a secret: her plans to circumvent the prison's computerised locking systems and release all the imprisoned women, a plan that the approaching cyclone will make possible.

The narrative is punctuated by Juna's transcriptions of pointed legal definitions copied out from books in the prison library, e.g. the definition of the state of Mauritius (from the Constitution of Mauritius Act), encompassing among other territories the Chagos Archipelago, including Diego Garcia.

Struggle/pronouns

The book is being written by Juna; there is a focus on the labour of her writing, her struggle to obtain materials. The book honours storytelling and writing as acts of resistance.

But what I am intrigued by, in connection with Collen's representation of a member of the Chagossian community, is her use of pronouns.

Collen has organised the narrative in sections named for pronouns, e.g. "We, us" (the three of them), "She, her" (the story of young Leila), "You in the plural" (the story of a nascent political party told by Juna), "I/me" (Juna's story) and "They/them" (the guards, or "Blue Ladies"). Throughout, Mama Gracienne is addressed directly, as "you": her introduction into the story is presented in the section "You in the singular".

As though this whole structuring device was about this "you"; created to support it.

This "you" feels like an acknowledgement, an honouring.

Lindsey Collen and Charlesia Alexis

Collen, a white South African woman, is writing from the POV of a woman of colour, a character apparently based on her friend also named Juna, a trade union activist who was wrongfully arrested on this same specious charge of "allegation".

I find it interesting to consider Collen's position in relation to the essay by Claudia Rankine and Beth Loffreda, "On Whiteness and The Racial Imaginary: Where writers go wrong in imagining the lives of others". Have you read it?

Arguments refuting cultural appropriation in Anglophone litfic seem to centre around the writer's right to have unimpeded extractive rights to the world's narrative resources. But Collen's project feels the opposite of extractive.

Her linguistic situation is interesting: the dominant language of literature in Mauritius is French; the language in which Shenaz Patel, Ananda Devi, Nathacha Appanah, and Barlen Pyamootoo write.

Collen is one of Mauritius' few Anglophone writers of literature.

Collen is a lifelong activist, involved in the anti-apartheid struggle and has lived for most of her adult life in Mauritius, a founder member of the radical leftwing political party Lalit. In the acknowledgements for *Mutiny* she writes:

> For sharing an arrest and a trial in Port Louis in 1981 with me, thanks to my seven co-accused, all women from Diego Garcia, the Chagos Islands and Mauritius Main Island; and to our lawyer Kader Bhayat.

> I wanted to know more about the trial. I looked online and found that one of the women who was tried with Collen – for protesting about the deportation, and in support of Chagossian women on hunger strike – was Charlesia Alexis.

I read more about these protests in "Charlesia Alexis: The Struggle of the Chagossian Women", an article by Laura Jeffery

> "We were just women; there were no men at all in those days," Charlesia mentions. Why not? "When we did demonstrations, the police beat the men ... so we decided to use a majority of women and a minority of men." The Chagossians' struggle was also supported by Mauritian members of the radical Women's Liberation Movement, who joined in the demonstrations. "The government doesn't care about us," the protesters chanted, "Send us back to Diego Garcia!"

That chant in Kreol is *Rann nu Diego* which also means: *Give us back Diego Garcia*. In other words, the Chagos Islands.

Here are some sentences I copied from *Mutiny*:

> *The same state that can bomb a market place can arrest a drunk beggar in another market place for disturbing the peace.*

In sizing up furniture as potential weapons:

> *legs can be arms.*

Also:

> *the beauty of the story is in the listener.*
>
> *She looks unbelieving. Disbelieving. Can I blame her? I can hardly believe it myself. That's what the state does to us. Puts us in a state of disbelief.*

What is it to read fiction but to willingly suspend disbelief?

That is what the UK and US governments wanted the world to do, with the fiction that they created.

There's an irrepressible spirit of political joy in the writing of Collen's that I have read so far.

She refutes Kafka's formulation, the one Daniel wrote back to so bleakly:

> *there is hope, but not for us.*

Collen's writing makes me believe there *is* hope, for all those who despair.

I note that *Mutiny* is dedicated to the memory of her brother John (1952–1975).

Saradha Soobrayen

Finally, an amazing text by the British Mauritian poet, Saradha Soobrayen, "Out of place, out of language, out of home: Fifteen pieces of poetic inquiry". In these 15 verses, Soobrayen gives an account of her experiences as poet in "non"-residence on the AHRC-funded project CHAGOS: Cultural Heritage Across Generations.

I love how Saradha Soobrayen makes visible in the poem the institutional framework of this project, staging the difficulties she experiences in trying to think through her poetic enquiry (and testimony). And how she shares her personal reflections on the complexity of this experience for her, how her time with the Chagossian community touches upon her own experience of diaspora.

What I loved most: some lines I have copied out from Saradha Soobrayen's work:

> *Having lacked the sinew and muscle for an essay*

She writes:

> *I have struggled to find a form that stays afloat, only to find my hands bloody with the guts of poetry and a Chagossian woman's lament, "not another book".* (from *ii*)

And:

> *I learned about sagren, the Chagos Islanders dying of sadness from the film* Stealing a Nation. *I rejected both of my governments. I was appalled and riddled with guilt, complacency and a wish for another poet to respond.* (from *vii*)

Also:

> *At the 2016 launch of "Kayo Chingonyi: A Creative/Critical Residency on Migration", I read a short poem on the long poem as a space for marginalized voices: "[a] poem can buckle under that kind of expectation to represent or speak for another, there needs to be self-doubt, writing with a sense of failure". I find myself questioning the ambition of such a poem while no one with a marginalized voice was present at this event or writing poetry, and why would they be? The Chagossians were writing letters to the UK Home Office, requesting visas for the children and family left in Seychelles and Mauritius.* (the whole of *viii*)

But most of all, this:

> *As a child, I could trace around the shape of Mauritius from a keyring, the souvenirs, a small blue photo album with a few outlines of the nine districts. As a British child I didn't completely understand the Kreol spoken aloud and I did not understand how much it would matter.* (from *xiii*)

I want to read more of Saradha Soobrayen's work.

Judge Gaja's Question

Did you notice the subject heading of my email? Did you get the reference? Lord Gaja's question. That was the one question asked by any of the 13 international court of justice judges in relation to the advisory opinion requested by Mauritius, about its partial decolonisation by Britain, which hived off the Chagos Islands before granting independence.

Judge Gaja's question has been tugging at me while I've been thinking about these texts: "In the process of decolonisation relating to the Chagos Archipelago, what is the relevance of the will of the population of Chagossian origin?"

I come back to Charlesia Alexis's album. To Clément Siatous' art.

I guess I am wondering why you and I felt – I still feel – so compelled to engage with this story as writers.

How as a writer do you tell a story that needs to be shared, if it is not *your* story?

I meet people all the time, people from the UK or the US who are otherwise well informed and politically engaged who've never heard about Chagos or the Chagossians or what the UK and US governments did to them in the name of "freedom"; what they continue to subject the Chagossian people to. How the Chagossian people are resisting. But are asking for support, solidarity.

I went to an online conference organized by Chagossian Voices, a platform for the global Chagossian diaspora. One of the organisers, Frankie Bontemps, spoke of the issues facing Chagossians in the UK today: the struggle and huge costs to secure British citizenship for younger members of Chagossian families excluded from the legal ruling on this. The struggle for Chagossian groups to secure any of the £40 million fund supposedly allocated to the Chagossian community in the UK.

At the webinar I saw blank squares with names I didn't recognise and wondered if one of them might be Diego.

Sometimes I think about the thing Diego wrote in his notebook. *Some poems are not for you.*

I thought perhaps you might like to write this essay with me?

writing with a sense of failure: I cherish these words of Saradha Soobrayen's.

Cake

I had Souad and Dina up here for tea and cake the other afternoon: I thought it might be nice for Souad to eat some cakes she hadn't made, for once. I found a recipe for napolitaines online: those little pink sugary cakes you get in Mauritius.

In Saradha Soobrayen's poem, she writes about learning to make a Chagossian coconut cake called matouftwa, a sweet coconut cake: *I will choke you.*

D. x

12 The British Courts and the Chagos Story

An Exercise in Colonial Justice

Satvinder Juss and Chris Monaghan

One and the Same: Empire and Constitutional Law

The decision to detach the Chagos Archipelago from the then British colony of Mauritius was sanctioned by the supremacy of British constitutional law, which gives a government the *carte blanche* ability to unilaterally carve up existing colonies and reallocate their constituent parts to other, or brand-new, colonial territories. This was classic imperialism. Much has been written, and will continue to be written, about the United Kingdom's approach to the creation of the British Indian Ocean Territory (see Allen and Monaghan, 2018; Allen, 2014; Sands 2022; Murray and Frost, 2018; Burri and Trinidad, 2021; Juss, 2017). In November 1965 as part of the Lancaster House Agreement, the Mauritian delegation, representing the independent political branch of the then British colony, agreed, with some persuasion and questionable encouragement to the detachment of the Chagos Archipelago and the creation of the British Indian Ocean Territory (for commentary see Sedley, 2015; Monaghan, 2023). The British Indian Ocean Territory was created within an imperial framework, with the dominant colonial state forcing the hand of its arguably subservient colony (however distasteful such a relationship seems today) to agree to a detachment of part of its territory. Arguably there was a sham of consent, as the UK could have unliterally detached Chagos using the prerogative powers, as it had previously done so to create the Seychelles as a separate colonial territory.

The detachment and creation of British Indian Ocean Territory (and its continued governance) is exercised under domestic prerogative powers by British politicians and civil servants based at the Foreign, Commonwealth and Development Office in London. The United Kingdom has used domestic constitutional law (i.e. the prerogative powers) to govern its empire and trade colonial possessions with other colonial powers, such as the decision to swap Heligoland (off the coast of Germany) for the island of Zanzibar in the Heligoland-Zanzibar Treaty 1890 (note that the Anglo-German Agreement Act 1890 gave Parliamentary assent to the transfer). (For commentary see Fossli Gjersø, 2015; Cohn, 2021; Kershaw, 2022; Darwin, 1997.)

The role of empire and the United Kingdom's view as to the role of the imperial power as controller of colonies and territories has always been highly contested. This chapter does not seek to, nor can it adequately do so, provide a thorough analysis of Britain's attitude towards the empire and the expectations of being an imperial power. The reason that we do offer a brief account here though is because of the direct relationship between imperialism and the Chagos Islands.

DOI: 10.4324/9781003390299-18

Firstly, the governance of Britain's remaining empire is still in the hands of the Foreign, Commonwealth and Development Office, with little effective parliamentary oversight regarding the laws that civil servants draft and ministers present to monarch to be approved as Orders in Council. Much has been written about the shortcomings of colonial law making through the Privy Council (see Sedley, 2015; Scott, 2020; Cormacain, 2013). As Paul Scott has argued, "the ongoing existence of the Privy Council is to create an artificial divide between the domestic and the imperial constitutions which both hinders the normal processes of democratic accountability and works to conceal the residue of the British Empire from the view of those who study the domestic constitution" (Scott, 2020, p. 262). Furthermore, Scott is clear that, "[t]o confront the anomalies of the Privy Council is to confront the UK's unambiguous imperial past and, more importantly, its ambiguous imperial present" (Scott, 2020, p. 271). Such a view is supported by Sir Stephen Sedley's views on the workings of the Privy Council and the absence of accountability and the absence of legislative control over laws made for overseas territories (Sedley, 2015, pp. 133–134).

Secondly, even though the established formulation that laws should be made for the peace, order and good government and the colony in question, which in itself is a lofty ideal and implicitly justifies the colonial rule as benign and enlightened, the interests of the imperial power can outweigh the needs of the colony's inhabitants (see "*R (on the application of Bancoult) v Secretary of State for Foreign and Commonwealth Affairs (No.2)*" and the view put forward by Professor John Finnis below) (Finnis, 2008) and also Hakeem O Yussuf (2013). Thirdly, the United Kingdom rode roughshod over the rights of the islanders and acted contrary to the rule of law, constitutional understandings, and provisions of Magna Carta. This was the view of the minority Lords Bingham and Mance in Bancoult (see Juss, 2017; Monaghan, 2012; Arvind, 2012).

Fourthly, whilst Britain has legislated to allow legislative independence for its colonies in the form of the Colonial Laws Validity Act 1865 and the Statute of Westminster Act 1931, this is not the case for the Chagos Islands. Fifthly, it is important to turn to history in order to appraise the legacy of empire (Veveers, 2023; Darwin, 1997). For example, the British use of martial law in its territories and the suspension of Habeas Corpus is well documented (see "*Phillips v Eyre*" (1870); Kostal, 2005; Halliday, 2012; Ryan, 2018). British conduct in the Caribbean and the system of slavery that existed demonstrated the limitations of civil liberties and the contradictions of the approach to slavery (see O'Brien, 2015). The conduct of the then Governor of Trinidad Sir Thomas Picton in ordering the torture of a child Luisa Calderon is now receiving appropriate coverage in the media, with calls to remove Picton's statue and portraits. Leighton James is clear that, "[a]t the heart of it were a clash of different times and values. Britain was becoming more enlightened and liberal, while the reality of life in the colonies remained dangerous and violent" (Bryan, 2022). Picton's defence was that he was applying local Spanish Law and although he was convicted at the subsequent trial, he later had his conviction overturned (Epstein, 2012). This can be contrasted to the trial and execution of Governor Joseph Wall in 1802 for killing a British soldier (Anon, 1802), which was depicted by James Gillray in "Governor Wall's Ghost!" (Gillray, 1802).

The next section will consider one of the most infamous episodes in British colonial history, the impeachment of Warren Hastings.

Burke and the Ideals of Empire

What does Edmund Burke and the impeachment trial of Warren Hastings have to do with the Chagos story? One answer is nothing; another would be that they are intrinsically linked as to how the United Kingdom has viewed its empire, treated its colonies upon independence, and views its former imperial role and now current position within the modern world. Burke viewed British rule in India (through the control of the East India Company) to be neither bringing benefits to, or in the interests of, the population that the Company ruled over (Marshall, 2019). Warren Hastings, the first Governor-General of Bengal, was viewed as being the epitome of all that was wrong, and Edmund Burke rejected Hastings' justification that he had adopted the local style of rulership (for commentary see Dirks, 2006; O'Brien, 2002; Marshall, 1965; Suleri, 1992, pp. 46–47; Greene, 2013, pp. 307–317). It is important to note that Burke was not a critic of empire, rather of empire done wrongly. O'Neill argued that Burke was a "lifelong proponent and defender" of Britain's Indian empire and saw it as a source of national pride and wealth (2016, p. 92). Furthermore, Burke was a reformer rather than an abolitionist of empire, and he believed that empire could work where the right individuals were sent to govern (2016, p. 123).

Critics of British rule in India were quick to draw comparisons between the exploitative nature of Company rule (which enriched the shareholders and Company servants) and the model of the Roman empire and the perceived benefits that went with Roman conquest (Mantena, 2010). Still the appeal to classical civilisations and their respective approaches to empire was a moot point as to what was the preferred imperial model to be adopted by Britain (see Rolli, 2019). Kumar observed that:

> [a]dherents of the Greek model… were inclined to regard empire as a temporary necessity, or perhaps as an honorable although burdensome responsibility, and looked forward to its disappearance as colonies grew to maturity and were given their freedom. Those with an eye on Rome saw empire as a noble aspiration and goal, one that the British were especially suited to promote and pursue.
>
> (2012, p. 83)

Robert Travers has observed that:

> The emergence in the nineteenth century of the powerful "Indian empire" as a distinct form of colonial rule, the site of a neo-Roman civilising mission, by contrast to the Grecian confederacy of the white settler colonies, exercised a powerful impact on the historiography of empire; the Atlantic and the Indian Ocean began to appear as quite different zones of imperialism mapping on to hardening hierarchies of civilisation and race.
>
> (2012, p. 126)

Returning to the importance of the fact that the House of Commons impeached Hastings and that he was tried before the House of Lords, Mithi Mukherjee explored the critical nature of the Hastings impeachment trial through the articulation of competing views of empire. Mukherjee made a distinction between the colonial (India) and the imperial (North America). She observed that "[i]t was in the Hastings's trial that these two visions of the future of empire in India dramatically clashed" (2005, p. 595). Empire should have a benefit for those under British rule and not just amount to a benefit for the commercial interest of Britain and the shareholders of the East India Company. Mukherjee is clear that:

> What is often overlooked about the Impeachment Trial of Warren Hastings is that it was also the first major public trial in which the legal and moral legitimacy of colonialism in the East itself was thrown into question. Indeed, it could be argued that it was on this occasion, and in this act of defending the rights of an alien population against an oppressive and brutal colonial regime, that some of Burke's long-held political and ethical convictions found their clearest expression …
>
> [Burke's] effort in the historical context of the eighteenth century to go beyond the territorially bounded discourses of political sovereignty and institutional practices of nation-states, and conceptualize a form of deterritorialized juridical-imperial sovereignty that would be exercised not in the pursuit of the exclusive interest of the colonizing nation but, rather, in ensuring that colonial administration in India remained firmly grounded in "native" society and prevented from exercising absolute and arbitrary power over it.
>
> (Mukherjee, 2023., pp. 84, 86)

Warren Hastings was and remains a controversial figure, and his legacy is contested (see Banks, 2022; Moon, 1947; Macaulay, 1841). Macaulay reflected, "Our feeling towards him is not exactly that of the House of Commons which impeached him in 1787; neither is it that of the House of Commons which uncovered [their heads] and stood up to receive him in 1813" (Macaulay, 1841, p. 160). The impeachment was brought against Hastings as a result of long-running concerns over the management of the East India Company and the behaviour of its employees who were deemed to be exploiting their position at the expense of the local population. Having then acquired too much wealth, they then posed a danger to the political and constitutional situation within Britain upon their return. These Nabobs, the quick rich of the late eighteenth century were vilified, and Hastings had been appointed by the Directors of the East India Company as Governor-General of Bengal under Lord North's Regulating Act of 1773, in order to curb their behaviour. The term Nabobs is an anglicisation of the Mughal term Nawab, which was the title of a regional ruler. It was intended as a derogatory term to criticise the conduct of Company servants and their new-found wealth (Nechtman, 2010). Although as O'Neill argues Burke did not see India as not corrupting the Company's servants, but rather he saw them as corrupting India (2016, pp. 122–123).

Hastings was viewed by many contemporaries as not only failing to do this but of behaving in a similar manner, oppressing local rulers and engaging in arbitrary rule. According to Conniff, "Burke felt that the story of the British venture in India was one of almost unmitigated depredation" and this disaster was caused by "a breach of trust by the British East India Company and its Indian Administration led by Warren Hastings" (1993, p. 300). The move to impeach Hastings was championed by Burke, Sheridan, Fox, and other members of the Whig opposition and was crucially supported in the House of Commons by their opponents, Pitt the Younger and Dundas (Monaghan, 2011, pp. 68–69).

Sen observed that:

> Burke's invective against the political ambitions and corrupt excesses of the East India Company in India, exemplified by… Hastings, was based not on the future prospect of British rule in India, but on its present state of governance, which Burke found to be an abdication of Britain's moral responsibility.
> (2015, p. 713)

This failure of moral responsibility was arguably epitomised by the excesses of the Company's officials and the failure of Parliament to effectively control the Company. Burke's solution was to advance the idea of trusteeship and the ideal of good governance, whereby the benefits of British rule did not just benefit the rulers but also those that they ruled. This is a point made succinctly by Conniff – "[i]n my view, realizing that the Indian people were incapable of controlling the East India Company, Burke turned to natural law and to a reformulated idea of trusteeship which made the British Parliament surrogates for the Indian people" (1993, p. 292). This proved to be a failure (1993, p. 301). Indeed, the use of martial law and the brutality metered out in terms of reprisals by the British in the aftermath of the 1857 mutiny (or Indian war of independence), is a case-in-point for the realities of empire, and the failure to investigate the propriety of such reprisals which contemporaries could seek to justify by the mutineers' treatment of British civilians (Kostal, 2005, pp. 206–207).

In the case of Chagos, the United Kingdom's control over the British Indian Ocean Territory neither brought benefits or civilisation; rather it exiled the population, handed over Diego Garcia, the largest island, to the United States to construct a military base and continued to block the population's return. Arguably, the United Kingdom fell below its own purported historical standards for doing empire, i.e., the justification for empire or the notion of trusteeship. The idea of trusteeship was betrayed by the United Kingdom's denial of a population to the United Nations and its long-running refusal to comply with its international law obligations regarding colonial territories. What would Burke have made of the Chagos story? The exile of an entire population does not compare unfavourably with the charges levelled against Hastings.

The UK Did Not and Continues to Refuse to Treat the Chagossians as Equals

Historically, the United Kingdom did not consult with the Chagossian community that lived on the archipelago. The population was deemed to be a transient one and not a genuine population with settled roots (Monaghan, 2018). The United Kingdom denied the existence of a permanent population which would have triggered the United Kingdom's responsibilities under Article 73 of the Charter of the United Nations. These responsibilities included the obligation to firstly "ensure, with due respect for the culture of the peoples concerned, their political, economic, social, and educational advancement, their just treatment, and their protection against abuses", and secondly, "to develop self-government, to take due account of the political aspirations of the peoples, and to assist them in the progressive development of their free political institutions, according to the particular circumstances of each territory and its peoples and their varying stages of advancement". It is somehow ironic and hard to reconcile as the United Kingdom was instrumental in the establishment of the United Nations and the precursor to the Charter in the declaration of 12 June 1941, which stated:

> [t]hat the only true basis of enduring peace is the willing co-operation of free peoples in a world in which, relieved of the menace of aggression, all may enjoy economic and social security; and that it is their intention to work together, and with other free peoples, both in war and peace to this end.
>
> (United Nations, Preparatory Years: UN Charter History)

The very purpose of the Charter of the United Nations was according to Article 1 "[t]o develop friendly relations among nations based on respect for the principle of equal rights and self-determination of peoples, and to take other appropriate measures to strengthen universal peace". The United Kingdom's treatment of, and indeed general attitude towards, the Chagossian population fell far short of this and stood in direct contrast to the Allied Powers' post-war lofty ambitions and fell within the classic tactics of nineteenth-century colonialism.

The exact status of the Chagossians (now recognised) as an indigenous people (Vine, 2008, Minority Rights Group), or (in the view of British officials) migrant workers with no roots to the territory, was highly contested. In *R (on the application of Bancoult) v Secretary of State for Foreign and Commonwealth Office (No.1)* (2000) Laws LJ was clear that the Chagossians were an indigenous people,

> They were an indigenous people: they were born there, as were one or both of their parents, in many cases one or more of their grandparents, in some cases (it is said) one or more of their great-grandparents. Some may perhaps have traced an earlier indigenous ancestry.
>
> (para 1)

The rights of indigenous people are protected by the United Nations Declaration on the Rights of Indigenous Peoples, with Article 3 confirming the right to self-determination, and Article 4 setting out their right to autonomy or self-government. Crucially, Article 6 is clear that "Every indigenous individual has the right to a nationality". Article 26 states that, "Indigenous peoples have the right to the lands, territories and resources which they have traditionally owned, occupied or otherwise used or acquired".

There had been permanent settlement on the islands by the then French colonial authorities since the late eighteenth century and by the 1930s,

> Nurseries and schools were established, and a refuse collection system provided. The infrastructure included small roads connecting different parts of the islands. Chagossians no longer solely worked on the plantations – some were blacksmiths or bakers, mechanics, carpenters or had carved out some other specialised roles.
>
> (Memorial of the Republic of Mauritius, 2012, para 2.27; see also Richard B. Allen's chapter on the history of the Chagos Islands)

The United Kingdom had good reason to emphasise the voluntary nature of the repatriation of the workers to Mauritius and the absence of compulsion on the part of the British authorities (see Monaghan, 2018). The British House of Commons was informed in 1967 by Mrs Hart MP that,

> The population of the islands is at present approximately 1,500. It fluctuates, as it consists mainly of contract labour, and their dependents, from Mauritius and Seychelles employed on the copra estates and in guano extraction and the turtle industry. The populations are of mixed African, European, Chinese and Indian origin.
>
> (1967, c305W)

This was the same message that was being articulated at the United Nations, thanks to guidance from London:

> The Foreign Office advised the UK Mission to "concert tactics with the United States Delegation" and sent additional Guidance to the UK Mission. The Guidance falsely stated that "[t]he islands chosen have virtually no permanent inhabitants". Lord Caradon, the British Ambassador at the UN, told London that there was nothing that could be done to prevent a debate on the detachment and that this position "may well lead to charges of failure to carry out our Charter obligations to those who are permanent inhabitants".
>
> (Memorial of the Republic of Mauritius, 2012, para 3.40).

The British officials knew that was bogus, and that the population had rights, even if at the time, it was not considered by the British to be indigenous:

> On the basis of the information available it seems to us difficult to avoid the conclusion that the new territory is a non- self-governing territory under Chapter XI of the Charter, particularly since it has and will or may have a more or less settled population, however small. We cannot disclaim Charter obligations to the inhabitants because they are not indigenous, since this

> would destroy our case on the Falklands and Gibraltar; nor apparently would the facts substantiate a plea that the inhabitants are not permanent – even if (which is not necessarily the case) Chapter XI of the Charter were confined to permanent populations.
>
> (Memorial of the Republic of Mauritius, 2012, n. 175)

However, even the government's position could not completely conceal the reality as to the population's factual status, as Lord Goronwy-Roberts informed the House of Lords on 14 October 1975,

> It is very difficult to define precisely the nature of this population. It was very largely made up of contract labour which moved about from one island to another, and there are a great many islands in this part of the world, as noble Lords will know. So that if I say that the majority returned to Mauritius, I feel that that is a fair statement. However, I agree that many others were born on islands in the BIOT.
>
> (1975, col 773)

Not everyone accepted this view, as Mr Cook MP informed the House of Commons, "[i]t must be a matter of some shame to this House that when the Government found themselves faced with a population of British subjects such as this, vulnerable and wholly dependent, they chose to sacrifice their interests" (1975, 1025). The United Kingdom doubled down on rejecting the idea of a Chagossian people, with Lord Trefgarne stating,

> My Lords, I am not sure, again, that it is accurate to say that the island of Diego Garcia was the homeland of these people. They were, generally speaking, migrant workers working in the copra plantations on that island. The copra plantations were being progressively run down, anyway, and the workers were in general moving away.
>
> (1980, cc540-1W).

The Chagossian people are today recognised as indigenous people, and the population denied the right to return to their homeland by the British Indian Ocean Territory (Constitution) Order 2004, live in Mauritius, Seychelles, and the United Kingdom. The distinct communities have developed a plurality of views and aims. In terms of the United Kingdom's position, the guidance on the government's website relating to Nationality and Borders Act 2022 gives the United Kingdom's current view of the Chagossians, "[t]he Chagossians are the former residents of the British Indian Ocean Territory (BIOT) also known as the Chagos Islands, who were removed from the islands, predominantly to Mauritius, between the mid-1960s and early-1970s". However, it is undeniable that the United Kingdom viewed the Chagossians as the "other", deploying racist language and colonial tropes in the 1960s and 1970s to negate the legitimacy of their belonging. The language used by officials at the Commonwealth Office was set out in Laws LJ's judgment "*R (on the application of Bancoult) v Secretary of State for Foreign &*

Commonwealth Office (No.1)" (2000): The Permanent Under-Secretary noted on 24 August 1966, that, "[w]e must surely be very tough about this. The object of the exercise was to get some rocks which will remain ours; there will be no indigenous population except seagulls who have not yet got a Committee (the Status of a Women Committee does not cover the rights of Birds)". In response, a Mr Greenhill, another civil servant, replied, "[u]nfortunately along with the Birds go some few Tarzans or Men Fridays whose origins are obscure, and who are being hopefully wished on to Mauritius etc. When that has been done I agree we must be very tough and a submission is being done accordingly" (at para 13).

More worryingly, although such language was inappropriate in the mid-20th century, there is an allegation that similar language, echoing back to the Crusoe-esque nature of the islanders, was allegedly used by Colin Roberts, the Commissioner for the British Indian Ocean Territory in 2009. Mr Roberts was alleged to have said the following at a meeting at the US Embassy, "Roberts stated that according to the HGM's [sic] current thinking on a reserve, there would be no 'human footprints' or 'Man Fridays' on the BIOT's uninhabited islands. He asserted that establishing a marine park would, in effect, put paid to resettlement claims of the archipelago's former residents…" ("*R (on the application of Bancoult) v Secretary of State for Foreign and Commonwealth Affairs (No.3)*" (2014), para 30. For a discussion see Monaghan, 2014). According to the Court of Appeal in *Bancoult (No. 3)*, the purported diplomatic cable, "purportedly summarised [the 12 May 2009 meeting] in the copy cable dated 15 May 2009 (para 76)." The Court of Appeal noted that "Mr Roberts denied making any reference to "Man Fridays"… Ms Yeadon [his colleague] also denied that Mr Roberts had used the words "Man Fridays"…' (para 76). The Supreme Court in "*R (on the application of Bancoult) v Secretary of State for Foreign and Commonwealth Affairs (No.3)*" (2018) later noted that the cable "purports to have been composed three days after the meeting took place. If it is authentic, or, perhaps more pertinently, if there is no reason to doubt its authenticity, it is, at least potentially, a significant source of evidence about the reasons for making the MPA" (para 82).

This is the central nub of the matter, if you (the colonial power) are incapable of treating someone as your equal (whether this is the population or the colony, as in the case of Mauritius), then the question must be why is this the case? This chapter does not seek to provide a full answer, rather it is our contention that the facts speak from themselves.

Firstly, Chagos remains administered from London by the Foreign, Commonwealth and Development Office. What percentage are white and elite? (UK Government, no date). In 2021, some 14.3% of civil servants were from an ethnic minority background (Foreign and Commonwealth Office, 2021).

Secondly, the continued position of the United Kingdom is fixed within a colonial mindset, where imperial considerations govern the decisions regarding Chagos (defence, foreign affairs and national interest), rather than the needs of the indigenous population. The United Kingdom's position was laid bare by Laws LJ's judgment in "*R (on the application of Bancoult) v Secretary of State for Foreign and Commonwealth Office*" (2000), about the limits of peace, order and good government:

> The authorities demonstrate beyond the possibility of argument that a colonial legislature empowered to make law for the peace, order and good government of its territory is the sole judge of what those considerations factually require. It is not obliged to respect precepts of the common law, or English traditions of fair treatment. This conclusion marches with the cases on the Colonial Laws Validity Act, and I have dealt with that. But the colonial legislature's authority is not wholly unrestrained; peace, order and good government may be a very large tapestry, but every tapestry has a border.
>
> (para 50)

The UK Misused the Provision of "Peace, Order, and Good Government" in the Law

Hakeem O. Yusuf has recently explained in his *Colonial and Post-colonial Constitutionalism in the Commonwealth: Peace, Order and Good Government,* how the "peace, order and good government (POGG) clause is found in the constitutions of almost all Commonwealth countries' and that "since its introduction, the clause has played a significant role in colonial and post-colonial constitutionalism in Commonwealth jurisdictions" (Yusuf, 2013). Nevertheless, "the peace, order and good government clause remains a relatively under-theorised and under-researched theme". The *Bancoult* decision is, however, one where it was considered by Sedley LJ in the Court of Appeal in "*R (on the application of Bancoult) v Secretary of State for Foreign and Commonwealth Affairs (No.2)*" (2007) and before that by Laws LJ in the High Court in "*R (on the application of Bancoult) v Secretary of State for the Foreign and Commonwealth Office (No.1)*" (2000).

First, Sedley LJ has explained how "the phrase, '*peace, order and good government*'" is one that "has a long legislative pedigree" but "has become a term of art in the sense that it is regularly used without further explanation to denote the delegation of large but undefined powers to a nominated rule-maker", even though it was, "a power of the greatest importance carrying commensurate responsibilities" (para 50). Indeed, "at its fullest it can bring about the creation of independent states", but, "it has limits, even if these are self-imposed" (para 50). These are, "directed to the wellbeing of a dependent territory and its population" as a way of deciding "what is best for a colony and to affirm that, like every discretion, it is limited by and to its own expressed objects" (para 51). As far as the courts were concerned, "it is their constitutional function to decide whether what has been enacted (or what it is proposed to enact) is rationally and legally capable of providing for a colony's wellbeing. If it is not, then it falls outside the prerogative power" (para 51). The situation may well be different during war-time exigencies, but the fact that "the words convey plenary or sovereign power does not necessarily import that the power is unlimited in scope" (para 53, quoting *Building Construction Federation v Minister for Industrial Relations* (1986), per Street CJ).

These sentiments were echoed by another great public law judge of the time, namely Laws LJ who observed that "peace, order and good government may be a very large tapestry, but every tapestry has a border" (para 55). So, two of the most eminent public law judges of the time had agreed on the nature of this power that the power given to the Commissioner by s.11 of the 1965 BIOT Order in Council to make laws for the *peace, order and good government* of the territory was held not to empower him to make an Ordinance exiling its entire population. In the felicitous language of Laws LJ,

> S.4 of the Ordinance effectively exiles the Ilois from the territory where they are belongers and forbids their return. But the *"peace, order, and good government"* of any territory means nothing, surely, save by reference to the territory's population. They are to be governed: not removed
>
> (para 57)

In a thunderous condemnation of Government action he further added that, "As Chitty said in 1820, the Queen has an interest in all her subjects, who rightly look to the Crown – today, to the rule of law which is given in the Queen's name" (para 57). Laws LJ drew attention to "*The Trustees Executors and Agency Co*" (1933), where Evatt J in the High Court of Australia stated at 234 that, "[t]he correct general principle is… whether the law in question can be truly described as being for the peace, order and good government of the dominion concerned" (para 55). So the Ordinance, as Sedley would have said in the Court of Appeal in "*Bancoult (No. 2)*", "it is ultra vires because it is unconnected with … governance" and so, "it falls to be quashed for irrationality" (para 48).

Second, Hooper LJ in the Divisional Court in "*R (on the application of Bancoult) v Secretary of State for the Foreign and Commonwealth Affairs (No.2)*" (2006) was also to provide an answer when he cited the Privy Council's decision in "*Liyanage v The Queen*" (1967), that the Colonial Laws Validity Act 1865 did not prevent challenge to the invalidity of a legislative measure, because the 1865 Act "abolished the vague doctrine of repugnancy" because "it was now necessary only for the colonial legislator to ascertain that there was no Imperial Act applicable and his field of action and choice of means became unfettered" (para 168). As a result, the Divisional Court held that "the 1865 Act does not preclude the public law irrationality challenge" because "we are not here concerned with repugnancy" since "'the act in question [was] the act of the executive.' As such it is amenable to judicial review" (para 169).

Third, as was stated by Sedley LJ in the Court of Appeal, it also became clear that any argument that, "an Order in Council is placed by the 1865 Act on a par with the Act of a colonial legislature and placed beyond challenge save for repugnancy to an imperial statute", cannot succeed because the 1865 Act creates a rule of priority and not of powers (para 21). This was explained by Sedley LJ when he explained that there is a way of limiting governmental power because the local colonial courts could nullify legislation that was *ultra vires* the imperial statute law, so that:

> [I]n my judgment the rule created by the 1865 Act is one of priority, not of powers: a colonial law, albeit validly enacted, is to be inoperative to the extent, but only to the extent, to which it conflicts with imperial statute law.

> That there exists a judicial power so to decide is assumed by the legislator: it is not a power created by the 1865 Act. Nor is the power of a colonial legislature unfettered: it will be limited by its own constitutive instrument and by the principle of territoriality, so that colonial judicatures remain able notwithstanding the 1865 Act to strike down local legislation which transgresses these limits. Likewise, those colonial Orders in Council made under statutory powers continued to be open to challenge not only for repugnancy to imperial legislation but, if they exceeded the powers which they purported to be exercising, for invalidity.
>
> (para 22)

Fourth, Sedley LJ relied on a series of classical constitutional cases to show that such an approach would not be inimical to colonial enactments based on the prerogative because "the modern power of public law to review the use by ministers of the royal prerogative was unrecognised in the nineteenth century" but that the "personal liability of ministers for breaches of private law in the exercise of their office under the Crown had been established by the courts during the eighteenth century' (given the well-known case of *Entick v Carrington*" (1765)). Further, *"the amenability of public authorities to the prerogative writs if they transgressed their powers was well established by 1865"* (given another classic case of see "*Cooper v Wandsworth Board of Works*" (1863)). As for *"the reviewability of the acts of ministers in the exercise of the royal prerogative*" this "was not *established until the landmark decision of the Divisional Court in Ex. Parte Lain* [1967] 2 QB 864" (para 23). So what this means is that whereas judicial review over Ministers use of prerogative goes back to the 19th century, Sedley LJ is saying that the personal liability of Ministers for breaches of private law in the exercise of their office goes back to *"Entick v Carrington"*. If so, this is an attempt by an eminent member of the English judiciary to square colonial constitutional law with that of the mother country, in a way which has rarely been done. In fact, the distinguishing feature of colonial law as confirmed by its history is that it was inherently different when it came to matters of individual liberty and coercive control. This is why Sedley LJ's attempts were in the end thwarted by the House of Lords in 2008.

Fifth, Sedley LJ says that the 1865 Act could not have taken account of the fact that, "the kind of challenge mounted in this case cannot therefore have been in the mind of either the draftsman or the legislature when the 1865 Act was written and passed". But today the "question … has been conclusively answered by the CCSU case" in a way that is "in favour of the amenability of the royal prerogative, where the subject matter is appropriate, to judicial review" (para 24). With impeccable logic Sedley LJ also relied on the elementary principle that, "the courts are reluctant to construe any but an unequivocal statutory provision as denying people access to them for the redress of justiciable wrongs, and …., the Colonial Laws Validity Act 1865 is anything but unequivocal on the question" (para 25).

Sixth, pressing forward with such water-tight logic, Sedley added that, "Repugnancy as a legislative term means an irreconcilable conflict between two laws". But here, "if an unconstitutional colonial statute is not law – as manifestly it is not – no question of repugnancy arises". As such, "the present dispute, equally, is not about whether the Constitution Order is repugnant to a superior statute or other legal provision but about whether it is law. It is accordingly not barred by the 1865 Act" (para 30).

Seventh, Sedley LJ reminded us of the fundamental issue here: namely, that the government's edicts could not have been put outside the reach of the jurisdiction of the courts by asking himself the next question "whether there are today at common law any larger constraints upon the prerogative power to legislate for the colonies" (para 31). Here Sedley LJ borrowed from the words of Lord Atkin in *Liversidge v Anderson* (1942) because in "*Bancoult*", when the Government retorted that "constitutionally and legally it is the Monarch and not the minister who makes a colonial Order in Council, and… this places the process outside the jurisdiction of the courts" (para 33), placing reliance on *Quark Fishing* UKHL 57 where Lord Bingham said that, "Such power and authority can be exercised only by the Queen, … It is in my view correct in constitutional theory to regard the Secretary of State as her mouthpiece and medium" (para 33). Sedley LJ disagreed. This is because there

> the context was not the making of a legislative instrument in the name of the Crown; it was the issuing by a minister of an instruction pursuant to an Order in Council which authorised Her Majesty to issue such instructions through a Secretary of State but gave ministers no independent powers.

Eighth, but in any event,

> What neither *Quark Fishing* nor any other case decides is that the theoretical source of a measure *in the Crown* protects it from legal challenge as an executive act, which is what it substantively and constitutionally is. Were it otherwise, no judicial review of central government action could ever take place.
>
> (para 33, emphasis added)

Ninth, in *"Bancoult"*, the older case of *"Ibralebbe v The Queen"* (1964), was discredited by Sedley LJ, who observed that in *"Ibralebbe"*:

> [T]he Privy Council held: "The words 'peace, order and good government' connote, in British constitutional language, the widest law-making powers appropriate to a Sovereign." In *Riel v The Queen* (1885) 10 App. Cas. 675, 678, their Lordships, per Lord Halsbury LC, described the same words in the British North America Act 1871 as "apt to authorise the utmost discretion of enactment for the attainment of the objects pointed to": "They are words under which the widest departure from criminal procedure as it is known and practised in this country have been authorised in Her Majesty's Indian empire. Forms of procedure unknown to the English common law have there been established and acted upon, and to throw the least doubt upon the validity of powers conveyed by those words would be of widely mischievous consequence."

In *"Bancoult"*, it was argued that "'where there are no such governing words, therefore, the prerogative power to legislate for the colonies must, Mr Howell submits, be a truly sovereign power: in the words of the Privy Council in *Liyanage'* (ante, 286), 'the full legislative powers of a sovereign independent state'" (para 63).

But against this, there was the argument on behalf of *"Bancoult"* that, "those powers must be exercised in accordance with the terms of the constitution from which the power derives", and that this is equally "true of a country such as the United Kingdom whose constitution, though unwritten, is no less real" and the Court of Appeal in *Bancoult* accepted this argument for the reasons it had given earlier in the judgment, namely, that

> the royal prerogative, while the common law accords it a very large area of judgment and discretion in colonial matters, is not unlimited or unreviewable. It may still be, as the decided cases from an earlier phase of Britain's imperial history hold, that it is not a sufficient objection that what has been enacted colonially would be improper or unconstitutional if done here.
>
> (para 64)

The reference to an earlier epoch of imperial history was a recognition of the fact, "that Lord Mansfield was right before his time when he held in *Campbell v Hall* (1774) 1 Cowp. 204, 209, that the colonial prerogative power was such that the Monarch 'cannot make any new change contrary to fundamental principles'" (para 64).

Tenth, in a thundering conclusion, Sedley LJ moved to suggest that, "unless the administration of the United Kingdom's remaining colonies is to be an Alsatia where the rule of law does not run, in my judgment the latter must today be the case" (para 65).

Eleventh, the reason for this was that,

> the governance of each colonial territory is in constitutional principle a discrete function of the Crown. That territory's interests will not necessarily be the interests of the United Kingdom or of its allies. This is not to say that the two things are mutually exclusive: they will often, perhaps usually, be interdependent, so that the defence of a colony from attack, and even its use as a base to protect the United Kingdom, may serve both its and the United Kingdom's interests. But that is not the case here.
>
> (para 67)

Twelfth, he pointed out that although "Lord Hoffmann said in *Quark Fishing* (ante) at §78: that an examination of the location and balance of the varying interests which a measure was designed to meet 'would be something for which a court is not at all well suited'", the fact was that, "he declined to hold that it was not justiciable" (para 68) and we know from even more difficult cases involving acts of state by foreign states, where torture has been used with the complicity of British officials, that the UK courts have now held that, such actions are "'justiciable' as is clear from *Belhaj*" (Juss, 2019).

Finally, there was the question of the reason given by the government for the Order in Council, namely, that the territory was to be "set aside to be available for the defence purposes of the Government", but Sedley LJ declared that this "single ground" even though "strategic" was one which, "on the evidence" was "in direct conflict with – the interests of the Chagossians" and so "consequently fails to justify the substantive provision because it lies beyond the objects, whether expressed in terms of peace, order and good government or in terms of the legitimate purposes of colonial governance, for which ministers are entrusted by law with the use of the royal prerogative" (para 69).

This approach was countered in "*R (on the application of Bancoult) v Secretary of State for Foreign and Commonwealth Affairs (No.2)*" (2008) by the majority in the House of Lords. Lord Hoffmann, was clear that:

> Her Majesty in Council is therefore entitled to legislate for a colony in the interests of the United Kingdom. No doubt she is also required to take into account the interests of the colony (in the absence of any previous case of judicial review of prerogative colonial legislation, there is of course no authority on the point) but there seems to me no doubt that in the event of a conflict of interest, she is entitled, on the advice of Her United Kingdom ministers, to prefer the interests of the United Kingdom. I would therefore entirely reject the reasoning of the Divisional Court which held the Constitution Order invalid because it was not in the interests of the Chagossians.
>
> (para 49)

But this was stated (after the publication of Professor John Finnis' Paper on "Common Law Constraints" asking "Whose Common Good Counts?" (Finnis, 2008) – which is addressed later below, and which appears to have been strangely influential on the Court).

Therefore, the constitution ultimately favoured the paramount interests of the colonial master, even if this meant exiling an entire population and preventing their return. Yes, there needed to be a tangential benefit for the colony, as Lord Carswell observed, "I am therefore willing to accept, as does Lord Rodger, that the Orders had to be laws made for the 'peace, order and good government' of the colony" (para 127); however, the removal of the islanders is not something for the courts to use as motivation for declaring the law invalid as

> However distasteful they may consider a provision such as those under consideration in the present case, I think that the rule of abstinence should remain unqualified and the courts should not pronounce on the validity of such a provision on the ground that it is not for the peace, order and good government of the colony in question.
>
> (para 130).

Lord Carswell spoke of "abstinence" and whilst there is a clear rationale for the courts to be careful when reviewing an essentially political decision, where this decision is of questionable legality and reinforces the exiled status of the islanders, this rationale reinforces the perception that constitutional law protects the interests of the colonial state over that of its disempowered colonial subjects.

Frost and Murray put this relationship in stark terms:

> Colonialism involves an assertion of dominance, both of the metropolis over the colony and the settler over the native … The effect of this power imbalance, simultaneously underpinning and undermining imperial relationships, is often magnified by an empire's need to accommodate budgetary and security concerns. These tensions are prominent in the UK's treatment of the Chagossians … [the] colonial administrators under London's direction considered themselves better placed than the Chagossians to administer the BIOT and maximise its benefit for the "undivided" *imperium*. The islanders' expulsion could be justified so long as it was cloaked in legal authority in a hat tip to liberal imperialism, as their contribution to the realisation of imperial security.
>
> (Frost and Murray, 2020, pp. 272 and 276)

They would subsequently note the subservience of the needs of the Chagossians to the needs of the imperial metropolis:

> The nature of imperial law helped dispossess both communities, and their exclusion was, in terms, their unwilling contribution to the commonweal … The Chagossians' expulsion and the subsequent litigation mirror aspects of an earlier example of colonial expropriation to advance imperial interests ... The Crown had no intention of shaping BIOT policy around the Chagossians, therefore their existence had to be denied. Their numbers were deliberately minimised.
>
> (Frost and Murray, 2020, pp. 765, 768 and 772)

It is important to note that this subservience is underpinned by the self-interest of the imperial power (or modern United Kingdom with its string of overseas territories around the globe) and reinforced by imperial constitutional law, which is arguably too rooted in the needs of empire and the "mother country", than the realities of a modern democracy clinging onto contested territories. The minority in *Bancoult (No.2)* used this imperial constitutional law to reinforce the rights of the Chagossians, allowing them to benefit from the inheritance of Magna Carta and the legacy of English constitutionalism and liberties, which entailed actively policing the limits of the purported prerogative power to exile and finding it a fictional fabrication. Whereas the majority in *"Bancoult (No.2)"* spoke in terms of deference, restraint, and the ultimate supremacy of the needs of the imperial power.

How the Supreme Court Ten Years Later Still Failed to Do Justice

On 29 June 2016 the Supreme Court in "*R (on the application of Bancoult) v Secretary of State for Foreign and Commonwealth Affairs (No 2)*" [2016] UKSC 35 (which replaced the House of Lords in October 2009) rejected a challenge by *"Bancoult"* to set aside the 2008 judgment of the House of Lords. In a majority ruling of 3/2 against, the justices said that a failure to disclose key Foreign Office documents in the form of a draft of a 2002 Feasibility Study would not have altered the outcome because Lord Mance in giving the leading judgment said there was "no probability, likelihood or prospect" (para 65) that a court would have made a different decision if it had seen the documents. Yet, when the Government removed the Chagossians right to return to their homeland it had relied on this 2002 Feasibility Study which examining how they could be settled, but this had never been presented to the original hearing, and the Government had concluded that the costs of long-term inhabitation of the outer islands would be prohibitive and life there precarious (Colley, 2016). A later Feasibility Study of 2014–15 was published by KPMG in March 2015, which in the words of Lord Mance, "assesses the risks differently" such that it finds, "that, at some cost and taking into account (for the first time) the possibility of resettlement on Diego Garcia itself" that, "there would be scope for supported resettlement". Lord Mance inferred from this that "in practical terms, the background has shifted, and logically the constitutional ban needs to be revisited" (para 72). The possibility of a favourable outcome for the Chagossians was thus raised. The Government's view after the latest judgment was expressed in terms that: "We remain committed to our current review of resettlement and will continue to keep Parliament, Chagossians and their supporters closely informed of progress on the issue" (Bowcott, 2016).

The Supreme Court's split decision fully acknowledged that its earlier 2008 decision had moved the law forward and that, in the words of Lord Mance who gave the majority decision, the exercise of prerogative powers was "susceptible to judicial review on ordinary principles of legality, rationality and procedural impropriety" (para 14). Even if "there has been a new 2104–2015 (sic) feasibility study, published by KPMG in March 2015, which assesses the risks differently" such that there is "the possibility of resettlement on Diego Garcia itself" so that "in practical terms, the background has shifted, and logically the constitutional ban needs to be revisited", the fact is that, "it is open to any Chagossian now or in the future to challenge" the government's position, "in the light of all the information now available" (para 17). But it is the dissenting judgments of Lord Kerr and Lady Hale that most clearly demonstrate how the law has moved forward, although the politics has yet to catch up. Lord Kerr reminds us how in 2008: "Lord Hoffmann decided that there was a power of review and that the main point in the appeal was 'the application of the ordinary principles of judicial review'" (para 112). The other two members of the majority, Lords Rodger and Carswell had agreed also, "that the courts had power to review" and could do so "on the normal judicial review grounds" (para 113, per Lord Kerr). The other two judges, Lords Bingham and Mance, gave "powerful dissenting speeches" and "concluded that the government did not have power by Order in Council to exclude the Chagossians from their homeland" (para 113, per Lord Kerr). Baroness Hale was brisk in her statement that,

> Any doubts about whether it is legally possible for the imperial power to exile a people from their homeland have to be rigorously suppressed. That question of law has been finally resolved in these proceedings by the decision of the majority in *Bancoult (No 2).*
>
> (para 189)

As David Snoxell has commented: "[t]he court's decision was a legal defeat, but a substantial moral and political victory for the Chagossians" (Prayag, 2016, p. 27). It is open to the Government to conduct a review and ultimately settle the issue once and for all. The litigation here is a good example of the limits of public law because ultimately the issue is one of political will and courage.

It is clear from this that if one locates the *"Bancoult"* litigation in its proper political context, against the background of the House of Lords in 2008, then the Supreme Court could – and indeed should – have taken a different decision. A decision that had already been made by Laws LJ in the Divisional Court in 2000 when the matter first arose and was affirmed resoundingly later by Sedley LJ in the Court of Appeal in 2007. One can start with the realisation that whereas the royal prerogative has in modern times been described as, "to all intents and purposes [a] government or even prime ministerial prerogative" (Markesinis, 1973, p. 288) it is not immune from judicial surveillance because as long ago as the *"Case of Proclamations"* (1611) 12 Co Rep 74 it was established that the English courts had jurisdiction to determine the existence and extent of the prerogative power. *"Bancoult"* has posed a challenge to that proposition. The case is troubling because it implied an absence of constitutional limits on the exercise of prerogative powers in circumstances where the rights of British subjects were involved. Yet, precisely because of its amplitude, the power has long been regarded even by the government as being anachronistic (Ministry of Justice, 2007). An example of this is The Governance of Britain paper, which stated:

> The flow of power from the people to government should be balanced by the ability of Parliament to hold government to account. However, when the executive relies on the powers of the royal prerogative – powers where government acts upon the Monarch's authority – it is difficult for Parliament to scrutinise and challenge government's actions.
>
> (Ministry of Justice, 2007, para 15)

The House of Lords judgment in *"Bancoult"* takes insufficient account of this anachronism. Indeed, writing in the wake of the Brexit judgment recently, Sir Stephen Sedley has explained how, "[f]or well over four hundred years British monarchs and their ministers have contested the claims of Parliament to have the last word on matters of state" and that "[t]he judges have arbitrated between them, laying down as part of the common law what ministers can lawfully doing the exercise of the royal prerogative" so that "[o]ver the centuries it has been rolling back ministerial claims to arbitrary power" (Sedley, 2017). Professor Mark Elliott and Amanda Perreau-Saussine had written then that *"Bancoult"* "constitutes an important and disappointing statement of contemporary judicial attitudes to the prerogative" (Elliot and Perreau-Saussine, 2009, p. 698).

Where the Supreme Court Went Wrong

The Courts in *"Bancoult"* lost the opportunity to affirm that the starting point to the modern exercise of the prerogative of colonial governance is that the power is anachronistic and that if it is to be exercised at all today then the legal obligations of trusteeship under Chapter XI of the UN Charter must be observed given that international law is an accepted source of English law. None of the judgments in the House of Lords fully developed this premise. The use of a "'colonial law" to affect purposes which a democratically elected Parliament would not otherwise endorse is also something not to be easily ignored by the Courts. There is reason to say that, as the Court of Appeal did in *R (on the application of Bancoult) v Secretary of State for Foreign and Commonwealth Affairs (No.2)*" (2007), "the permanent exclusion of an entire population from its homeland for reasons unconnected with their collective well-being cannot have [the] character [of governance] and accordingly cannot be lawfully accomplished by the use of prerogative power of governance" (para 67). In *Shergill & Ors v Khaira & Ors* (2014) the Supreme Court explained how under the doctrine of the Separation of Powers, an issue is treated beyond the constitutional competence of the courts if, for example, it involves certain transactions of foreign states, "although the boundaries of the category of 'transactions' of states which will engage the doctrine now are a good deal less clear today than they seemed to be forty years ago" (para 42, see Juss, 2016). The constitutional limits of the court's competence are "as against that of the executive in matters directly affecting the United Kingdom's relations with foreign states" (para 42). Here there was no question of relations with foreign states. Accordingly, the matter could not be said, "to be inherently unsuitable for judicial determination by reason only of its subject-matter".

The question, of course, is whether a different view was possible back in 2008. It is now clear from the 2016 decision that it was. The dissenting judgment of Lord Kerr was unequivocal that, "a decision to remove the Chagossians from their homeland with little or no provision for their future would indeed be a profoundly intrusive measure and one for which compelling justification would be required" (para 117). So much so that:

> In accordance with the standard set by Lord Hoffmann, the decision to remove the Chagossians without making adequate provision for them and their subsequent actual removal when that provision was not in place must therefore have been irrational when those events occurred. The fact that their removal, when it in fact occurred, was unreasonable cannot, … be left out of account in assessing whether the subsequent decision to perpetuate the Chagossians' exile was rational.
>
> (para 118)

Lady Hale in her dissenting judgment helpfully reminded us of the elementary principles at play, namely, that "Courts have … to do justice according to law" and that "the decision to exile a people has to be taken in accordance with the law; and the people to whom it is of such momentous importance are entitled to expect the highest standards of decision-making and the most scrupulous standards of fairness from the institutions of imperial government". Yet here the earlier feasibility study of 2002 relied upon by the government "showed that the government had made it plain to the consultants what it wanted the conclusions to be" and that "important changes had been made to the conclusion" so that "the central findings about climate change had been changed" when it was clear that "the islands were not in a cyclone belt". In a rare judicial statement, highlighting the central role played by judicial personalities in hard cases arising before the courts, Lady Hale also added for good measure that:

> The question whether this might have made a difference has to be answered objectively rather than by reference to the particular judges who were then sitting on the case.
>
> (para 193)

Some of the judges in the *Bancoult* litigation took cognisance of this limitation (i.e. the power was anachronistic). Sedley LJ considered that it was only in the specific context of the allocation and assignment of authority to colonial legislatures that the formula of "peace, order and good government" acquired the status of plenary power but that the Crown's remaining powers of colonial governance were still subject to a limitation through these very words.

This meant that, in *"R (on the application of Bancoult) v Secretary of State for Foreign and Commonwealth Affairs (No.2)"* (2007), "the permanent exclusion of an entire population from its homeland for reasons unconnected with their collective well-being cannot have [the] character [of governance] and accordingly cannot be lawfully accomplished by the use of prerogative powers" (para 67). Given that the Crown has to exercise governance over the Colonies as a Crown function, the territories' interests are not coterminous with interests of the UK state and its allies. As a result, "[t]he governance of each colonial territory is in constitutional principle a discrete function of the Crown" such that "[t]hat territory's interests will not necessarily be the interests of the United Kingdom or of its allies" (para 67). This is a different constitutional theory from that of Professor Finnis, but all the more apposite given that we are in the 21st century now, and not in the heyday of the Empire in the nineteenth.

In *"R (on the application of Bancoult) v Secretary of State for Foreign and Commonwealth Affairs (No.2)"* (2008) Lord Bingham had little doubt that Section 9 of the Constitution Order could not be enacted (para 71), and Lord Mance said that only the proper governance of the territory could be countenanced (para 157). Lord Hoffmann believed the prerogative's exercise by the Crown to be "in the interests of her undivided realm, including both the United Kingdom and the colony" (para 47). Whilst Lords Rodger (para 109) and Carswell (para 131) took a markedly different approach, suggesting that it was a matter for the Crown and not the Court, on grounds that was non-justiciable question, that position is difficult to sustain given that they also held that the question whether the power was exercised rationally was a justiciable question (para 109). Lord Rodger did not accept the contention that, "that judicial review of an order in council would trespass against the rule that prerogative orders are regularly made against Ministers in their official capacity, but never against the Crown" (para 106) and where Lord Carswell noted that, "It must be borne in mind that it is the *Wednesbury* standard which must be applied to the Secretary of State's decision to have the Orders in Council enacted" (para 131).

Returning to *"Shergill & Ors v Khaira & Ors"* (2014) and the Supreme Court's approach to the separation of powers in relation to transactions of foreign states, it is clear that in "*Bancoult*" there was no question of relations with foreign states. Accordingly, the matter could not be said, "to be inherently unsuitable for judicial determination by reason only of its subject-matter" (para 41).

In the light of this Lord Carswell's reservations in *"R (on the application of Bancoult) v Secretary of State for Foreign and Commonwealth Affairs (No.2)"* (2008) that the courts should not make judgments of this sort because, "they could very easily get into the area of challenging what is essentially a political judgment, which is not for courts of law" (para 130) are untenable. One is inclined to agree with Mark Elliott and Amanda Perreau-Saussine that: "[i]t is difficult to resist the conclusion that a measure of unnecessary deference lives on in relation to the prerogative merely because it *is* the prerogative" and that "our highest court remains in thrall to what Lord Roskill referred to 'as the clanking of medieval chains of the ghosts of the past'" (Elliot and Perreau-Saussine, 2009, pp. 710–711). All the more reason then why this landmark case falls outside the rule of law. A different view was possible. Sedley LJ had already held in the Court of Appeal that although a court may not substitute its view for that of the Executive, it may decide whether prerogative legislation is "rationally and legally capable of providing for a territory's wellbeing" (para 51). This was echoed by Lord Mance that: "[a] Constitution which exiles a territory's population is a contradiction in terms" (para 157).

Frost and Murray had in 2015 referred to the competing forces of "liberal imperialism" and "'utilitarian imperialism' and in her dissenting judgment in *R (on the application of Bancoult) v Secretary of State for Foreign and Commonwealth Affairs (No 2)*" (2016) Lady Hale had quoted their words that in 2008, "Lord Hoffmann acknowledged that a choice between the liberal and utilitarian faces of imperialism did rest with the court, and decisively affirmed the utilitarian importance of the imperial interests at stake" (Frost and Murray, 2015, p. 287). Yet there is every reason to doubt now whether this "utilitarian" view of imperialism, about "how best to appropriate colonial possessions for the benefit of the imperial power", will prevail over the "liberal" view of imperialism, about "the civilising nature of empire and focuses on the good governance of colonies" (Frost and Murray, 2015, p. 266). Even the majority in *"R (on the application of Bancoult) v Secretary of State for Foreign and Commonwealth Affairs (No 2)"* (2016) accepted that given that, in the words of Lord Clarke, "there is a critical factor which is in any event conclusive", namely, "2014–2015 feasibility study' which considers, among other things, "the possibility of resettlement on Diego Garcia" then "that is not the end of the road" because this "new factor" is such that it "concludes that there would be scope for supported resettlement", so that quite simply "the background has now shifted and logically the constitutional ban needs to be revisited" (para 78). This view was shared by Lord Mance (para 72). The result in 2016 is likely to be a pyrrhic victory for the government.

In addition to the argument above, in fact, there are other reasons why a different view was entirely possible in 2008, whatever the judicial personalities. It is one that fully exposes the internal incoherence and confusion of thought in the majority's collective judgment back in 2008. In a bizarre three-page letter – allegedly written by Rose Likins, the acting Assistant Secretary of State at the US State Department, to Denise Holt of the UK Foreign Commonwealth Office a case against resettlement of Chagossians in their homelands is made out on the grounds that, "the United States is seriously concerned that repopulating the outer islands would provide terrorists the cover and concealment to establish permanent operating bases from which they could monitor island operations with minimum risk of counter detection" (Letter on File with Satvinder Juss, paras 2–3). This was a risk which could not be run because, "Diego Garcia is an important forward operating base from which the United States can conduct rapid and tailored air, sea, land operations in four of the seven continents of the world" and that "[f]rom a defense position, the repopulation of the outer islands presents an unacceptable risk to military operations" (paras 2–3).

This letter was not the creation of the US State Department but was written after consultation with the FCO officials in London who ventriloquised it so that it could be used in the legal proceedings (Snoxell, 2009). Snoxell makes it clear that the FCO in London was under no pressure from the Americans to remove the population from all the Islands. The policy to do so was driven entirely by the FCO officials themselves. If the Americans had objected, the policy would not have been implemented. As long ago as April 1969 the UK Prime Minister, on the recommendation of the Foreign Secretary, had given authority for the wholesale removal of the Chagossian population from their homeland, but the FCO only affected that policy from 1971 to 1973. This is clear from a 1980 letter to the British High Commission in Mauritius:

> I am sure the Americans do not want to get mixed up in this. They look to us to sort it out and I should think they consider that we made a hash of the Diego Garcia clearance. Our agreement with them leading to the 1966 Exchange of Notes required only Diego Garcia to be empty. They had no objections to the other Chagos Islands remain populated; it was our decision to clear the lot and resettle in Mauritius.
>
> (Snoxell, 2009)

Even more than that, it was roundly castigated by House of Lords when in his judgment Lord Hoffmann said that "[s]ome of these scenarios might be regarded as fanciful speculations". Lord Hoffmann had all the more reason not to proceed to conclude that, "but, in the current state of uncertainty, the government is entitled to take the concerns of its ally into account" (para 56). It was surely little more than lame to suggest that:

> It is true that the Chagossians will now require immigration consent even to visit the islands. But the government have made it clear that such visits, to tend graves and so forth, will be allowed, and since in practice they are funded by the BIOT administration, immigration consent will be no more than an additional formality. Furthermore, there is no reason why, if at some time in the future, circumstances should change, the controls should not be lifted.
>
> (para 55)

The judgment of Laws LJ, on the other hand, was much more to be preferred in *"Bancoult (No 1)"*, namely, that a rationality review was entirely possible in the proper circumstances of this case because a reference to, "the peace, order and good government" of any territory means nothing, surely save by reference to the territory's population. They are to be *governed* not removed (para 57). It may confidently be asserted that, that view of the predominance and pre-eminence of the rule of law in public law proceedings is now likely to prevail over considerations of political expediency in any future legal action.

The Contested Legacy of Empire

Why was Lord Hoffmann in the Supreme Court so influenced by Professor John Finnis' paper on the *"Bancoult"* litigation (Finnis, 2008)? Why was that Paper considered so decisive in Lord Hoffmann reaching his view as to how to treat the requirement of peace, order, and good government? Finnis had taken the view that the Orders in Council:

> They are acts of the UK Government in the exercise of its responsibility for the common good – the peace, order and good government – of the United Kingdom and all its dependencies, including but not exclusively the BIOT. The legal doctrine that there is one undivided realm and Crown of the United Kingdom and its dependent territories corresponds to the moral and political reality that the common good of each part is dependent on the common good of the whole. If the UK is conquered or subverted or economically ruined or impoverished, the common good of each dependent territory is more or less radically affected, presumptively for the worse.
>
> (Finnis, 2008, para 20)

This is sound reasoning, as if we view the British Empire as a family of nations and each part benefiting from benign and enlightened imperial rule, then sacrificing the needs of a component part for the benefit of the imperial power to benefit the inhabitants of every other colony could be justified. Finnis' account rests on the assumption of the common good. But can we really say that there has ever been an assumption or exercise of common good in relation to how the United Kingdom treated the Chagossian Islanders? The dependent territories included colonies (alongside royal dependencies inherited from the Duchy of Normandy in the case of the Channel Islands), and these colonies are the legacy of empire, built upon global domination of the seas (in the case of the Chagos Islands) and the system of slavery in the West Indies. The legacy of empire and the United Kingdom's responsibilities towards its former and remaining colonies is heavily contested. The Oxford theologian Professor Nigel Biggar in *Colonialism: A Moral Reckoning* has presented a view that is contested by some historians (Biggar, 2023). Kenan Malik viewed Biggar's book as seeking to defend the legacy of empire,

> Biggar's real concern is not with the past but with the present. Denigrating colonialism, he claims, is an "important way of corroding faith in the west". Yet, in seeking to challenge what he regards as cartoonish views of imperial history, Biggar has produced something equally cartoonish, a politicised history that ill-serves his aim of defending "western values".
>
> (Malik, 2023)

Alan Lester was highly critical of Biggar's "straw man caricature" that historians "tend not to focus solely on the 'costs' of colonialism while denying its 'benefits'" (Lester 2022, 2023). Lester is clear that whilst colonialism can be criticised, historians do not ignore "the legacies of colonial schooling, education and public health initiatives that tended to come in the later stages of imperialism". Even Jonathan Sumption opined about the need for a balance sheet approach to Empire:

> Unless we draw up a balance sheet of empire, we will never understand one of the most significant forces in the making of the modern world. Inevitably, it will be an incomplete balance sheet. There will be credits and debits, but no bottom line.
>
> (Sumption, 2023)

Nonetheless, balance sheet or no balance sheet, we need as a country to have a serious and frank conversation about empire. Individuals are doing this already, such as the broadcaster Laura Trevelyan and members of her wider family, in acknowledgement of how their family has directly benefitted from slavery (Mohdin, 2023).

The disquiet about colonialism and Chagos is not a new concern. The then Colonial Secretary, Anthony Greenwood, was reflective about the United Kingdom's creation of the British Indian Ocean Territory, at a time when colonies should be given their independence, and here was a Labour government creating a new colony (Monaghan, 2023). Now in light of the death of George Floyd in 2020 and the Black Lives Matter movement, it is imperative that collectively we acknowledge that an African indigenous people were exiled from their homeland and have been subsequently prevented from returning home. The late legal academic and barrister, Anthony Bradley QC (Hons) summed up the broader issue,

> I was listening to a radio programme this morning about history and the teaching about slavery etc ... if you think that the Chagossians were descendants of slaves... it gives extra depth to what Sedley and Bingham and others were

> saying about the importance of having somewhere to live and the importance of the mother country and so I think from that point of view that has been re-emphasized the value of somebody, you know you can't just move them from anywhere and take away all their roots.
>
> (Monaghan, 2020)

The issue of a colonial power's treatment of an African indigenous population surely hinges on race and the implicit prejudices that do exist. Regardless of the motivation of individual decision makers, the exile of a black population by a white colonial power, who then prevented their return, cannot be separated from race. This is reflected by the racist language used as the time, and allegedly in 2009, to justify the United Kingdom's action. Olivier Bancoult was interviewed by *The Guardian* in 2022, upon his return to the Chagos Islands as part of a Mauritian trip to the archipelago. Bancoult informed the reporters that:

> he suspected that the treatment of the Chagossians amounted to racism. "The British government says it is in favour of human rights yet they make a difference between the treatment of Falkland Islanders, for example, and Chagossians," he said. "Is it because we are black?"
>
> (Bowcott and Rinvolucri, 2022)

There is clearly a colonial mindset at play (see Monaghan, 2021).

The 2023 report by Human Rights Watch is particularly stark in its use of language:

> The forced displacement of the Chagossians and ongoing abuses amount to crimes against humanity committed by a colonial power against an Indigenous people. UK colonial rule in the Chagos Archipelago, unlike in most of its other colonies in Africa, did not end in the 1960s, and it has continued at extraordinary cost to the people of Chagos. This colonial rule was built on systematic racism and ethnic and racial discrimination in the treatment of the Chagossians.
>
> (Human Rights Watch, 2023)

The uncomfortable fact remains that the United Kingdom is clinging on to its empire, in the face of international opposition (the United Nations Generally Assembly resolution (United Nations, 2019) and the International Court of Justice's Advisory Opinion in *"Legal Consequences of the Separation of the Chagos Archipelago from Mauritius in 1965*)", and as it moves to potentially decolonise Mauritius, it adopts a colonial mindset towards the islanders. Arguably how does the United Kingdom show its true position: the Chagos Islands are an example of where liberal and enlightened rhetoric meets imperial self-interest.

Apologies

Although the United Kingdom has apologised for its treatment of the Chagossians, the apologies have often been made as part of the litigation strategy. Jonathan

Crow QC, who took over as the lead counsel for the government in *"Bancoult (No.2)"*, adopted a very different strategy to his predecessor and conceded on behalf of the government the appalling way the Chagossians had been treated. This change of approach, that focused on the legality of the 2004 Orders in Council, as opposed to the historic conduct of British officials, was viewed as a decisive factor in the government's success at the House of Lords. As Maya Lester KC stated,

> in the House of Lords Jonathan Crow took an entirely different approach, very wisely from the Government's perspective, and focused much more on the merits of the decision about whether to repopulate in 2004 ... he was much more focused not on anything to do with [initially] clearing the islands but what were the factors that went into the Government's decision at that time ... I think that different approach made a massive difference.
>
> (Monaghan, 2023b;. see also Paterson, 2013, p. 55; Paterson, 2011,p. 51).

More recently, Robert Buckland KC MP, the then Solicitor General, made an apology as part of the oral proceedings in *"Mauritius v the United Kingdom"*. (Oral Proceedings, 2018). An apology made as part of a litigation strategy is still an apology but is it a genuine one that is accompanied by a desire to make amends. The answer is complicated. Apologies made within the context of Britain's colonial role are controversial, such as the refusal to issue a full apology for the massacre at Amritsar in 1919 (McKie, 2019), or for the slave trade.

The United Kingdom has compensated the islanders. The initial agreement with Mauritius involved compensation to be paid for the islanders (albeit insufficient to support them economically),[1] the United Kingdom again agreed to additional compensation as a way to settle litigation in 1982 that had been commenced by Michael Vencatassen in 1975, and finally in 2016 the United Kingdom announced a substantial compensation package (see Wintour, 2016; Armour, 2021). Sir Alan Duncan MP who was Minister for Europe and the Americas informed the House of Commons that "[t]he Government have now considered all the available information and decided against the resettlement of the Chagossian people on the grounds of feasibility, defence and security interests, and the cost to the British taxpayer" (2016, c385). Duncan said that "in looking forward, the Government intend to allocate £40 million, shared between the Department for International Development and the Foreign Office, to address the needs of Chagossians wherever they are – whether in Mauritius, the Seychelles or the United Kingdom" (ibid., c388). The Chagossians had sought additional compensation since the 1982 settlement and had been unsuccessful in the England and Welsh Courts in *"Chagos Islanders v The Attorney-General"* (2004), and the European Court of Human Rights in *"Chagos Islanders v the United Kingdom (application no. 35622/04)"*.

The 2016 decision to compensate the islanders and exclude the right to return was unsuccessfully challenged in the Court of Appeal in *"R (on the application of Hoareau and Bancoult) v The Secretary of State for Foreign and Commonwealth Affairs"* (2020). Previously, in the decision of the Divisional Court in *"R (on the application of Hoareau and Bancoult) v The Secretary of State for Foreign and Commonwealth Affairs"* (2019), Singh LJ and Carr J had been critical of the use of judicial review to advance political causes:

> Judicial review is an important mechanism for the maintenance of the rule of law. It serves to correct unlawful conduct on the part of public authorities. However, judicial review is not an appeal against governmental decisions on their merits. The wisdom of governmental policy is not a matter for the courts and, in a democratic society, must be a matter for the elected government alone. We stress these fundamentals in this case because there have been times when sight appears to have been lost of them … Judicial review is not, and should not be regarded as, politics by another means.
>
> (para 326)

Negotiations, but an Inherent Failure to Consult

There has been a failure to include the Chagossian people as equals in negotiations with Mauritius regarding the status of the Chagos Islands. In 2022 it was announced that negotiations had begun between Mauritius and the United Kingdom. The Chagossian Voices, an organisation that represents members of the Chagossian community who live in the United Kingdom, pointed out that the negotiations between two countries did not involve representatives of the Chagossian population (Boffey, 2023). In response Bernadette Dugasse from Chagossian Voices has commenced judicial review proceedings (Chagossian Voices, 2023). Dugasse's claim *inter alia* argues on a failure to consult and that "[s]uch negotiations without the consultation with or involvement of my Client is contradictory to the Chagossian people's right of self-determination and who were ruled as the '*belongers*' on the islanders in a Divisional Court judgement… [*Bancoult (No.1)*]" (van Dellen, 2023, p. 20). Members of the Chagossian community living in the United Kingdom were featured as part of a video produced by Chagossian Voices. The message advanced was clear, concerning the inequity of negotiations without the involvement of the Chagossian people. "No-one can start any negotiations on my behalf without my consent" was the view of Yolande who had been born on Peros Banhos. Lucette Martin who had also been born on Peros Banhos, was clear that "I should be the one making the decisions concerning my homeland". "The British Government took away our Homeland but I don't want the Mauritian Government to take decisions on my behalf. I want to decide about the future of my homeland" was the view of Louis Vivian Marie who had been born on the Salomon Islands (for more of the views of Chagossians on not being included, see Chagossian Voices (2022).

It is interesting to note the possibility of future legal challenges being brought against Mauritius if and when the United Kingdom gives back the Chagos Islands. In this case, could the community demand self-determination and a special constitutional status within Mauritius? As Frost and Murray noted in 2020,

> If the London courts do not take steps to recognise the Chagossians' interest in the Chagos archipelago, then even the eventual transfer of sovereignty over the islands to Mauritius will not address their exclusion; Mauritius maintains that they are a minority group within the Mauritian people.
>
> (Frost and Murray, 2020, p. 793)

Unilateralism: The United Kingdom's Treatment of Mauritius

Equally Mauritius was not treated as a genuine equal. The historic inequality in negotiating positions of the then colony of Mauritius and the United Kingdom at Lancaster House in 1965 can hardly be disputed, then or indeed now (see also the chapters by Milan Meetarbhan and Samuel Bashfield).[2] The decision of the United Kingdom to unilaterally create the Marine Protected Area around the Chagos Islands, without consulting Mauritius and in clear violation of the Lancaster House Agreement as it infringed on Mauritius' commercial rights such as the right to fish in the Chagos waters, is an example of imperialism, albeit in the guise of the noble cause (see above for alleged comments made by Colin Roberts in 2009; see also Tomkins, 2018). The need to protect the marine environment gained the support of the environmental lobby. One noted environmentalist and television presenter Ben Fogle was critical of the creation of the Marine Protected Area, arguing that, "I was duped into supporting the creation of the marine sanctuary under false pretences" (see Lunn, 2012; Gregory, 2011). Fogle summed up the dilemma, "The marine protectorate is undoubtedly important for conservation science but at what cost?" (Fogle, 2012) (see also the chapter by Sue Farran).

Notes

1 It is interesting to note Sedley LJ's account, "A compensation payment of £650,000 from the British government, with accrued interest, was distributed in 1977–8 to a total of 595 displaced families then in Mauritius. It did little if anything to relieve their massive problems of rudimentary housing, unemployment and social isolation" [9] (*"Chagos Islanders v The Attorney-General"*, 2004).

2 For the inequality in negotiation positions, see the Memorial of the Republic of Mauritius (2012, 3.49). Mauritius argued that "Further criticism of the detachment of the Chagos Archipelago was made at meetings of Sub-Committee I, as reported to London by the UK Mission to the UN in New York, on 1, 9 and 12 September 1966 [and that] … Mr. Malecela representing Tanzania, the Chairman of the meeting held on 9 September, reiterated the predominant view of Afro-Asian countries, opposing the establishment of military bases in the Indian Ocean, and asked for assurances from the UK that such bases would not be established. He stated that negotiations between a colony and the colonial Power could not be valid as these 'could not be on an equal basis'". See also Monaghan, 2023a.

References

Allen, S. (2014) *The Chagos Islanders and International Law*. Oxford: Hart Publishing.

Allen, S. and Monaghan, C. (eds.) (2018) *Fifty Years of the British Indian Ocean Territory: Legal Perspectives*. Cham: Springer.
Anon. (1802) *Life, Trial and Particulars of Execution of Governor Wall, Who was Executed on Thursday Morning Last, fronting Newgate, for the Murder of Benjamin Armstrong, Nearly 20 Years ago, at Goree, in Africa*. London: J Davenport.
Armour, K. (2021) 'Just £12,000 of £40m fund for displaced Chagos islanders has been spent'. *The Guardian*, 21 January. Available at: https://www.theguardian.com/world/2021/jan/31/just-12000-of-40m-fund-for-displaced-chagos-islanders-has-been-spent (Accessed: 1 September 2023).
Arvind, T.T. (2012) '"Though it shocks one very much": Formalism and Pragmatism in the Zong and Bancoult'. *Oxford Journal of Legal Studies,* 32(1), pp. 113–151.
Banks, A. (2022) 'The imperial afterlife of warren hastings, 1818-1947'. *The Journal of Imperial and Commonwealth History,* 50(3), pp. 498–531.
Biggar, N. (2023) *Colonialism: A Moral Reckoning.* London: William Collins.
Boffey, D. (2023) 'Chagos Islanders demand say as UK-Mauritius sovereignty talks begin'. *The Guardian,* 2 January. Available at: https://www.theguardian.com/world/2023/jan/02/chagos-islanders-demand-say-as-uk-mauritius-sovereignty-talks-begin (Accessed: 1 September 2023).
Bowcott, O. (2016) 'Chagos islanders lose supreme court bid to return to homeland'. *The Guardian,* 29 June. Available at https://www.theguardian.com/world/2016/jun/29/chagos-islanders-lose-supreme-court-bid-to-return-to-homeland (Accessed: 1 September 2023).
Bowcott, O. and Rinvolucri, B. (2022) 'Exiled Chagos Islanders return without British supervision for first time'. *The Guardian,* 8 February. Available at: https://www.theguardian.com/world/2022/feb/08/mauritian-ship-takes-scientific-team-to-contested-chagos-islands (Accessed: 01 September 2023).
Bryan, N. (2022) 'Slave owner Sir Thomas Picton portrait returns in bid to reframe past'. *BBC News*. Available at: https://www.bbc.co.uk/news/uk-wales-62350923 (Accessed: 1 September 2023).
Burri, T. and Trinidad, J. (eds.) (2021) *The International Court of Justice and Decolonisation: New Directions from the Chagos Advisory Opinion.* Cambridge: Cambridge University Press.
Chagossian Voices (2022) 'Chagos Islanders talk about the chagos sovereignty negotiations between Mauritius and the UK'. Available at: https://www.youtube.com/watch?v=bfu4gwvI28U and https://www.youtube.com/watch?v=sLj-3QsoaF4 (Accessed: 1 September 2023).
Chagossian Voices [@ChagossianVoic2] (2023) [Twitter, 9 January]. 'Bernadette Dugasse of Chagossian Voices,born on Diego Garcia has instructed a barrister to prepare a judicial review'. Available at: https://twitter.com/ChagossianVoic2/status/1612485834292318210 (Accessed: 1 March 2024).
Cohn, M. (2021) *A Theory of the Executive Branch: Tension and Legality.* Oxford: Oxford University Press.
Colley, J. (2016) 'Chagos Islands residents forcibly removed from homeland lose Supreme Court appeal'. *The Independent,* 29 June. Available at https://www.independent.co.uk/news/uk/home-news/chagos-islands-lose-supreme-court-appeal-home-diego-garcia-us-air-force-base-a7108741.html (Accessed: 1 September 2023).
Conniff, J. (1993) 'Burke and India: The Failure of the Theory of Trusteeship'. *Political Research Quarterly*, 46(2), pp . 291–309.
Cook, R. (1975) 'Hansard: House of Commons debates'. 3 November, 899, 1025. Available at: https://hansard.parliament.uk/commons/1975-11-03/debates/f4d69c4b-1a1c-4d8e-b844-ff999ac01a76/HouseOfCommons (Accessed: 1 September 2023).
Cormacain, R. (2013) 'Prerogative legislation as the paradigm of bad law-making: The Chagos Islands'. *Commonwealth Law Bulletin,* 39(3), pp. 487–508.
Darwin, J. (1997) 'Imperialism and the victorians: The dynamics of territorial expansion'. *The English Historical Review*, 112(447), pp. 614–642.

van Dellen, A. (2023) 'Letter to government legal department'. 2 January. Available at: https://twitter.com/ChagossianVoic2/status/1612485834292318210 (Accessed: 1 March 2024).

Dirks, N. (2006) *The Scandal of Empire*. Cambridge MA: Harvard University Press.

Duncan, A. (2016) 'Hansard: House of Commons debates'. 17 November, 617, c385, c88. Available at: https://hansard.parliament.uk/commons/2016-11-17/debates/3BCB7C20-20B6-41C2-9208-482E911FCF6B/HouseOfCommons (Accessed: 1 September 2023).

Elliott, M. and Perreau-Saussine, A. (2009) 'Pyrrhic public law: Bancoult and the sources, status and content of common law limitations on prerogative power'. *Public Law,* October.

Epstein, J. (2012) *Scandal of Colonial Rule: Power and Subversion in the British Atlantic during the Age of Revolution*. Cambridge: Cambridge University Press.

Finnis, J. (2008) 'Common law constraints: Whose common good counts?, Colloquium on common law, royal prerogative and executive legislation'. Available at: https://www.cpl.law.cam.ac.uk/sites/www.law.cam.ac.uk/files/images/www.cpl.law.cam.ac.uk/legacy/File/Finnis_J_Paper%281%29.pdf (Accessed: 1 September 2023).

Fogle, B. (2012) 'The Chagos islanders' plight makes me ashamed to be British'. *The Guardian,* 21 May. Available at: https://www.theguardian.com/environment/2012/may/21/chagos-islanders-plight-ashamed-british (Accessed: 1 September 2023).

Foreign and Commonwealth Office (2021) 'Corporate report: Foreign and Commonwealth diversity and equality report 2019 to 2020'. 7 April. Available at: https://www.gov.uk/government/publications/fco-diversity-and-equality-report-2020/foreign-commonwealth-office-diversity-and-equality-report-2019-to-2020 (Accessed: 01 September 2023).

Frost T. and Murray C. (2015) 'The Chagos Islands Cases: The Empire Strikes Back' *Northern Ireland Legal Quarterly,* 66 (3), pp. 263-288.

Frost, T. and Murray, C.R.G. (2020) 'Homeland: Reconceptualising the chagossians' litigation'. *Oxford Journal of Legal Studies,* 40(4), pp. 764–794.

Gillray, J. (1802) *Governor Wall's Ghost!*. London: Hannah Humphrey.

Gjersø, J.F. (2015) '"Continuity of moral policy": A reconsideration of British motives for the partition of East Africa in light of anti-slave trade policy and imperial agency, 1878-96'. Unpublished PhD thesis. London: London School of Economics and Political Science.

Goronwy-Roberts, G. (1975) 'Hansard: House of Lords debates'. 14 October, 364. Available at: https://hansard.parliament.uk/Lords/1975-10-14/debates/ebcc46b1-8a58-4f3f-a075-f442adc0aafd/DiegoGarciaInhabitants?_gl=1*1y673b4*_up*MQ..*_ga*MTc0MDk1NDYyOC4xNzEyNzQyMjY1*_ga_Z1C97N01BT*MTcxMjc0MjI2NC4xLjAuMTcxMjc0MjI2NC4wLjAuMA (Accessed: 1 September 2023).

Greene, J.P. (2013) *Evaluating Empire and Confronting Colonialism in Eighteenth-Century Britain.* Cambridge: Cambridge University Press.

Gregory, P. (2011) 'The Secret Falklands that's still in conflict'. *The Times*, 2 June. Available at: https://www.thetimes.co.uk/article/the-secret-falklands-thats-still-in-conflict-3bdnvlg2w0z (Accessed: 1 September 2023).

Halliday, P. (2012) *Habeas Corpus: From England to Empire*. Cambridge MA: Harvard University Press.

Hart, J. (1967) 'Hansard: House of Commons debates'. 12 May, 746, c. 305W. Available at: https://api.parliament.uk/historic-hansard/written-answers/1967/may/12/zambia-british-detainees#column_305w (Accessed: 1 September 2023).

Human Rights Watch (2023) '"That's when the nightmare started": UK and US forced displacement of the chagossians and ongoing colonial crime'. 15 February 2023. Available at: https://www.hrw.org/report/2023/02/15/thats-when-nightmare-started/uk-and-us-forced-displacement-chagossians-and (Accessed: 1 September 2023).

Juss, S. (2016) 'Back to the future: justiciability, religion, and the figment of 'judicial no-man's land'. *Public Law*, April, pp. 198–206.

Juss, S. (2017) 'Bancoult and the royal prerogative in colonial constitutional law'. In S. Juss and M. Sunkin (eds.), *Landmark Cases in Public Law*. Oxford: Hart Publishing, pp. 239–270.
Juss, S. (2019) 'Belhaj, justiciablity, and the "silhouette-like" act of state doctrine'. *Public Law,* 1, pp. 8–19.
Kershaw, D. (2022) 'Revolutionary amnesia and the nature of the prerogative power'. *International Journal of Constitutional Law*, 20(3), pp. 1071–1102.
Kostal, R.W. (2005) *A Jurisprudence of Power: Victorian Empire and the Rule of Law*. Oxford: Oxford University Press.
Kumar, K. (2012) 'Greece and rome in the British Empire: Contrasting role models'. *Journal of British Studies*, 51(1), pp. 76–101.
Lester, A. (2022) 'What are the British Empire's "Legacies"?'. *University of Sussex*, 10 October. Available at: https://blogs.sussex.ac.uk/snapshotsofempire/2022/10/10/what-are-the-british-empires-legacies/#:~:text=For%20conservatives%20these%20legacies%20of,%2C%20railways%2C%20education%20and%20medicine (Accessed: 1 September 2023).
Lester, A. (2023) 'The British empire rehabilitated?'. *Bella Caledonia*, 7 March. Available at: https://bellacaledonia.org.uk/2023/03/07/the-british-empire-rehabilitated/ (Accessed: 1 September 2023).
Lunn, J. (2012) 'The Chagos Islanders'. *House of Commons Library*, SN04463, 20 April. Available at https://researchbriefings.files.parliament.uk/documents/SN04463/SN04463.pdf (Accessed: 1 September 2023).
Macaulay, T.B. (1841) 'Warren hastings'. *Edinburgh Review*, October, p. 160.
Malik, K. (2023) 'Colonialism by Nigel Biggar review – a flawed defence of empire'. *The Guardian*, 20 February. Available at: https://www.theguardian.com/books/2023/feb/20/colonialism-a-moral-reckoning-by-nigel-biggar-review-a-flawed-defence-of-empire (Accessed: 1 September 2023).
Mantena, R.S. (2010) 'Imperial ideology and the uses of rome in discourses on Britain's Indian empire'. In M. Bradley (ed.), *Classics and Imperialism in the British Empire*. Oxford: Oxford University Press. pp. 54–76.
Markesinis, B. (1973) 'The royal prerogative revisited'. *The Cambridge Law Journal*, 32(2), pp. 287–309.
Marshall, P.J. (2019) *Edmund Burke and the British Empire in the West Indies: Wealth, Power, and Slavery*. Oxford: Oxford University Press.
Marshall, P.J. (1965) *The Impeachment of Warren Hastings*. Oxford: Oxford University Press.
McKie, R. (2019) 'UK "deeply regrets" Amritsar massacre – but no official apology'. *The Guardian*, 13 April. Available at: https://www.theguardian.com/world/2019/apr/13/uk-deeply-regrets-amritsar-massacre-but-no-official-apology-india. (Accessed: 1 September 2023).
Memorial of the Republic of Mauritius (2012) 'Republic of Mauritius v Untired Kingdom of Great Britain and Norther Ireland'. 1 August 2012. Available at: https://pcacases.com/web/sendAttach/1796 (Accessed: 1 September 2023).
Ministry of Justice (2007) 'The Governance of Britain'. CM 7170. Available at: https://www.gov.uk/government/uploads/system/uploads/attachment_data/file/228834/7170.pdf (Accessed: 1 September 2023).
Minority Rights Group International, 'Directory of minorities and indigenous people'. Available at: https://minorityrights.org/minorities/chagossiansilois/ (Accessed: 1 September 2023).
Mohdin, A. (2023) 'Laura Trevelyan quits BBC to campaign for reparative justice for Caribbean'. *The Guardian*, 16 March. Available at: https://www.theguardian.com/world/2023/mar/16/laura-trevelyan-quits-bbc-to-campaign-reparative-justice-slavery-caribbean (Accessed: 1 September 2023).

Monaghan, C. (2011) 'In defence of intrinsic human rights: Edmund Burke's controversial prosecution of Warren Hastings, Governor-General of Bengal'. *Law, Crime and History*, 2, p.58.

Monaghan, C. (2012) 'Lord Mance's dissent in *R (Bancoult) v Secretary of State for Foreign & Commonwealth Affairs (No2)* [2008] UKHL 61'. In N. Geach and C. Monaghan (eds.), *Dissenting Judgments in the Law*. London: Wildy, Simmonds and Hill, pp. 239–262.

Monaghan, C. (2014) 'The marine protected area and WikiLeaks: *R (Bancoult) v Secretary of State for Foreign & Commonwealth Affairs (No. 3)* [2014] EWCA Civ 708'. *Judicial Review*, 19(3), pp. 151–159.

Monaghan, C. (2018) 'An imperfect legacy: The significance of the Bancoult litigation on the development of domestic constitutional jurisprudence'. In S. Allen and C. Monaghan (eds.), *Fifty Years of the British Indian Ocean Territory: Legal Perspectives*. Cham: Springer, pp. 111–146.

Monaghan, C. (2020) 'Unpublished Interview between Anthony Bradley and Chris Monaghan'. October.

Monaghan, C. (2021) 'Reflections on the United Kingdom's assertion of sovereignty over the Chagos Archipelago in the wake of the Chagos Advisory Opinion'. In T. Burri and J. Trinidad (eds.), *The International Court of Justice and Decolonization: New Directions from the Chagos Advisory Opinion*. Cambridge: Cambridge University Press, pp. 144–158.

Monaghan, C. (2023a) 'The fight to achieve full decolonisation: Mauritius Versus the United Kingdom'. In G. Baldacchino (ed.), *The Success of States in International Relations: Mice That Roar?*. Abingdon: Routledge, pp. 148–169.

Monaghan, C. (2023b) 'Returning to Bancoult: New Perspectives'. *Judicial Review*, 27(4), 337–359.

Moon, P. (1947) *Warren Hastings and British India*. London: English Universities Press.

Mukherjee, M. (2005) 'Justice, War, and the Imperium: India and Britain in Edmund Burke's prosecutorial speeches in the impeachment trial of Warren Hastings'. *Law and History Review*, 23(3), pp. 589–630.

Mukherjee, M. (2023) 'Edmund Burke, India, and the impeachment trial of Warren Hastings'. In C. Monaghan and M. Flinders (eds.), *British Origins and American Practice of Impeachment*. Abingdon. Routledge., pp. 84–113.

Murray, C.R.G. and Frost, T. (2018) 'The Chagossians' struggle and the last bastions of imperial constitutionalism'. In S. Allen and C. Monaghan (eds.), *Fifty Years of the British Indian Ocean Territory: Legal Perspectives*. Cham: Springer, pp. 147–174.

Nechtman, T.W. (2010) *Nabobs: Empire and Identity in Eighteenth-Century Britain*. Cambridge. Cambridge University Press.

O'Brien, C.C. (2002) *Edmund Burke*. London: Vintage Lives.

O'Brien, D. (2015) 'Magna Carta, the "Sugar Colonies" and "Fantasies of Empire"'. In R. Hazell and J. Melton (eds.), *Magna Carta and Its Modern Legacy*. Cambridge: Cambridge University Press, pp. 99–122.

O'Neill, D.I. (2016) *Edmund Burke and the Conservative Logic of Empire*. Oakland: University of California Press.

Oral Proceedings (2018) 'Legal consequences of the separation of the Chagos Archipelago from Mauritius in 1965'. 3 September. Available at: https://www.icj-cij.org/sites/default/files/case-related/169/169-20180903-ORA-02-00-BI.pdf (Accessed: 1 September 2023).

Paterson, A. (2011) *Lawyers and the Public Good: Democracy in Action?* Cambridge: Cambridge University Press.

Paterson, A. (2013) *Final Judgment: The Last Law Lords and the Supreme Court*. Oxford: Hart Publishing.

Prayag, T. (2016) 'Passing the dossier to the next government will lead to more prolonged delay'. *La Sentinelle,* 14–20 July, pp. 27–29.

Rolli, C. (2019) *The Trial of Warren Hastings: Classical Oratory and Reception in Eighteenth-Century England.* London: Bloomsbury Academic.

Ryan, L. (2018) 'Martial Law in the British Empire'. In P. Dwyer and A. Nettlelbeck (eds.), *Violence, Colonialism and Empire in the Modern World.* Basingstoke: Palgrave Macmillan, pp. 93–110.

Sands, P. (2022) *The Last Colony: A Tale of Exile, Justice and Britain's Colonial Legacy.* London: Weidenfield and Nicolson.

Scott, P.F. (2020) 'The Privy Council and the constitutional legacies of empire'. *NILQ*, 71(2), p. 261

Sedley, S. (2015) *Lions under the Throne: Essays on the History of English Public Law.* Cambridge: Cambridge University Press.

Sedley, S. (2017) 'The judges verdict'. *London Review of Books,* January.

Sen, S. (2015) 'Liberalism and the British Empire in India'. *The Journal of Asian Studies,* 74(3), pp. 711–722.

Snoxell, D. (2009) 'Anglo-American complicity in the removal of the inhabitants of the Chagos Islands, 1964-73'. *Journal of Imperial & Commonwealth History,* 37, pp. 127–134.

Suleri, S. (1992) *The Rhetoric of English India.* Chicago: University of Chicago Press.

Sumption, J. (2023) 'Cruel Britannia?'. *Literary Review*, February. Available at: https://literaryreview.co.uk/cruel-britannia (Accessed: 1 September 2023).

Tomkins, A. (2018) 'Environmental protection v the right of abode: A case-study in the misuse of power'. In S. Allen and C. Monaghan (eds.), *Fifty Years of the British Indian Ocean Territory: Legal Perspectives.* Cham: Springer, pp. 43–54.

Travers, R. (2012) 'Constitutions, contact zones, and imperial ricochets: sovereignty and law in British Asia'. In H. Bowen *et al.* (eds.), *Britain's Oceanic Empire: Atlantic and Indian Ocean Worlds.* Cambridge: Cambridge University Press, pp. 98–129.

Trefgarne, D. (1980) 'Hansard: House of Commons debates'. 25 March, vol 1980, cc540-1W. Available at: https://hansard.parliament.uk/Commons/1980-03-25/debates/81fa3683-6727-4684-9f37-57cc5ba91878/DiegoGarciaSalamonAndPerosBunhos?_gl=1*t8u1o7*_up*MQ..*_ga*MTk4NjQ1NTk0NS4xNzEyNzQzMTg4*_ga_Z1C97N01BT*MTcxMjc0MzE4OC4xLjAuMTcxMjc0MzE4OC4wLjAuMA (Accessed: 1 September 2023).

UK Government. (n.d.) 'Civil service diversity and inclusion dashboard'. Available at: https://www.gov.uk/government/publications/civil-service-diversity-inclusion-dashboard/civil-service-diversity-and-inclusion-dashboard (Accessed: 01 September 2023).

United Nations. 'Preparatory years: UN charter history'. Available at: https://www.un.org/en/about-us/history-of-the-un/preparatory-years (Accessed: 1 September 2023).

United Nations. (2019) 'Advisory opinion of the International Court of Justice on the legal consequences of the separation of the Chagos Archipelago from Mauritius in 1965'. Resolution A/RES/73/295. Available at: https://documents-dds-ny.un.org/doc/UNDOC/GEN/N19/151/29/PDF/N1915129.pdf?OpenElement (Accessed: 1 September 2023).

Veveers, D. (2023) *The Great Defiance: How the World Took on the British Empire.* London: Ebury Press.

Vine, D. (2008) 'Decolonizing Britain in the 21st century? Chagos Islanders challenge the crown, house of Lords, 30 June–3 July 2008'. *Anthropology Today*, 24(4), pp. 26–28.

Wintour, P. (2016) 'Chagos Islanders denied right to return home'. *The Guardian,* 16 November. Available at: https://www.theguardian.com/world/2016/nov/16/chagos-islanders-denied-right-to-return-home (Accessed: 1 September 2023).

Yusuf, H.O. (2013) *Colonial and Post-colonial Constitutionalism in the Commonwealth: Peace, Order and Good Government.* Abingdon: Routledge.

List of Cases

Building Construction Employees and Builders' Labourers Federation of New South. Wales v Minister for Industrial Relations (1986) 7 NSWLR 372. (New South Wales Court of Appeal)
Case of Proclamations (1611) 12 co rep 74; 77 ER 1352. *BAILII.* Available at: http://www.bailii.org/ew/cases/EWHC/KB/1610/J22.html (Accessed: 1 March 2023).
Chagos Islanders v Attorney General & Anor (2004) [2004] EWCA Civ 997. *BAILII.* Available at: http://www.bailii.org/ew/cases/EWCA/Civ/2004/997.html (Accessed: 1 March 2023).
Chagos Islanders v the United Kingdom (application no. 35622/04) (2012) ECHR. *HUDOC.* Available at: https://hudoc.echr.coe.int/sites/eng-press/pages/search.aspx?i=003-4207010-4992253 (Accessed: 1 September 2023).
Hourigan v The Trustees Executors and Agency Co. Ltd [1933] VLR 470. Supreme Court of Victoria.
International Court of Justice, *Legal Consequences of the Separation of the Chagos Archipelago from Mauritius in 1965.* Available at: https://www.icj-cij.org/case/169 (Accessed: 1 September 2023).
R (Bancoult) v. Secretary of State for Foreign and Commonwealth Office (No 1) (2000) [2000] EWHC 413 (Admin). *BAILII.* Available at: http://www.bailii.org/ew/cases/EWHC/Admin/2000/413.html (Accessed: 8 September 2023).
R (on the application of Bancoult) v Secretary of State for Foreign and Commonwealth Affairs (No.2) (2007) [2007] EWCA Civ 498. *BAILII.* Available at: http://www.bailii.org/ew/cases/EWCA/Civ/2007/498.html (Accessed: 1 September 2023).
R (Bancoult) v. Secretary of State For Foreign and Commonwealth Affairs (No 2) (2008) [2008] UKHL 61. *BAILII.* Available at: https://www.bailii.org/cgi-bin/format.cgi?doc=/uk/cases/UKHL/2008/61.html (Accessed: 8 September 2023).
Phillips v Eyre (1870) LR 6 QB 1
R (on the application of Bancoult) v Secretary of State for Foreign and Commonwealth Affairs (No.3) (2014) [2014] EWCA Civ 708. *BAILII.* Available at: http://www.bailii.org/ew/cases/EWCA/Civ/2014/708.html (Accessed: 1 September 2023).
R (on the application of Bancoult (No 3)) v Secretary of State for Foreign & Commonwealth Affairs (2018) [2018] UKSC 3. *BAILII.* Available at: http://www.bailii.org/uk/cases/UKSC/2018/3.html (Accessed: 1 September 2023).
R (on the application of Hoareau and Bancoult) v The Secretary of State for Foreign and Commonwealth Affairs (2020) [2020] EWCA Civ 1010. *BAILII.* Available at: http://www.bailii.org/ew/cases/EWCA/Civ/2020/1010.html (Accessed: 1 September 2023).
R (on the application of Hoareau and Bancoult) v The Secretary of State for Foreign and Commonwealth Affairs (2019) [2019] EWHC 221 (Admin). *BAILII.* Available at: http://www.bailii.org/ew/cases/EWHC/Admin/2019/221.html (Accessed: 1 September 2023).
R (on the application of Bancoult (No 2)) (Appellant) v Secretary of State for Foreign and Commonwealth Affairs (Respondent) (2016) [2016] UKSC 35. *BAILII.* Available at: https://www.bailii.org/uk/cases/UKSC/2016/35.html (Accessed: 1 September 2023).
R (on the application of Bancoult) v Secretary of State for Foreign & Commonwealth Affairs Rev 1 (2006) [2006] EWHC 1038 (Admin). *BAILII.* Available at: http://www.bailii.org/ew/cases/EWHC/Admin/2006/1038.html (Accessed: 1 September 2023).
Shergill & Ors v Khaira & Ors (2016) [2014] UKSC 33. *BAILII.* Available at: http://www.bailii.org/uk/cases/UKSC/2014/33.html (Accessed: 1 September 2023).

13 Stakeholders or Bystanders?

An Attempt by Seychellois Chagossians to Intervene in the International Tribunal for the Law of the Sea

Stephen Allen, Thomas Burri, and Jamie Trinidad

In 2019, the International Court of Justice (ICJ) held in a ground-breaking Advisory Opinion that the separation of the Chagos Archipelago from Mauritius by the UK in 1965 was an unlawful violation of the right to self-determination of the Mauritian people (ICJ, 2019; see also Allen, 2019; Burri and Trinidad, 2021a). A Special Chamber of the International Tribunal for the Law of the Sea (ITLOS) subsequently endorsed the ruling of the ICJ and used it as a basis for treating Mauritius as the coastal state in the Chagos Archipelago in the context of maritime delimitation proceedings with the Maldives (ITLOS, 2021; see also Burri and Trinidad, 2021b). These decisions were no doubt influential in pushing the UK towards the negotiating table.

In the ICJ, the participation of several Chagossians as part of the Mauritian delegation, and in particular the powerful testimony of Liseby Elysé, had a profound impact in setting the tone of the proceedings and foregrounding the human catastrophe that lay at the heart of the case.[1]

By contrast, the attempt by the Chagossian Committee Seychelles (CCS), led by Pierre Prosper, to intervene in the maritime delimitation proceedings between Mauritius and the Maldives in ITLOS was rejected. The Special Chamber hearing that case decided not to allow the intervention or place the CCS's amicus submission on the case file, despite the parties expressing no objection and deferring to the Special Chamber's discretion.

Both these episodes serve to highlight the potential and limits of using international courts and tribunals, and international law more generally, as a platform for the expression and vindication of Chagossian rights and interests, noting that these may not always align with the rights and interests of Mauritius.

Sub-state groups like the Chagossians lack formal standing in "statist" forums like the ICJ and ITLOS. Certain creative forms of participation are possible, especially with the support of participating states, as we saw in the ICJ advisory proceedings. However, attempts to intervene that are not underwritten by participating states are unlikely to have an impact. Indeed, they are often not even acknowledged in the official record of the case.

It was against this backdrop, with the procedural odds stacked against them, that the CCS attempted to intervene in the maritime delimitation proceedings between Mauritius and Maldives in ITLOS. They did so in the wake of a remarkable preliminary decision on jurisdiction, where the ITLOS Special Chamber had

DOI: 10.4324/9781003390299-19

held that Mauritian sovereignty over the Chagos Archipelago could be inferred from the Advisory Opinion of the ICJ, and that therefore "Mauritius should be regarded as the coastal state of the Archipelago" (ITLOS, 2021, supra n. two, para 15).

The CCS, represented by us, submitted a written brief to ITLOS in which they placed reliance on the distinct rights of the Chagossians as the Indigenous people of the Chagos Archipelago, rather than as a sub-set of the people of Mauritius. Included among these rights, they submitted, was the right to be consulted over, and derive benefit from, the use of marine spaces and resources surrounding the Chagos Archipelago.

There is no detailed record of how the CCS intervention was considered by the Special Chamber and by the parties, but a basic indication can be found in paragraphs 34–36 of the judgment on the merits:

> 34. With regard to the request by the "Chagossian Committee Seychelles" referred to in paragraph 29, the Agent of the Maldives, by letter dated 15 December 2021, stated that "in the absence of any express rules concerning amicus curiae submissions by non-governmental entities such as the Committee, the acceptance of this request by the Committee is for determination by the Special Chamber in the exercise of its inherent powers over procedural questions."
> 35. By letter dated 16 December 2021, the Agent of Mauritius indicated that Mauritius "is comfortable leaving it to the discretion of the Special Chamber to determine whether this communication should be included in the case file … and would have no objection should it be so included."
> 36. By letter dated 11 January 2022, the Registrar informed the Agents of the Parties that the Special Chamber, after reviewing the amicus curiae submissions and the comments thereon made by the Parties, decided that the request should not be accepted and that the amicus curiae submissions by the "Chagossian Committee Seychelles" should not be included in the case file. By letter of the same date, the Registrar also communicated the decision of the Special Chamber to the "Chagossian Committee Seychelles".

The Special Chamber's decision to reject the CCS submission and not to include it in the case file could well have been based on a narrow assessment that the intervention was not useful for the immediate technical purpose of delimiting the maritime zones of the parties. However, in the absence of any pushback from Mauritius and Maldives, it seems to us that the Special Chamber has passed up a rare and valuable opportunity to give a platform to Indigenous voices, unmediated by the parties to the proceedings.

The written intervention submitted by CCS to the ITLOS Special Chamber is set out here in full. It is hoped that its contents might help to inform future discussion of the rights of the Chagossians over the land and maritime spaces of the Archipelago.

BEFORE A SPECIAL CHAMBER OF THE INTERNATIONAL TRIBUNAL FOR THE LAW OF THE SEA

CASE NO. 28

Dispute Concerning Delimitation of the Maritime Boundary Between Mauritius and Maldives in the Indian Ocean
***AMICUS CURIAE* SUBMISSION**
BY THE CHAGOSSIAN COMMITTEE SEYCHELLES 23 NOVEMBER 2021

A. Introduction

1. We are a group of Chagossians who are resident in the Republic of Seychelles. None of us are citizens of the Republic of Mauritius. A number of us were born in, and then unlawfully removed and/or prohibited from returning to, the Chagos Archipelago prior to Mauritian independence. The rest of us are directly descended from members of that displaced community. All of us hope, one day, to be able to return to our ancestral homeland. Some of us hope to resettle there.
2. We are making this *amicus* submission because we have an interest of a legal nature in these proceedings, and we would like our interest to be taken into consideration by the Special Chamber. Simply put, as part of the people whose right to self-determination was violated when the United Kingdom detached the Chagos Archipelago from the Non-Self-Governing Territory of Mauritius in 1965, we are specially affected by, and have a direct stake in, the outcome of the delimitation dispute that is presently before the Special Chamber.
3. The essence of our submission is that *all Chagossians* – regardless of whether they are citizens of the Republic of Mauritius – have a special interest in these proceedings. As the Indigenous people of the territory, we have a right to be consulted regarding the use of the maritime spaces around the Chagos Archipelago, and a right to share in any economic and other benefits that may flow therefrom.
4. In section B we explain the nature of our legal interest in these proceedings. In part C we explain what we hope to achieve in putting these *amicus* submissions before the Special Chamber.

B. The legal basis of our entitlement

5. The substantive phase of these proceedings is premised on the validity of the findings of the International Court of Justice in its *Chagos* Advisory Opinion (ICJ, 2019). Concretely, the ICJ held that the Chagos Archipelago had been unlawfully separated from the Non- Self-Governing Territory of Mauritius in 1965.

6. In reaching its Opinion, the ICJ rejected the contention that it should decline to exercise its advisory jurisdiction because the proceedings concerned a bilateral sovereignty dispute to which the UK had not consented (ibid., para 83). It observed that, given the significance of decolonization for the United Nations; and the leading role played by the General Assembly in that process, the issues raised in the Assembly's request were located in the broader frame of decolonization and were inseparable from it (ibid., para 86-88). Having decided to answer the request, the ICJ found the Mauritian people to be the beneficiaries of the right to self-determination and, as a corollary, the UK was obligated to maintain the territorial integrity of Mauritius pending its decolonization (ibid., paras 150-153; 173). The Court went on to rule that the detachment of the Chagos Archipelago from Mauritius in 1965 could only be validly undertaken if the Mauritian people had freely consented to such an excision (ibid., paras 160; 172).
7. On the facts, the ICJ concluded that such consent had not been secured, and, as a result, Mauritius' decolonization had not been lawfully completed in 1968, when it acceded to independence (ibid., para 174). The Court also decided that the UK's administration of the Archipelago constituted an international wrongful act of a continuing character for which it bears responsibility (ibid., para 177). Accordingly, the UK was required to withdraw from the Archipelago as rapidly as possible (ibid., para 178). To that end, the Court reaffirmed the *erga omnes* character of the principle of self-determination and that, as a result, all States are under a duty to co- operate with the UN in order for this entitlement to be fulfilled (ibid., paras 180; 182).
8. The ICJ left the modalities for the completion of Mauritius' decolonization to the General Assembly (ibid., para 179). The Assembly subsequently set these out in resolution 73/295, which was adopted on 22 May 2019 by 116 votes in favour, 6 against and 56 abstentions. In this resolution, the Assembly asserted that, in accordance with the Advisory Opinion, '[t]he Chagos Archipelago forms an integral part of the territory of Mauritius' (para 2(b)). It demanded that the UK withdraw its administration from the Archipelago within six months (para 3), and it reiterated that all Member States are under a duty to co-operate with the UN to bring about the completion of Mauritius' decolonization while refraining from any action that would impede or delay this process (paras 2(e) and 5). Further, the Assembly instructed all UN agencies to 'recognize that the Chagos Archipelago forms an integral part of the territory of Mauritius' and, to refrain from 'giving effect to any measure taken by or on behalf of, the "British Indian Ocean Territory"' (para 6).
9. In the preliminary phase of the present proceedings, the Special Chamber endorsed the ICJ's findings (ITLOS, 2021).
10. In its judgment of 28 January 2021, the Special Chamber acknowledged the close relationship between decolonization and sovereignty as far as the longstanding dispute between Mauritius and the UK was concerned (ibid., paras 166; 188; 242). In this context, the Chamber considered that the ICJ's determinations in the Chagos Advisory Opinion had 'unmistakable implications' for the UK's sovereignty claim (ibid., para 173). Likewise, those determinations had

'considerable implications' for Mauritius' claim that the Chagos Archipelago forms an integral part of its national territory (ibid., para 174). The Chamber also considered resolution 73/295 to be relevant to its assessment of the legal status of the Chagos Archipelago for the purpose of adjudicating the dispute between Mauritius and the Maldives (ibid., paras 226-229).

11. Ultimately, the Special Chamber decided that Mauritius' sovereignty over the Chagos Archipelago could be inferred from the determinations made by the ICJ in its *Chagos* Advisory Opinion, despite the process of Mauritius's decolonization remaining incomplete (ibid., para 246). Further, it concluded that Mauritius qualifies as the Archipelago's coastal state, by virtue of those determinations (ibid., para 250). In sum, the Chamber, therefore, held that the Chagos Advisory Opinion generated legal effects for the legal status of the Chagos Archipelago by necessary implication, a conclusion that was strengthened by the content of resolution 73/295 (ibid., para 246).
12. The appalling treatment of the Chagossians in the lead up to Mauritian independence, and during its aftermath, is well documented, in the Advisory Opinion and elsewhere. Many were displaced to Mauritius. Others, like ourselves and our families, were displaced to the Seychelles.
13. We are part of the people whose right to self-determination and permanent sovereignty over natural resources was breached in 1965. Our right was not extinguished by the UK's unlawful act, nor was it extinguished by the creation of the Republic of Mauritius in 1968. It was vested in us prior to 1965, before the concept of Mauritian citizenship existed.
14. We submit moreover that as the Indigenous people of the Chagos Archipelago, we and our fellow Chagossians have a special interest in any proceedings where the status of the Archipelago, and/or the maritime spaces around it, are at issue.
15. It was the Chagossians, after all, who were unlawfully expelled from, and/or prevented from returning to, the Archipelago by the British authorities, with the connivance of the pre-independence Mauritian authorities. Our way of life and means of subsistence were stolen from us, at a time when most of the inhabitants of the island of Mauritius – over 2000 kilometres away – were oblivious to our suffering, and while the politicians who led Mauritius to independence treated us as bargaining chips.
16. We strongly submit, therefore, that our legal interest in these proceedings cannot legitimately be viewed as a mere subset of the international legal rights enjoyed and invoked by the Republic of Mauritius.
17. While this last point holds true for Chagossians in general, it is of particular importance for Chagossians who, like us, are not Mauritian citizens. We have no legal relationship with the Republic of Mauritius, and no formal means through which to influence political decision making in Mauritius.
18. In our submission, once the Special Chamber has established the extent of the maritime entitlements generated by the Chagos Archipelago, Mauritius will be under a duty to consult Indigenous Chagossians regarding the use and exploitation of these marine spaces, and to share with them the economic and other benefits that flow from these maritime entitlements. This duty, we submit, is owed not only to Chagossians who are Mauritian citizens but to *all Chagossians*.

19. This leads us to our reasons for wanting to put these submissions before the Special Chamber, and to set out what we hope to achieve in doing so.

C. Our aim in putting these submissions to the Special Chamber

20. During the ICJ advisory proceedings, Judge Gaja put the following question to the Republic of Mauritius: 'In the process of decolonization relating to the Chagos Archipelago, what is the relevance of the will of the population of Chagossian origin?'
21. The Written Reply of the Republic of Mauritius is set out here in full for ease of reference (with emphasis supplied):
    1. The Chagos Archipelago having always been an integral part of the territory of Mauritius, the "“process of decolonization relating to the Chagos Archipelago” ***could only be treated as a part of the decolonization of Mauritius as a whole***.
    2. Accordingly, the position in international law, as at November 1965 (when the right of self-determination was already established in international law), was that ***the Chagos Archipelago could not be detached from the territory of Mauritius, unless the express consent of the people of Mauritius, including Mauritians residing in the Chagos Archipelago or of Chagossian origin, to such a detachment had been obtained.***
    3. No such consent was obtained either prior to 12 March 1968 when Mauritius achieved independence, nor was any consent obtained thereafter.
    4. Accordingly, as at that date, and continuing until today, the purported “detachment” of the Chagos Archipelago has been, and continues to be, unlawful under international law. The process of decolonization of Mauritius therefore remains incomplete. As a consequence, the United Kingdom is under an obligation under international law to complete the decolonization of Mauritius, by taking immediate steps to withdraw its unlawful colonial administration and restore the integrity of the territory of Mauritius.
    5. ***As regards the “will” of the population of Chagossian origin, this was required to be taken into account by the administering power in determining whether the consent of the people of Mauritius as a whole had been obtained to the purported “detachment”*** of the Chagos Archipelago from the territory of Mauritius. As noted above, ***the will of the people of Mauritius, including the “will of the population of Chagossian origin”,*** was not taken into account prior to the detachment of Chagos Archipelago in 1965, or prior to the independence of Mauritius. This was a manifest violation of ***the right of the people of Mauritius, including its population of Chagossian origin, to self-determination.***
    6. The withdrawal of the unlawful colonial administration, the recognition of the territorial integrity of Mauritius as including the Chagos Archipelago and the exercise of sovereignty over the totality of its territory by Mauritius, will allow the return to the Chagos Archipelago, and

the resettlement there of all individuals of Chagossian origin wishing to do so, in accordance with the laws of Mauritius.

7. Mauritius reaffirms its commitment to respect the 'will of the population of Chagossian origin', by facilitating resettlement. Whether to return and resettle is a matter of free choice to be decided on an individual basis by each person of Chagossian origin (ICJ, 2018).

22. This carefully worded Written Reply deems the will of the population of Chagossian origin to be relevant, but only insofar as Chagossians are also part of the broader entity, the 'people of Mauritius'. This framing of the issue gives rise to two points of concern. The first is that it ignores the rights that Chagossians hold under international law as the Indigenous people of the Chagos Archipelago. The second is that it does not acknowledge the existence of Chagossians who are not citizens of Mauritius.

(i) The rights of Chagossians as the Indigenous people of the Chagos Archipelago

23. The Chagossians are the Indigenous people of the Archipelago. As a population we were – and continue to be – uniquely affected by the United Kingdom's unlawful actions. Chagossians, we submit, have rights to their land and waters *qua* Chagossians, and not merely as a subset of the population of Mauritius.
24. In the *Chagos* Advisory Opinion, the ICJ took the view that the subject of the right to self-determination – the 'people' – must be defined by reference to the colonial unit as a whole for the purpose of effecting decolonization (ICJ, 2019, para 160). However, as the Canadian Supreme Court observed, in *Re Secession of Quebec*, the notion of a 'people' is not necessarily coterminous with the total population of a given State. Indeed, in that case, the Court observed that a 'people' may include only a portion of the population of a State in relation to the exercise of the right to self-determination (Supreme Court of Canada, 1998, para 124). This is particularly true in relation to the rights of Indigenous peoples.
25. In this respect, it is worth noting that Article 3 of the UN Declaration on the Rights of Indigenous Peoples (General Assembly resolution 61/295 (13 September 2007)) declares that Indigenous peoples possess the right to self-determination notwithstanding the fact that, pursuant to Article 4 UNDRIP, the exercise of the Indigenous-specific variant of this entitlement does not give rise to a presumptive right to independent statehood. The Chagossians have embraced their status as an Indigenous people and have self-identified as such (United Nations, 1999, para 63). Consequently, the Chagossians are entitled to enjoy an array of Indigenous-specific rights relating to the Chagos Archipelago.
26. In particular, Article 15(1) of ILO Convention 169 on Indigenous and Tribal Peoples in Independent Countries (1989), provides that the rights of Indigenous peoples 'to the natural resources pertaining to their lands shall be specially safeguarded. These rights include the right of these peoples to participate in the use, management and conservation of these resources'. It is

well established that the concept of 'lands' underpinning this provision is a broad one. In this context, Article 13(2) states that: 'The use of the term lands in Articles 15 and 16 shall include the concept of territories, which covers the total environment of the areas which the peoples concerned occupy or otherwise use'.

27. In fact, Article 25 UNDRIP specifically refers to 'lands, territories, waters, coastal seas and other resources' in this regard. Accordingly, the concept of territories clearly encompasses both terrestrial and marine space and resources. Moreover, Article 26, which has now acquired customary international law status as far as Indigenous natural resources rights are concerned, provides that: (1) 'Indigenous peoples have the right to the lands, territories and resources which they have traditionally owned, occupied or otherwise used or acquired'; (2) they 'have the right to own, use develop and control the lands, territories and resources that they possess…'; and (3) 'States shall give legal recognition and protection to these lands, territories and resources [...]'.
28. Indigenous peoples have the right to be consulted and to participate in decision-making processes that concern them with a corresponding duty on States to secure their Free, Prior and Informed Consent before adopting and implementing legislative or administrative measures that may affect them (United Nations General Assembly, 2011, Article 19). In addition, the duty to consult is specifically engaged in certain situations, including where decisions about the exploration and exploitation of natural resources relating to Indigenous lands (Article 15(2), Convention 169), and by necessary implication, to their marine territories, are being considered.
29. Further, Article 28(1) UNDRIP recognizes that Indigenous peoples have the right to redress, which may include restitution, where, 'lands, territories and resources which they have traditionally owned or otherwise occupied or used, [are] confiscated, taken, occupied, used or damaged without their free, prior and informed consent.'

(ii) The need to avoid the disenfranchisement of Chagossians who are not Mauritian citizens

30. The Republic of Mauritius' Written Reply to Judge Gaja's question ignores the fact that many Chagossians, like us, were part of the 'people of Mauritius' in 1965 but did not become citizens of the Republic of Mauritius when it was created in 1968. The continuing effects of the United Kingdom's unlawful act (see paragraph 4 of Mauritius' Written Reply) are felt by us today just as intensely as they are felt by fellow Chagossians who happen to be Mauritian citizens.
31. When control of the Chagos Archipelago eventually passes to Mauritius, the return and resettlement of Chagossians will of course be subject to 'the laws of Mauritius' (paragraph 6 of Mauritius' Written Reply). However, the conditions of our return and resettlement are not *exclusively* governed by Mauritian domestic law. As members of the Indigenous people of the Archipelago, we have rights under *international law* that Mauritius and other States are under

a duty to respect, including rights over the natural marine resources of the Archipelago.

32. The Republic of Mauritius has done much to advance the Chagossian cause in recent years, and it is understandable that it should seek to frame the issue in 'statist' terms. Indeed, it must be acknowledged that Chagossians – who have no standing before tribunals like the ICJ or ITLOS – have benefited from pinning their interests onto the litigation strategy of the Republic of Mauritius.
33. We accept that Mauritius is correct when it asserts that the right to self-determination of the 'people of Mauritius', which included the Chagossians, was violated in 1965. However, another proposition is simultaneously true: the Chagossians were, and remain, uniquely affected by the detachment of the Archipelago, and as an Indigenous people we have special legal interests in the land and waters of the Archipelago, *which cannot be entirely subsumed under the interests of the Republic of Mauritius in the present case.*
34. We therefore respectfully request an acknowledgment from the Special Chamber that all Chagossians, including those who are not Mauritian citizens:

(a) are specially affected by the outcome of these delimitation proceedings;
(b) should be consulted regarding any exploitation of the maritime spaces around the Chagos Archipelago; and
(c) are entitled to an equitable share of any economic and other benefits that may be derived from the maritime spaces around the Chagos Archipelago.

SIGNATORY

Pierre Prosper

Chairperson of the Chagossian Committee Seychelles
(La Misere, Mahé, Seychelles, 23 November 2021)

ADVISORS

Sebastian Schnitzenbaumer
Jamie Trinidad

Fellow, Wolfson College, Cambridge and Lauterpacht Centre for International Law

Stephen Allen

Senior Lecturer in Law, Queen Mary, University of London

Thomas Burri

Professor of International Law University of St. Gallen

Note

1 This testimony was included in Judge Robinson's Separate Opinion (para 104). Nevertheless, it raises awkward questions for the Mauritian government of the late 1960s and early 1970s notwithstanding the UK government's predominant position and its actions pursuant to the excision of the Chagos Archipelago from the Mauritian colonial unit. See Allen (2020).

References

Allen, S. (2019) 'Introductory note: legal consequences of the separation of the Chagos Archipelago from Mauritius in 1965 (ICJ)'. *International Legal Materials,* 58(3), pp. 445–447.

Allen, S. (2020) 'Self-determination, the *Chagos Advisory Opinion* and the Chagossians'. *International & Comparative Law Quarterly,* 69, pp. 203, 214–215.

Burri, T. and Trinidad, J. (eds.) (2021a) *The International Court of Justice and Decolonization: New Directions from the Chagos Advisory Opinion.* Cambridge: Cambridge University Press.

Burri, T. and Trinidad, J. (2021b) 'Introductory note: Dispute concerning delimitation of the maritime boundary between Mauritius and Maldives in the Indian Ocean, preliminary objections (ITLOS)'. *International Legal Materials,* 60(6), pp. 969–972.

International Court of Justice (2018) 'Written Reply of the Republic of Mauritius to the question put by Judge Gaja at the end of the hearing held on 3 September 2018'. Available at: https://www.icj-cij.org/index.php/sites/default/files/case-related/169/169-20180906-OTH-01-00-EN.pdf.

International Court of Justice (2019) 'Legal consequences of the separation of the Chagos Archipelago from Mauritius in 1965. Advisory opinion'. Available at: https://www.icj-cij.org/public/files/case-related/169/169-20190225-01-00-EN.pdf.

International Labour Organization (189) 'Convention (No. 169) concerning indigenous and tribal people in independent countries'. 27 June 1989, 1650 U.N.T.S. 383. Available at: https://www.investorstatelawguide.com/documents/documents/OTI-0120%20-%20International%20Labour%20Organization%20Convention%20No.%20169%20(1989)%20(citation%20and%20source).pdf.

International Tribunal for the Law of the Sea (2021) 'Dispute concerning delimitation of the maritime boundary between Mauritius and Maldives in the Indian Ocean (Mauritius/Maldives) preliminary objections- judgment'. Available at: https://jusmundi.com/en/document/decision/en-dispute-concerning-delimitation-of-the-maritime-boundary-between-mauritius-and-maldives-in-the-indian-ocean-mauritius-maldives-judgment-preliminary-objections-thursday-28th-january-2021#decision_14650.

Supreme Court of Canada (1998) 'Reference re secession of Quebec, [1998] 2 SCR 217'. Available at: https://scc-csc.lexum.com/scc-csc/scc-csc/en/item/1643/index.do.

United Nations (1999) 'Report of the 17th session of the UN working group on indigenous populations'. 12 August 1999. E/CN4/Sub2/1999/19. Available at: https://digitallibrary.un.org/record/278132/files/E_CN.4_Sub.2_1999_19-EN.

United Nations General Assembly (2011) 'Final report of the study on indigenous peoples and the right to participate in decision-making: Report of the expert mechanism on the rights of indigenous peoples'. UN Doc A/HRC/18/42. Available at: file:///C:/Users/mairi/Documents/A_HRC_18_42-EN.pdf.

14 The 1966 BIOT Agreement and Polaris

Samuel Bashfield

Many contemporary accounts of British Indian Ocean Territory (BIOT) history note that Britain received discounted Polaris nuclear weapons in exchange for allowing the United States to militarise the Chagos Archipelago (Wenban-Smith and Carter, 2016, p. 474; Vine, 2011, pp. 87–88; Bandjunis, 2001, pp. 26–27). However, the finer details and significance of this deal are little analysed or understood. How various remote Indian Ocean islands and Polaris submarine-launched ballistic missiles (SLBM) – one of Britain's most secretive and significant military technologies – were intertwined is worthy of renewed attention. Indeed, BIOT may never have been created and Diego Garcia not militarised if not for this Anglo-US deal, which softened the financial burden BIOT created for the economically fragile United Kingdom in the mid-1960s. This deal allowed Britain to create another colony, despite the Cold War wave of decolonisation concurrently sweeping the globe. This analysis affords a glimpse into how decolonisation was inconsistently implemented.

This chapter first provides contextual background on Britain's nuclear deterrent in the early-1960s, before examining Her Majesty's Government (HMG) plans to acquire Polaris SLMBs from the United States and the unexpected research and development (R&D) costs. Second, this chapter assesses the costs associated with creating BIOT in 1965. Third, it examines how BIOT and Polaris were intertwined in 1966 and the coverup which took place in 1967 to keep these financial details secret.

This chapter illuminates how creating and militarising BIOT had far-reaching ramifications for British statecraft – enabling it to acquire an independent nuclear deterrent and remain an influential global power above its station throughout the Cold War. It also sheds light on Anglo-US negotiations pertaining to BIOT's creation, demonstrating how the Chagos Archipelago was used by Britain to offset its other defence acquisitions. Lastly, the chapter re-examines the 1966 BIOT agreement, which will need to be terminated should the Chagos Archipelago be transferred to Mauritius – negotiations for which are ongoing at the time of writing in 2024. While much contemporary attention is focussed on Anglo-Mauritian sovereignty negotiations, Anglo-US negotiations pertaining to cancelling the 1966 BIOT Agreement are, arguably, equally vital.

This chapter cites a variety of primary and secondary sources to draw conclusions. Of note, a range of declassified papers from the UK National Archives are

DOI: 10.4324/9781003390299-20

referenced, as well as primary formerly classified records from both the John F. Kennedy and the Lyndon B. Johnson presidential libraries in Boston and Austin respectively. However, before examining how BIOT and Polaris were intertwined, some background on Britain's sensitive nuclear deterrent is necessary.

Skybolt, Polaris, and Unexpected R&D Surcharges

Britain's acquisition of Polaris SLBM technology was precipitated on Skybolt's controversial cancellation. Skybolt, an air-launched ballistic missile developed by the United States, was designed to be dropped by strategic bombers. The United Kingdom joined Skybolt in early-1960, agreed to by President Eisenhower, and intended to deploy the system via its V-bomber force (Jones, 2019, p. 62). However, from the outset Skybolt was plagued by cost blowouts, technical issues, developmental delays, and concerns over its eventual reliability and utility (Klein, 1963, p. 11). President Kennedy decided to cancel Skybolt on 23 November 1962, and the project was formally ended on December 5 (Klein, 1963, p. 2).

This decision blindsided Britain, which was counting on Skybolt as its sole nuclear deterrent, after it cancelled Blue Steel II in 1959 and Blue Streak in 1960. The October 1962 Cuban Missile Crisis preoccupied many US officials, which contributed to poor communication with British officials on Skybolt's uncertain future. According to a White House post-mortem after Skybolt's cancellation: "at the critical moments in the SKY BOLT [sic] exercise there appears to have [been] an insufficient appreciation of the political problems likely to result from the decision, and over-optimism about our ability to cope with those that were identified" (Klein, 1963, p. 3). Despite Britain being promised sufficient time to process any US decision, when US Secretary of Defense Robert McNamara finally discussed the issue with UK Secretary of State for Defence Peter Thorneycroft on 11 December 1962, the pair could only discuss alternatives since the project had already been cancelled (Klein, 1963, p. 5). The decision caused a major crisis for Britain and a significant Anglo-US bilateral spat.

Both sides convened an emergency meeting at Nassau, Bahamas, between 18 and 21 December 1962 to discuss Britain's nuclear deterrent options following Skybolt's untimely cancellation. Despite Skybolt's cancellation, Kennedy offered UK Prime Minister Harold MacMillan American readiness to jointly develop Skybolt, with each side contributing equally to future development costs, but this option was deemed unacceptable due to costs and uncertainty on timelines (Bligh, 1962, p. 1). Second, Kennedy offered to sell Hound Dog missiles, but MacMillan deemed it too onerous to retrofit these missiles to British V bombers (Bligh, 1962, 2). Finally, Kennedy's offer of Polaris SLBMs (less warheads), in concert with the North Atlantic Treaty Organization (NATO), was accepted by MacMillan (Bligh, 1962, p. 2). According to the 21 December joint communique, while the SLBMs would be made available to NATO's multilateral nuclear force and be used to defend the "Western Alliance", at MacMillan's insistence, HMG may use the SLBMs if Britain's "supreme national interests are at stake" ("Text of the Joint Communique by the President and Prime Minister Harold MacMillan Following

Discussions Held in Nassau, Bahamas", 1962, p. 2). This statement provided for the independence of Britain's prized "independent" nuclear deterrent.

Attaining Polaris – far superior to Skybolt – was a coup for Britain after its bruising experience with Skybolt. Despite initial US reluctance to furnish Britain with this potent technology, the Skybolt crisis had forced Kennedy's hand and initiated a highly favourable technology transfer across the Atlantic. In an excited 22 December memorandum dictated by the British Controller of the Navy (Third Sea Lord), which he intended to put in the recipients' "Christmas stocking[s]", he proclaimed "we are now 'IN' POLARIS in a big way. We are in the big time. The Americans are psychologically ready to go" ("Notes on Bahamas Meeting", 1962, pp. 5–7).

MacMillan, though, took a far more cautious approach. In preparing to send a negotiating team to Washington, in his personal minute of 26 December, he wrote: "There are a lot of snags to be watched very carefully here" (MacMillan, 1962, p. 1). Indeed, MacMillan's circumspect approach was warranted, as almost immediately a major "snag" emerged.

Upon negotiating the Polaris deal in January 1963, British officials were surprised to learn that an R&D fee was being sought from Washington. According to a report by British negotiators:

> One unexpected development was the American insistence that the U.K. should, with effect from 1st January 1963, bear, on a pro rata basis to be negotiated, a share of any research and development still to be done on any equipment which we wish to procure from them under the POLARIS agreement. This could mean significant payments in future years.
>
> ("Report of Polaris Fact Finding Mission to Washington", 1963)

The British had historically never paid such fees and were blindsided by the request, which was not discussed at Nassau. On 16 January 1963, McNamara wrote to Thorneycroft about the R&D issue. McNamara noted that the "Nassau Agreement did not purport to address itself to costs", and he proposed that "each of us pay a fair share of all costs … What I am suggesting is that the cost of such items as you choose to buy include a proper proportion of the R. & D. [sic] costs since January 1st of this year" (McNarama, 1963, p. 1). Under this formulation, Britain would not be liable for any Polaris R&D expenditure prior to 1963 but would be charged an estimated $17 million in surcharges over Polaris' lifetime.

In the end, MacMillan acquiesced and agreed to pay a five per cent R&D surcharge on British Polaris SLMBs ("Polaris Sales Agreement Between the United States and the United Kingdom", 1963, 601). The Polaris Sales Agreement was inked in Washington on 6 April 1963 between US Secretary of State Dean Rusk and UK ambassador to the US David Ormbsy Gore, and applied to R&D from 1 January 1963 onwards. With the Polaris Sales Agreement in place, and the R&D issue begrudgingly agreed to, Britain was on track to acquire its first undersea nuclear deterrent. British officials could never have known at the time, that the

R&D charge would be partially waived in exchange for US military access to various small Indian Ocean islands several years subsequent.

BIOT's Detachment Costs

By the end of April 1965, HMG had agreed, subject to the assent of Mauritius and Seychelles, to detach the Chagos, Aldabra, Farquhar, and Desroches, but at an anticipated £10 million [$28 million] cost, a US contribution was requested. According to the original 1964 understanding, the United Kingdom would finance the compensation (to Mauritius and Seychelles) and detachment costs, while the United States would construct the facilities. However, during the Spring of 1965, Britain's ability to absorb the expenses was uncertain, owing to its precarious overall economic predicament and balance of payments problem. As a result, an American contribution was sought. In a 15 April 1965 meeting at the White House with US Secretary of State, Dean Rusk, UK Prime Minster Harold Wilson stated that:

> We, for our part, were anxious to press ahead with this project as rapidly as possible, despite the political embarrassment to which we might be subjected in the United Nations and elsewhere. On the other hand it would involve us in very heavy expenditure, not only as regards compensation for the commercial interests concerned but also in terms of the price which we should have to pay to the parent Governments for the detachment of the Islands in question. We should wish to discuss this question further with the United States Government, in the light, among other things, of further consideration of the legalities of the situation, i.e. the extent to which the parent Governments could really sustain a claim for compensation in respect of the detachment of the Islands.
>
> (Record of a Meeting at the White House, 1965, pp. 3–4)

One month subsequent, at a 14 May Anglo-US meeting, further details were agreed to, including the geographic scope of the new territory, which would include the entire Chagos Archipelago, as well as Aldabra, Farquhar, and Desroches. However, the financial arrangements were yet to be settled. On the financial contribution request:

> In answer to a question from Mr Kitchen [Department of State], Mr Peck [Foreign Office] explained that the American contribution which we hoped for need not be publicly related to the project. In approaching the Mauritius and Seychelles authorities we should anyway maintain that it was HMG, and not "the bottomless American purse" which would foot the bill. Mr Kitchen then said that, speaking personally, he was prepared (on his return to Washington) to look into the possibility of making a payment through offsets in US/UK research and development programmes. Mr. Burlace [UK Ministry of Defence] said that if this turned out to be practicable from the American point of view, it might be feasible from the British side.
>
> (Defence Facilities in the Indian Ocean, 1965, p. 2)

Another month later, on 24 June 1965 George Newman of the US Embassy in London delivered a memorandum to Geoffrey Arthur, Head of the Permanent Under-Secretary's Department at the Foreign Office, advising that the American government was prepared in principle to contribute up to one half of the detachment costs through a "deduction of an agreed amount of United Kingdom payments due in research and development surcharges" ("Memorandum", 1965, p. 1). Exactly what the research and development surcharges applied to was a mystery at the time to both men. The memorandum called for meetings post-haste in order for both sides to discuss specifics ("Memorandum", 1965, p. 1). In response to a question about which R&D project was involved, Newman told Arthur that Washington did not provide him specifics, but were "convinced that there would be no difficulty in finding the sum required through a waiver of surcharges" (Arthur, 1965). Arthur sent the Memorandum to the Ministry of Defence the following day reporting that Newman had informed him that the US Government would stipulate that this financial contribution should remain secret and commenting that "it seems to me that the American offer is a pretty handsome one considering that our original agreement implied that we should provide the real estate whilst they bore the cost of the facilities" (Arthur, 1965).

By July 1965, the Ministry of Defence had completed its examination of the feasibility of the US proposal. Replying to Geoffrey Arthur, FJ Burlace at the Ministry of Defence informed him that it would not be possible to offset any R&D levies on aircraft purchases (Hercules C130, Phantom and F111), but the Royal Navy had identified the Polaris R&D surcharge as a possibility, and the US Assistant Secretary of Defense, Mr McNaughton, had mentioned Polaris to the UK Defence Secretary a fortnight earlier. However, Burlace expressed concern as to whether the Americans could square away the Polaris R&D charge and the BIOT contribution "without revealing the link between the two transactions" observing that since the surcharge was specifically stated in the Polaris sales agreement of 1963 "the [US] Special Projects Office might have to give awkward explanations to awkward people if they failed to collect" (Burlace, 1965).

Despite financial repayment via Polaris R&D surcharges remaining unresolved for the time being, US agreement to contribute towards Britain's detachment costs spurred on detachment negotiations.

BIOT's Creation

By September 1965, final arrangements were being made to create BIOT. Britain was consulting with the leaders of Mauritian political parties who were present in London for talks on independence, while also holding talks with a US Department of State and Department of Defense team also in London. Meanwhile, Cabinet was meeting to coordinate.

As for the soon-to-be independent Mauritius, the first round of constitutional negotiations had failed to reach agreement, due to Britain's intention to detach some of its islands. At the final round of talks in London's Lancaster House on 23 September 1965 (see also Chapter 1), Wilson pressed Seewoosagur in a private side meeting that, although the United States was interested in the islands, that Mauritius' compensation demands should not be "too high" (Record of a Conversation Between the Prime Minister and the Premier, 1965, p. 2). On Diego Garcia, Wilson said that "it was a purely historical accident that it was administered by Mauritius. Its links with Mauritius were very slight" (Record of a Conversation Between the Prime Minister and the Premier, 1965, p. 3). Wilson also noted that:

> The Premier and his colleagues could return to Mauritius either with Independence or without it. On the Defence point, Diego Garcia could either be detached by order in Council or with the agreement of the Premier and his colleagues. The best solution of all might be Independence and detachment by agreement, although he could not of course commit the Colonial Secretary at this point.
>
> (Record of a Conversation Between the Prime Minister and the Premier 1965, p. 3)

Both sides agreed in principle to detach the Chagos, in exchange for £3 million compensation directly to Mauritius, not including resettlement and land acquisition costs ("Mauritius Defence Matters", 1965, pp. 4–5).[1] Both parties also agreed to an undertaking that Britain would return the Archipelago to Mauritius when it was no longer required for defence purposes ("Mauritius Defence Matters", 1965, p. 5). The following day on 24 September 1965 Britain announced its support for granting Mauritius independence.

Simultaneously on 23 and 24 September, a US Department of State and Department of Defense team were in London to negotiate with British counterparts over the Indian Ocean islands. Agreement was reached on modifying the Polaris Sales Agreement, to offset detachment costs up to $14 million ("Memorandum: Subject: Indian Ocean Islands", 1965, p. 2). Both sides also agreed to the conditions and terms of US access to the islands to be constitutionally detached (barring minor details related to civil and criminal jurisdiction matters), as well as a deal to allow an American satellite tracking station in Mahé, Seychelles, subject to some language modifications ("Memorandum: Subject: Indian Ocean Islands", 1965, p. 2). The American side noted the "friendly and cooperative atmosphere" of the 23–24 September 1965 talks in London ("Memorandum: Subject: Indian Ocean Islands", 1965, p. 2). Despite these ad-referendum agreements, the negotiations were protracted due to Britain's pending Defence Review, and how this review would affect Indian Ocean (island) policy, as well as the issue of Mauritian independence ("Background Memorandum", 1965, p. 4).

Finally, British officials decided on 24 September to formally to detach and retain the Chagos Archipelago, Aldabra, Farquhar, and Desroches ("Memorandum: Subject: Indian Ocean Islands", 1965, p. 1). Apparently, some officials considered, but discarded, the name "Limuria"[2] for the new territory (Edis, 2004, p. 80). In addition to compensating Mauritius, to compensate Seychelles for dismembering its three islands, the British agreed to construct an airport on Mahé, which was expected to cost £3 million.

With Mauritius' independence agreed to, Seychelles compensated, and the Anglo-US negotiations settled, the Indian Ocean islands were ready to be detached. As it happened, Queen Elizabeth II approved the British Indian Ocean Territory Order 1965 at the Court at Buckingham Palace on 8 November 1965 ("The British Indian Ocean Territory Order", 1965, p. 1). Under this Order, the Chagos Archipelago, Farquhar Islands, the Aldabra Group, and the Islands of Desroches "shall together form a separate colony which shall be known as the British Indian Ocean Territory" (The British Indian Ocean Territory Order, 1965, p. 1). In an era of decolonisation, Britain had created a new colony. On 10 November, the British Secretary of State made a statement in the House of Commons, in which he noted that:

> The islands will be called the British Indian Ocean Territory and will be administered by a Commissioner. It is intended that the islands will be available for the construction of defence facilities by the British and United States. Governments, but no firm plans have yet been made by either Government.
> (Outward Telegram: U.K./U.S. Defence Interests, 1965)

Conveniently for American and British officials, BIOT's creation was overshadowed by Rhodesia's illegal declaration of independence on 11 November (Harrison, 1966, p. 1). Regardless, British officials prepared for criticism at the United Nations. According to an internal British brief, "there is bound to be criticism of our action in the United Nations, on the grounds that we are starting a new colony in an era of de-colonization, and that we are setting up new military bases at a time when we should be pulling out of our old ones" (Indian Ocean Islands, 1965, p. 1). Indeed, the UN did condemn Britain's creation of BIOT on 16 December 1965 via Resolution 2066 (XX), which called on the United Kingdom to "take no action which would dismember the Territory of Mauritius and violate its territorial integrity" ("United Nations General Assembly A/RES/2066(XX) – Question of Mauritius", 1965). However, this resolution was made too late as the British Indian Ocean Territory had been born.

Intertwining Polaris and BIOT

In the Spring of 1966, the United States provided Britain drafts on both the BIOT Agreement, as well as the Financial Arrangements. While BIOT had been created, these agreements would stipulate conditions attached to US military access. The BIOT Agreement would be public, but the Financial Arrangements would remain classified. According to a Cabinet Office official in May 1966: "None of this arrangement for a United States contribution will be made public. The United States administration would become involved in Congressional difficulties if an indirect payment to British Colonial territories became known" (Harrison, 1966, p. 4). Also, the financial arrangements referred to the then still security classified Polaris Sales Agreement, which would be compromised if publicly cited. While the draft BIOT Agreement was largely acceptable, several edits were sought. The most pertinent being that an initial 50 year agreement period was deemed to be too long and instead proposed the agreement be valid initially for 30 years only. The British understood 30 years to be more appropriate "for presentational reasons" (Harrison, 1966, p. 4).

The draft classified Financial Agreement was also largely acceptable to British officials. The draft proposed the United States contribute up to half of BIOT's administrative detachment costs, up to a limit of $14 million (then equivalent to £5 million), whichever was less (Harrison, 1966, p. 4). As had been discussed in 1965, this payment would be concluded by reducing Britain's Polaris R&D expenditure obligation. According to American officials, both agreements should be signed simultaneously, as well as an agreement over a US satellite tracking station in Mahé (Harrison, 1966, p. 5).

By late-June 1966, negotiations pertaining to the first Exchange of Notes and the Financial Arrangements had reached an advanced stage. British officials noted on the Polaris deal:

> The exchange of letters on financial arrangements is, by agreement between the two Governments, to be kept secret. It should not therefore be couched in a form which would make it registerable under the United Nations Charter, for such registration would involve publication. It is therefore necessary that the word "agreement" should be avoided in the text. For this reason the concluding paragraph has been redrafted so as to request confirmation of the financial arrangements, rather than to propose that the arrangements should constitute an inter-governmental agreement.
>
> ('British Indian Ocean Territory: Amended Draft: Financial Arrangement', 1966, p. 11)

The Exchange of Notes and financial deal was inked on 30 December 1966. The two parties agree that:

> Since the United Kingdom is assuming the costs of the administrative detachment of the Indian Ocean islands and of the acquisition of the lands thereon the United States will forego the R&D surcharge to the extent of $14 million or one half of the foregoing Indian Ocean island costs incurred by the United Kingdom, whichever is the less.
>
> (Bruce, 1966, pp. 1–2)

The published Exchange of Notes for BIOT was also concluded on 30 December 1966 and registered on 22 August 1967. While the Agreement stated that "each Government shall normally bear the cost of site preparation, construction, maintenance, and operation for any facilities developed to meet its own requirements", section four makes clear that the "the required sites shall be made available to the United States authorities *without charge* [emphasis added]" (Government of the United Kingdom of Great Britain and Northern Ireland 1966, p. 276). This published agreement was to be superseded by the financial deal which stipulated the offset.

The Agreement also concluded that BIOT's islands would be available for Anglo-US defence needs for an "indefinitely long period" – initially 50 years (to

2016) and a further 20 years (to 2036) unless notice of termination is given by either side (Government of the United Kingdom of Great Britain and Northern Ireland, 1966, p. 278). Prior to signing off, then UK Prime Minister Harold Wilson was briefed that, while British officials pushed for 30 years, the "exceptional nature" of BIOT, the US contribution, and the requirement for long tenure warranted a 50 year initial period, as argued by US officials (Brown, 1966, p. 3). It had also been argued by the Americans that such a long tenure would discourage Mauritian and Seychellois officials from pressing for the islands' return ("Agreements on British Indian Ocean Territory", 1966, p. 20).

The Polaris-Diego Coverup

The American financial contribution to BIOT's creation would not stay secret for long and fears the details would leak caused a crisis in Whitehall. As early as March 1967, knowledge of the secret financial contribution outside authorised circles was reported, causing angst in both capitals.

On 23 March 1967 at a US National Academy of Sciences meeting, scientist Dr Talbot from the Smithsonian said he understood that "the cost of creating BIOT was about $28 million and that the US had shared half the cost" (Campbell, 1967, p. 1). According to the Foreign Office, US officials believed the leak originated from the Royal Society, during conservation work on Aldabra, but some British officials believed the leak came from the American side (Campbell, 1967, p. 1). One British official noted that the Royal Society was responsible, as they "apparently gleaned some information about the American contribution and may leak" (McDonnell 1967, p. 2). Alternatively, Dr Talbot may have gleaned his controversial information from a May 1965 Easterbrook *Washington Post* article, which mentioned a $28 million total figure and the possibility of a US contribution ("Draft Telegram to: Washington from Foreign Office, B.I.O.T", 1967, pp. 2–3). Regardless, knowledge of the contribution had reached the scientific community, and a coordinated response from London and Washington was required.

While American decisionmakers had insisted the deal be kept secret in 1966 to avoid difficulties with Congress, just several months subsequent they were no longer willing to categorically deny the contribution if pressed ("Draft Note for Minister of Defence to Send to S. of S. for Foreign Affairs", 1967, p. 2). The American side felt the cat was out of the bag, and that if pressed, they would admit to a contribution. HMG was particularly concerned about these arrangements leaking for several reasons. Firstly, HMG made unusual arrangements with its comptroller and the auditor-general in order to exclude any reference to the Polaris payment in votes submitted to parliament ("Letter: B.I.O.T Financing", 1967, p. 1). Second, the Prime Minister had denied Mauritius further compensation using the line that no American contribution had been received. As such, one Foreign Office official noted that due to these reasons, "the issue is one of immense potential embarrassment" (Letter: B.I.O.T Financing, 1967, p. 1).

In early-August, both the British and American sides agreed to a public statement on US contributions related to BIOT's establishment. While the British intended for "absolute secrecy", officials in Washington feared the backlash should such a denial be proved a lie (Skyes, 1967, p. 1). The British, conscious that the secret deal created plausibility issues when fielding enquiries on the topic, devised the following cryptic formulation which was subsequently agreed by the US:

> There was no direct payment by the United States. The British Indian Ocean Territory is, however, available to serve both British and American purposes and in consideration of the arrangements made by the United Kingdom the United States have made some *adjustments in other fields* which are more favourable to the United Kingdom than would otherwise be the case [emphasis added].
>
> ('British Indian Ocean Territory: Reports in the "Guardian" of 10 and 11 September 1975. Note by the Foreign and Commonwealth Office and the Ministry of Defence', 1975)

Since there was no immediate need to make such an admission, the Foreign Office considered that the agreement could be "put on ice", ready to be deployed when "awkward questions are really likely to be asked" (Skyes, 1967, p. 1). However, before long the statement was necessarily deployed.

On 16 August 1967, *The Times* newspaper published an article by journalist Charles Douglas-Home on Aldabra's planned militarisation, which sent London into a spin, and forced the statement's release sooner than anticipated. In the article Douglas-Home incorrectly claimed that, in exchange for establishing BIOT, the United States "contributed two-thirds of the cost of the islands, which came to about £5m., and will pay half the costs of any military development of them" (Douglas-Home, 1967). He had telephoned the British Ministry of Defence (MOD) two days earlier to confirm that this was the case, which prompted a MOD spokesman to inform Douglas-Home of the new Anglo-US disclosure. A Foreign Office official expected the admission to create a "fair-sized and well-publicised rumpus", but apparently Douglas-Home had "reacted scarcely at all" according to the MOD spokesman, and appeared to have "no intention of making political capital out of the information, the damaging significance of which he did not seem to appreciate" (Seller, 1967, p. 1). Several days later, a cable to various British diplomatic missions told its officials that "The question of an American contribution to the cost of establishing BIOT is, for your information only, an extremely delicate issue … Please report any serious questioning on this point" ("Guidance No. 208: British Indian Ocean Territory (B.I.O.T)", 1967, p. 5). Even though Douglas-Home published incorrect details, his supposed knowledge of this secretive financial arrangement spooked planners in London and Washington. Details of the financial arrangement would not become public until the 1970s.

Conclusion

This chapter examined the trouble Britain faced in acquiring a credible nuclear deterrent in the early-1960s, before analysing the secretive BIOT financial arrangement and how Polaris was intertwined with Diego Garcia's militarisation. The chapter concluded by illuminating the Polaris-Diego coverup, which vexed British officials who intended the link remain secret.

Historically this deal is significant for two reasons. First, by trading US access to Diego Garcia for nuclear weapon technology, the transfer enabled Britain to maintain a global status far higher than its economic output would otherwise allow. Britain was already financially stretched by procuring Polaris, and the R&D cost would have further limited British spending in other areas of defence. By lessening these charges and enabling Britain to acquire a potent nuclear capability, its global standing and influence could be maintained for the foreseeable future, which was also in the US national interest. This chapter demonstrated how the islands comprising BIOT were used as a tool by Britain to maintain its global status and influence through nuclear deterrence.

Second, the secrecy of the Polaris-Diego deal is worthy of comment. The deal was kept secret for a variety of reasons: to avoid general parliamentary and congressional scrutiny, to limit the compensation amount payable to Mauritius and Seychelles, and to protect the classified nature of Polaris technology. However, by insisting the contribution remain secret and maintaining a fiction that the United States did not contribute financially to BIOT's establishment for many years, extraordinary effort was expended by American and British officials to maintain the lie. Arguably, this lie, as well as the Ilois "contract labour" lie, contributed to the immense public and political backlash Diego Garcia's militarisation generated in the 1970s and beyond. Put simply, the number and variety of people mislead in the 1960s regarding BIOT's creation and Diego Garcia's militarisation contributed to its pariah status.

Contemporarily, this historical narrative demonstrates the importance of Anglo-US negotiations and dealmaking. Writing in 2024, international attention is focussed upon Anglo-Mauritian negotiations and how these two nations can/will reconcile sovereignty over the Chagos Archipelago. However, the United States' role is conspicuously understudied, especially so considering its outsized geopolitical influence and military might (see Chapter 15 for an in-depth discussion of the role of the United States). Any agreement reached by the United Kingdom and Mauritius will need American assent. It is hoped that by revisiting the 1966 BIOT Agreement via this chapter, light can be shed on how BIOT was created, to contemplate its dissolution.

Acknowledgements

Particular thanks is due to Richard P. Dunne for assistance accessing various British archives.

Notes

1 In 2019 the International Court of Justice opined that due to the separation of the Chagos Archipelago in 1965, Mauritius' decolonisation was not lawfully completed in 1968.

2 Limuria (also spelt Lemuria) refers to a mythical ancient continent supposedly situated in the now-Indian Ocean. Limuria played a central role in how British officials perceived the island cluster and even features in sanctioned heraldry. Upon BIOT's 25th anniversary, the British Government gave BIOT a coat of arms with the motto "In tutela nostra Limuria", translated to "Limuria is in our trust".

References

'Agreements on British Indian Ocean Territory' (1966) Defence and Oversea Policy (Official) Committee: Sub-Committee on Defence Facilities in the Indian Ocean: OPD(O)(IO)(66). CAB 148/76. National Archives, United Kingdom.

Arthur, G.G. (1965) 'Memorandum'. Defence Interests Overseas: US/UK Discussions on Diego Garcia'. FO 371/184525. National Archives, United Kingdom.

'Background Memorandum' (1965) Indian Ocean (Including IOTF) - December 1963 - March 1966. National Security Files, Files of Robert W. Komer, Box 26. Lyndon B. Johnson Presidential Library.

Bandjunis, Vytautas B. (2001) *Diego Garcia: Creation of the Indian Ocean Base*. Lincoln: Writer's Showcase Press.

Bligh (1962) 'No. Codel 16. 'From Nassau to foreign office (United Kingdom delegation to bahamas meeting)'. 20 December 1962, ADM 1/28839. National Archives, United Kingdom.

'British Indian Ocean Territory: Amended Draft: Financial Arrangement' (1966) United Kingdom Vol. VIII Cables 1/66 - 7/66, National Security Files, Country File, Box 209 [2 of 2]. Lyndon B. Johnson Presidential Library.

'British Indian Ocean Territory: Reports in the "Guardian" of 10 and 11 September 1975. Note by the Foreign and Commonwealth Office and the Ministry of Defence' (1975) PREM 16/1156/25. The National Archives, United Kingdom.

Brown, G. (1966) 'Note to the Prime Minister, The British Indian Ocean Territory, PM/68/112'. U.K/U.S Agreements for Providing Defence Facilities in the British Indian Ocean Territories, T 225/2871. National Archives, United Kingdom.

Bruce, D. (1966) 'Letter from David Bruce to George Brown'. Exchange of Notes and Agreed Minutes Concerning Defence Co-Operation in the British Indian Ocean Territory, FO 93/8/401. National Archives, United Kingdom.

Burlace, F.J. (1965) 'Indian Ocean Islands'. DO 164/118. National Archives, United Kingdom.

Campbell, A. (1967) 'Letter: US/UK agreement on the British Indian Ocean Territory'. BIOT Defence Discussions with United States, FCO 32/117. National Archives, United Kingdom.

'Defence Facilities in the Indian Ocean: Meeting Between United States and United Kingdom Officials' (1965) US Defence Interests in Indian Ocean Territories, CO 1036/1323. National Archives, United Kingdom.

Douglas-Home, C. (1967) 'Scientists fight defence plans for Island of Aldabra'. Cited in: Defence Discussions with the USA, FCO 32/118. National Archives, United Kingdom.

'Draft Financial Agreement between the United Kingdom and the United States Governments' (1966) CAB 148/69/12. National Archives, United Kingdom.

'Draft Note for Minister of Defence to Send to S. of S. for Foreign Affairs' (1967) Defence Discussions with the USA, FCO 33/117. National Archives, United Kingdom.

'Draft Telegram to: Washington from Foreign Office, B.I.O.T' (1967) BIOT Defence Discussions with United States, FCO 32/117. National Archives, United Kingdom.

Edis, R. (2004) *Peak of Limuria: The Story of Diego Garcia and the Chagos Archipelago*. London: Chagos Conservation Trust.

Government of the United Kingdom of Great Britain and Northern Ireland (1966) 'Exchange of notes between the government of the United Kingdom of great britain and Northern Ireland and the government of the United States of America concerning the availability for defence purposes of the British Indian Ocean Territory'. Available at: https://

treaties.un.org/doc/Publication/UNTS/Volume%20603/volume-603-I-8737-English.pdf (Accessed: 1 September 2023).

'Guidance No. 208: British Indian Ocean Territory (B.I.O.T)' (1967) Defence Discussions with the USA, FCO 32/119/85. National Archives, United Kingdom.

Harrison, F.A.K. (1966) 'Draft agreement with the United States government on the use of the British Indian Ocean Territory. Note by the Chairman of the sub-committee on defence facilities in the Indian Ocean'. OPD(O)(66)12, CAB 148/69/12. National Archives, United Kingdom.

'Indian Ocean Islands' (1965) Defence Interests Overseas: US/UK Discussions on Diego Garcia, FO 371/184530. National Archives, United Kingdom.

International Court of Justice (2019) 'Legal Consequences of the Separation of the Chagos Archipelago from Mauritius in 1965. Advisory opinion'. Available at: https://www.icj-cij.org/public/files/case-related/169/169-20190225-01-00-EN.pdf (Accessed: 1 September 2023).

Jones, M. (2019) 'Prelude to the Skybolt Crisis: The Kennedy administration's approach to British and French strategic nuclear policies in 1962'. *Journal of Cold War Studies,* 21(2), pp. 58–109.

Klein, D. (8 March 1963) 'Memorandum: Subject: Skybolt: Post-mortem'. 'Skybolt Post-Mortem II'. National Security Files, Series 02, Regional Security, Box 227. John F. Kennedy Presidential Library.

'Letter: B.I.O.T. Financing' (1967) Defence Discussions with the USA, FCO 33/117. National Archives, United Kingdom.

MacMillan, Harold (1962) 'Polaris, Prime Minister's personal minute'. Prime Minister's Office, UK. ADM 1/28839. National Archives, United Kingdom.

'Mauritius Defence Matters, Record of a Meeting Held in Lancaster House' (1965) UK Bases in Indian Ocean: US Use; Opposition from India, Ceylon and Pakistan, DO 164/119. National Archives, United Kingdom, 23 September 1965.

McDonnell, C.T. (1967) 'Letter to Mr. Nicholls and Mr. Bancroft: British Indian Ocean Territory – Financial Arrangements'. U.K./U.S. Agreements for Providing Defence Facilities in the British Indian Ocean Territories, T 225/3052/49. National Archives, United Kingdom.

McNamara, R. (1963) 'Copy of a Letter from the Hon. Robert McNamara to the minister of defence dated 16 January 1963', 16 January 1963. DEFE 7/2162. National Archives, United Kingdom.

'Memorandum' (1965). Defence Interests Overseas: US/UK Discussions on Diego Garcia, FO 371/184525, National Archives, United Kingdom.

'Memorandum: Indian Ocean Islands' (1965) Indian Ocean (Including IOTF) - December 1963 - March 1966. National Security Files, Files of Robert W. Komer, Box 26. Lyndon B. Johnson Presidential Library.

'Notes on Bahamas Meeting' (1962) ADM 1/28839. National Archives, United Kingdom.

'Outward Telegram: U.K./U.S. Defence Interests' (1965) Defence Interests Overseas: US/UK Discussions on Diego Garcia, FO 371/184530. National Archives, United Kingdom.

'Polaris Sales Agreement Between the United States and the United Kingdom' (1963) *International Legal Materials* 2 (3): 595–607.

'Record of a Conversation Between the Prime Minister and the Premier of Mauritius' (1965) Defence Interests Overseas: US/UK Discussions on Diego Garcia, FO 371/184528. National Archives, United Kingdom, 23 September 1965.

'Record of a Meeting at the White House' (1965) US Defence Interests in Indian Ocean Territories, CO1036/1322/38. National Archives, United Kingdom, 15 April 1965.

'Report of Polaris Fact Finding Mission to Washington' (1963) DEFE 7/2162. National Archives, United Kingdom, 15 January 1963.

Seller, C.A. (1967) 'Draft Letter to Mr. Trafford Smith'. Defence Discussions with the USA, FCO 33/117/80. National Archives, United Kingdom.

Skyes, R.A. (1967) 'Letter: British Indian Ocean Territory'. Defence Discussions with the USA, FCO 33/117/66. National Archives, United Kingdom.

'Text of the Joint Communique by the President and Prime Minister Harold MacMillan Following Discussions Held in Nassau, Bahamas' (1962) JFKPOF-042-013-p0002. John F. Kennedy Presidential Library, 21 December 1962. Available at: https://www.jfklibrary.org/asset-viewer/archives/JFKPOF/042/JFKPOF-042-013 (Accessed: 1 September 2023).

'The British Indian Ocean Territory Order' (1965) British Indian Ocean Territory (BIOT): Order-in-Council and Royal Instructions; Powers and Functions of the Commissioner and Administrator, FCO 141/1452. National Archives, United Kingdom.

United Nations (1965) 'Resolution A/RES/2066(XX) - Question of Mauritius'. United Nations. Available at: https://undocs.org/en/A/RES/2066(XX). (Accessed 1 September 2023).

Vine, D. (2011) *Island of Shame: The Secret History of the U.S. Military Base on Diego Garcia*. Princeton: Princeton University Press.

Wenban-Smith, N. and Carter, M. (2016) *Chagos: A History: Exploration, Exploitation, Expulsion*. London: Chagos Conservation Trust.

15 The Power behind the Throne

The US Government Must Face Its Responsibility for the Chagossian Exile

David Vine

In 2023 Human Rights Watch published a groundbreaking report, "That's When the Nightmare Started", finding the US and UK governments guilty of "crimes against humanity" in their treatment of the Chagossians (2023). The report was the first of its kind by a major international human rights organisation after more than 50 years of Chagossian exile.[1]

Despite its importance in documenting human rights abuses committed against the Chagossians, the report troublingly mischaracterises responsibility for the crimes by exaggerating the role of the UK government and significantly diminishing the US government's role. The report's first sentence reads,

> About 60 years ago, the United Kingdom government secretly planned, with the United States, to force an entire Indigenous people, the Chagossians, from their homes in the Chagos Archipelago.
>
> [Human Rights Watch, 2023, p. 1]

This description is, if not factually inaccurate, deeply misleading.

The "planning" referenced *started* with US government officials *not* with UK officials. US officials, not UK officials, conceived the idea for the base. US officials proposed the idea to the UK government – not the other way around. US, not UK, officials insisted on the expulsion of the Chagossians and paid the British government $14 million to carry it out.

Human Rights Watch's first sentence and its punctuation reverse the responsibility and minimise US culpability with a comma-demarcated, dependent clause. To be accurate, the sentence should read in the opposite direction:

> About 60 years ago, *the United States government* secretly planned, with the United Kingdom, to force....

or

> About 60 years ago, the United States *and* United Kingdom governments secretly planned to force....

The problem is not confined to the first sentence. Throughout the pages of the report, Human Rights Watch repeatedly overlooks the leading role of the US government.

DOI: 10.4324/9781003390299-21

Unfortunately, Human Rights Watch is not alone, nor the most egregious example, in a disturbing pattern: the US government's role in exiling the Chagossians has been underestimated, overlooked, and at times erased entirely by many journalists, human rights organisations, and scholars, among others. Consistently, many have ignored the leading role that US officials played in initiating, orchestrating, and funding a crime in which British officials were effectively junior partners recruited to provide land and perform the outsourced colonial violence of deportation.

To be clear, both the US and UK governments bear responsibility for the crimes committed against the Chagossians (and the people of Mauritius). However, the US government was always the senior partner – the power behind the throne. I don't say this to lessen the responsibility of the UK government or its officials. I say this because the crimes have two authors, one of whom – the US government – has almost completely escaped responsibility.

My point is pragmatic and strategic as much as moral and historical: ignoring the power and role of the US government in the past risks ignoring the power and responsibility of the US government to correct this injustice in the present. Overlooking the US role also risks allowing the US government to get away with a plan embedded in the original Diego Garcia deal: US officials paid not just for the expulsion and base access but also for the UK government to answer to any international criticism and legal liability. To this point, that's almost entirely what has happened.

Here I insist that the US government finally must acknowledge its responsibility for the exile and the profound suffering it has inflicted. Beyond acknowledgement, the US government must help repair as much of the damage suffered by Chagossians as possible.

Following Chagossians' longstanding demands, I outline how major pillars of repair should include at least the right of return, resettlement assistance, and proper financial and non-financial compensation. The chapter updates a 2012 reparations calculation guided by a 2005 UN resolution on reparations for victims of human rights abuses (Vine, Harvey, and Sokolowski, 2012). I argue that the US should be responsible for paying at least half of all total compensation totalling between $7.76 billion and $18.97 billion.

Before outlining how the US government, with the UK government, should repair the damage inflicted, I attempt to remove any ambiguity about the US government's leading role in exiling the Chagossians. I will do so by detailing eight major ways the US government was the senior partner, in addition to two ways the US and UK governments conspired together to hide the expulsion and cover up their crimes. First, in the next section, I provide prominent examples of people overlooking the US government's role and responsibility.

Overlooking the US Government's Role

There are many examples of observers underestimating, overlooking, or erasing the US government's role. The pattern frequently appears in titles that fail to mention the United States at all. These include "How Britain Forcefully Depopulated a Whole Archipelago; And Managed to Cover It Up" (Pilger, 2019) and *The Chagos*

Betrayal: How Britain Robbed an Island and Made Its People Disappear (Grosset, 2021). Both of these otherwise important works, and others like them, discuss, to varying degrees, the US government's role in their main text. Still, titles (which are often selected by editors concerned with online clicks and sales) can shape readers' impressions and public perceptions, including through the minds of people who never read the main text.

An article in the major US news magazine *The Atlantic* (Murphy, 2022) is more problematic in largely overlooking the US role throughout its pages. While beautifully written, the article notably fails to mention the US payment of $14 million and US officials asking for the expulsion and the excision of Chagos from Mauritius. The article's misleading online subtitle reflects the omissions: "Half a Century Ago, the British Government Forcibly Removed 2,000 People from a Remote String of Islands in the Middle of the Indian Ocean". The *Atlantic's* primarily US-based audience makes it particularly surprising the subtitle did not read correctly as "Half a Century Ago, the *US and* British Government*s* Forcibly Removed …".

The problem exists among some scholars, lawyers, and human rights advocates as well. Most troublingly, some, like Human Rights Watch, reverse the culpability, attributing all or nearly all responsibility to the UK government. Some claim incorrectly that "the UK itself made the decision to remove the population not only from Diego Garcia but also the outlying islands" (Raoof, 2014: 2; Raoof is not wrong about the UK's role in expelling Chagossians from the Chagos islands *other than* Diego Garcia – see point 4 in this chapter's next section). Some wrongly suggest the expulsion "was more London's doing than Washington's. In fact, it was engineered by a handful of FCO officials in London themselves" (Juss, 2017, p. 248).[2]

Other observers scarcely mention the US role. The introduction to an edited legal volume contains a single parenthetical reference to the US government, describing "the involuntary displacement of the Chagos Islanders (pursuant to the construction of a US naval facility on Diego Garcia)" (Allen and Monaghan, 2018, p. 1).

At the International Court of Justice (ICJ), the sole defendant was the UK, not the US. The ICJ's 2019 decision finding UK sovereignty over the Chagos islands "unlawful" neglected the role of the US government in proposing and paying for the excision of Chagos from Mauritius and the creation of the British Indian Ocean Territory. The subsequent 2019 UN resolution likewise ordered Britain, alone, to "withdraw its colonial administration". The resolution did not mention the US government's role in supporting British colonial rule on an island where the US exercises considerable de facto sovereignty. While the base is technically a joint installation, the British role is negligible. Diego Garcia is the only place in the United Kingdom, other than Gibraltar, where cars drive on the right side of the road. Both the ICJ and UN let the US government escape justice. Both overlooked the crime's senior partner: the US government.

The ICJ and UN were constrained to some extent by the Mauritian government's decision to take only the UK to the court. This decision was understandable. Taking on both governments would have made a difficult case even harder legally and diplomatically. Mauritius already effectively was taking on both governments given the support the US government provided the UK through its friendly submissions to the ICJ, its UN vote, and its public statements. The presence of a US judge with deep links to the US government at the ICJ would have made a case against both governments even more difficult, as evidenced by Judge Joan E. Donoghue providing the single vote for the UK in the court's main 13–1 decision.[3]

The frequent diminishment or erasure of the US role is further understandable given the perceived significance of sovereignty in the international system. UK sovereignty over Chagos and Chagossians' status as UK citizens has meant that many rightly have criticised the British government and held it accountable for the expulsion and exile. That the vast majority of Chagos litigation has taken place in British courts or involved the UK government has further tilted attention towards the UK government.

Overlooking the leading US role also likely derives from the fact that UK citizens have produced much of the work about the exile. Proximity and access to government documents and officials often can shape the focus of research and analysis. I suspect many UK citizens feel a responsibility, as UK citizens, to hold their government accountable. As a US citizen, I have a similar feeling about holding the US government accountable. That said, my primary motivation for focusing on the US role throughout my scholarship has been scholars' and journalists' overwhelming focus on the UK role and the dearth of research about the US government.

Ultimately the neglect of the central role the US government played in initiating, orchestrating, and paying for the expulsion is troubling. Such depictions are like describing a paid hitman murdering someone without explaining who ordered and paid for the hit. Or, perhaps more accurately, it's like describing a paid thief stealing someone's property without explaining who ordered and paid for the theft.

US Responsibility: The Historical Record

To remove any doubt about the primary responsibility of the US government in expelling the Chagossians, I will briefly outline the US role (for more details, see Vine, 2011).[4]

1. US – not UK – officials conceived the idea for the base found today on Diego Garcia: Beginning around 1958, Stuart Barber and other US Navy officials identified and developed the idea for building a base on Diego Garcia as part of their "Strategic Island Concept." (The small British military outpost found on Diego Garcia during World War II closed at war's end and was not the foundation for today's base.) Barber's key role is well documented (e.g., Vine, 2011, 2023; Bandjunis, 2001; Ryan, 1984). In an unpublished letter, Barber explained, "The concept of setting aside Diego Garcia and surrounding islands as an unpopulated strategic territory for joint US-UK use was initially mine" (Barber, 1971).

2. US officials subsequently proposed the idea to the UK government – not the other way around: US Navy and other government leaders embraced Barber's "Strategic Island Concept" and its identification of Diego Garcia as a leading candidate for base development. In 1960, US Navy officials approached their British counterparts about creating one or more military bases on Diego Garcia and other islands in the Indian Ocean (Vine, 2011, pp. 68–69).

3. US – not UK – officials first proposed the creation of the British Indian Ocean Territory (BIOT) and violating UN rules on decolonisation: US officials proposed the creation of the new colony to secure permanent colonial control of the Chagos islands amid Mauritius's push for independence. The Strategic Island Concept was premised on gaining control of strategic islands under direct US sovereignty or the sovereignty of a close European ally such as the UK or Australia. Barber explained in an unpublished letter to the *Washington Post* how "in May 1960 ... I was the individual who proposed the detachment of these islands from Mauritius [and] the establishment of the British Indian Ocean Territory" (Barber, 1991). The US Navy subsequently "initiated negotiations ... to persuade London to detach the Diego Garcia atoll" and other Chagos islands from Mauritius to create the BIOT (Bezboruah, 1977, p. 58). Multiple accounts confirm: "BIOT was thus the brainchild of the US Navy" (Bezboruah, 1977, p. 58; see also Bandjunis, 2001, pp. 1–3; Ryan, 1984, p. 133; Vine, 2004, p. 119, 2011, p. 69).

4. US – not UK – officials insisted on the expulsion of the Chagossians from Diego Garcia and secured the possibility of expulsion from all the Chagos islands: During secret negotiations in 1964 (if not earlier) US officials indicated they wanted basing rights on Indian Ocean islands, including Diego Garcia, on the condition that they have "exclusive control (without local inhabitants)" (US Embassy London, 1964). UK officials agreed.

The two governments sealed the deal in the 1966 US–UK agreement. In a confidential, unpublished "agreed minute" attached to the published agreement, Britain committed to take "administrative measures" necessary to make all of Chagos and other BIOT islands available for US use. The administrative measures, the secret notes show, were any actions necessary for closing down the island plantations and "resettling the inhabitants" (Chalfont, 1966).[5]

(Ultimately, evidence suggests that US officials only requested the expulsion of Chagossians from Diego Garcia. UK officials appear to have made the decision to remove Chagossians from the other Chagos islands of Peros Banhos and Salomon (Snoxell, 2009). They did so, however, in a context in which US officials refused to guarantee their UK counterparts that they would refrain from building military facilities and asking for expulsions on Peros Banhos and Salomon for a period of 20 years or else compensate the UK government for any such decision (Stoddart, 1969). While UK officials appear to have had additional motivations for exiling Chagossians from Peros Banhos and Salomon (Snoxell, 2009), the looming prospect of US officials requesting additional deportations seems to have shaped their decision significantly.[6])

5. The US government secretly paid $14 million for the expulsion of the Chagossians and basing rights, hiding the payment from Congress, Parliament, and the world: As part of secret minutes attached to the 1966 US–UK agreement, US government officials arranged to pay the $14 million by wiping away $14 million in debt the UK government owed the US government for the development of the Polaris missile system (Vine, 2011, pp. 87–88; Bandjunis, 2001, p. 46; US House, 1975, pp. 42–43). By erasing the UK debt, US officials avoided having to ask Congress for an authorisation of funds, further concealing the plans. The payments were to reimburse the British for "all costs pertaining to the administrative detachment of the Indian Ocean islands in question and to the acquisition of the lands thereon". This was diplomatic legalese for the costs of deporting the Chagossians, buying out the plantation owners, and paying off Mauritius and the Seychelles.

When the two governments quietly published the 1966 Diego Garcia agreement in 1967, the agreement deceptively said the UK would make the BIOT islands available to the United States "without charge" (United Kingdom, 1966). The US government perpetuated the falsehood of non-payment in recent years when describing to the International Court of Justice "the absence of any 'lease' *or payment* by the United States" (United States of America, 2018, p. 37, 4.7).

You don't need to be an accountant to know that removing a debt is one way one party can pay another. The US embassy in Mauritius admitted the truth in 1972, saying that the Pentagon "acknowledged its responsibility for the removal of the Ilois [Chagossians] by *payment* of $14 million to HMG [Her Majesty's Government]" (Brewer, 1972, pp. 2, 5; emphasis added).

6. US officials ordered the final deportation of Chagossians from Diego Garcia: In late 1970 and early 1971, as the US Navy was beginning construction on Diego Garcia, US officials asked UK officials to complete the deportation of the remaining Chagossians on the island. On 7 December 1970, a joint State Department–Pentagon message told the London embassy to inform British officials that it was time "for the UK to accomplish relocation of the present residents of Diego Garcia to some other location". The message continued, "All local personnel should be moved from the western half of the island before the arrival of the construction force in March 1971. We hope that complete relocation can be accomplished by the end of July 1971" (Rogers, 1970).

When a Navy commander on the island warned of "possible bad publicity" from deporting a people who had lived there for generations, the highest-ranking official in the US Navy, Admiral Elmo Zumwalt, held firm. In exactly three words, Zumwalt cut off internal discussion and delivered what amounted to the final deportation order: "Absolutely must go" (1971).

7. US officials also ordered and assisted in the killing of Chagossians' pet dogs, showing direct US involvement in the deportation – contrary to later US government assertions: While Chagossians were awaiting their deportation, US military officials ordered the killing of all dogs on Diego Garcia to avoid their interfering in military operations. The British agent on Diego Garcia, plantation manager Marcel Moulinie, coordinated the killing of what he estimated as around 800 dogs. US Navy personnel assisted in the killing first by attempting to shoot and then poison the dogs. When both methods failed as efficient killing mechanisms, US Navy personnel helped herd the pets into sealed sheds, where they were gassed with exhaust from US Navy vehicles, after which their carcasses were burned (Moulinie, 1999; Vine, 2011, pp. 113–114).

When in 1975 Congress held the only day of hearings it has ever held to investigate the expulsion, President Gerald R. Ford's administration falsely claimed, "All went willingly .... No coercion was used and no British or US servicemen were involved" (US House of Representatives, 1975, p. 42).

8. US officials inhibited resettlement planning and refused British and Mauritian government requests that Chagossians be allowed to work on the base (as at most other US bases abroad): US officials prevented the British government from discussing the resettlement of Chagossians with the Mauritian government until after the US Navy secured funding for the base in late 1970. The US embassy in London quickly understood that the British were facing serious difficulties in arranging the deportations as a result. In January 1971, State Department Legal Adviser John R. Stevenson warned US officials:

> Although the responsibility for carrying out measures to ensure the welfare of the inhabitants lies with the UK, the US is charged under the [1966] Agreement with *facilitating these arrangements* .... The US *constrained the UK* from discussing the matter with the GOM pending the outcome of our Congressional appropriations legislation. In light of this, we are under a particular responsibility not to pressure the UK into meeting a time schedule which may not provide sufficient time in which to satisfactorily arrange for the welfare of the inhabitants. Beyond this, their removal is to accommodate US needs, and the USG will, of course, be considered to *share the responsibility* with the UK by the inhabitants and other nations if satisfactory arrangements are not made.
>
> [Stevenson, 1971; emphasis added]

US officials ignored this and other warnings. After construction on the base began, US diplomats began pressuring their British counterparts to complete the deportations as quickly as possible. One official later acknowledged, "In order to meet our self-imposed timetable, their evacuation was undertaken with a haste which the British could claim has prevented careful examination of resettlement needs" (Newsom, 1972, p. 1).

The US embassy in Mauritius noted, too, that the US government had "resisted" Mauritian and British government "efforts to permit Ilois [Chagossians] to remain as employees of the facility" (Brewer, 1971).

9. US officials, with UK officials, intentionally hid the development of the base and the expulsion of the Chagossians from the UN, lying about Chagossians' indigenous status to avoid the responsibilities related to the right to self-determination: The US and UK delegations to the United Nations jointly suggested a slow implementation of base construction and the deportation "to minimize adverse reaction at the UN and throughout the world". Each step should have "some logical cover", they said. "The transfer of population", they warned, "is a very sensitive issue at the UN" (see Vine, 2011, p. 80).

The US State Department suggested "that the term 'migrant laborers' be used" to describe the Chagossians, whom they knew to have lived in the islands for generations. "Withdrawal of 'inhabitants' obviously would be more difficult to justify to [Indian Ocean] littoral countries and [UN] Committee of Twenty-four" responsible for decolonisation (Rusk, 1968). US officials wanted a base without the risk of eviction or local protest by a self-governing population. They protected against that risk by ensuring there would be no "inhabitants" or any indigenous population that could assert its right to self-determination at the UN (Vine, 2011, pp. 89–92).

10. US officials, with UK officials, covered up their crimes and perpetuated Chagossians' exile by censoring media and lying to Congress, the media, and the world since the 1960s: As early as 1964, for example, the State Department pressured both the *Washington Post* and the *Economist* to hold stories for months that threatened to break news about the secret planning for Diego Garcia (Vine, 2011, pp. 80–82). The published article described the population of Diego Garcia as consisting "largely of transient laborers" (Estabrook, 1964, p. A1, A6).

Misrepresenting the Chagossians as "transient contract workers" and migrant "copra workers" became official US–UK policy to avoid public criticism. In late 1970, the State Department sent instructions to its embassies to tell the press, "The population consists of a small number of contract laborers from the Seychelles and Mauritius engaged to work on the copra plantations" (Rogers, 1970). For Congress, the Navy described Diego Garcia's population as "negligible .... For all practical purposes ... uninhabited" (Leddick, 1969).

The role of the US government in shaping UK policy and maintaining the Chagossians' exile since the expulsion from Diego Garcia remains unclear due to the lack of transparency in US–UK intergovernmental relations and the inability to consult relevant government documents that officials have refused to provide public access to by maintaining classified status. Human Rights Watch (2023) and others may be right in attributing the majority of responsibility for perpetuating the exile post-expulsion to the British government. Alternatively, US officials may have continued to play a leading role in determining UK policy. The US government's support, at very least, for UK policy is clear given public statements under presidents Obama, Trump, and Biden.

For those who may think I'm exaggerating the US role, I would ask simply: If the US government had never shown any interest in or taken any steps towards building a base in Chagos, would the Chagossians have been exiled? The historical record shows that the answer is almost certainly *No.* There is no evidence that the UK government had any plans for or consideration of separating Chagos from Mauritius and exiling the Chagossians. If the US government had not initiated, paid for, and orchestrated this colonial crime, Chagossians would likely be living to this day in Chagos, as part of Mauritius, just as people live on the small Mauritian islands of Agalega and Rodrigues.

The Colonial Mastermind

The US government's ability to escape most international criticism, protest, and legal proceedings has been no accident. It has been by design. This was part of US strategy embedded in the original 1966 Diego Garcia agreement: the US government paid $14 million not just for basing rights and the deportation of the Chagossians but also for the UK government to assume responsibility for any criticism received at the UN, in other international fora, and in the media. For only $14 million, US officials secured the legal and political alibi that Great Britain was the sovereign and thus responsible for the local population.

US officials saw the value of avoiding the responsibilities and challenges of direct sovereignty and outsourcing the colonial dirty work and bureaucratic logistics of exiling the Chagossians to the British government.[7] Outsourcing the colonial dirty work – which is to say, violence – of expulsion was in keeping with US colonial practice since the start of the 20th century. US officials, like imperial rulers throughout history, realised the value of indirect rule, avoiding direct sovereignty and outsourcing the violence of displacement, especially amid the decolonisation movement of the 1950s and 1960s.

The recruitment of the UK government to displace the Chagossians was part of a pattern of "base displacement" in which US officials enlisted (mostly) colonial powers to displace local, often indigenous populations during the construction and expansion of overseas military installations (Vine, 2011, pp. 65–68, 2020, pp. 226–234). Examples include Trinidad and Newfoundland (UK), Greenland (Denmark), Okinawa (Japan), and Daechuri (South Korea). The US government also displaced people directly in US colonies including Puerto Rico, Guam, Hawaiʻi and Alaska before statehood, and the Marshall Islands when it was a US colony (Vine, 2020, pp. 228–233).

Among all the peoples displaced, only one (Newfoundland) was of European ancestry and considered white. The racism of US policy has been clear.

US Responsibility to Repair

Given its leading role, the US government is more than five decades overdue in redressing its responsibility for inflicting gross human rights abuses against the Chagossians. Given the passage of time and the proportion of the population that has died in exile there will be no way to repair most of the damage. Repairing as much of the damage as possible remains urgent.

Chagossians' right to comprehensive reparations is clearly established under international law (United Nations, 2005). Such reparations include but are not limited to monetary compensation for "any economically assessable damage" suffered as a result of a human rights violation. Those entitled to reparations include both direct victims displaced from Chagos and indirect victims such as descendants born in exile (United Nations, 2005, Principles 20, 8).

Reparations practice demands that Chagossians, as victims, must decide what reparations and repair look like (Johnston, 2000). Following longstanding Chagossian demands, the US government should be responsible for at least: (1) immediately supporting Chagossians' right to return home to live and visit Diego Garcia and the other Chagos islands; (2) assisting with Chagossians' resettlement of their islands, as well as visitation, with the full cooperation of the base (whether it remains operational or not); and (3) collaborating with the UK government to provide proper financial and/or non-financial compensation to all Chagossians regardless of where they live. The US government – unless Chagossians disagree – should provide other forms of reparations including a public apology, a guarantee of non-repetition, and the publication of all documents related to the expulsion (Human Rights Watch, 2023, pp. 92–95).

Calculating monetary compensation is difficult, given that money cannot adequately measure or reflect harms suffered. Still, we can and must calculate compensation so Chagossians can receive fair financial reparation in keeping with international law (courts do this every day when people suffer lost property or other damages).

To estimate proper compensation that accords with the highest standards of international human rights law, colleagues and I developed a "Human Rights Standards Damages Model" (Vine, Harvey, and Sokolowski, 2012). We call it this because the model assumes that proper compensation owed to Chagossians is the difference between the lives Chagossians have led since their expulsion and the lives they could have expected if the UK and US had lived up to their human rights obligations under international law.

The model estimates the value of land and possessions taken, and economic, psychological, and sociocultural damage suffered as a result of being forcibly displaced, including consequential damages since the expulsion (see, e.g., Vine, 2011).

We subtract compensation of about $6,000 per recipient received previously by some Chagossians (Vine, Harvey, and Sokolowski, 2012, p. 154). Updating our 2012 calculations to 2023, we conclude that proper compensation ranges between $7.76 billion and $18.97 billion (expressed in 2008 Purchasing Power Parity dollars, inflation adjusted to 2023).

Given the US government's leading role in the crime, the US should be responsible for paying *at least* half of total compensation, or between $3.88 billion and $9.49 billion.

Conclusion

Unfortunately the US government's position has remained largely unchanged since the time of the expulsion. The position the Ford administration articulated to Congress in 1975 appears to remain US policy: "There is no outstanding US obligation to underwrite the cost of additional assistance for the persons affected" (US House, 1975, pp. 42–45). In a letter responding to Human Rights Watch's report, the US government ignored the demand to join reparations efforts (Human Rights Watch, 2023, p. 125). A State Department spokesperson said only that the US government "acknowledges the challenges faced by Chagossian communities".

To date the US government's strategy to outsource the colonial violence of displacement and the international obligations of sovereignty to the UK sadly has worked. The US government has remained in the background, obscured and shielded from most criticism and legal action despite having been the senior partner in this crime, the power behind the throne.

This cannot continue. Justice demands that the US government face its responsibility for exiling the Chagossians and the profound damage the exile has caused.

Those who care about justice and the Chagossians must ensure that we no longer overlook or underplay the US role. This is no academic matter: US officials possessed the majority of power when they proposed, paid for, and requested the base and the expulsion. They possess the majority of power now to correct this injustice.

We now must ensure that US officials, with UK officials, do just that.

Notes

1 Thank you Laura Jeffery, Chris Monaghan, and Mairi O'Gorman for the hard work of organising an edited book and the conference that preceded it. Thank you to many Chagossian friends and organisations, including the Chagos Refugees Group, for making all of my scholarship and career possible. Thanks to Phillip Harvey and S. Wojciech Sokolowski who collaborated to produce the reparations model discussed here. Thanks to the authors in this book and many others who have written about the Chagossians and Diego Garcia for inspiration and endless assistance through the years.

2 Juss seems to indicate that the "the decision to depopulate the islands [including Diego Garcia] was a British decision" (2017, p. 250). Juss cites Snoxell's conclusion that UK officials decided on the expulsion from the Chagos islands *other than* Diego Garcia but fails to note Snoxell saying "the US had indicated only that they required Diego to be depopulated" (Snoxell, 2009, p. 133). Juss doesn't provide additional evidence showing that UK officials made the decision to forcibly remove Chagossians from Diego Garcia or that UK officials "engineered" the entirety of the expulsions. By contrast, Snoxell's (2009) characterisation of "Anglo-American complicity" is accurate.

3 See Judge Donoghue's official ICJ biography at https://www.icj-cij.org/sites/default/files/donoghue_en.pdf.

4 Most of the US government documents and others cited are available at www.chagosarchive.org.

5 The 1966 US–UK Diego Garcia agreement and inter-governmental negotiations allowed for forced removals from other islands to make way for additional US military facilities. There is no evidence that US officials exercised this facet of the Diego Garcia agreement or ordered the removal of Chagossians from the other Chagos islands; however, this possibility exists.

6 In requesting the 20-year guarantee, UK officials appear to have been seeking assurance that they could make financial investments in Peros Banhos and Salomon without the danger of losing those investments and incurring the additional costs of deporting the Chagossians and closing the island plantations (Snoxell, 2009, pp. 132–133). Other motivations may have included the desire to avoid scrutiny from the UN's decolonisation committee and the belief that it was "altogether more convenient not to be saddled with the administrative burden of a new populated colony with its UN reporting requirements" (Snoxell, 2009, p. 134).

7 UK officials appear to have embraced US officials' plans for three main reasons: (1) a desire to maintain the "special relationship" with the UK's closest ally amid rapidly declining British power globally; (2) wanting to maintain a symbolic British military presence in Asia following the decision to close all UK military bases "east of Suez"; and (3) the $14 million offered by the US government amid a serious British economic crisis.

References

Allen, S. and Monaghan, C. (2018) 'Introduction'. In Stephen Allen and Chris Monaghan (eds.), *Fifty Years of the British Indian Ocean Territory: Legal Perspectives*. Cham, Switzerland: Springer, pp. 1–12.

Bandjunis, V.B. (2001) *Diego Garcia: Creation of the Indian Ocean Base*. San Jose, CA: Writer's Showcase.

Barber, S.B. (1971) 'Unpublished letter to the editor of the *Honolulu Star-Bulletin*'. 16 March 1971. Available at: https://thechagosarchive.omeka.net/ (Accessed: 1 March 2023).

Barber, S.B. (1991) 'Unpublished letter to the editor of the *Washington Post*'. 9 March 1991. Available at: https://thechagosarchive.omeka.net/ (Accessed: 1 March 2023).

Bezboruah, M. (1977) *U.S. Strategy in the Indian Ocean: The International Response*. New York: Praeger Publishers.

Brewer, W.D. (1971) 'Memorandum to department of state'. 20 December 1971. National Archives and Records Administration: RG 59/150/67/27/6, Subject-Numeric Files 1970–1973, Box 3010, 4.

Brewer, W.D. (1972) 'Letter to Herman J. Cohen'. 5 January 1972. National Archives and Records Administration: RG 59/150/67/1/5, Subject-Numeric Files 1970–1973, Box 1715.

Chalfont, A.A.G.J. (1966) 'Letter to David K. E. Bruce'. 30 December 1966. National Archives and Records Administration, RG 59/150/64-65, Subject-Numeric Files 1964–1966, Box 1552.

Estabrook, R.H. (1964) 'U.S., Britain consider Indian Ocean bases'. *Washington Post*, 29 August 1964, pp. A1, A6.

Grosset, F. (2021) *The Chagos Betrayal: How Britain Robbed an Island and Made Its People Disappear*. Oxford: Myriad Editions.

Human Rights Watch (2023) *"That's When the Nightmare Started": UK and US Forced Displacement of the Chagossians and Ongoing Colonial Crimes*. New York: Human Rights Watch.

Johnston, B.R. (2000) 'Reparations and the right to remedy'. Contributing paper, World Commission on Dams, 1 July.

Juss, S.S. (2017) 'The royal prerogative in colonial constitutional law'. In Satvinder Juss and Maurice Sunkin (eds.), *Landmark Cases in Public Law*. Oxford: Hart/Bloomsbury Publishing, pp. 247–262.

Leddick, R.S. (1969) 'Memorandum for the record'. 11 November 1969. Naval Historical Center: 00 Files, 1969, Box 98, 11000.

Moulinie, M. (1999) '"Statement of marcel moulinie," application for judicial review, *Queen v. The Secretary of State for the Foreign and Commonwealth Office, ex parte Bancoult [1999]*', para. 14; Vine, Island of Shame, pp. 113–114.

Murphy, C. (2022) 'They bent to their knees and kissed the sand: Half a century ago, the British government forcibly removed 2,000 people from a remote string of islands in the middle of the Indian Ocean'. *The Atlantic,* 15 June 2022. Available at: https://www.theatlantic.com/magazine/archive/2022/07/reclaiming-chagos-islands-british-colonization/638444/ (Accessed: 1 March 2023).

Newsom, D.D. (1972) 'Letter to James K. Bishop, Jr'. 1 February 1972. National Archives and Records Administration: RG 59/150/67/1/5, Subject-Numeric Files 1970–1973, Box 1715.

Pilger, J. (2019) 'How britain forcefully depopulated a whole archipelago; And managed to cover it up'. *Al Jazeera*, 25 February 2019. Available at: https://www.aljazeera.com/opinions/2019/2/25/how-britain-forcefully-depopulated-a-whole-archipelago (Accessed: 1 March 2023).

Raoof, A. (2014) 'Still dispossessed—The battle of the Chagos Islanders to return to their homeland'. Briefing, Minority Rights Group International.

Rogers, W.P. (1970) 'Telegram to the U.S. Embassy London'. 14 December 1970, National Archives and Records Administration: RG 59/150/67/1/5, Subject-Numeric Files 1970–1973, Box 1744.

Rusk, D. (1968) 'Telegram to U.S. Embassy London'. 7 August 1968. National Archives and Records Administration: RG 59/150/64–65, Subject-Numeric Files 1967–1969, Box 1552.

Ryan, P.B. (1984) 'Diego Garcia'. *Proceedings,* 110(9/979), pp. 133–138.

Snoxell, D. (2009) '"Anglo-American complicity in the removal of the inhabitants of the Chagos Islands, 1964–73'. *Journal of Imperial & Commonwealth History,* 73, pp. 127–134.

Stoddart, J.D. (1969) Letter to Richard A. Sykes. February 22, 1969. UK National Archives (Public Records Office) FCO 31/401 DG 1969.

United Kingdom of Great Britain and Northern Ireland (1966) 'Availability of Certain Indian Ocean Islands for defense purposes'. *Exchange of Notes*, 30 December 1966.

United Nations (2005) *Basic Principles and Guidelines on the Right to a Remedy and Reparation for Victims of Gross Violations of International Human Rights Law and Serious Violations of International Humanitarian Law*, G.A. Res. 60/147, Principle 18, U.N. Doc. A/RES/60/147.

United States of America (2018) *Written Comments to the International Court of Justice, Advisory Opinion on the "Legal Consequences of the Separation of the Chagos Archipelago from Mauritius in 1965"*. Washington: United States of America.

US Embassy London (1964) 'Telegram to secretary of state'. February 27, 1964. Naval Historical Center: 00 Files, 1964, Box 20, 11000/1B.

US House of Representatives (1975) *Diego Garcia, 1975: The Debate over the Base and the Island's Former Inhabitants*. Special Subcommittee on Investigations, Committee on International Relations, June 5 and November 4, 94th Cong., 1st sess. Washington, DC: US Government Printing Office.

Vine, D. (2004) 'War and forced migration in the Indian Ocean: The U.S. Military base at Diego Garcia'. *International Migration,* 42(3), pp. 111–143.

Vine, D. (2011[2009]) *Island of Shame: The Secret History of the U.S. Military Base on Diego Garcia*. Princeton, NJ: Princeton University Press.

Vine, D. (2020) *The United States of War: A Global History of America's Endless Conflicts, from Columbus to the Islamic State*. Oakland: University of California Press.

Vine, D. (2023) 'The U.S. Base at Diego Garcia holds a dirty secret'. *Inkstick*, February 16, 2023. Available at: https://inkstickmedia.com/the-us-base-at-diego-garcia-holds-a-dirty-secret/ (Accessed: 1 March 2023).

Vine, D., Harvey, H., and Wojciech Sokolowski, S. (2012) 'Compensating a People for the Loss of Their Homeland: Diego Garcia, the Chagossians, and the Human Rights Standards Damages Model'. *Northwestern Journal of International Human Rights*, 11(1), pp.152–185.

Zumwalt, E. (1971) 'Attachment to E. L. Cochrane, Jr., memorandum for the deputy chief of naval operations (plans and policy)'. March 24, 1971. US Navy Archives, 00 Files, 1971, Box 174, 11000.

"UK Ambassador Lobbied Senators To Hide Diego Garcia's Role In Rendition" "L'ambassadeur britannique lobbied les sénateurs cachera le rôle de Diego Garcia dans la restitution"

Saradha Soobrayen

What gives Diego Garcia its unique identity is not where it is situated
geographically – south of the equator, 2200 miles east of the coast

of Africa and 1000 miles south-west of the southern tip of India –
but how it is situated in the minds of the politicians who tell it slant,

circumnavigating the facts and the fiction: "embarrassed Miliband
admits two US rendition flights refuelled on British soil" – the legal minds

finding joy in metaphor and irony: "the land where human rights
hardly ever happened", Richard Gifford, lawyer for the Chagossians.

Clive Stafford Smith, human rights campaigner: "on Diego Garcia
you may be arrested for violating the rights of a Warty Sea Slug …

but no-one will object if you land a plane with a kidnapped, shackled,
hooded man trapped in a coffin shaped box". Legal expert, Peter H Sands:

"a legal black hole" – Political Scientist, Peter Harris: "reforming Diego Garcia
is entirely within the grasp of those in London. It is high time that action

was taken to do the right thing" – his paper "America's Other Guantánamo:
British Foreign Policy and the US Base on Diego Garcia" telling it simply.

DOI: 10.4324/9781003390299-22

16 The Indo-Pacific and the Chagos Archipelago

Two Logics, Two Futures

Peter Harris

Introduction

Mauritius is an Indo-Pacific nation. Indeed, Mauritian membership of the Indo-Pacific – a newly conjured "megaregion" that encompasses the Indian Ocean, Western Pacific, and the littoral states of these oceanic expanses – can be considered the most important shift in the country's external environment since at least the end of the Cold War. At least in nominal terms, Mauritius is now part and parcel of geopolitics in the world's largest and most consequential world region. In this chapter, I explore what belonging to the Indo-Pacific region will mean in particular for the future of Mauritius and its Chagos Archipelago. Namely, I trace the relevance for the Chagos Islands of two distinct logics of international relations that are coinciding to give the Indo-Pacific construct its shape and meaning: (1) the logic of great power competition between the United States and China; and (2) the logic of a rules-based international order. On the one hand, the Indo-Pacific label is clearly the product of the US-China rivalry (Pan, 2014). Especially in the West, the discourse of a unified Indo-Pacific community has been adopted in large part because it captures (and reifies) the idea that the littoral states of the Indian Ocean and Western Pacific share common interests in the shadow of China's rise – and, moreover, that they should work together to counter Beijing's growing influence. On the other hand, however, the Indo-Pacific is supposed to be a region defined by adherence to international rules. Indeed, the rules-based character of the Indo-Pacific order is often portrayed as giving the region a sort of specialness in comparison to other world regions, where rules do not always apply. In recent years, both of these distinct logics of international relations – one rooted in *realpolitik* and the other in *idealpolitik* – have been evident in official discourse on the Indo-Pacific, despite the fact that they are somewhat in tension with one another.

The point of this chapter is that Mauritius's newfound belonging to the Indo-Pacific region will be enormously consequential for its political development and foreign policy going forward, including with specific reference to the Chagos Archipelago. For Mauritius and the Chagossians, much will depend upon how the conflicting demands and implications of the two sides of the Indo-Pacific construct are resolved in practice. If the logic of great power competition comes to dominate the words and deeds of those engaged in Indo-Pacific politics, Britain's unlawful occupation of Chagos Islands is more likely to endure. The prospects for

DOI: 10.4324/9781003390299-23

decolonisation and resettlement, meanwhile, will be slim. This is because British control of the Chagos Archipelago is easier to justify if the islands are conceptualised as belonging to a region where military competition with China is of paramount importance; the narrative of an existential struggle ("strategic competition" or a "new cold war") between China and the West is one that permits London and Washington to plausibly invoke *raison d'état* when violating established rules on decolonisation (Bashfield, 2021). However, if the narrative of the Indo-Pacific as a rules-based international system is elevated over the discourse of great power competition, then Mauritius will have a stronger chance of reclaiming control of the Chagos group. As well, the ambitions of some Chagossians to resettle their islands will be easier to fulfil. This is for the obvious reason that Britain's administration of the Chagos Archipelago is in clear contravention of the established rules-based order (Bashfield and Proukaki, 2022), and so London has no choice but to decolonise if its leaders want to be seen as conforming with international rules.

The rest of the chapter is organised as follows. First, I sketch a basic theoretical framework for understanding international organisation in the Indo-Pacific, and the mechanisms by which ideas about world regions can influence the behaviour of states. Second, I explain how the logic of strategic competition with China undergirds the Indo-Pacific concept in much of the West. While this narrative has met with opposition among some regional states, especially those of Southeast Asia, it is highly prevalent among the United States and its allies. I show how this logic can be (and has been) used to justify the continued occupation of the Chagos Archipelago by Britain (Thorpe, 2019; McDevitt, 2020; Bashfield, 2021). Third, I turn to discuss the nominal existence of a rules-based order in the Indo-Pacific. I argue that British control of the Chagos Islands is repugnant to the idea of a regional order defined by shared rules that apply equally to states large and small (Bashfield and Proukaki, 2022). If taken seriously, then, the logic of rules-based order implies that the territory ought to be decolonised – which, in turn, would allow Mauritius to implement its stated commitment to permitting a right of return and resettlement by the Chagossians. Fourth, I consider a "missing" third logic of international organisation as it applies to the Indo-Pacific: the logic of human rights and especially indigenous rights. This narrative decentres the role of states, foregrounding instead the interests of marginalised and dispossessed populations such as the Chagossians. It is a frame that some actors are trying to apply to the Chagos dispute, but so far with limited success. The final section concludes with a discussion of how the intertwined evolution of the Indo-Pacific order and the Chagos dispute might proceed in the future.

Regions and Regional Order

Scholars of International Relations have long argued that the behaviour of states is influenced by the type of international order (or international society) within which these states operate (see, *inter alia*, Bull, 2012[1977]; Finnemore, 1996). The insight here is that states neither exist in a vacuum nor a "thin" international realm consisting merely of other states. Rather, the international system is a "thick" milieu that weaves together norms, ideas, institutions, organisations, and routinised patterns of behaviour. The impact of this thick external environment – one replete with social interaction, political pressure, and institutional barriers – is that states cannot behave in any way they see fit. Rather, they must usually comport themselves with the prevailing international order to a greater or lesser extent. This is true both because of a logic of consequences (i.e., because states perceive costs to deviating from international strictures) and a logic of appropriateness (i.e., because states are socialised into choosing to behave in "proper" ways) (Finnemore, 1996, p. 29). The overall point is that international orders vary in terms of the ideas and patterns of behaviour that inhere within them, but that all international orders affect states to a non-trivial degree. In short, the behaviour of states on the world stage is largely a product of what is permitted and encouraged by their external environment.

There is also some scholarly agreement that international orders can sometimes exist at the regional level, as opposed to the global level alone (Hurrell, 2007; Stivachtis, 2013). In other words, discrete geographic zones in world politics can sometimes be observed to possess a unique set of rules, norms, and institutions that dictates the pace and character of international politics within that space. This might be because of a regional hegemon that undertakes an ordering role within its "near abroad" (such as the United States in the Western Hemisphere today, or China during its height as an imperial power in East Asia); because of geographic isolation that prevents the region in question from fully being incorporated into a global system (such as Mesoamerica prior to contact with Europeans); or because neighbouring states choose to pursue a form of regionalism that suits their specific interests or values (e.g., the European Union). Of course, the notion that the world's various regions are home to different sorts of international order is somewhat intuitive: most people would readily acknowledge that the regional politics of Europe is different to the regional politics of, say, Latin America, sub-Saharan Africa, or Oceania.

What, though, does it mean to live in the Indo-Pacific? The answer depends upon who you ask. To Shinzo Abe, the man most closely associated with the concept's emergence, the Indo-Pacific was a megaregion defined by *interconnectedness* – social, political, and economic. When Abe (2007) talked about the "confluence of the two seas", he meant simply that states and peoples on each side of the Strait of Malacca belonged to a unified geopolitical and geoeconomic space as a matter of empirical reality. According to Abe, the unprecedented volumes of trade and investment passing between the Indian Ocean and Western Pacific were what mattered most; observation alone was enough to conclude that a new megaregion had superseded the old (discrete) regional orders (Abe, 2007; Harris, 2022, p. 38).

Others disagree, however. As will be shown in the next two sections, the narrative of economic interconnectedness has been replaced in recent years by new narratives about great power competition and a rules-based order. During his second stint as prime minister of Japan, Abe played a role in shaping the latter by putting forward the concept of a Free and Open Indo-Pacific (FOIP) (Abe, 2016; Hosoya,

2019; Koga, 2020). According to this view, the Indo-Pacific is (or can be) a unique regional space in the sense that it is a place where international rules are dominant. Membership of the Indo-Pacific is defined not by trade relations but by respect for cardinal norms such as sovereignty, territorial integrity, non-intervention, free trade, and the peaceful resolution of disputes. As yet, however, few institutions or organisations have been created to embed this narrative about the Indo-Pacific (He and Feng, 2020), meaning that the rules-based order is more of an aspiration than a reality. Even so, the aspiration of achieving and concretising an FOIP has begun to define the official discourse used by governments across the region and beyond in some noticeable ways. It is an idea that has demonstrated great potential to mobilise political opinion.

The other major factor shaping discourse on the Indo-Pacific is the rise of China. In particular, China's rise seems to have been instrumental in persuading US leaders to exchange the language of the Asia-Pacific for that of the Indo-Pacific (such as by renaming US Pacific Command, or USPACOM, to US Indo-Pacific Command, or USINDOPACOM, in 2018). From the US perspective, embracing the language of the Indo-Pacific is attractive because it helps to frame Asia in strategic terms that centre the United States as the region's leading power (Pardesi, 2020). For Washington and its allies, the defining characteristic of the Indo-Pacific megaregion is neither economic interconnectedness nor the prevalence of international rules, but a common strategic understanding that the geographic expanse from the Persian Gulf to Northeast Asia faces the so-called China Threat. The formation of the Quadrilateral Security Dialogue ("Quad") is the clearest attempt to institutionalise the idea that the Indo-Pacific label reflects this underlying material reality of strategic competition (Harris, 2022). That said, some states have pushed back against the idea of the Indo-Pacific as a theatre of geopolitical competition. The member states of ASEAN, for example, have been particularly vocal about their desire to avoid the region being defined in such terms; and even Japan and India (members of the Quad) have gone to lengths to insist that their respective visions of an FOIP are not meant to exclude or contain China.

As can be seen, then, the Indo-Pacific is a contested space: the region's geographic expanse is contested, the contents of the supposed order are contested, and even the usage of the term "Indo-Pacific" is contested by some (most notably China). This is an important point. It means that states and non-state actors (internal and external to the region) are presently involved in a struggle over how to define the Indo-Pacific. In the following sections, I explore how the contested application of the Indo-Pacific as a political construct will help to determine the opportunity structures open to the various actors involved in the Chagos dispute. To be sure, it is also true that the causal arrow can point in the other direction, too, in the sense that what happens in the Chagos Archipelago will influence the larger contours of Indo-Pacific order in some non-trivial ways. But the overall point is that the Chagos dispute is bound up with wider questions of international political development in the Indo-Pacific region.

The China Threat and the Chagos Archipelago

It is commonplace in the West to define the Indo-Pacific as a theatre of great power competition. Beijing, it is implied, poses a grave threat not only to the United States and its core allies, but also to the security and sovereignty of small and middle powers in Africa and Asia, from the Seychelles to the South China Sea. For this reason, it matters little what side of the Malacca Strait you are on; China's rise means that the states of the Indo-Pacific megaregion ought to consider themselves as belonging to the same region for all intents and purposes. The Indo-Pacific idea captures this material reality, while also helping to reify the idea of strategic competition.

The so-called China threat and its infusion into the Indo-Pacific construct has elevated the perceived need for Western cooperation in military terms. In this context, the base on Diego Garcia has taken on special importance. Some commentators even seem to be rewriting the history of the base on Diego Garcia to fit the new narrative about China's rise. Michael McDevitt (2020), for example, has written that,

> it was China, not the Soviet Union, that spurred Washington to focus on acquiring a base. The policy trigger was the 1962 Sino-Indian War, when Prime Minister Jawaharlal Nehru had pressed Washington for military assistance to India, including an urgent request for U.S. air power to actually intervene.

This claim cuts against the conventional historiography that the Soviet Union constituted the primary impetus for US power projection during the Cold War, especially in the Indian Ocean region. McDevitt appears to rely upon a single source to justify the contention (Andersen, 1989). But given the weakness of China's navy during the early 1960s, it strains credulity that leaders in the United States judged Beijing to represent more of a proximate threat to US and allied security than the Soviet Union.

Whatever the merits of this revisionist history, however, the contemporary narrative of strategic competition with China can be observed to have shaped official discourse over Diego Garcia in some important ways. First, it explains why statements by Britain and Mauritius on the potential decolonisation of the Chagos Islands almost always include caveats that the base on Diego Garcia will be protected as part of any settlement to the sovereignty issue. Both London and Port Louis know that a deal to hand over control over the islands will never enjoy the support of the United States unless audiences in Washington – who are preoccupied with competition against China – are reassured on these points. Second, however, some commentators seem to be using the China threat to argue that British control of the Chagos Islands is more justifiable and ethical when judged against the Mauritian claim. Whereas London wants only to use Diego Garcia as a bulwark against Chinese expansionism, the argument goes, Port Louis is far grubbier and more cynical. As one retired British military officer wrote in 2019, "Behind [the] false narrative of championing the Chagossian cause, two other factors are really fuelling Mauritius' sovereignty claim: revenge and money" (Thorpe, 2019).

The allegation that Mauritius is interested in reclaiming the Chagos islands for reasons for revenge and money is unsupported by evidence. But the general idea that Britain has a strong (security-based) claim to the Chagos group has gained traction in London and Washington. In Britain, Daniel Kawczynski MP is perhaps the most prominent proponent of the idea that Mauritius cannot be trusted to govern its own territory in the shadow of China's rise. At times, Kawczynski has explicitly put forward the argument that breaking international rules (e.g., on decolonisation) can be justified in the context of trying to defeat China. Writing in the *Daily Express*, for example, Kawczynski (2020) gave the following unabashed defence of imperialism in an article titled, "Don't Let China In!"

> To those MPs who claim that our retaining this territory challenges the rules-based international order, I say quite the opposite: that this order can only be maintained if the UK, United States, and other like-minded countries are able to defend it, wherever in the world it is challenged. Far from being an imperial relic, the BIOT is essential to safeguarding British interests, allies, and values in the region. Outposts such as this, and the Royal Air Force station on Ascension Island, are valuable NATO assets and a key part of what "Global Britain" can offer the Western alliance as we face the threats of the 21st Century.

Kawczynski's ideas have been taken up by Mike Waltz (2022), a member of the US House of Representatives, who argued in a letter to Secretary of State Antony Blinken and Secretary of State Lloyd Austin that "Should the U.K. cede control of the Chagos to Mauritius, I have no doubt that China will take advantage of the resulting vacuum". This is a strong claim – and Waltz has not given any evidence for why he can be so sure that Mauritius is plotting to hand over the Chagos Islands to China. But the general logic is nothing new. Indeed, this is merely a repeat of the earlier arguments used during the Cold War and the post-9/11 era for why the expulsion and exile of the Chagossians was a strategic necessity. Then, imperialism was justified in the name of containing the Soviet Union. Now, the same illegal practices are deemed necessary as a means to defeat China. As far as Diego Garcia is concerned, the ongoing "contest for supremacy" between the United States and China is just the latest in a series of global narratives that have served to justify US military primacy in general and the UK-US occupation of Diego Garcia in particular.

It is worth asking: Why do politicians like Kawczynski and Waltz not trust Mauritius given that Port Louis has offered the United States a 99-year lease on Diego Garcia? In the past, racism played a large part in the Cold War-era dismemberment of Mauritius and the forced depopulation of the Chagos Islands. It was only because postcolonial Mauritius would not be run by white Europeans that UK and US officials perceived a need to transform the Chagos Archipelago from a Lesser Dependency of Mauritius into a new – and empty – British-administered colonial jurisdiction. The archival record is clear that the Anglo-American powers viewed it as far too risky to entrust a Third World government ("a newly emergent independent state") with stewardship of the base on Diego

Garcia (Allen, 2014, p. 78). The Chagossians, meanwhile, were disparaged as "Tarzans" and "Man Fridays", a population to be "wished away" and hidden from international observers such as the UN's Special Committee on Decolonization (Vine, 2009, pp. 89–98; see also Jeffery, 2011). This discrimination between reliable Anglophone nations and dubious postcolonial peoples was a textbook case of what W.E.B. Du Bois (Du Bois, 2007[1903], p. v) once called the global "color-line".

There are eerie similarities with what is being said about Mauritius today. But there is also something else at play: the literal disappearance of Mauritians from official discourse. To be fair to Rep. Waltz, for example, his opposition to a handover of control is borne out of animosity toward China – Washington's *bête noire du jour* – rather than any obvious animus towards Mauritius in particular. But in his letter to Blinken and Austin, Waltz (2022) argued that Mauritian control over Chagos would create a "vacuum" to be filled by the expansionist Chinese. Clearly, Beijing is the enemy in Waltz's eyes; Mauritius is spared the indignity of direct insult. But the colour-line stands out brightly. For Waltz, it is as if Mauritian sovereignty does not count; Diego Garcia can be British, American, or Chinese, but it cannot be African. Mauritius is incapable of exercising meaningful control in its own right; for Mauritius to be allowed ownership of strategic islands would be to create a "vacuum". This is the inevitable conclusion of a political discourse that foregrounds great power competition over the concerns of local actors; it is the "great game" all over again, with states such as Mauritius frequently erased from the conversation.

The Rules-Based Order, Decolonisation, and the Right of Return

At the same time, however, the Indo-Pacific region is supposed to be defined by rules and international law (Byrne, 2020). This is the "friendly face" of the Indo-Pacific concept, one meant to attract states to its banner via soft power (attractiveness) rather than fear or anxiety. One version of the rules-based order can be found in the FOIP concept popularised first in Japan, and later disseminated throughout the region. Other states do not use the FOIP acronym, but nevertheless insist that a rules-based order exists in the Indo-Pacific, and caution that it must be protected against those who would undermine its operation. For obvious reasons, the promise of a rules-based order is meant to be attractive to small and middle states, who might otherwise worry about their national interests being fairly protected in the absence of strong international rules.

The narratives of great power competition and rules-based order are interconnected, of course, via the prevalent idea that the rise of China constitutes the primary threat to the Indo-Pacific's supposed rules-based order. As the realist scholar Stephen Walt (2021) has argued, China supports the existence of a rules-based international order, too, but disagrees with the West about what these rules should be. Walt's point is that Westerners and their allies should not overreact to China's challenge to international order. But the conventional wisdom is exactly the opposite: that Beijing is plotting to overturn the present rules-based system and institute

China-centric rules that will suit its own national interest at the expense of everybody else who inhabits the system.

For the purposes of this chapter, however, it is most important to stress that the narrative of a rules-based order is a threat to Britain's continued occupation of the Chagos Archipelago. Simply put, the version of rules-based order that has been embraced by the United States and Britain is difficult to square with their occupation of the Chagos Islands. In the past, Britain sought to tether its claims to Chagos to well-understood artefacts of law: the Treaty of Paris, which handed sovereignty of Mauritius from France to Britain; the Lancaster House agreement, which codified the terms of Mauritian independence and now has the force of an international treaty; the oft-repeated claim that Mauritius had never exercised sovereignty over the islands; and, most importantly of all, the fact that there had been no dispositive ruling on the legal question until the 2019–2021 era. Over time, however, Britain's violation of the rules-based order became impossible to disguise.

The sheer illegality of Britain's handling of the Chagos issue was etched into the public record in stages. First, the Permanent Court of Arbitration ruled in March 2015 that London had breached international law by designating a marine protected area in the Chagos Islands without first consulting Mauritius (Harris, 2015). Two years later, the UN General Assembly adopted a resolution that called upon the International Court of Justice to give an advisory opinion on the question of sovereignty itself (Bowcott, 2017). This advisory opinion was forthcoming in 2019, and unambiguously held Mauritius to be the sovereign authority over the islands (Jeffery, 2019). Soon after, an overwhelming majority of states in the UN General Assembly voted to accept the ICJ's opinion and call on the British government to decolonise the territory (Bowcott and Borger, 2019). Finally, a special chamber constituted under auspices of the International Tribunal of the Law of the Sea ruled in 2021 that the ICJ's legal opinion could be considered a definitive answer to the question of sovereignty (Klein, 2021). This case was between Maldives and Mauritius, concerning their dispute over the boundary between their respective Exclusive Economic Zones. Soon after, even the Maldives abandoned the ship and switched to recognise Mauritian sovereignty (Shivamurthy, 2022; Ghafoor, 2023).

Despite strong incentives to maintain the status quo, this avalanche of adverse legal and political decisions seems to have been too much for the United States and Britain to ignore. By mid-2022, the British government had decided to begin negotiations with Mauritius over sovereignty (BBC, 2022). As Sarah Gray (2022, p. 83) puts it,

> As a sovereign state Mauritius was able to flex its international muscle, demonstrating how small island countries continue to shape the processes that define their relationships to imperial powers. The case offers a new precedent with which to fight the history wars contributing to subtle shifts in global hierarchies the world over.

The Missing Third Logic: Indigenous Rights and People Politics

So far, I have argued that two dominant logics are at play when it comes to defining international politics in the Indo-Pacific: *realpolitik* and *idealpolitik*. But there is another logic that is often wished for by scholars and activists who are closely associated with the Chagossians' struggle: the logic of indigenous rights and what might be called "people politics". From this view, it is frustrating that the Indo-Pacific order is not designed to further the interests of local communities, including indigenous peoples such as the Chagossians. It would be better, the argument goes, if world politics were decentred, and indigenous peoples could become sovereign over their own political destinies rather than relying upon the forbearance of states. But is there a pathway to securing justice for the Chagossians that obviates the need to work through the states-system structure?

In theoretical terms, people-centric politics is a powerful alternative logic and mode of international organisation to both *realpolitik* and *idealpolitik*. Indeed, it is a logic that has been articulated and discussed in practice. The International Conference on the Status of the Chagos Islands, for example, is a recent case in point. At this conference, which was held in Pretoria in October 2022, an international cast of scholars, activists, and practitioners gathered to foreground the interests of the Chagossians. A sizable number of attendees expressed distrust of the government of Mauritius, preferring instead that the Chagossians be given a form of statehood and independence from both Britain and Mauritius, a popular idea among some segments of the Chagossian diaspora (Holloway, 2022).

Yet such arguments have scant footing the corpus of public international law. While most proponents of the rules-based international order would agree that self-determination is a cardinal principle of international law, it is alas an ill-defined principle. Sometimes, self-determination is conceptualised as meaning freedom from external control, while at other times it implies a right to democratic government. What self-determination does not mean is that every national, ethnic, linguistic, religious, or indigenous group in the world is entitled to sovereign statehood. For better or worse, the idea of Chagossian statehood is entirely unsupported by the current framework of international rules, norms, and processes that make up the African and Indo-Pacific orders. On the contrary, international politics in these regions is heavily biased in favour of maintaining the territorial integrity of existing states.

This is why indigenous rights and people-politics constitute only a *potential* third logic of international affairs when it comes to the Indo-Pacific and the Chagos Islands: without a state of their own, groups such as the Chagossians are entirely dependent upon existing states as interlocutors and conduits for interfacing with the outside world (Zhu, 2023). By design, the international system is *of* states, *by* states, and *for* states; indigenous peoples have been organised out of the state-system, reduced in power and made to direct their entreaties towards state entities rather than availing themselves of intergovernmental forums. While there are some international-level rules with regard to the rights of indigenous peoples – the UN Declaration on the Rights of Indigenous Peoples, for example – these exist only because states have agreed to them, which implies that states consider such rules to be non-threatening or unenforceable. It would be highly unlikely for states to limit their own sovereign authority by agreeing to binding international rules on the treatment of indigenous peoples.

Support from organisations such as Human Rights Watch (2023) can mean only so much in this context. Grassroots movements can succeed in international politics, but even organised movements that operate across state borders cannot hope to influence international law and order without the compliance of states, who are the only actors with legal personality and thus the ability to conclude international agreements. Simply put, the international system affords groups like the Chagossians no opportunities to shape regional politics other than the opportunity to lobby national governments such as the British and Mauritian administrations; international order still treats indigenous issues as mostly domestic affairs, with little role for international organisations, courts, or other states. This is why the Chagossians' hopes of returning to their islands now depend upon the willingness of Port Louis to organise a resettlement in the event of assuming full control over the archipelago (Harris, 2013).

Conclusion

The Chagos dispute has not unfolded in a vacuum. It has taken place in the context of a wider struggle over international and regional order. From this view, it matters how international order is defined, and what international actors want to see from regional organisation. In this chapter, I have argued that the logic of *realpolitik* (great power competition) is helping to drive Indo-Pacific politics. This logic emboldens actors such as Britain and the United States to uphold the status quo and dismiss Mauritian and Chagossian requests for justice. Indeed, Mauritius and the Chagossians are not even viewed as meaningful participants in this type of international order, which foregrounds the role of great powers over small states and non-state actors. Another logic that has been shaping the Chagos dispute, however, is *idealpolitik*, or the logic of a rules-based order. This logic differs from *realpolitik* in that it widens the aperture to include small states like Mauritius, and encourages a focus on questions of right and wrong. Using the logic and language of a rules-based order, Port Louis has enjoyed some success at pressing its claims to the Chagos Islands during recent years.

Neither logic foregrounds the interests of non-state actors such as the Chagossians. For centuries, the international system has been regarded as a members-only club for sovereign states – and the Indo-Pacific is no exception. The Chagossians' various court cases against the British government no doubt played a major role in pushing London to accept the need for negotiations with Mauritius, but all movement towards a resolution of the Chagos dispute look certain to be channelled through the fabric of international law as it concerns state sovereignty and territorial integrity. As frustrating as it might be, the fate of the Chagossians will not be decided (or even discussed) at the international level; the question of resettlement will necessarily be left as a domestic matter for Mauritius to decide once the islands have been handed over. This is a cold consequence of the Chagossian people not having a state of their own.

References

Abe, S. (2007) 'The confluence of the two seas. Speech to the parliament of the Republic of India'. 22 August 2007. Available at: https://www.mofa.go.jp/region/asia-paci/pmv0708/speech-2.html (Accessed: 1 March 2023).

Abe, S. (2016) *Address at the Opening Session of the Sixth Tokyo International Conference on African Development*. Nairobi: Kenyatta International Convention Centre, 27 August 2016. Available at: https://www.mofa.go.jp/afr/af2/page4e_000496.html (Accessed: 1 March 2023).

Allen, S. (2014) *The Chagos Islanders and International Law*. London: Bloomsbury.

Andersen, W.K. (1989) 'Emerging security issues in the Indian Ocean: An American perspective'. In Selig S. Harrison and K. Subrahmanyanm (eds.), *Superpower Rivalry in the Indian Ocean*. Oxford: Oxford University Press, pp. 12–83.

Bashfield, S.M. (2021) 'Military security obstacles to decolonizing the Chagos: A reply to Harris'. *Journal of the Indian Ocean Region*, 17(2), pp. 230–234.

Bashfield, S.M. and Katselli Proukaki, E. (2022) 'The rules-based order, international law and the British Indian Ocean territory: Do as I Say, Not as I Do'. *German Law Journal*, 23(5), pp. 713–737.

BBC (2022) 'UK to open negotiations over future of Chagos Islands'. *BBC*, 3 November 2022. Available at: https://www.bbc.com/news/uk-politics-63498137 (Accessed: 1 March 2023).

Bowcott, O. (2017) 'EU members abstain as Britain defeated in UN vote on Chagos Islands'. *The Guardian*, 23 June 2017. Available at: https://www.theguardian.com/world/2017/jun/22/un-vote-backing-chagos-islands-a-blow-for-uk. (Accessed: 1 March 2023).

Bowcott, O. and Borger, J. (2019) 'UK suffers crushing defeat in UN vote on Chagos Islands'. *The Guardian*, 22 May 2019. Available at: https://www.theguardian.com/world/2019/may/22/uk-suffers-crushing-defeat-un-vote-chagos-islands (Accessed: 1 March 2023).

Bull, H. (2012[1977]). *The Anarchical Society: A Study of Order in World Politics*. New York: Columbia University Press.

Byrne, C. (2020) 'Securing the "Rules-based order" in the indo-pacific'. *Security Challenges*, 16(3), pp. 10–15.

Finnemore, M. (1996) *National Interests in International Society*. Ithaca: Cornell University Press.

Ghafoor, M. (2023) 'Why maldives sided with Mauritius on the Chagos Islands'. *The Diplomat*, 10 January 2023. Available at:https://thediplomat.com/2023/01/why-maldives-sided-with-mauritius-on-the-chagos-islands/ (Accessed: 1 March 2023).

Gray, S. (2022) 'Fighting one Island to claim another: Mauritius' journey to international justice'. *Small States & Territories*, 5(1), pp. 71–86.

Harris, P. (2013) 'Dead end or crossroads? The chagossians fail in strasbourg'. *Anthropology Today*, 29(3), p. 26.

Harris, P. (2015) 'Why law and politics matter for marine conservation: The case of the chagos marine protected area'. *Environmental Policy and Law*, 45(5), pp. 204–207.

Harris, P. (2022) 'The indo-pacific power: The United States, the quad, and the making of a Megaregion'. In Srabani Roy Choudhury (ed.), *The Indo-Pacific Theatre Strategic Visions and Frameworks*. New Delhi: Routledge, pp. 35–49.

He, K. and Feng, H. (2020) 'The institutionalize of the indo-pacific: Problems and prospects'. *International Affairs*, 96(1), pp. 149–168.

Holloway, L. (2022) 'Chagos islanders fear they will disappear'. *The Voice*, 29 December 2022. Available at: https://www.voice-online.co.uk/news/world-news/2022/12/29/chagos-islanders-fear-they-will-disappear (Accessed: 1 March 2023).

Hosoya, Y. (2019) 'FOIP 2.0: The evolution of Japan's free and open IndoPacific strategy'. *Asia-Pacific Review*, 26(1), pp. 18–28.

Human Rights Watch (2023) '"That's when the nightmare started": UK and US forced displacement of the chagossians and ongoing colonial crimes'. *Human Rights Watch*, February 2023. Available at: https://www.hrw.org/sites/default/files/media_2023/04/chagos0223web.pdf (Accessed: 1 March 2023).

Hurrell, A. (2007) 'One world? Many worlds? The place of regions in the study of international society'. *International Affairs*, 83(1), pp. 127–146.

Jeffery, L. (2011) *Chagos Islanders in Mauritius and the UK: Forced Displacement and Onward Migration*. Manchester: Manchester University Press.

Jeffery, L. (2019) 'The international court of justice: Advisory opinion on the Chagos Archipelago'. *Anthropology Today*, 35(3), pp. 24–27.

Kawczynski, D. (2020) 'Don't let China in! Beijing will pounce if UK sacrifices islands'. *Daily Express*, 20 June 2020. Available at: https://www.express.co.uk/comment/expresscomment/1298649/china-new-chagos-islands-british-indian-ocean-territory-diego-garcia-Daniel-Kawczynski (Accessed: 1 March 2023).

Klein, N. (2021) 'Chagos: A boundary dispute tips over a sovereignty ruling'. *Lowy Interpreter*, 8 February 2021. Available at: https://www.lowyinstitute.org/the-interpreter/chagos-boundary-dispute-tips-over-sovereignty-ruling (Accessed: 1 March 2023).

Koga, K. (2020) 'Japan's "Indo-Pacific" question: Countering China or shaping a new regional order?' *International Affairs*, 96(1), pp. 49–73.

McDevitt, M. (2020) 'America's interest in Diego Garcia'. *War on The Rocks*, 3 June 2020. Available at: https://warontherocks.com/2020/06/americas-interest-in-diego-garcia (Accessed: 1 March 2023).

Pan, C. (2014) 'The "Indo-Pacific" and geopolitical anxieties about China's rise in the Asian regional order'. *Australian Journal of International Affairs*, 68(4), pp. 453–469.

Pardesi, M.S. (2020) 'The indo-pacific: A "New" region or the return of history?' *Australian Journal of International Affairs*, 74(2), pp. 124–146.

Shivamurthy, A.G. (2022) 'Maldives' Chagos conundrum: Continuing inconsistency and its politicization'. *Observer Research Foundation*, 22 November 2022. Available at: https://www.orfonline.org/research/maldives-chagos-conundrum/ (Accessed: 1 March 2023).

Stivachtis, Y.A. (2013) 'The regional dimension of international society'. In Cornelia Navari and Daniel M. Green (eds.), *Guide to the English School in International Studies*. Oxford: Wiley Blackwell, pp. 109–125.

Thorpe, R. (2019) 'Mauritius scores a pyrrhic victory in the Indian Ocean'. *War on The Rocks*, 12 July 2019. Available at:https://warontherocks.com/2019/07/mauritius-scores-a-pyrrhic-victory-in-the-indian-ocean/ (Accessed; 1 March 2023).

Vine, D. (2009) *Island of Shame: The Secret History of the U.S. Military Base on Diego Garcia*. Princeton, NJ: Princeton University Press.

Walt, S.M. (2021) 'China wants a "rules-based international order" too'. *Foreign Policy*, 31 March 2021. Available at: https://foreignpolicy.com/2021/03/31/china-wants-a-rules-based-international-order-too/ (Accessed: 1 March 2023).

Waltz, M. (2022) 'Letter to secretary of state Antony Blinken and secretary of defense Lloyd Austin'. 19 December 2022. Available at: https://waltz.house.gov/uploadedfiles/2022-12-19_waltz_letter_to_blinken_and_austin_re_diego_garcia.pdf (Accessed: 1 March 2023).

Zhu, Y.Y. (2023) 'A real decolonisation dispute Nobody has asked the Chagos Islanders if they wish to be independent of Britain'. May 2023. Available at: https://thecritic.co.uk/issues/may-2023/a-real-decolonisation-dispute/ (Accessed: 1 September 2023).

17 Flagpole Fights, Courtroom Clashes, and Coconut Crabs

Owen Bowcott

Invited to Embark

The invitation to join a voyage across the Indian Ocean was not entirely a surprise. As *The Guardian's* legal affairs correspondent, I, and newsroom colleagues, had for years followed court cases and political battles over the enforced depopulation of the Chagos Islands. There had been talk of a Mauritian-organised landing on the outer islands. My account is a passenger's perspective of the expedition.

A Tale of Two Ships

This is a tale of two ships; of dispossession and return. It encompasses the deportation of every inhabitant of the Chagos Islands on the cargo ship *Nordvaer* and a homecoming voyage on the *Bleu de Nîmes* 50 years later.

For the five Chagossian exiles gathering at Eden Island marina in the Seychelles, the journey would take them back to the beginning of their lives. For the rest of the passengers and crew, it offered an exploration of a remote archipelago and an unresolved colonial dispute.

Departure had been fixed for Tuesday 8 February 2022. Dazzling, white rows of yachts were moored side by side. Above swabbed sundecks, thickets of aerials and radar domes glinted in the midday sun. Of our vessel, the *Bleu de Nîmes*, however, there was no sign. The mooring piers, it turned out, were too small to accommodate the 72-metre ship.

Promptly on time, uniformed crew arrived in matching navy blue tops. They scooped up suitcases and broadcast equipment. The converted, former British minesweeper was waiting in the bay. The dark hull and white superstructure of the *Bleu de Nîmes* soon appeared; its elegant bulk inspired confidence. We were welcomed aboard and shown around air-conditioned and wood-panelled rooms.

It was not a pleasure cruise; nor was it quite gunboat diplomacy. The plan was for the ex-Royal Navy ship – chartered by the Mauritian government – to sail into the normally forbidden waters of the British Indian Ocean Territory (BIOT), asserting Mauritian sovereignty over reefs and atolls that the United Nations' highest court had ruled were illegally confiscated by the UK in 1965.

The need for such a large vessel became apparent as we were briefed about distances. From the Seychelles to the Chagos Islands, it is 1,015 nautical miles

DOI: 10.4324/9781003390299-24

(1,880 kilometres). It takes four or five days on a route bordering the track of cyclones which slam into Madagascar with increasing regularity.

The initial intention had been to sail from Malé, capital of the Maldives, only 565 miles (1,048 kms) away – a shorter, two-day trip. But there was a difficulty. As Professor Philippe Sands KC, of University College, London, the lawyer retained by Mauritius, explained:

> The Maldives … informed Mauritius it would exercise a right of veto over the delegation and made it clear journalists would not be permitted. One can assume the UK had a role in encouraging the Maldives to take steps to limit who participated.

Departing from Mauritius, further to the south, would have meant crossing the path of developing cyclones. Leaving from the Seychelles, north of incoming storms, was deemed a wiser course.

There were other reasons for choosing a spacious vessel. The prime minister of Mauritius, Pravind Jugnauth, had originally intended to be on board. His planned presence was an indication of how much national pride is bound up in efforts to recover the Chagos Archipelago from British occupation. A prime minister needs a stable platform and high-tech communications to stay in touch with his government.

The other rationale was the need for smaller craft capable of survey work. The *Bleu de Nîmes* carries a flotilla of inflatables and tenders. The main purpose of the voyage, as explained by Mauritius to the UK Foreign Office, was the examination of Blenheim Reef, gathering information about its height above water.

Why, though, should Mauritius be allowed to gather precious seabed data around islands the UK governs as BIOT? To answer that requires explanation of the legal battles over ownership. I will come to that shortly.[1]

At this point it is sufficient to appreciate that the UK's grasp on the Chagos Archipelago is slipping. "Early in December," Sands revealed, "Mauritius informed the UK it would be visiting the Chagos Archipelago, to follow up a case before the International Tribunal for the Law of the Sea [ITLOS]. It asked for confirmation from the UK that it would not impede the visit.

The Mauritius government made clear that if information was not received by 20 December [2021], it would start fresh proceedings against the UK. The UK blinked and sent a note saying they would not impede the voyage".

Ultimately the Mauritian prime minister decided not to join the expedition. Given subsequent communications problems, it was probably a sensible decision.

The Bleu de Nîmes

The *Bleu de Nîmes*, or at least most of it, was constructed on Tyneside. Completed in 1980 as the Royal Marine Auxiliary Service *Lodestone*, it specialised in degaussing – removal of magnetism from a ship so it can deal with mines. The vessel was sold in 1997 and underwent two refits, slotting in additional sections that extended its length. In early 2022, it was available both for charter and sale – 430,000 euros a week, according to the charter website, or it could be purchased outright for 47 million euros.

The Italian owner, whose fortune derives from clothing, renamed the vessel "*Bleu de Nîmes*" in tribute to the resilient cloth from the French city. (The "denim" cotton was dyed deep blue to make trousers for Genoese sailors, later known in French as "bleu de Genes" – giving the world the name "jeans".)

Although registered in Rarotonga, on the Cook Islands in the Pacific, the ship's regular port is Genoa. It has been around. The owner previously sailed to Greenland and into uncharted waters surrounding. Papua New Guinea. The captain of *the Bleu de Nîmes* is Mascia Poma. A dedicated mariner, she has been in charge since 2007 and relished the adventure of exploring unvisited destinations.

The passengers included journalists, marine surveyors, Mauritian officials, international lawyers, a medical team, and the five exiled Chagossians. The media included the BBC, *The Atlantic* magazine, the Mauritius Broadcasting Corporation, and *The Guardian*.

Jagdish Koonjul, who, at 69, is the country's ambassador to the United Nations, led the Mauritian team. A veteran diplomat with decades of experience in New York and Europe, his cheerful and calm demeanour concealed encyclopaedic knowledge about the protracted dispute.

That afternoon, as clouds began to build from another cyclone, the *Bleu de Nîmes* weighed anchor, edged out into the Indian Ocean, and pointed east. Soon a fluorescent pink sunset spread across the horizon astern.

The Voyage Out

The five Chagossians on board were among those most determined to return home. Olivier Bancoult, Rosemonde Berthin, Liseby Elysé, Marie Suzelle Baptiste, and Marcel Humbert had been forcibly deported, or prevented from returning, by British officials – along with 1,500 other islanders, known in French Creole as "Îlois".

The history of the Chagos Islands is complex. They were occupied by the French in the 18th century who established coconut plantations. Workers were initially taken from Mozambique and Madagascar as slaves; after 1840 they were freed. The archipelago, more than 60 islands clustered in seven atolls, was administered from Mauritius, formerly a French colony, which passed into British hands in 1814 after the defeat of Napoleon (for more of this history, see Chapters 2 and 3).

In the 1960s, as pressure for independence grew, Britain entered into negotiations with the USA which wanted a military base in the Indian Ocean. The Americans selected the island of Diego Garcia. The UK detached the Chagos Islands from the rest of Mauritius, creating a new colony, the British Indian Ocean Territory. UK diplomats forced Mauritian politicians to accept partition and signed an agreement with Washington promising to remove "any inhabitants". In return, Britain received a $14 million discount on the cost of Polaris missiles purchased for its submarines.

As the ship pitched and rolled, Berthin and Elysé kept to their cabin but were happy to talk. Berthin was only 17 when British officials arrived on Salomon Atoll in 1972. Everyone, she recalled, was ordered to gather at the manager's office on the coconut plantation. She did not remember any advance warning.

The commissioner ordered them to leave because the Americans were setting up a military base on Diego Garcia. For Berthin, who used to clean the house of the plantation manager, Mr Doffay, and look after a baby, it was the moment her island life vanished forever. "It had been wonderful", she said. "There were about 300 people and we lived as one big family". They fished and processed coconuts.

> The authorities put pressure on people, saying we needed to go or otherwise we wouldn't survive. Provisions in the store had been run down. There was only one bag of sugar. I can't understand how those who lived freely could be removed.

The islanders boarded the *Nordvaer*, the supply vessel operated by the British government. Half were taken directly to Mauritius, half to a neighbouring island before eventual removal from the archipelago the following year. After they left, their pets were shot or gassed.

"I felt very sad", Berthin remembered. "They put mattresses on the decks. It was in a very bad state: the vessel normally carried animals and fertiliser. Conditions were so bad one lady gave birth prematurely".

Fifty years later Berthin still lives in exile in Mauritius. She had been permitted "heritage visits" twice before, in 2006 and 2009, under close supervision of UK officials. Like the other Chagossians, she brought along her birth certificate. "I don't want to be a visitor", she explained. "Salomon is my birthplace".

Her cabin mate, Liseby Elysé, born on a nearby atoll, Peros Banhos, was expelled in 1973 when she was 20. "Life was lovely. We ate what we grew. There was fish and fresh fruit", she explained. "We had a garden and cultivated tomatoes, aubergine, pumpkins and lettuce. My father grew food for the whole community".

She worked on the plantation until "two men turned up, the commissioner and a company director. They said we would all be removed and taken to Mauritius". She had to leave her ducks, chickens, and two dogs: Ali Baba and Vainqueur. "When we went onboard, the dogs swam out and tried to jump into the ship". The Chagossians themselves felt like slaves or animals aboard the *Nordvaer*, she said. "The officials told us we would have houses and gardens just like we had on Peros Banhos". Those promises never materialised. The exiles were dumped in the Black River district of Port Louis, the Mauritian capital. "I felt very sad, heartbroken. There was no choice about leaving".

Elysé, a mother of five, has lived in Mauritius since then. "My children have never seen Peros Banhos. It was a paradise. I would like to go back and live there permanently". She had been on one previous UK-arranged "heritage visit" in 2006.

Marcel Humbert, 66, joined the voyage to show scientists examining Blenheim Reef where, historically, they fished in outrigger sailing canoes. "We used to catch red snapper, tuna, sharks, parrot fish and kingfish", he said. "But always with hooks – not nets".

He was 11 when he left Peros Banhos for Mauritius in 1967. He and his family were then prevented from returning. He now works as a fisherman and owns a boat. Until the UK government introduced a Marine Protected Area (MPA) around the Chagos in 2010, he could obtain fishing licences for the surrounding waters.

One crustacean with alarming, predatory capabilities, Humbert explained, is the metre-wide coconut or robber crab. It has become dominant on some islands and been observed killing seabirds. "You have to be careful. Their claws are very powerful. They cut coconuts in two".

Marie Suzelle Baptiste, secretary of the Chagos Refugees Group, brought flowers for the cemeteries on Peros Banhos and Salomon. She was born on Diego Garcia, the largest island. "I'm very sad we don't have permission to go there", she said. She was 11 months old in 1965 when she travelled to the Seychelles with her mother because her brother needed medical attention. After he had been treated, her mother tried to book their return passage. "'Chagos is closed', my mother was told. So I couldn't go back".

In 2006, she was allowed a "heritage visit" to Diego Garcia. "My father told me where our house was. It's a military base now. I'd still like to go back and live there". She carried onboard the Chagos refugees' orange, black, and blue flag. Orange represents the sunset when they were deported, black the misery of exile, and blue the ocean and future hopes.

Olivier Bancoult, leader of the refugees group, celebrated his 58th birthday during the voyage. Born on Peros Banhos in 1964, he was four when he sailed with his family to Mauritius so that his sister could receive medical treatment after a cart drove over her foot. The family were prevented from returning.

The most outspoken activist, he has brought so many legal challenges against the British government; they are numbered – *Bancoult No 1* (2000), *Bancoult No 2* (2008), *Bancoult No 3* (2018), *Bancoult No 4* (2016), and *Bancoult No 5* (2020) – for convenience of legal reference. Sitting in the hushed surroundings of the London courts down the years, listening to lawyers arguing his claims about mistreatment of the islanders, I witnessed an emotional rollercoaster as the exiles' hopes of returning home soared only to be repeatedly dashed by switches in Foreign Office policy or judgements that refused to admit as evidence leaked, diplomatic cables.

"I have never given up taking legal cases because I believe our struggle is a just cause", he said. "My dream is to be able to settle in my birthplace. I have spent [decades] in exile". Official treatment of the Chagossians, he believes, constitutes racism.

> The British government says it's in favour of human rights, yet they make a distinction between Falkland Islanders, for example, and Chagossians. Is it because we are black? We have ideas for eco-tourism and fishing jobs, too. We want to develop Chagos and create jobs. Lots of young people would join us.

Entering BIOT Territorial Waters

Mauritius was diplomatically adept in its preparations for the *Bleu de Nîmes'* voyage: the US had been reassured it could continue leasing its military base on Diego

Garcia even after Britain left, a new MPA was announced to reassure environmentalists, and Chagossians promised a right of return. Everything was done to align the interests of Mauritius and the Chagossian exile community.

As the ship crossed into BIOT Territorial waters, it sounded its horn. Music was played on the top deck where the Chagossians danced and sang in the warm rain, raising glasses of champagne in anticipation of homecoming.

One of the strangest facts to emerge during the voyage is that the waters around the Chagos Archipelago are almost 100 metres below average sea level. Different densities inside our planet cause fluctuations in gravity which affect the oceans; additionally, the Earth is not a perfect sphere but more like a lumpy potato. "Mean sea level is not constant", explained Ola Oskarsson, the Swedish marine surveyor retained for the voyage. Oskarsson's task would be to establish if any part of Blenheim Reef, a northern outcrop of the archipelago, was above water – thereby enabling Mauritius to extend its claim to a 200-mile exclusive economic zone in a forthcoming ITLOS case.

As we approached, a telephone interview was arranged with Pravind Jugnauth, the Mauritian prime minister, who had hoped to be on board. His country's first expedition to the Chagos Islands was "not in any way a hostile act", he declared. "It is merely an exercise of our sovereignty over part of our territory and that is in accordance with international law.

> We totally condemn the way Chagossians have been treated by the UK. Uprooting people from their place of birth without any warning, putting them on a ship, leaving them at the quay in Mauritius and preventing them from going back – that clearly is a crime against humanity".

The Foreign Office retaliated with a statement asserting that:

> The UK has no doubt as to our sovereignty over [BIOT]. Mauritius notified the UK about its plans to conduct a scientific survey close to the Chagos islands. The UK shares this interest in research and environmental protection and gave assurances to Mauritius it would not interrupt the survey.

That welcome was less confrontational than the reception given to the journalist Simon Winchester – formerly of *The Guardian* and the *Sunday Times* – when he sailed into Diego Garcia's harbour in 1984. Recorded in his book *Outposts – Journeys to the Surviving Relics of the British Empire*, his unannounced arrival panicked British officials who ordered his boat out to sea after only one night moored alongside the US military base.

While Chagossians are forbidden from living in their homeland (punishment for illegal entry into BIOT waters is up to three years in prison), yachts are allowed to purchase permits to explore the outer islands. We would see the results of this policy.

First Sight of Land

Land! On Saturday, after four days at sea, a dark smudge appeared on the horizon. Soon the islands forming Peros Banhos Atoll resolved into palm trees breaking the skyline. The captain steered through a narrow passage into shallow inner waters. Olivier, Marie Suzelle, Liseby, Rosemonde, and Marcel, beaming with exuberance, were on deck sporting t-shirts emblazoned with the words: "Everyone has a right to their birthplace" and "Chagos my home".

The anchor chain rattled down off the Île du Coin, the largest in the atoll. A line of white breakers ringed the beach and flocks of seabirds passed overhead. "It's idyllic", remarked Koonjul. "I understand how people feel about being uprooted. You could resettle. There's great potential for eco-tourism".

A decaying jetty and buoys in the anchorage were the only sign of human activity. Creepers had engulfed houses. "We are back home!" sighed Oliver Bancoult. "This is where I embarked on a boat to Mauritius in 1968. My grandfather's grave is here". We were ferried ashore. The five Chagossians gathered on the beach, kissed the sand and stood – hands joined together – in thanksgiving prayers. "Welcome everyone to our birthplace!" smiled Bancoult.

Inland, the railway track which once transported copra (coconut) oil to the jetty had rusted away. Homes and warehouses had fallen into ruin. The ground was littered with rotting coconut shells.

In what had been the administrator's two-storey house, a banyan tree grew through steps up to the first floor. Nearby was the island's chapel, Saint Sacrement. "This is where I was christened", gestured Bancoult. The roof had collapsed; walls were covered in yellow and ochre mould.

With his fellow Chagossians, he set to work clearing the floor. Sprouting coconuts were hurled out through empty windows. Humbert hacked at palm fronds with a machete, trying to push back the jungle. "I was baptised here, too", said Liseby. "This is my church".

Survey of Blenheim Reef

Overnight we sailed north to Blenheim Reef. Surveying the semi-submerged coral atoll might provide Mauritius with evidence for an extended claim on the seabed in its dispute over marine boundaries with neighbouring Maldives. ITLOS has ruled that the UK has no legitimate claim.

Oskarsson and a colleague departed in an inflatable to place tide gauges on the seafloor to measure water levels. The expedition was hoping to find rocks that stayed dry all the time. They could be used as an outer base point for extending the 200-mile exclusive economic zone (EEZ). "If you see bird shit", he explained, "that's a sign a rock is permanently above water".

A second boat, with the media onboard, set off to examine the 13-mile perimeter of the reef, searching for boulders or sand bars above the ocean swell. At one point, a protruding rock was visible in troughs between waves. From the far side of the reef, the mothership receded into the distance. Dolphins leapt out of the water alongside us. Flying fish erupted from the sea, gliding for hundreds of feet. Soaked by salt spray, we returned to the *Bleu de Nîmes*. No one had spotted any guano.

On Sunday afternoon, we turned south to Salomon Atoll. On Île Boddam, the jetty was also overgrown and crumbling. Rosemonde Berthin led the way to what was once a hospital. "I had my baby here", she said. "William was born in 1972". A rusting, enamelled bedpan lay half concealed by ferns. Beside the hospital stood St Bridget's chapel. Creepers and roots had penetrated the walls. The roof had disappeared. Orange and black coconut crabs lurked in crevices. "My church is abandoned", wailed Berthin. "I was baptised here. I made my first communion here. Families came to services every Sunday".

Near the beach there was evidence of more recent settlers. Plastic buoys were strung across an entrance to an encampment made by visiting yacht crews. A polystyrene box, bottles, and debris lay around. Nearby a BIOT sign, clearly ignored, read "Do not discard any rubbish on this island". A larger placard declared that setting up an encampment or taking wildlife would be punished by a fine or imprisonment "by order of the BIOT commissioner's representative". The UK government's commitment to a pristine MPA does not appear to be rigorously enforced.

A torrential downpour required 10 minutes' shelter under the trees. Down a track through coconut palms, Berthin led the way to the island's cemetery. Predatory frigate birds drifted overhead. Rusting iron rails surrounded some tombs. Gravestones were covered in moss and ferns with few legible inscriptions. One read: "Ici repose Dookie décédé le 9 Mars 1880". Berthin found the name "Madame Yvon Dyson", the midwife who had helped deliver her in 1954.

Mauritius Demonstrates Its Authority

Monday morning found the *Bleu de Nîmes* moored again inside Peros Banhos Atoll. From the deck, a donkey was spotted trotting along the sand. A small herd has evaded capture since 1973.

We went ashore for a ceremony to celebrate Mauritian ownership of the archipelago – formally challenging the UK over possession of the Chagos Islands. No British officials had been invited, or presumably, forewarned.

At 10.30 am local time, Mauritian officials sang their country's national anthem. Ambassador Koonjul, in a short-sleeved shirt, declared: "We are performing the symbolic act of raising the flag as the British have done so many times to establish colonies. We, however, are reclaiming what has always been our own". A prerecorded message by the Mauritian prime minister was played. "This is the first time Mauritius has led an expedition to this part of its territory", Pravind Jugnauth said. "I'm delighted our Chagossian brothers and sisters are able to travel to their birthplace without any foreign [i.e. British] escort". A metal plaque cemented beneath the flagpole read: "Visit of the Mauritius delegation to Peros Banhos archipelago, Republic of Mauritius, in the context of the scientific survey of Blenheim Reef".

The prime minister also gave a telephone interview, explaining: "The international community and international institutions have already decided this is our territory. What we are doing is legitimate". Asked what would happen if Britain removed the Mauritian flag, Jugnauth said: "This will amount to a provocation. The UK is not abiding by international law judgments".

Afterwards, the ship's crew organised a barbecue on the beach. They danced with Olivier, Marie Suzelle, Liseby, Rosemonde, and Marcel to the Creole anthem "Peros Vert", an elegy for lost island lives. I dictated my story of the ceremony over a satellite phone to a *Guardian* news editor in London. The onboard wifi communication on the ship had stopped working.

At Blenheim Reef the following morning, tide gauges were lifted from the seabed so recordings could be analysed. Captain Poma had been in touch with the Wi-Fi provider. The communications breakdown was proving to be a mystery. A BIOT-retained fisheries protection vessel, the *Grampian Frontier*, was then identified eight miles away. It had been shadowing the *Bleu de Nîmes* at a constant distance. Poma spoke over the radio to its captain, who said he was "carrying out fisheries patrols". Intriguingly, he referred to Poma as "Ma'am" – implying he knew precisely what ship he was following.

There were suspicions that the *Bleu de Nîmes'* Wi-Fi problems could be due to signal jamming. Software patches were downloaded and the apparatus stripped down. Not until the vessel was hundreds of miles beyond the Chagos Islands days later did the broadband function again.

In the afternoon, we returned to Salomon but could not enter the atoll due to heavy seas. A tender sent out to land was unable to penetrate the breakers. Floral wreaths, intended for the cemetery, were floated away on the current. The following day, the expedition returned to Blenheim Reef. A Mauritian flag was planted on a sandbank that emerged at low tide. It would be visual evidence for the ITLOS hearing. With everyone back onboard, the *Bleu de Nîmes* turned west and headed for the Seychelles. The *Grampian Frontier* accompanied us until late evening.

The Journey Home

The return trip took six days due to headwinds and currents. We detoured once to follow whale spouts moving across undulating seas. It was a time for reflection. For Ambassador Koonjul, one of the achievements of the trip was "what the press did". Mauritius had been able to offer an alternative narrative to "the lies and deceits hidden for so long by certain powers" – a reference to the United Kingdom. International coverage of the voyage "had helped the cause extremely well", he concluded.

Not only did the BBC, *The Guardian*, and Mauritius Broadcasting Corporation report from onboard but the developing story was picked up by media outlets around the world. Raising the Mauritian flag over what Britain claims as overseas territory was a buccaneering, David vs Goliath tale.

In terms of timing, the expedition was fortunate. It offered unfamiliar and exotic images just as the world was tiring of Covid and before the Russian invasion of Ukraine swamped the international news agenda. Deployment of drones, to film lustrous, aerial images of tropical islands helped secure slots in television bulletins. *The Guardian* also sent a multimedia journalist, Bruno Rinvolucri, to produce online films, spreading the story across social media.

As a story, the fate of the Chagossians involves multiple injustices of exile, diplomatic deception, the betrayal of an exploited people, behaviour approaching racism, environmental pressures, and British political subservience to the United States – not forgetting the use of Diego Garcia as a "black site" (or secret detention centre) for rendition of jihadist suspects. Furthermore, it raises the awkward question of how the UK can urge others to comply with international law while itself refusing to respect the UN-adopted, ICJ ruling.

The remoteness of the archipelago had been deployed for decades as a means of discouraging critical coverage. The *Bleu de Nîmes* voyage provided a platform for eyewitness reporting.

At the back of many minds were anxieties over parallels with the Falkland Islands. Philippe Sands believed the UK's resistance was partially because it feared handing over BIOT would set a precedent for the loss of the Falklands and Gibraltar. "But there's no other UK [territory] that involves … dismemberment [before independence]", he pointed out.

Loss of international status post-Brexit may have intensified unease. On one level it is a familiar tale of the long, slow retreat from Empire and disentangling that relationship. Two months before we sailed, for example, Barbados dropped Queen Elizabeth II as head of state and became a republic.

Seen from another perspective, Mauritius resembles Ireland: their northern extremities are both held by the UK. In both cases, the government in London contemplates eventual handover – promising to "cede sovereignty to Mauritius once BIOT is no longer required for defence purposes" and return Northern Ireland if a majority vote to end partition.

It was the plight of the surviving exiled Chagossians, their tireless campaigning, and court battles that kept the issue alive for decades. Interviews with members of the Chagossian diaspora serve as reproaches to Foreign Office policy-making that privately described them as "Man Fridays" and denied them their homeland.

Despite limited compensation and belated apologies, the UK's protracted refusal to offer Chagossians British citizenship reinforced the sense of injustice. It may have been a coincidence but the government's decision in spring 2022 to provide a route for Chagossians and their descendants to obtain UK citizenship suggests lessons have eventually been learnt.

Resting on the quarterdeck as the Indian Ocean rolled by, Olivier Bancoult felt satisfied:

> Our message has been sent out to the world, to show that there was a population living there in peace and harmony on the Chagos Islands. How can you support a government which continues to banish the rights of my people?

He was going to work on a resettlement plan.

Liseby Elysé felt lucky to have been able to see her birthplace again. "I'm sad to leave. I want to return before I die." Marcel Humbert, who regularly proved his angling skills by hooking red snappers and grouper, believed he could survive alone on Peros Banhos; he wanted his family come and live with him. Rosemonde Berthin could "still see" her dog, Haydoker, whom she was forced to abandon when deported from Salomon. Marie Suzelle Baptiste's three children are in the UK but, she said, "they want to go to Chagos".

Seychelles and the Nordvaer

The *Blue de Nîmes* anchored off the Seychelles on Tuesday 22 February. We went ashore and visited the National Museum in the capital Victoria. Displays showed how the island was used as a prison for politicians from Africa and the Middle East who opposed colonial rule – the Siberia of the British Empire. The last exile sent to the Seychelles was the Greek Cypriot leader Archbishop Makarios who arrived in 1956.

In the afternoon, we drove into the hills to interview Captain Rowley Samynaden. Aged 72, he went to sea when he was 17, serving with the British Royal Fleet Auxiliary. In 1970, he joined the *Nordvaer* first as mate then chief officer.

The 500-ton cargo vessel was built in Germany in 1958 and purchased by BIOT 10 years later. It carried supplies for the Chagos Islands; stores would be delivered and copra oil exported. The *Nordvaer* featured on British Indian Ocean Territory commemorative stamps in 1974. Five years later it was driven aground to serve as a breakwater in the Seychelles.

"The islands were developed and there were lots of animals", Samynaden recalled. "People liked the way they lived. When the boat arrived, they would barter for provisions – giving us vegetables and salted fish".

The *Nordvaer* was also the vessel that carried Chagossians into exile.

> We first removed people from Diego Garcia. They were not happy. They were crying because they were leaving everything behind. Later we closed Salomon and Peros Banhos. There was a big tent in the forward hatch. We got tables and chairs. People lived down in the hold. There was trouble when we reached Mauritius. They didn't want to leave. They were not treated like animals [but] those in the cabins were different from those in the holds. If you had any problems there, no one was interested.

Asked whether he felt bad about what he had done, Samynaden replied:

> You had to do your duty. I would like the islands to reopen. I was told one lady gave birth, the child died and was buried at sea. Even the crew knew it was wrong. But what could they do? I would not put people in the hold now.

He recalled people's pets swimming out to the boat. "I know they destroyed all the dogs but I didn't see it". Preparing to leave Salomon, Samynaden remembered noticing an old man sitting on the shore. "We had to pick him up. He didn't know what was happening".

Britain Runs Its Sovereignty Up and Down the Flagpole

Two weeks after our return, in March 2022, the Foreign Office minister Amanda Milling told MPs:

> The UK is in no doubt about its sovereignty over BIOT. We were disappointed that Mauritius turned a scientific survey into a political stunt; the raising of Mauritian flags on outer islands of BIOT was an unhelpful way to approach a bilateral dispute. We removed the flags planted by Mauritius.
> (Milling, 2022)

In November, however, parliament was informed of an abrupt policy reversal. The Foreign Secretary, James Cleverly (2022), announced that: "the UK and Mauritius have decided to begin negotiations on the exercise of sovereignty over the British Indian Ocean Territory (BIOT)/Chagos archipelago".

Note

1 For further discussion of the legal disputes surrounding ownership of the archipelago and the rights of the Chagossians, see Chapters 1, 5, 6, 7, 12, and 13.

References

Cleverly, J. (2022) 'Chagos Archipelago'. *Hansard: House of Commons Debates*, 3 November, 721, 27WS. Available at: https://hansard.parliament.uk/commons/2022-11-03/debates/22110340000007/ChagosArchipelago (Accessed: 1 September 2023).

Milling, A. (2022) 'Topical questions'. *Hansard: House of Commons Debates*, 8 March, 710, c192. Available at: https://hansard.parliament.uk/commons/2022-03-08/debates/A1D7EE7C-07F7-4ACD-A5B8-CB7D8BCA10CB/TopicalQuestions (Accessed: 1 September 2023).

(Bancoult No 1) R (Bancoult) v. Secretary of State for Foreign and Commonwealth Office (No 1) (2000) [2000] EWHC 413 (Admin). *BAILII.* Available at: http://www.bailii.org/ew/cases/EWHC/Admin/2000/413.html (Accessed: 8 September 2023).

(Bancoult No 2) R (on the application of Bancoult) v Secretary of State for Foreign and Commonwealth Affairs (No 2) (2008) [2008]UKHL 61. *BAILII.* Available at: https://www.bailii.org/cgi-bin/format.cgi?doc=/uk/cases/UKHL/2008/61.html&query=(bancoult) (Accessed: 1 September 2023).

(Bancoult No 4) R (on the application of Bancoult (No 2)) (Appellant) v Secretary of State for Foreign and Commonwealth Affairs (Respondent) (2016) [2016] UKSC 35. *BAILII.* Available at: https://www.bailii.org/uk/cases/UKSC/2016/35.html (Accessed: 1 September 2023).

(Bancoult No 3) R (Bancoult) v Secretary of State for Foreign and Commonwealth Affairs (2018) [2018] UKSC 3. *BAILII.* Available at: http://www.bailii.org/uk/cases/UKSC/2018/3.html (Accessed: 8 September 2023).

(Bancoult No 5) R (Hoareau and Bancoult) v Secretary of State for Foreign and Commonwealth Affairs (2020) [2020] EWCA Civ 1010. *BAILII.* Available at: http://www.bailii.org/ew/cases/EWCA/Civ/2020/1010.html (Accessed: 8 January 2023).

18 Why Has It Taken 25 Years for the UK to Start Negotiating an Overall Settlement on Chagos with Mauritius?

David Snoxell

Introduction

After 25 years a settlement of the issues concerning the future of the Chagos Islands and of the expelled Chagossians is hopefully nearing a conclusion. As of August 2024, details of an agreed settlement are not available, nor whether it would be a compromise that all interested parties could endorse.

This chapter discusses the reasons for the prolonged delay and a likely outcome of the current negotiations between the UK and Mauritius.

Historical Background

Although the British Indian Ocean Territory (BIOT) was created in 1965 and the Chagossians expelled between 1968 and 1973, the international community, UK Parliament, and the public remained largely unaware of the true extent of what had happened until details emerged in the late 1990s with the release of Government files to the National Archives. This led to the first court case in a long series of litigation that progressively laid bare the full story and a tangled web of deception. Known as the Bancoult litigation, these cases have provided much insight into the secretive nature of what occurred between 1965 and 1973 and also the foundation for recent litigation in international courts and tribunals.

The collective memory of the early years of the BIOT during the 1960/70s was largely forgotten in the British Foreign Office (FCO) as officials retired or moved on to new postings, and briefings for incoming ministers omitted the more unsavoury aspects. Unawareness of these issues in 1999, even by those who were responsible for BIOT in the FCO (I was Deputy Commissioner of BIOT 1995–97) is not therefore surprising. A blanket coverup had deceived officials and ministers, Parliament, the public, and the UN into believing that the population were contract workers from Mauritius and Seychelles and that Chagos was a legitimate albeit new overseas territory under British sovereignty, renamed the British Indian Ocean Territory (Snoxell, 2020).

If Chagos Had Not Been Detached from Mauritius in 1965

But where would the Chagos Archipelago and its people be today if the UK had not detached the islands from Mauritius, three years before independence? The answer

DOI: 10.4324/9781003390299-25

is obvious. Chagos would have continued to remain an integral part of Mauritius and many of the people would still be living there today. As with Rodriguans, the inhabitants of the Mauritian island of Rodrigues 390 miles east of Mauritius, Chagossians would likely have had a measure of devolved self-government, an Executive and elected Assembly to represent them and to enact local legislation. The current UK/Mauritius negotiations hold out a similar prospect.

First, I will consider what the influences and developments were that brought the previous British government to agree to negotiate an overall settlement when successive governments and their officials since 2001 had opposed any compromise and used a smokescreen of historical and legal misrepresentation to defend their position. For the long and convoluted history behind British intransigence, I refer readers to my chapters in Fifty Years of the British Indian Ocean Territory (2018) and the International Court of Justice and Decolonisation (2021).

External and Domestic Influences on UK Policy

It was the accumulation of numerous external and domestic factors that brought about a change of heart in government. This included domestic and international litigation – the Bancoult cases, the International Court of Justice (ICJ) Advisory Opinion and its implementation by the UN system and Specialised Agencies, the International Tribunal on the Law of the Sea (ITLOS) judgment. Also UN General Assembly resolutions, UN human rights bodies such as the Human Rights Committee and the Committee for Elimination of Racial Discrimination (CERD); intergovernmental bodies – the African Union, Southern Africa Development Community (SADC), the Commonwealth, the European Parliament and the EU. Also the UK Parliament and the Chagos Islands (BIOT) All-Party Parliamentary Group (APPG), the media, Non-Governmental Organisations such as the Chagos Support Association and Human Rights Watch, academics, lawyers, novelists, playwrights, and diplomats. Even Wikileaks in 2010 played a part in revealing the truth as did the Chagossian people who have not ceased to campaign for their right to return and resettle.

Several historical accounts, novels, films, and a play on the Chagos saga have been published over the years. The most recent was by Philippe Sands KC, titled "The Last Colony, a Tale of Exile, Justice and Britain's Colonial Legacy" (2022). This book reaches back to 1945 and blends the author's personal experience of Chagossians with the litigation, historical and political narratives. It is the human and personal aspects which bring the "tale" alive and engages the reader that a legal analysis could not do. The book provides an incisive and accurate understanding of this long and complex story.

What Finally Changed Official Attitudes?

What broke the logjam were international judgments and UK isolation in the UN brought on by the UK's diminishing reputation due to a disregard for international comity and law, and later the UK stand on Russia's invasion of Ukraine which exposed HMG to charges of hypocrisy. The UK seemed to be saying that international law applied to Russia's illegal occupation of parts of Ukraine but not to the UK's illegal occupation of Chagos. The Biden Administration may have concluded that HMG's refusal to recognise the ICJ and UNGA decisions on Chagos and to negotiate with Mauritius weakened the West's cohesion on Ukraine. Furthermore, the UK's unprecedented expulsion and callous treatment of the Chagossians undermined its claims to be an upholder of humanitarian and human rights law. It is a combination of all these factors, influences, and international developments that forced a U-turn in UK policy. A settlement could have been achieved at any time since 2000, but there was never sufficient political will to bring it about. The present government and its immediate predecessor should therefore be acknowledged for having made the decision to negotiate a settlement.

Six Failed Policies, 2002–2019

My article in *L'express* of Mauritius on 20 October 2022 titled "Six blunders of UK Chagos policy – time to wind-up Britian's last colony" unintentionally heralded a change of policy which occurred two weeks later. I wrote, "The UK's current position that international law applies to Russia's illegal occupation of Ukraine but not to the UK's illegal occupation of Chagos, which remains a part of Mauritius, is double standards and hypocrisy". The six policy failures were: the 2002 flawed resettlement feasibility study; the 2004 Orders in Council banning return; the 2010 declaration of the Chagos Marine Protected Area; the 2016 rejection of the KPMG feasibility study which concluded that resettlement was feasible; the automatic rollover without any conditions of the 1966 UK/US agreement until 30 December 2036; and the 2019 rejection of the ICJ Advisory Opinion and the UNGA resolution which required the UK to implement the ICJ ruling within 6 months by 22 November 2019.

Announcement of Policy U-turn in 2022

This policy sea change was announced on 3 November 2022, coincidentally the 22nd anniversary of the 2000 English High Court judgment, which allowed Chagossians to return to the Outer Chagos Islands. The UK and Mauritius jointly stated that they would:

> begin negotiations on the exercise of sovereignty over BIOT/Chagos Archipelago taking into account relevant legal proceedings to secure an agreement on the basis of international law to resolve all outstanding issues, including those relating to the former inhabitants. This will allow the UK and Mauritius, as close Commonwealth partners, to work even more closely together to tackle the regional and global security challenges that face us all. We will seek to strengthen significantly our co-operation on Indian Ocean security, maritime security and maritime protection, conservation of the environment, climate change and respect for human rights, and on tackling illegal migration, illegal fishing, drugs and arms trafficking, as well as

> bilateral cooperation on a range of other issues. We will work to do this in cooperation with key allies and partners in the region.
>
> The UK and Mauritius have reiterated that any agreement between our two countries will ensure the continued effective operation of the joint UK/US military base on Diego Garcia, which plays a vital role in regional and global security. We recognise US and India's interests and will keep them informed of progress.
>
> The UK and Mauritius have agreed to engage in constructive negotiations, with a view to arriving at an agreement by early next year.
>
> (Cleverly, 2022)

UK/Mauritius Negotiations

Other items on the agenda ("bilateral cooperation on a range of other issues") which include environment, conservation, climate change, law enforcement, illegal migration, illegal fishing, piracy, drug trafficking, money laundering, organised crime are issues which the UK and Mauritius could take forward within the bilateral relationship.

Clearly the target of an agreement by early 2023 could not be achieved, which is not surprising given such an ambitious agenda to work through. There have been seven negotiating sessions and four online consultations with Chagossians. The negotiations have been proceeding in quiet secrecy between a handful of officials from both sides in London and Port Louis (Mauritius). Neither government has said anything of substance, only that constructive and encouraging discussions have taken place.

In a written ministerial statement to Parliament on 17 March 2023, the Foreign Secretary announced that

> "These discussions have built understanding between the two sides, and covered issues relating to ensuring the continued effective operation of the joint UK/US military base on Diego Garcia; resettlement of the former inhabitants of the Chagos Archipelago; strengthening our cooperation on a range of issues such as environmental and marine protection, improving security and tackling illegal activities in the region. The UK and Mauritius have taken stock of negotiations and agreed next steps. The two Prime Ministers spoke on 14 February, welcomed the progress to date and agreed to continue negotiations, with a view to arriving at an agreement in the coming months.
>
> (Cleverly, 2023)

Slow Progress

During a Commons debate on the Overseas Territories on 11 May 2023, the FCDO Minister said "Although the negotiations are clearly between UK and Mauritius, we recognise the diversity of views among Chagossians. We take those views seriously and have a further engagement planned for the coming weeks". In an oral question to the Foreign Secretary on 13 June 2023, Jeremy Corbyn MP, Hon President of the APPG, said:

> I thank the Foreign Secretary for his answer. I would be grateful if he could assure the House that these negotiations are going on in the spirit of the International Court of Justice advisory opinion and the decision of the UN General Assembly in 2019 on the reunification of the Chagos islands with Mauritius. Can he give us some idea of when he expects these negotiations to come to fruition?

Mr Cleverly replied:

> I am not able to give a date or a projected date of when we will conclude these negotiations. We want to ensure that we conclude them successfully. Our shared objective is to ensure the continued effective operation of the joint UK-US defence facility on Diego Garcia, protecting the vital role it plays in both regional and global security.

Parliamentary Involvement and the APPG

Parliamentary involvement goes back to the 1970s. In 2007–8 the House of Commons Foreign Affairs Committee (FAC) held hearings on Chagos and concluded that "there is a strong moral case for the UK permitting and supporting a return to BIOT for Chagossians. The FCO has argued that such a return would be unsustainable, but we find these arguments less than convincing" (Foreign Affairs Committee, 2008, para 69). In December 2023 the FAC established a sub-committee to examine the situation regarding BIOT/Chagos Islands and invited written and oral evidence which has since been published (Foreign Affairs Sub-Committee on the Overseas Territory, 2024). The Committee met with Chagossian communities and on 28 February 2024 held an oral evidence session in Parliament. Witnesses invited to give oral evidence were David Snoxell, Dr Walter C. Ladwig 111, Sir Robert Buckland, and Prof Philippe Sands KC. On 8 March Jeremy Corbyn MP wrote to the Chair and FAC members, setting out what should be done to bring about a resolution of the issues.

On 12 March 2024, the FAC Chair wrote to the Foreign Secretary concerning Chagossian engagement, resettlement, the support package, and environmental protection (Kearns, 2024). The letter said that the Government should immediately begin the process of preparing for a pilot resettlement programme on an outlying island in partnership with the Mauritian and US Governments, Chagossian groups, and with the input of the scientific community. The letter also noted, "We understand that negotiations regarding sovereignty are ongoing and we are fully supportive of a successful conclusion and outcome that ensures continued operation of the base at Diego Garcia, which plays a fundamental role in global security". The letter asked for a response by 25 March 2024.

In 2008 the Chagos Islands (BIOT) APPG had been established with the purpose "To help bring about a resolution of the issues concerning the future of the Chagos Islands (BIOT) and of the Chagossians". It has been an important player, keeping government feet to the fire for 15 years. Currently there are 53 members of the APPG from all seven political parties in Westminster, several of whom were FCO and other ministers. The 93rd meeting was on 7 November 2023. The APPG supports the current UK/Mauritius negotiations to reach an overall settlement of all issues pertaining to Chagos and the Chagossians, based on international law. Neither Britain nor Mauritius can accept non-governmental participation in the negotiations as these are inter-state talks but both governments are consulting Chagossian groups. The FCDO conducted four online consultations with Chagossians in 2023. The APPG has always advocated the right of Chagossians to return to the islands and to resettle, irrespective of how many may wish to do so permanently. The APPG also strongly supports further compensation to Chagossians though this is a matter for the UK and US, not Mauritius.

On the issue of sovereignty, the APPG has accepted the ICJ Advisory Opinion of 2019, the resolution of United Nations General Assembly (2019) endorsing it which set a deadline of 22 November 2019 for implementation. An ICJ Advisory Opinion advises the General Assembly on the obligations and requirements of international law on an issue of international importance. The APPG has also supported the findings by other international courts such as the Permanent Court of Arbitration (2015) and the International Tribunal for the Law of the Sea (2023) which have confirmed the sovereignty of Mauritius over the Chagos Archipelago. The ITLOS judgment on 28 April 2023 delimiting the maritime boundary between Mauritius and Maldives reconfirms that Chagos is part of Mauritius. Both governments have an obligation to inform the UNGA of progress towards resolving these issues which are both bilateral and international.

Defence and Security Issues

Defence and Security is a more complex aspect of the negotiations. India has built a small defence facility, airstrip, and jetty on Agalega Island which belongs to Mauritius; the French have a base on Reunion (130 miles from Mauritius); and the UK/US on Diego Garcia. The potential for an alliance comprising the UK, US, Mauritius, France, Australia, and India would act as a bulwark in the Indian Ocean against supposed Chinese threats. Such an alliance would reflect the objectives of the UK's 2021 updated defence review (2023) which states that a core tenet of the UK's approach in the Indo-Pacific is that "territorial integrity is respected and disputes resolved".

The China "threat"

The Indian Ocean is hardly threatened by China and may never be. A campaign by the Daily Mail alleging that Mauritius wants the islands to hand them over to China to build a military base is fanciful. In a clear attempt to destabilise the negotiations, the press has reported alarmist claims by several politicians and academics in the US and UK, that Mauritius would hand the islands over to China for a military base, and/or that Britain is breaking off the negotiations. As a member of the Commonwealth, Mauritius' closest ties have long been with India, and it maintains excellent relations with the UK, US, and France. It is inconceivable that Mauritius would prioritise future relations with China over an agreement with the UK/US concerning the security of Diego Garcia. An agreement with Mauritius will give her a stake in protecting the base and ensure she is not drawn into the Chinese sphere of influence and will remain a close ally of the West.

The UK's claim to sovereignty over the islands was backed by a Policy Exchange Report in November 2023. But the report is flawed, ignoring as it does that the claim is invalidated by the customary international law norm of self-determination which applied in 1965 when the UK detached the Chagos Islands from the colony of Mauritius. An analogy often made with Falklands and Gibraltar is false since Chagos was always part of Mauritius. Under international law, self-determination belongs collectively to all Mauritians, whether in Mauritius, Chagos, Agalega, or Rodrigues. In contrast, the right of the inhabitants of Gibraltar and Falklands to decide their own future is independent of what Spain and Argentina may think.

Reaching Agreement on Protecting the UK/US Base

The most likely cause for the present delay is reaching agreement on the UK/US base (or facility) on Diego Garcia. In answer to a parliamentary question on 22 June 2023 the Foreign Office minister said, "The US fully supports the process of bilateral negotiations between the UK and Mauritius on the exercise of sovereignty over the Chagos Archipelago" (Rutley, 2023). This was confirmed by the US Secretary of State Anthony Blinken when he met the new Foreign Secretary David Cameron on 7 December 2023 with Blinken telling the Press "This is a bilateral matter for the UK and Mauritius to work out and we support their engagement to resolve the differences". In answer to a Question on 5 February 2024 in the House of Lords, Lord Ahmad replied: "…talks with the Government of Mauritius continue. The UK's priority is to ensure the long term continued effective operation of the joint UK/US military base on Diego Garcia. Mauritius has also publicly committed to this goal" (Ahmad, 2024).

Mutual confidence is at the heart of achieving a satisfactory solution. Mauritius has made its support for the base clear by offering a 99-year lease. Although the Mauritian government holds firmly to its position that in accordance with international law it must exercise full sovereign rights over the territory, the use of the term "exercise of sovereignty" in the 2022 joint statement would not rule out an interim solution whereby the UK administers Diego Garcia on behalf of Mauritius for a defined period, say until 2036 when the 1966 UK/US agreement comes to an end. A continuing temporary administration by the UK or the US over Diego Garcia could be a way of resolving the confidence issue. The US could conclude a separate agreement with Mauritius which gave the US temporary control of the island.

Alternatively, all islands could be subject now to Mauritian law but with jurisdiction over the base and UK and US personnel governed by visiting forces agreements as is standard practice elsewhere in the world. Others have suggested an arrangement such as the sovereign base agreement that the UK has with Cyprus. It is likely that the bilateral talks have discussed these possible solutions. A treaty, registered with the UN between the three parties, which enshrined arrangements for the future of the base, should be enough to reassure the US and UK on the security of the base in an increasingly hostile and unstable world, reminiscent of the Soviet-era Cold War period.

Mauritian Commitment to Chagossian Resettlement

Mauritius has offered to facilitate and contribute financially to resettlement of Chagossians wherever they live in the world. While the UK is opposed to resettlement, the Mauritian Prime Minister has said repeatedly that Mauritius will facilitate and help fund resettlement for Chagossians wishing to return, but as he made clear to a question on 4 July 2023 from the Leader of the Opposition, Mauritius needs to conduct surveys and an assessment mission to Chagos of the practicalities and requirements (Jugnauth, 2023, p. 10). The 2015 KPMG study is out of date and its estimated costs exaggerated. Since 2020 the Mauritian budget has set aside funds for resettlement. The UK government remains silent about resettlement, though would probably be relieved if Mauritius took on a resettlement programme to which the UK and US could contribute. Under Mauritian control, the Chagossians would be able to return to all the islands and resettle though the UK and US would be expected to contribute to the costs. Resettlement organised by Mauritius is the most likely outcome.

The Marine Protected Area

The policing of the Chagos Marine Protected Area (MPA) created in 2010 is complex and expensive with no sign that illegal fishing has been effectively reduced. An agreement on its handover and continuation should be straightforward and satisfy the conservationists. Mauritius would implement a zoned MPA. The reefs and islands are a valuable resource for research. Hopefully, Mauritius will take on the current scientific, conservation, environmental research capacity and the UK assist Mauritius in this regard. It has long been argued that Chagossians would make the best custodians of this unique marine environment and could be employed to enforce and monitor the MPA (Snoxell, 2010).

BIOT – an artificial construct

There are other pressures on the UK which make its continued occupation of the Chagos increasingly unmanageable, costly to the taxpayer and damaging to the UK's standing and reputation. Legitimacy of BIOT and its sham legal system is increasingly challenged. The BIOT Supreme Court consists of a single judge sitting in London. BIOT itself is an artificial construct, in practice administered by

FCDO officials in London. Britain's denial of the application to BIOT of human rights conventions and law, including the 1951 UN Refugee Convention, makes the UK look hypocritical in its approach to international law.

The arrival in Diego Garcia from October 2021 to December 2022 of boatloads of Sri Lankan asylum seekers (some 350) has caused a major logistical and legal problem though the majority have since departed. Following challenges in 2023 in the BIOT Supreme Court, the Commissioner was forced to withdraw his decisions to return them to Sri Lanka and to conduct an independent review of each claim for protection on non-refoulement grounds. The UK had not extended the UNHCR Refugee Convention to BIOT which prohibits states from returning refugees to countries in which they face persecution on account of their race, religion, nationality, membership of a particular social group, or political opinion. Nonetheless, the customary international law principle of non-refoulement applies to the Territory.

Postscript

The sooner BIOT, the UK's post-colonial creation nearly six decades ago, is returned to Mauritius, the sooner Chagossians can return to their islands, the UK's international reputation is restored, and UK/Mauritius relations put on a productive course for the benefit of both nations. For the UK, an architect of international law and a founding father of the UN system, a negotiated settlement to this long-standing dispute is inescapable.

The new Labour government, elected on 4 July 2024, has resumed the UK/Mauritius negotiations which have dragged on since first announced on 3 November 2022. On 10 July 2023, the then shadow Foreign Secretary, David Lammy, committed Labour to a resolution of the issues in a speech at the Bingham Centre for the Rule of Law. He said:

> For years the government ignored the opinions of the ICJ, the International Tribunal for the Law of the Sea and the UN General Assembly about the Chagos Islands. Only belatedly has the government sought what we have called for: a new settlement that brings the UK into compliance with international law, redresses the historical injustices done to the Chagossians, maintains the marine protected environment, and meets strategic security concerns.

Mr Lammy, now the Foreign Secretary, is likely to prioritise this commitment. The Chagos Islands APPG will be re-established in the new Parliament. Two of the APPG members were former shadow foreign affairs ministers, Stephen Doughty and Catherine West, who have been appointed FCDO ministers. They will no doubt continue to support an overall settlement. I expect the APPG to press the government to conclude an agreement expeditiously, providing for Chagossian resettlement and return of the territory to Mauritian sovereignty. A final settlement after nearly six decades would be a major foreign and defence policy achievement for the new government. The new British Government is set to negotiate a settlement with Mauritius.

Personal Postscript

Soon after arriving in Mauritius in September 2000 as British High Commissioner, I concluded that the problems of Chagos could be resolved but that it would require a negotiated settlement with Mauritius, getting the US on side, and providing for resettlement of Chagossians who wanted to return. After retirement I had a letter published in *The Times* asking,

> Is it not time that HMG brought together Chagossian leaders, Mauritius and the US to sort out this relic of the Cold War and rectify one of the worst violations of fundamental human rights perpetrated by the UK in the twentieth century?
>
> (Snoxell, 12 February 2007)

Appreciations

I would like to end by paying tribute to the relentless work of Richard Gifford, Olivier Bancoult's Solicitor, who has retired after 25 years of representing the Chagossian cause in English litigation. I would also like to commend Parliamentarians going back to the 1970s and the Members of the Chagos Islands APPG, especially the late Lord Avebury (died 2016) who founded the Group in 2008 and Lord Ramsbotham (died in 2022) who served as a Vice Chairman since its establishment. They gave generously of their time and energy in promoting the Chagossian cause and in holding the government to account for their mistreatment of the Chagos Islanders. Their efforts will be vindicated by a successful conclusion to the UK/Mauritius negotiations.

References

Ahmad, T. (2024) 'British Indian Ocean territory: Sovereignty, answer to a parliamentary question'. *UK Parliament,* 5 February. Available at: https://questions-statements.parliament.uk/written-questions/detail/2024-01-22/hl1784 (Accessed: 30 March 2024).

Cleverly, J. (2022) 'British Indian Ocean territory / Chagos Archipelago'. *House of Commons*, 3 November, HCWS354. Available at: https://questions-statements.parliament.uk/written-statements/detail/2022-11-03/hcws354 (Accessed: 1 September 2023).

Cleverly, J. (2023) 'British Indian Ocean territory / Chagos Archipelago'. *House of Commons*, 17 March. Available at: https://questions-statements.parliament.uk/written-statements/detail/2023-03-17/hcws645?fbclid=IwAR2SIJ_JNQzBMavmRofO5dHRvNbtf1prhTBM_XiPQ8UAJejDdyFs3G3yS-A (Accessed: 1 September 2023).

Foreign Affairs Committee (2008) 'Seventh report, session 2007-8'. *UK Parliament.* Available at: https://publications.parliament.uk/pa/cm200708/cmselect/cmfaff/147/14702.htm (Accessed: 1 September 2023).

Foreign Affairs Sub-Committee on the Overseas Territories (2024) 'The UK Government's engagement regarding the British Indian Ocean territory: Inquiry'. *UK Parliament.* Available at: https://committees.parliament.uk/work/8116/the-uk-governments-engagement-regarding-the-british-indian-ocean-territory/publications/ (Accessed: 1 September 2024)

HM Government (2023) *Integrated Review Refresh 2023: Responding to a More Contested and Volatile World.* London: the Stationery Office. Available at: https://assets.publishing.service.gov.uk/media/641d72f45155a2000c6ad5d5/11857435_NS_IR_Refresh_2023_Supply_AllPages_Revision_7_WEB_PDF.pdf (Accessed: 1 September 2023).

International Tribunal for the Law of the Sea (2023) Dispute Concerning Delimitation of the Maritime Boundary between Mauritius and Maldives in the Indian Ocean. Hamburg.

Jugnauth, P.K. (2023) 'Oral answers to questions: Exercise of sovereignty over the Chagos Archipelago – negotiations between Mauritius & UK'. *Hansard: Mauritius National Assembly*, 4 July, 20. Available at: https://mauritiusassembly.govmu.org/mauritiusassembly/index.php/download/329/2023/16720/debate-no-18-of-2023-tuesday-20-june-2023.pdf (Accessed: 1 September 2023).

Kearns, A. (2024) 'Letter to the foreign secretary relating to Chagossians'. *UK Parliament*, 12 March 2024. Available at: https://committees.parliament.uk/work/8116/the-uk-governments-engagement-regarding-the-british-indian-ocean-territory/publications/3/correspondence/ (Accessed: 30 March 2024).

Permanent Court of Arbitration (2015) Award in the Arbitration regarding the Chagos Marine Protected Area between Mauritius and the United Kingdom of Great Britain and Northern Ireland. The Hague.

Rutley, D. (2023) 'British Indian Ocean territory: Sovereignty, answer to a parliamentary question'. *UK Parliament*, 22 June. Available at: https://questions-statements.parliament.uk/written-questions/detail/2023-06-19/190051. (Accessed 1 September 2023).

Sands, P. (2022) *The Last Colony, A tale of exile, Justice and Britain's Colonial Legacy.* London: Weidenfeld and Nicolson.

Snoxell, D. (2007) 'Justice for the Chagos Islands'. *The Times*, 12 February. Available at: http://www.thetimes.co.uk/tto/opinion/letters/article2056377.ece (Accessed: 1 September 2023).

Snoxell, D. (2010). 'Chagossians would be the best custodians of their unique islands'. *The Guardian*, 16 April. Available at: https://www.theguardian.com/commentisfree/2010/apr/16/chagos-islands-marine-protected-area (Accessed: 1 September 2023).

Snoxell, D. (2018) 'The politics of Chagos: Part played by Parliament and the Courts towards resolving the Chagos tragedy'. In S. Allen and C. Monaghan (eds.), *Fifty Years of the British Indian Ocean Territory: Legal perspectives.* Cham: Springer, pp. 359–379.

Snoxell, D. (2020) '26 Chagos misunderstandings, myths and mantras 1966-2020'. Unpublished.

Snoxell, D. (2021) 'Prospects of the Chagos advisory opinion and the subsequent UN general assembly resolution helping to resolve the future of the Chagos Archipelago and its former inhabitants: A political perspective'. In T. Burri and J. Trinidad (eds.), *The International Court of Justice and Decolonisation, New Directions form the Chagos Advisory Opinion.* Cambridge: Cambridge University Press, pp. 262–279.

United Nations General Assembly (2019) 'Advisory opinion of the International Court of Justice on the legal consequences of the separation of the Chagos Archipelago from Mauritius in 1965'. Resolution 73/295. Available at: https://digitallibrary.un.org/record/3806313/files/A_RES_73_295-EN.pdf (Accessed: 1 September 2023).

Ode to Chagossian Zistwar

Chrisyl Wong-Hang-Sun

Down where the river meets the sea,
An old man sits beside me.
His long white beard and skin, a rich ***Nwar***
He begins to share with me our ***zistwar***

Long ago we knew these waters,
Long lived our sons and our daughters.
Together we moved to the beat of the shore,
A harmony that cannot exist anymore.

At the source of the river flowed abundant life
Without any tension, pain, or strife.
We had balance, at peace with our land,
As she nurtured us with her generous hand.

But now, all of that is lost.
A disrupted balance, and at what cost?
And as you strive to reach for the stars,
Is it worth the money, power, and call to arms?

Down where the river meets the sea,
An old man sits beside a coconut tree.
Weaving his basket to harvest to some fruit,
I realised I was wrong in my pursuit.

For greed and desire can never be satisfied,
And the lust for more must be cast aside,
To make space for the things that bring us life,
With the river, sea, and land, we must unite.

Returning to the source of my being,
I no longer succumb to that which is fleeting.
Down where the river meets the sea,
A wise old man has set me free.

DOI: 10.4324/9781003390299-26

Afterword

Sabrina Jean

The Chagossian community has suffered for over 50 years since their banishment from the Chagos islands, when they lost access to their homes and to their homeland. The UK government, the US government, and the Mauritian government – and all those involved in the deportation of the Chagossians – should be held accountable for these injustices and should work towards restitution. The UK Government says it can't turn the clock back, but I think it's time to turn the clock forward and let Chagossians decide their own futures.

DOI: 10.4324/9781003390299-27

Index

For Product Safety Concerns and Information please contact our EU representative GPSR@taylorandfrancis.com
Taylor & Francis Verlag GmbH, Kaufingerstraße 24, 80331 München, Germany

www.ingramcontent.com/pod-product-compliance
Ingram Content Group UK Ltd.
Pitfield, Milton Keynes, MK11 3LW, UK
UKHW021828101126
477531UK00020B/550
* 9 7 8 1 0 3 2 4 8 6 9 2 5 *